# The Diwan

of the Shaykh and Gnostic of Allah
Sayyidi Muhammad ibn al-Habib
al-Amghari al-Idrisi al-Hasani

# The Diwan

of the Shaykh and Gnostic of Allah
Sayyidi Muhammad ibn al-Habib
al-Amghari al-Idrisi al-Hasani

*The Desire of Journeying Murids
and the Gift to Wayfaring Gnostics*

# Contents

# Preface

SHAYKH MUHAMMAD AL-MURTADA AL-BOUMAS-HOULI

بسم الله الرحمن الرحيم وصلى الله وسلم وبارك على سيدنا ونبينا ومولانا محمد
وعلى آله وصحبه وسلم تسليما. ولا حول ولا قوة الا بالله العلي العظيم.

In the name of Allah, the All-Merciful, the Most Merciful, and may Allah
bless and send baraka upon our master and Prophet, Mawlana Muhammad
and his family and Companions and grant them abundant peace.
There is no power and no strength but by Allah, the High, the Vast.

مِنَ الْمُؤْمِنِينَ رِجَالٌ صَدَقُوا مَا عَاهَدُوا اللَّهَ عَلَيْهِ ۖ فَمِنْهُم مَّن قَضَىٰ نَحْبَهُ
وَمِنْهُم مَّن يَنتَظِرُ ۖ وَمَا بَدَّلُوا تَبْدِيلًا

(Surat al-Ahzab 33:23)

The book of Sayyidi Muhammad ibn al-Habib, may Allah be pleased with
him and make him contented – which contains his noble wirds, the
Hafidha, and qasidas that strike home – has an effect on everyone who
reads or hears it all over the world, particularly after its translation into other
languages when it became possible for Westerners and others to understand its
contents. This is all by the overflowing favour of Allah and the secret of the
idhn from him, may Allah be pleased with him.

When he granted idhn to Shaykh Abdalqadir as-Sufi, may Allah be pleased with him, to instruct others in the wirds and to print his Diwan, its blessings became manifest in people engaging with it, since every murid has a copy of the Diwan in his satchel and in his library. The increase in the numbers of murids is shown by our need for more copies.

For that reason, Shaykh Abdalqadir, may Allah be pleased with him, gave permission for this new edition of the Diwan and asked that I write this Preface to it. On our part we give our blessing to this idhn, hoping from Allah that He make it sincerely for His face and beneficial to His slaves and for everyone who reads, hears or looks into it not merely for research.

May Allah bless our intermediary with Him and our model, our Master Muhammad and his family and Companions and grant them abundant peace.

The servant of the people of Allah
Muhammad al-Murtada al-Boumas-houli
Allah is His Guardian Friend

# Introduction to the Diwan

SHAYKH MUHAMMAD IBN AL-HABIB

The Shaykh said, may Allah be pleased with him: Praise belongs to Allah Who has established men in every age to revive His Tariqa. He has revealed to them the lights of Muhammad, from which all the lovers who followed them would derive aid, be they couples or individuals.

We praise Him, the Glorious and Exalted, for the secrets with which He has entrusted us, and for the sciences, gnoses and lights He has poured out on us. We greatly thank Him, may His Majesty be exalted, in recognition of all the blessings that have come to us and all the slaves of Allah, free or in bondage.

We declare that our master Muhammad is His slave and His Messenger, sent by Allah as a mercy to the creation, may Allah bless him and grant him peace, and his family and companions who spent themselves and their wealth in the revival of His way and the setting up of His sunna, and who did not turn to the destruction of the hypocrites and the veiled.

Brothers of the Darqawiyya-Shadhiliyya order and all others of the Lord's slaves in all of Allah's countries who desire to emulate a master, know, that Allah the Exalted has destined for this noble path in every age one who sets right its deviations and manifests its secrets and its lights. He is the Shaykh who unites the Haqiqa and the Shari'a with the idhn of Allah and His Messenger and all the awliya of Allah. He is the unique man of Muhammad of whom there is only one in every age. If there are numerous Shaykhs in his age, he rules over them all, whether they are aware of it or not. Many have laid claim to the Station of uniqueness with falsehood and lies because they seek leadership and desire to possess this passing world. The pretender is unaware that whoever claims what is not in him is exposed by the witnesses of the test, since in their presence a man is either exalted or humiliated. True Shaykhs are satisfied with the knowledge of Allah and depend only on Allah. All that emanates from them speaks of the blessing of Allah. He, may He be exalted said:

*'As for the blessing of your Lord – declare it.'*

So let Muhammad ibn al-Habib, al-Amghari al-Hasani by lineage, dwelling in Fez, the poor slave of his Master, yet enriched by Him with other-than-Him – declare, in speaking of Allah's blessing – that *idhn* (authorisation) has come to him from Allah and the Messenger of Allah and all the awliya of Allah, and that Allah has singled him out with sciences and secrets which only the unique man of Muhammad possesses.

Had we wished to reveal all that Allah has blessed us with we would need volumes, we shall however relate to the fuqara only that tribute with which our Shaykh and teacher Sayyidi Muhammad ibn 'Ali favoured us. When he, may Allah be pleased with him, became head of the order, we wrote him a letter renewing our contact with him although we had taken Tariq from the Shaykh and gnostic of Allah, Sayyidi al-'Arabi ibn al-Huwari. He, may Allah be pleased with him, wrote to us and ordered us to come to his presence. So we obeyed his command and went to Marrakesh. When we went in to him he was filled with limitless joy and happiness and said to us: 'The whole order came to me when you came!' On another occasion he said to us in a prophecy, may it long be remembered, 'Your rank with us in our order is that of Ibn 'Ata'llah in the Shadhiliyya order. As Allah revived the Shadhiliyya path through Ibn 'Ata'llah, so also He will revive this blessed Tariqa through you, if He wills!' And Allah has realised his hope in us.

By Allah and by Allah we have not passed through a city, a village or a desert but that the people testified that love had come to them and life flowed in their hearts. Such is the secret of Allah's idhn. Praise be to Allah, no faqir has sat with us without gaining a knowledge that was not his before, and getting from it humility and a contrite heart. No murid of the Tariqa has sat with us without a strengthening of his innate condition and the heightening of his himma in the quest for gnosis of Allah. There has been no Shaykh of the Shaykhs of the age who has not increased in his immediate tasting and gained something of benefit which he did not have before. All that is from the secret of the idhn and its baraka.

Ibn 'Ata'llah says in his 'Hikam' (Book of Wisdom):

'He to whom the idhn of discourse has been given, his declaration is understood in the ears of creation, and the evidence of his selection is made plain to them.'

2

The one with idhn is the one who speaks by Allah and for Allah, and so his words have an effect on the heart, and all the elect and the beloved are guided to him. The Shaykh of our Shaykh, Sayyidi Muhammad al-'Arabi, may Allah be pleased with him, said, 'By Allah, none has come to me who was not acceptable.' I say, speaking of the blessing of Allah, 'By Allah, none has come to me who was not beloved.'

Muhammad, may Allah bless him and grant him peace, said to me in a prophecy, 'Know, my son, that Allah will honour you with sweet and pleasant waters.' I said, 'O Messenger of Allah, are these the waters of Islam, Iman and Ihsan?' He said to me, may Allah bless him and grant him peace, 'They are.' I said, 'You and all of my community who follow you shall drink them.' And Allah realised for us what He promised. By Allah, we have drunk these waters, and soon all of those who accompany us with sincerity will drink them too. So, my lords, give praise to Allah ta'ala and thank Him for what He has honoured you with in your time.

He has said, may He be exalted, *'Whenever we abrogate an ayat or cause it to be forgotten, We bring one better than it or equal to it.'* Allah ta'ala has given precedence here to the better over the like as an indication that the heir to the perfect Wali must appear even after some time has passed. And that he will be more perfect than him in knowledge and gnosis of Allah ta'ala. He is the miracle of that perfect Wali. So the overflowing energy from Allah continues to increase. The Shaykh, our lord and master, Ahmad al-Badawi, may Allah be pleased with him, said:

'Your overflowing increases
Your existence is uninterrupted.'

I have indicated some of what Allah has granted me in the qasida that speaks of the blessing from Allah, entitled 'The Robe of Nearness':

'Invocation of the Beloved clothed us in beauty and radiance, exaltation and joy.
In drawing near we cast aside every restraint and openly proclaimed the One we love to glorify.'

When the Shaykh Sayyidi Muhammad ibn 'Ali, may Allah be pleased with him, died, and the idhn was renewed in me, I regarded my self as worthless and undeserving of that station until the four Shaykhs came to me. They are: Sayyidi Muhammad ibn 'Ali, Sayyidi al-'Arabi ibn al-Huwari, Sayyidi Muhammad al-'Arabi, and Sayyidi Ahmad al-Badawi, may Allah be pleased with them. They commanded me to go out to the creation and guide them to the true King. They said: 'The water which you have drunk from us is the coolest and sweetest of waters, so stretch out your hand to the east and the west, and fear no-one!' Then the idhn came from the Chosen One, may Allah bless him and grant him peace, and I was awed into going forth. So I went out to creation by Allah and for Allah, saying as Ibn 'Ata'llah said in his 'Hikam': 'My God, you have ordered me to return to the existence-traces, so return me to it with a robe of lights and the guidance of discrimination so that I may return to You from it, as I came to You from it – my secret pure of regard for it and my himma elevated above dependence on it. You have power over all things.'

Know, my lords, that it is obligatory on every murid who seeks the presence of Allah to take the living Shaykh. The proof of this obligation is His word, may He be exalted: 'O you who have iman, fear Allah, and be with the truthful ones.' Being with them necessitates accompanying them in body, not just in spirit. He has said, may He be exalted: 'Follow the path of whoever turns away from self to Me.' In this ayat, He, may He be exalted, orders the walad (beginner/lit. youth) to follow the spiritual father, not the father of form, because the spiritual father teaches the inner meaning and the father of the body teaches you sensory meaning. What a difference there is between the one whose himma is for the meaning and the one whose himma is for the sensory! He said, may Allah bless him and grant him peace: 'A man follows the Deen of his friend, so let each of you look to who he takes as a companion.' There has always been agreement in this community of Muhammad that the first thing required of a murid once he has become aware of his state of distraction is that he should rely on a Shaykh of good counsel and guidance who knows the defects of the self, its motives, and the remedies for its ailments, and who has done with the putting right of his own self and its desires. He will give the murid insight into the faults of his self and draw him out beyond the perimeter of his senses. Whoever has no Shaykh to direct him will most certainly be directed by shaytan to the path of destruction.

Murid is derived from will (irada) and it depends on sincerity (ikhlas). The true meaning of murid is one who has stripped himself of his own will and accepted what Allah wills for him, which is the worship of Allah ta'ala, for as He said: 'I have not created jinn and men except to worship Me.' When the murid is weak in disciplining his self – since the inner rule belongs to the self and shaytan – he places himself under the rule of the Shaykh and in the protection of his power. He, in his turn will help the murid to obey and worship Allah through his himma which operates by the idhn of Allah and through his words which are made effective by the gift of Allah. So a murid must cling to whoever of the Shaykhs of the age are well disposed towards him.

Sayyidi 'Abd al-Wahid ibn 'Ashir says:

'The murid keeps company with a Shaykh who knows the ways of behaviour,
and who protects him from dangers on his way.
The murid is reminded of Allah when he sees the Shaykh,
who then leads the slave to his Master.'

Look at our commentary on these verses and confusion will leave you.
Ibn 'Ata'llah, may Allah be pleased with him, says in his *Hikam*:

'Do not accompany one whose state does not change you,
and whose speech does not guide you to Allah.'

The elevation of your state, and the guidance of his speech are the result of
this companionship. So whoever does not find such a state from his companion
let him abandon him to Allah and seek one of this description. The murid will
gain a master in accordance with his own sincerity and strength of resolution.
Allah is the one to ask for help.

Explaining the attributes of the teaching Shaykh, I said in one of my qasidas
ending in *ta'*:

*La ilaha illa'llah* banishes all whisperings
with the instruction of a Shaykh who knows the Haqiqa.
His signs are: a light which shines appearing outwardly,
and a secret which appears inwardly, with himma.
He elevates you with a glance even before he speaks,
and from this glance comes a Robe of Honour.

By that I mean the secrets which flow rapidly into the
heart of the murid seeking the truth free of any shirk.
The staff of his journey is his *zuhd* among people,
and his concern lies in seeking the Beloved alone in vision.
His speech is by *idhn* from the Best of Creation
upon whom the glorious truthful ones depend.
If you attain the goal of finding someone like this,
then set out and offer up the self without delay.
Consider nothing except what I have described here,
for it is enough and it contains every happiness.

Al-Junayd, may Allah be pleased with him said:

'Purify yourself with the water of the Unseen if you are one possessing a secret. If not, do *tayammum* with dust or stone. Go before an Imam in front of whom you stand, and pray the noon prayer at the beginning of the afternoon. This is the prayer of those who are the gnostics of their Lord. If you are one of them, then moisten the dry land with the sea.'

He, may Allah be pleased with him, commanded the murid to purify himself with the water of the Unseen. It is understood that purification is of two sorts: sensory purification which is the sensory water, and pertains to the whole body if it is a major impurity, and to specific limbs if it is a minor impurity. This is not what the poet meant, may Allah be pleased with him. The second sort is spiritual purification which is the purification of the hearts from the ailments which veil them from the presence of the Knower of the Unseen. This purification is only done with spiritual water which is the water of sciences, gnoses and secrets that flow from the presence of the Unseen into the heart of the Shaykh who is a gnostic of Allah, purified of fault. The Shaykh pours it over the murid and so he purifies his heart from otherness and it is filled with gnoses and secrets. This is if the murid himself possesses a secret, that is to say inner sight, which brings him into contact with the one who takes him by the hand, that is, the Shaykh who draws his power from the presence of the Unseen as we have stated. If the murid does not possess this secret and inner sight then he must do *tayammum* with the dust of outward deeds and formal knowledge until Allah endows him with the secret and the inner sight.

He indicates, may Allah be pleased with him, by his statement: 'Go before an Imam in front of whom you stand,' that the murid must go before an Imam, a Shaykh, a gnostic of Allah, to copy him in the spiritual prayer which is the direct perception of the worshipped King, as it is necessary for the one behind the Imam in the prayer to do *ruku'* and *sujud* (bowing and prostrating). His words: 'In front of whom you stand,' indicate to the murid that he should not follow any Shaykh except one he already knew in the world of spirits. The Prophet, peace by upon him, said: 'The spirits are numerous hosts, whoever of them become acquainted will be in harmony, and those not acquainted will be at variance.' The meaning then is: 'Go before in the world of spirits. Because of the encounter and acquaintance which occurred in the world of the spirits, harmony will occur in the world of forms.'

By his words, 'Pray the noon prayer at the beginning of the afternoon,' he means pray the dhuhr prayer (noon prayer), that is the manifestation (*dhuhur*) of your desire for your Lord, which is uninterrupted witnessing of the worshipped King, as we have said. 'Asr (afternoon prayer) means 'being together' (*mu'asara*) with your Shaykh and the negation of your will for him. He does not refer, may Allah be pleased with him, to the prayers of dhuhr and 'asr containing *ruku'* and *sujud*, because it is known that dhuhr is set to be prayed at the beginning of its time and not at the beginning of 'asr. Thus the meaning falls into place, so understand and you will be guided – and Allah has charge of our guidance and the guidance of creation. Amin.

As regards his statement: 'This is the prayer of those who are gnostics of their Lord,' it means this is uninterrupted contemplation of the worshipped King. Their prayer is not interrupted because it is constant. They persevere in the witnessing of their Lord. His word: 'If you are among them, then moisten the dry land with the sea,' means if you are one of the gnostics – and they are not veiled by creation from the truth, nor by the truth from creation – then moisten, that is sprinkle, the dry land of your road (*Shari'a*) with the sea of your reality (*Haqiqa*), and be among those who unite the two. Likewise, our Imam, Malik, may Allah be pleased with him, said: 'He who follows the Shari'a and does not ascertain (i.e. have direct experience) has strayed from the proper course. He who ascertains and does not follow the Shari'a has become a heretic. Whoever unites the two has realised!' That is, he has realised the two forms of worship (*'ubudiyya*), the worship of obligation and the worship of instruction.

وَهَذَا وِرْدُنَا الشَّرِيفُ لِمَنْ أَرَادَهُ وَطَلَبَهُ فَهُوَ كَفِيلٌ بِكُلِّ خَيْرٍ
دَافِعٌ لِكُلِّ شَرٍّ وَبِالْمُوَاظَبَةِ عَلَيْهِ بِإِذْنٍ مِنَ الشَّيْخِ أَوِ الْمُقَدَّمِ
الْمَأْذُونِ مِنَ الشَّيْخِ يَجْمَعُ اللهُ لِلْعَبْدِ بَيْنَ الشَّرِيعَةِ وَالْحَقِيقَةِ
وَنَصُّهُ:

This is our noble Wird for whoever wishes it and seeks it.
Its recital guarantees every good and repels every evil.

If the slave perseveres in it with idhn from the Shaykh,
or from a muqaddam who has idhn from the Shaykh,
Allah will unite the Shari'a and Haqiqa for him.

# The Wird

مِفْتَاحُ الْوِرْدِ

The Key to the Wird

اَللّٰهُمَّ صَلِّ عَلَىٰ سَيِّدِنَا مُحَمَّدٍ عَبْدِكَ وَرَسُولِكَ النَّبِيِّ الْأُمِّيِّ وَعَلَىٰ
ءَالِهِ وَصَحْبِهِ وَسَلِّمْ تَسْلِيمًا. عَدَدَ خَلْقِكَ وَرِضَا نَفْسِكَ
وَزِنَةَ عَرْشِكَ وَمِدَادَ كَلِمَاتِكَ.

O Allah pour blessings upon our master Muhammad, Your slave
and Messenger, the unlettered Prophet, and upon his Family and
Companions and grant them perfect peace, as great as the number of
Your creations and Your pleasure and the weight of Your throne
and the ink of Your words.

أَعُوذُ بِاللّٰهِ السَّمِيعِ الْعَلِيمِ مِنَ الشَّيْطَانِ الرَّجِيمِ.

I take refuge with Allah, the All-Hearing, the All-Knowing
from the accursed shaytan.

بِسْمِ اللّٰهِ الرَّحْمٰنِ الرَّحِيمِ

In the name of Allah, the All-Merciful, the Most Merciful

وَلَا حَوْلَ وَلَا قُوَّةَ إِلَّا بِاللّٰهِ الْعَلِيِّ الْعَظِيمِ.

There is no power and no strength but by Allah, the High, the Vast.

أَسْتَغْفِرُ اللهَ. (ثلاثا)

I seek forgiveness of Allah. (3)

اَللّٰهُمَّ صَلِّ عَلَى سَيِّدِنَا مُحَمَّدٍ عَبْدِكَ وَرَسُولِكَ النَّبِيِّ الْاُمِّيِّ
وَعَلَى ءَالِهِ وَصَحْبِهِ وَسَلِّمْ. (ثلاثا)

O Allah pour blessings upon our master Muhammad, Your slave and
Messenger, the unlettered Prophet, and upon his Family and Companions
and grant them peace. (3)

لَا إِلَهَ إِلَّا اللهُ وَحْدَهُ لَا شَرِيكَ لَهُ. لَهُ الْمُلْكُ وَلَهُ الْحَمْدُ.
وَهُوَ عَلَى كُلِّ شَيْءٍ قَدِيرٌ. (ثلاثا)

There is no god except Allah alone, without partner. His is the kingdom,
all praise belongs to Him and He is Powerful over all things. (3)

سُبْحَانَ اللهِ وَالْحَمْدُ لِلَّهِ وَلَا إِلَهَ إِلَّا اللهُ وَاللهُ أَكْبَرُ.
وَلَا حَوْلَ وَلَا قُوَّةَ إِلَّا بِاللهِ الْعَلِيِّ الْعَظِيمِ. (ثلاثا)

Glory be to Allah and all praise belongs to Allah, there is no god except
Allah, Allah is greater! There is no power and no strength but by Allah,
the High, the Vast. (3)

سُبْحَانَ اللهِ وَبِحَمْدِهِ سُبْحَانَ اللهِ الْعَظِيمِ. (ثلاثا)

Glory be to Allah by His praise, glory be to Allah the Vast. (3)

اَلْحَمْدُ لِلَّهِ وَالشُّكْرُ لِلَّهِ. (ثلاثا)

Praise is due to Allah and thanks be to Allah. (3)

لَقَدْ جَاءَكُمْ رَسُولٌ مِّنْ أَنْفُسِكُمْ عَزِيزٌ عَلَيْهِ مَا عَنِتُّمْ. حَرِيصٌ عَلَيْكُمْ. بِالْمُؤْمِنِينَ رَءُوفٌ رَّحِيمٌ.

A Messenger has come to you from among yourselves; your suffering is
distressing to him; he is deeply concerned for you;
he is gentle and merciful to the muminun.

فَإِنْ تَوَلَّوْا فَقُلْ حَسْبِيَ اللَّهُ. لَا إِلَهَ إِلَّا هُوَ. عَلَيْهِ تَوَكَّلْتُ. وَهُوَ رَبُّ الْعَرْشِ الْعَظِيمِ. (ثلاثا)

But if they turn away, say, "Allah is enough for me. There is no god but
Him. I have put my trust in Him. He is the Lord of the Mighty Throne." (3)

بِسْمِ اللَّهِ الرَّحْمَنِ الرَّحِيمِ قُلْ هُوَ اللَّهُ أَحَدٌ. اللَّهُ الصَّمَدُ. لَمْ يَلِدْ وَلَمْ يُولَدْ. وَلَمْ يَكُنْ لَّهُ كُفُؤًا أَحَدٌ. (ثلاثا)

In the name of Allah, All-Merciful, Most Merciful, say: "He is Allah,
Absolute Oneness. Allah, the Everlasting Sustainer of all. He has not
given birth and was not born. And no one is comparable to Him." (3)

تَبَّرَكَ اللَّهُ. (ثلاثا)

Blessed is Allah. (3)

بِسْمِ اللهِ الرَّحْمَـٰنِ الرَّحِيمِ الْحَمْدُ لِلَّهِ رَبِّ الْعَالَمِينَ الرَّحْمَـٰنِ الرَّحِيمِ مَلِكِ يَوْمِ الدِّينِ. إِيَّاكَ نَعْبُدُ وَإِيَّاكَ نَسْتَعِينُ. اِهْدِنَا الصِّرَاطَ الْمُسْتَقِيمَ صِرَاطَ الَّذِينَ أَنْعَمْتَ عَلَيْهِمْ غَيْرِ الْمَغْضُوبِ عَلَيْهِمْ وَلَا الضَّالِّينَ. ءَامِين. (ثلاثا)

In the name of Allah, the All-Merciful, the Most Merciful,
praise be to Allah, the Lord of all the worlds, the All-Merciful,
the Most Merciful, the King of the Day of Judgment. You alone we
worship, You alone we ask for help. Guide us on the Straight Path, the
Path of those whom You have blessed. Not of those with anger upon
them, nor the misguided. Amin. (3)

سُبْحَانَ رَبِّكَ رَبِّ الْعِزَّةِ عَمَّا يَصِفُونَ. وَسَلَامٌ عَلَى الْمُرْسَلِينَ. وَالْحَمْدُ لِلَّهِ رَبِّ الْعَالَمِينَ.

Glory be to your Lord, the Lord of might, above all else that they
describe. And peace be upon the Messengers. And all praise belongs to
Allah, the Lord of all the worlds.

اَللّٰهُمَّ صَلِّ عَلَىٰ سَيِّدِنَا مُحَمَّدٍ عَبْدِكَ وَنَبِيِّكَ وَرَسُولِكَ النَّبِيِّ الْأُمِّيِّ وَعَلَىٰ ءَالِهِ وَصَحْبِهِ وَسَلِّمْ تَسْلِيمًا. بِقَدْرِ عَظَمَةِ ذَاتِكَ فِي كُلِّ وَقْتٍ وَحِينَ. (ثلاثا) ءَامِين (ثلاثا)

O Allah pour blessings upon our master Muhammad, Your slave,
Your Messenger, the unlettered Prophet, and upon his Family and

Companions and grant them perfect peace, by the measure of the sublimity of Your Essence at every time and in every age. (3) Amin. (3)

سُبْحَانَ رَبِّكَ رَبِّ الْعِزَّةِ عَمَّا يَصِفُونَ. وَسَلَامٌ عَلَى الْمُرْسَلِينَ.
وَالْحَمْدُ لِلَّهِ رَبِّ الْعَٰلَمِينَ.

Glory be to your Lord, the Lord of might, above all else that they describe. And peace be upon the Messengers. And all praise belongs to Allah, the Lord of all the worlds.

اَللّٰهُمَّ إِنِّي أَسْأَلُكَ إِسْلَامًا صَحِيحًا
يَصْحَبُهُ الِاسْتِسْلَامُ لِأَوَامِرِكَ وَنَوَاهِيكَ.

O Allah! I ask You for sound Islam
accompanied by submission to Your orders and prohibitions;

وَإِيمَانًا خَالِصًا رَاسِخًا ثَابِتًا مَحْفُوظًا مِنْ جَمِيعِ الشُّبَهِ وَالْمَهَالِكَ.

and for pure Iman, firmly established, enduring,
protected from all ambiguities and dangers;

وَإِحْسَانًا يَزُجُّ بِنَا فِي حَضَرَاتِ الْغُيُوبِ.

and for Ihsan that will drive us into the presence of the Unseen,

وَنَتَطَهَّرُ بِهِ مِنْ أَنْوَاعِ الْغَفَلَاتِ وَسَائِرِ الْعُيُوبِ.

and by which we will be purified from every kind of negligence
and all other defects;

وَإِيقَانًا يَكْشِفُ لَنَا عَنْ حَضَرَاتِ الأَسْمَاءِ وَالصِّفَاتِ.

and a certainty which will reveal to us the presences
of the Names and the Attributes,

وَيَرْحَلُ بِنَا إِلَىٰ مُشَاهَدَةِ أَنْوَارِ تَجَلِّيَاتِ الذَّاتِ.

and by which we will be carried into witnessing
the lights of the Manifestations of the Essence;

وَعِلْمًا نَافِعًا نَفْقَهُ بِهِ كَيْفَ نَتَأَدَّبُ مَعَكَ

وَنُنَاجِيكَ فِي الصَّلَوَاتِ.

and for useful knowledge by which we may understand how to conduct
ourselves in Your presence and how to confide in You in the prayers.

وَامْلأْ قُلُوبَنَا بِأَنْوَارِ مَعْرِفَتِكَ حَتَّى نَشْهَدَ قَيُّومِيَّتَكَ السَّارِيَةَ

فِي جَمِيعِ الْمَخْلُوقَاتِ.

Fill our hearts with the lights of Your Ma'rifa so that we may witness
Your All-Sustaining Gatheredness that flows in all created things.

وَاجْعَلْنَا مِنْ أَهْلِ دَائِرَةِ الْفَضْلِ الْمَحْبُوبِينَ لَدَيْكَ.

Let us be among the circle of Your bounty, beloved to You.

وَمِنَ الرَّاسِخِينَ الْمُتَمَكِّنِينَ فِي التَّوَكُّلِ
وَصِدْقِ الْاعْتِمَادِ عَلَيْكَ.

And among the firmly grounded and enduring in reliance
and sincerity of dependence on You.

وَحَقِّقْ رَجَاءَنَا بِالاِجَابَةِ يَا كَرِيمُ يَا وَهَّابُ
فِي كُلِّ مَا سَأَلْنَاكَ.

Realise our hope with the answer, O Generous, O Giving,
in all that we ask You.

وَلَا تَكِلْنَا يَا مَوْلَانَا فِي جَمِيعِ حَرَكَاتِنَا وَسَكَنَاتِنَا
إِلَى أَحَدٍ سِوَاكَ.

Do not entrust us, O Master, in all our movements and stillness,
to anyone other than You.

فَإِنَّكَ عَوَّدْتَنَا إِحْسَانَكَ مِنْ قَبْلِ سُؤَالِنَا
وَنَحْنُ فِي بُطُونِ الْأُمَّهَاتِ.

For You have accustomed us to Your Ihsan before we even asked for it
while we were in our mothers' wombs.

وَرَبَّيْتَنَا بِلَطِيفِ رُبُوبِيَّتِكَ تَرْبِيَةً
تَقْصُرُ عَنْ إِدْرَاكِهَا الْعُقُولُ الْمُنَوَّرَاتُ.

You have raised us with the Gentleness of Your Lordship over existence
in a manner far beyond the perception of illuminated intellects.

فَنَسْأَلُكَ اللّٰهُمَّ بِنَبِيِّكَ الَّذِي فَضَّلْتَهُ
عَلَىٰ سَآئِرِ الاَنْبِيَآءِ وَالْمُرْسَلِينَ.

We ask You, O Allah, by Your Prophet, whom You have preferred
above all other Prophets and Messengers,

وَ بِرَسُولِكَ الَّذِي جَعَلْتَ رِسَالَتَهُ عَآمَّةً وَرَحْمَةً لِّلْخَلاَئِقِ أَجْمَعِينَ.

and by Your Messenger whose message You made universal
and a mercy to all creation,

أَنْ تُصَلِّيَ وَتُسَلِّمَ عَلَيْهِ وَعَلَىٰ ءَالِهِ صَلاَةً وَسَلاَمًا نَنَالُ بِهِمَا مَحَبَّتَهُ
وَمُتَابَعَتَهُ فِي الاَقْوَالِ وَالاَفْعَالِ وَالْمُرَاقَبَةِ وَالْمُشَاهَدَةِ وَالآدَابِ
وَالاَخْلاَقِ وَالاَحْوَالِ.

to bless him and his family and grant them a peace by which we may
attain his love and follow him in words, in deeds, in watching, in
witnessing, in adab, in character and states.

وَنَسْأَلُكَ يَا مَوْلَانَا بِجَاهِهِ أَنْ تَهَبَ لَنَا عِلْمًا نَافِعًا يَنْتَفِعُ بِهِ كُلُّ سَامِعٍ.

We ask You, O Master, by his rank, to grant us useful knowledge by
which every listener may profit,

وَتَخْشَعُ لَهُ الْقُلُوبُ وَتَقْشَعِرُّ مِنْهُ الْجُلُودُ وَتَجْرِي لَهُ الْمَدَامِعُ.

and every heart may be made humble, and at which the skin may
tremble and tears flow.

إِنَّكَ أَنْتَ الْقَادِرُ الْمُرِيدُ الْعَالِمُ الْحَيُّ الْوَاسِعُ.

You are the All-Powerful, the One who wills,
the Knowing, the Living, the Vast.

سُبْحَانَ رَبِّكَ رَبِّ الْعِزَّةِ عَمَّا يَصِفُونَ. وَسَلَامٌ عَلَى الْمُرْسَلِينَ. وَالْحَمْدُ لِلَّهِ رَبِّ الْعَالَمِينَ.

Glory be to your Lord, the Lord of might, above all else that they
describe. And peace be upon the Messengers. And all praise belongs to
Allah, the Lord of all the worlds.

ثُمَّ تُصَلِّي بِهَذِهِ الصَّلَاةِ الْمُسَمَّاةِ بِكَنْزِ الْحَقَائِقِ فِي الصَّلَاةِ عَلَى أَشْرَفِ الْخَلَائِقِ الَّتِي تَلَقَّاهَا

شَيْخُنَا عَنِ الْمُصْطَفَى صَلَّى اللهُ عَلَيْهِ وَسَلَّمَ وَهِيَ.

*Then you pray the prayer called the Treasury of Truths asking for blessings on the*
*most noble of creatures, which our Shaykh received from the Chosen One, may*
*Allah bless him and grant him peace.*

اَللّٰهُمَّ صَلِّ وَسَلِّمْ بِأَنْوَاعِ كَمَالَاتِكَ فِي جَمِيعِ تَجَلِّيَاتِكَ

عَلَى سَيِّدِنَا وَمَوْلَانَا مُحَمَّدٍ

أَوَّلِ الْأَنْوَارِ الْفَائِضَةِ مِنْ بُحُورِ عَظَمَةِ الذَّاتِ.

O Allah bless and grant peace with every one of Your perfections in all
Your manifestations upon our lord and master Muhammad, the first of
the lights emanating from the oceans of the sublimity of the Essence,

اَلْمُتَحَقِّقِ فِي عَالَمَيِ الْبُطُونِ وَالظُّهُورِ

بِمَعَانِي الْأَسْمَآءِ وَالصِّفَاتِ.

who realised in the two worlds – the hidden and the seen – the
meanings of the Names and the Attributes.

فَهُوَ أَوَّلُ حَامِدٍ وَمُتَعَبِّدٍ بِأَنْوَاعِ الْعِبَادَاتِ وَالْقُرُبَاتِ.

He is the first to give praise and worship
with every kind of adoration and good action.

18

وَالْمُمِدُّ فِي عَالَمَيِ الْاَرْوَاحِ وَالْاَشْبَاحِ بِجَمِيعِ الْمَوْجُودَاتِ.

He is the helper of all created beings
in the world of spirits and the world of forms.

وَعَلَىٰ ءَالِهِ وَأَصْحَابِهِ صَلَاةً تَكْشِفُ لَنَا النِّقَابَ
عَنْ وَجْهِهِ الْكَرِيمِ فِي الْمَرَآئِي وَالْيَقَظَاتِ.

And blessings be upon his family and Companions with a blessing
that will lift the veil from his noble face for us
in visions and in the waking state,

وَتُعَرِّفُنَا بِكَ وَبِهِ فِي جَمِيعِ الْمَرَاتِبِ وَالْحَضَرَاتِ.

and will acquaint us with You and with him
in all ranks and presences.

وَالْطُفْ بِنَا يَا مَوْلَانَا بِجَاهِهِ
فِي الْحَرَكَاتِ وَالسَّكَنَاتِ وَاللَّحَظَاتِ وَانْخَطَرَاتِ. (ثلاثا)

Be gracious to us, O Mawlana, by his rank,
in movements and in stillness, in looks and in thoughts. (3)

سُبْحَانَ رَبِّكَ رَبِّ الْعِزَّةِ عَمَّا يَصِفُونَ. وَسَلَامٌ عَلَى الْمُرْسَلِينَ.
وَالْحَمْدُ لِلّٰهِ رَبِّ الْعَٰلَمِينَ.

Glory be to your Lord, the Lord of might, above all else that they
describe. And peace be upon the Messengers. And all praise belongs to
Allah, the Lord of all the worlds.

أَعُوذُ بِاللهِ مِنَ الشَّيْطَانِ الرَّجِيمِ.

I seek refuge with Allah from the accursed Shaytan:

اَلَّذِينَ قَالَ لَهُمُ النَّاسُ إِنَّ النَّاسَ قَدْ جَمَعُوا لَكُمْ
فَاخْشَوْهُمْ فَزَادَهُمْ إِيمَانًا وَقَالُوا

Those to whom people said,
'The people have gathered against you, so fear them,'
but that merely increased their Iman and they said:

حَسْبُنَا اللهُ وَنِعْمَ الْوَكِيلُ. (عشراً)

"Allah is enough for us and the best of Guardians." (10)

فَانْقَلَبُوا بِنِعْمَةٍ مِنَ اللهِ وَفَضْلٍ لَمْ يَمْسَسْهُمْ سُوءٌ (ثلاثاً)

So they returned with blessings from Allah,
and no evil touched them. (3)

وَاتَّبَعُوا رِضْوَانَ اللهِ. وَاللهُ ذُو فَضْلٍ عَظِيمٍ. (ثلاثاً)

They pursued the pleasure of Allah.
Allah's favour is indeed immense. (3)

وَإِنْ يُرِيدُوا أَنْ يَخْدَعُوكَ فَإِنَّ حَسْبَكَ اللهُ.

And if they intend to deceive you, Allah is enough for you.

هُوَ الَّذِيٓ أَيَّدَكَ بِنَصْرِهِۦ وَبِالْمُومِنِينَ وَأَلَّفَ بَيْنَ قُلُوبِهِمْ ۚ

It is He Who supported you with His help,
and with the muminun, and unified their hearts.

لَوْ أَنفَقْتَ مَا فِي الْأَرْضِ جَمِيعًا مَّآ أَلَّفْتَ بَيْنَ قُلُوبِهِمْ ۚ

Even if you had spent everything on the earth,
you could not have unified their hearts.

وَلَٰكِنَّ اللَّهَ أَلَّفَ بَيْنَهُمْ ۚ إِنَّهُۥ عَزِيزٌ حَكِيمٌ ۚ

But Allah has unified them. He is the Almighty, All-Wise.

يَٰٓأَيُّهَا النَّبِيُّ حَسْبُكَ اللَّهُ ۚ وَمَنِ اتَّبَعَكَ مِنَ الْمُومِنِينَ ۚ (ثلاثا)

O Prophet! Allah is enough for you,
and for the muminun who follow you. (3)

أَلَا يَا لَطِيفُ يَا لَطِيفُ لَكَ اللُّطْفُ

O Gentle, O Knower of subtleties, gentleness is Yours!

فَأَنْتَ اللَّطِيفُ مِنْكَ يَشْمَلُنَا اللُّطْفُ

You are the Gentle, and from You gentleness engulfs us.

لَطِيفُ لَطِيفُ إِنَّنِي مُتَوَسِّلٌ

Latif, Latif, I seek nearness to You

بِلُطْفِكَ فَالْطُفْ بِي وَقَدْ نَزَلَ اللُّطْفُ

by means of Your lutf – be latif to me – and lutf has descended!

بِلُطْفِكَ عُذْنَا يَا لَطِيفُ وَهَا نَحْنُ

Ya Latif, we have sought refuge in Your lutf – we have

دَخَلْنَا فِي وَسْطِ اللُّطْفِ وَانْسَدَلَ اللُّطْفُ

gone into the centre of lutf – and lutf has come down.

نَجَوْنَا بِلُطْفِ اللهِ ذِي اللُّطْفِ إِنَّهُ

We have been freed by the lutf of Allah, the Possessor of lutf,

لَطِيفٌ لَطِيفٌ لُطْفُهُ دَائِمًا لُطْفُ

He is Latif, Latif, His lutf is always that.

أَلَا يَا حَفِيظُ يَا حَفِيظُ لَكَ الْحِفْظُ

O Preserver, O Guardian, guardianship is Yours!

فَأَنْتَ الْحَفِيظُ مِنْكَ يَشْمَلُنَا الْحِفْظُ

You are the Preserver, and from You guardianship engulfs us.

حَفِيظُ حَفِيظُ إِنَّا نَتَوَسَّلُ

Hafidh, Hafidh, We seek nearness to You

بِحِفْظِكَ فَاحْفَظْنَا وَقَدْ نَزَلَ الْحِفْظُ

by means of Your hifdh – be hafidh to us – and hifdh has descended.

22

بِحِفْظِكَ عُذْنَا يَا حَفِيظُ وَهَا نَحْنُ

Ya Hafidh, we have sought refuge in Your hifdh – we have

دَخَلْنَا فِي وَسْطِ الْحِفْظِ وَانْسَدَلَ الْحِفْظُ

gone into the centre of hifdh – and hifdh has come down.

نَجَوْنَا بِحِفْظِ اللهِ ذِي الْحِفْظِ إِنَّهُ

We have been freed by the hifdh of Allah, the Possessor of hifdh.

حَفِيظٌ حَفِيظٌ حِفْظُهُ دَائِمًا حِفْظُ

He is Hafidh, Hafidh, His hifdh is always that.

بِجَاهِ إِمَامِ الْمُرْسَلِينَ مُحَمَّدٍ

By the rank of the Imam of the Messengers, Muhammad,

فَلَوْلَاهُ عَيْنُ الْحِفْظِ مَا نَزَلَ الْحِفْظُ

If it were not for him, the source of hifdh,
hifdh would not have descended.

عَلَيْهِ صَلَاةُ اللهِ مَا قَالَ مُنْشِدٌ

Blessings be upon him as long as there is one who chants:

أَلَا يَا حَفِيظُ يَا حَفِيظُ لَكَ الْحِفْظُ

Ya Hafidh, ya Hafidh, the hifdh is Yours!

لَآ إِلَهَ إِلَّا اللهُ. (عشرا)

No god – except Allah (10)

لَآ إِلَهَ إِلَّا اللهُ. سَيِّدُنَا مُحَمَّدٌ رَسُولُ اللهِ.

No god – except Allah;

our master Muhammad is the Messenger of Allah.

صَلَّى اللهُ عَلَيْهِ وَسَلَّمَ وَعَلَىٰ ءَالِهِ.

May Allah bless him and his family and grant them peace.

ثَبِّتْنَا يَا رَبِّ بِقَوْلِهَا. وَانْفَعْنَا يَا مَوْلَانَا بِذِكْرِهَا.

O Lord, make us firm by its recital.

O Mawlana, give us benefit from its invocation.

وَأَدْخِلْنَا فِي مَيْدَانِ حِصْنِهَا. وَاجْعَلْنَا مِنْ أَفْرَادِ أَهْلِهَا.

Let us enter into the fortress of its protection.

And let us be among its people,

وَعِنْدَ الْمَوْتِ نَاطِقِينَ بِهَا. عَالِمِينَ بِهَا.

who at the time of death say it, having knowledge of what is in it.

وَاحْشُرْنَا فِي زُمْرَةِ سَيِّدِنَا وَمَوْلَانَا مُحَمَّدٍ صَلَّى اللهُ عَلَيْهِ وَسَلَّمَ

وَعَلَىٰ ءَالِهِ وَأَصْحَابِهِ وَعَلَىٰ جَمِيعِ عِبَادِ اللهِ الْمُؤْمِنِينَ.

Gather us into the company of our lord and master Muhammad, may

Allah pour blessings upon him and grant him peace, and his family and Companions and all the believing slaves of Allah.

ءَامِين (ثلاثًا)

Amin. (3)

وَسَلَامٌ عَلَى الْأَنْبِيَآءِ وَالْمُرْسَلِينَ • (ثلاثًا)

And peace be upon the Prophets and the Messengers. (3)

وَعَلَىٰ جَمِيعِ عِبَادِ اللهِ الصَّالِحِينَ.

And on all the Right-acting slaves of Allah (Saliheen).

وَءَاخِرُ دَعْوَانَآ أَنِ الْحَمْدُ لِلَّهِ رَبِّ الْعَٰلَمِينَ.

The end of our call is: Praise be to Allah, the Lord of the worlds.

وَلَا حَوْلَ وَلَا قُوَّةَ إِلَّا بِاللهِ الْعَلِيِّ الْعَظِيمِ.

There is no power and no strength but by Allah,
the High, the Vast.

وَمَا تَوْفِيقِي إِلَّا بِاللهِ. عَلَيْهِ تَوَكَّلْتُ. وَإِلَيْهِ أُنِيبُ.

My success is only by Allah. In Him I have put my trust.
And to Him I turn in renewal.

وَالْحَمْدُ لِلَّهِ عَلَىٰ نِعْمَةِ الْإِسْلَامِ وَكَفَىٰ بِهَا نِعْمَةً.

Praise belongs to Allah for the blessing of Islam,
and it is blessing enough.

يَا أَوَّلُ يَاۤ ءَاخِرُ يَا ظَاهِرُ يَا بَاطِنُ. اِسْمَعْ نِدَآئِي بِمَا سَمِعْتَ بِهِ نِدَآءَ

O First! O Last! O Manifest! O Hidden!
Hear my cry as you heard the cry

عَبْدِكَ سَيِّدِنَا زَكَرِيَّاۤءَ عَلَيْهِ السَّلَامُ.

of Your slave, our master Zakariyya', peace be upon him.

وَانْصُرْنِي بِكَ لَكَ.

Give me victory by You – for You.

وَأَيِّدْنِي بِكَ لَكَ.

Support me by You – for You.

وَاجْمَعْ بَيْنِي وَبَيْنَكَ.

Join me to You.

وَحُلْ بَيْنِي وَبَيْنَ غَيْرِكَ.

Separate me from other-than-You.

اللّٰه (عشرا)

Allah (10)

وإن أردت الزيادة من ذكر الاسم المفرد في غير الورد فلك ذلك ، ومن زاد زاده الله ،
وقد ذكر العارفون بالله للاسم المفرد فوائد لا تعد ولا تحصى

*If you want to do more of the dhikr of the Unique Name outside of the Wird you may do so, and whoever does more, Allah will give more, and the 'arifun of Allah have mentioned innumerable benefits from the Unique Name.*

# The Lesser Wird

بِسْمِ اللهِ الرَّحْمٰنِ الرَّحِيمِ.

In the name of Allah, All-Merciful, Most Merciful.

اَللّٰهُمَّ إِنِّي أَسْأَلُكَ بِسِرِّ الذَّاتِ.

O Allah, I ask You by the secret of the Essence.

وَبِذَاتِ السِّرِّ. هُوَ أَنْتَ وَأَنْتَ هُوَ.

And by the Essence of the secret. He is You and You are He.

اِحْتَجَبْتُ بِنُورِ اللهِ. وَبِنُورِ عَرْشِ اللهِ.

I have veiled myself with the light of Allah,
and by the light of the Throne of Allah,

وَبِكُلِّ إِسْمِ اللهِ مِنْ عَدُوِّي وَعَدُوِّ اللهِ.

and with all the Names of Allah from my enemy
and the enemy of Allah.

بِمِائَةِ أَلْفٍ لَا حَوْلَ وَلَا قُوَّةَ إِلَّا بِاللهِ.

With one hundred thousand "there is no power
and no strength but by Allah."

خَتَمْتُ عَلَى نَفْسِي وَعَلَى دِينِي وَعَلَى كُلِّ شَيْءٍ أَعْطَانِيهِ رَبِّي.

I have set a seal upon my self and my Deen
and upon everything given to me by my Lord.

بِخَاتِمِ اللهِ الْمَنِيعِ الَّذِي
خَتَمَ بِهِ أَقْطَارَ السَّمَٰوَاتِ وَالْاَرْضِ.

With the protecting seal of Allah
with which He has sealed the heavens and the earth.

وَحَسْبُنَا اللهُ وَنِعْمَ الْوَكِيلُ. نِعْمَ الْمَوْلَىٰ وَنِعْمَ النَّصِيرُ.

Allah is enough for us and He is the best Guardian.
The best Protector, the best Helper.

وَصَلَّى اللهُ عَلَى سَيِّدِنَا وَمَوْلَانَا مُحَمَّدٍ

The blessings of Allah be upon our lord and master Muhammad,

وَعَلَى ءَالِهِ وَأَصْحَابِهِ أَجْمَعِينَ.

and upon all his family and Companions.

وَسَلَّمَ تَسْلِيمًا كَثِيرًا.

And grant them great peace.

وَالْحَمْدُ لِلَّهِ رَبِّ الْعَٰلَمِينَ.

Praise belongs to Allah, the Lord of the worlds.

ثم تقول الدعاء المبارك وهو :

*Then you may say this blessed du'a*

يَا وَدُودُ. (ثلاثا)

O Lover! (3)

يَا ذَا الْعَرْشِ الْمَجِيدِ. (ثلاثا)

O Possessor of the glorious Throne! (3)

يَا مُبْدِئُ يَا مُعِيدُ. (ثلاثا)

O You Who Originate, O You Who Bring back to life! (3)

يَا فَعَّالًا لِمَا يُرِيدُ. (ثلاثا)

O He Who does whatever He wills! (3)

أَسْأَلُكَ بِنُورِ وَجْهِكَ الَّذِي مَلَأَ أَرْكَانَ عَرْشِكَ. (ثلاثا)

I ask You by the light of Your face
that fills every corner of Your Throne, (3)

وَأَسْأَلُكَ بِالْقُدْرَةِ الَّتِي قَدَرْتَ بِهَا عَلَى خَلْقِكَ. (ثلاثا)

and I ask You by the power You exercise over Your creation, (3)

وَبِرَحْمَتِكَ الَّتِي وَسِعَتْ كُلَّ شَيْءٍ. (ثلاثا)

and by Your mercy that encompasses all things: (3)

لَآ إِلَهَ إِلَّا أَنْتَ يَا مُغِيثُ أَغِثْنَا. (ثلاثا)

No god but You – O Rescuer – rescue us! (3)

سُبْحَانَ رَبِّكَ رَبِّ الْعِزَّةِ عَمَّا يَصِفُونَ. وَسَلَامٌ عَلَى الْمُرْسَلِينَ.
وَالْحَمْدُ لِلَّهِ رَبِّ الْعَلَمِينَ.

Glory be to your Lord, the Lord of might, above all else that they
describe. And peace be upon the Messengers. And all praise belongs to
Allah, the Lord of all the worlds.

اَللَّهُ لَطِيفٌ بِعِبَادِهِ. يَرْزُقُ مَنْ يَشَاءُ. وَهُوَ الْقَوِيُّ الْعَزِيزُ. (تسعا)

Allah is gentle with His slaves. He provides for anyone He wills, and He
is the Most Strong, the Almighty. (9)

سُبْحَانَ رَبِّكَ رَبِّ الْعِزَّةِ عَمَّا يَصِفُونَ. وَسَلَامٌ عَلَى الْمُرْسَلِينَ.
وَالْحَمْدُ لِلَّهِ رَبِّ الْعَلَمِينَ. ○

Glory be to your Lord, the Lord of might, above all else that they
describe. And peace be upon the Messengers. And all praise belongs to
Allah, the Lord of all the worlds.

وعند الصباح تزيد :

*At Subh you add:*

30

لَاۤ إِلَهَ إِلَّا اللهُ وَاللهُ أَكْبَرُ. وَسُبْحَانَ اللهِ وَبِحَمْدِهِ وَأَسْتَغْفِرُ

اللهَ. وَلَا حَوْلَ وَلَا قُوَّةَ إِلَّا بِاللهِ. هُوَ الْاوَّلُ وَالْآخِرُ وَالظَّاهِرُ

وَالْبَاطِنُ. بِيَدِهِ الْخَيْرُ. يُحْيِي وَيُمِيتُ.

وَهُوَ عَلَى كُلِّ شَيْءٍ قَدِيرٌ. (عَشْرًا)

There is no god except Allah and Allah is greater. Glory be to Allah
and by His praise, and I seek forgiveness from Allah. And there is no
power and no strength but by Allah. He is the First and the Last and the
Outwardly Manifest and the Inwardly Hidden. Good is in His hand, He
makes to live and makes to die, and He is powerful over all things. (10)

وَصَلَّى اللهُ عَلَى سَيِّدِنَا وَمَوْلَانَا مُحَمَّدٍ وَعَلَى ءَالِهِ وَصَحْبِهِ وَسَلَّمَ

تَسْلِيمًا. عَدَدَ خَلْقِكَ وَرِضَا نَفْسِكَ وَزِنَةَ عَرْشِكَ

وَمِدَادَ كَلِمَاتِكَ.

And blessings of Allah upon our lord and master, Muhammad, and upon
his family and Companions and grant them perfect peace – as great as
the number of Your creations and Your pleasure and the weight of Your
Throne and the ink of Your words.

سُبْحَانَ رَبِّكَ رَبِّ الْعِزَّةِ عَمَّا يَصِفُونَ. وَسَلَامٌ عَلَى الْمُرْسَلِينَ.

وَالْحَمْدُ لِلَّهِ رَبِّ الْعَلَمِينَ.

Glory be to your Lord, the Lord of might, above all else that they
describe. And peace be upon the Messengers. And all praise belongs to
Allah, the Lord of all the worlds.

سُبْحَانَ اللهِ وَالْحَمْدُ لِلَّهِ وَلَا إِلَهَ إِلَّا اللهُ وَاللهُ أَكْبَرُ.

وَلَا حَوْلَ وَلَا قُوَّةَ إِلَّا بِاللهِ الْعَلِيِّ الْعَظِيمِ. عَدَدَ مَا عَلِمَ

وَزِنَةَ مَا عَلِمَ وَمِلَا مَا عَلِمَ. (ثَلَاثًا)

Glory be to Allah and praise be to Allah and there is no god except
Allah and Allah is greater. There is no power and no strength but by
Allah, the High, the Vast, in quantity as great as what He knows, in
weight as much as He knows and in volume as much as He knows. (3)

سُبْحَانَ رَبِّكَ رَبِّ الْعِزَّةِ عَمَّا يَصِفُونَ. وَسَلَامٌ عَلَى الْمُرْسَلِينَ.
وَالْحَمْدُ لِلَّهِ رَبِّ الْعَٰلَمِينَ ۝

Glory be to your Lord, the Lord of might, above all else that they
describe. And peace be upon the Messengers. And all praise belongs to
Allah, the Lord of all the worlds.

# The Seal of The Wird

أدعية ختام الورد

اَللّٰهُمَّ افْتَحْ بَصَآئِرَنَا لِمُرَاقَبَتِكَ وَمُشَاهَدَتِكَ بِجُودِكَ وَفَضْلِكَ.

O Allah, open our inner sight for us to watch You and witness You
by Your generosity and overflowing.

وَنَوِّرْ سَرَآئِرَنَا لِتَجَلِّيَاتِ أَسْمَائِكَ وَصِفَاتِكَ بِحِلْمِكَ وَكَرَمِكَ.

And illuminate our secret to the manifestations of Your Names and
Attributes through Your forbearance and noble generosity.

32

وَأَفْنِنَا عَنْ وُجُودِنَا الْمَجَازِي
فِي وُجُودِكَ الْحَقِيقِي بِطَوْلِكَ وَمَنِّكَ.

And annihilate us from our metaphorical existence
in Your real existence, by Your favour and gifts.

وَأَبْقِنَا بِكَ لَا بِنَا مُحَافِظِينَ عَلَى شَرِيعَتِكَ وَسُنَّةِ نَبِيِّكَ.

And make us continue by You, not by us, preserving Your Shari'a
and the Sunna of Your Prophet.

إِنَّكَ عَلَى كُلِّ شَيْءٍ قَدِيرٌ. وَبِالْإِجَابَةِ جَدِيرٌ.

You are powerful over all things — and are disposed to answer.

بِسِرِّ وَبَرَكَةِ بِسْمِ اللهِ الرَّحْمَنِ الرَّحِيمِ الْحَمْدُ لِلَّهِ رَبِّ الْعَالَمِينَ
الرَّحْمَنِ الرَّحِيمِ مَلِكِ يَوْمِ الدِّينِ. إِيَّاكَ نَعْبُدُ وَإِيَّاكَ نَسْتَعِينُ. اهْدِنَا
الصِّرَاطَ الْمُسْتَقِيمَ صِرَاطَ الَّذِينَ أَنْعَمْتَ عَلَيْهِمْ غَيْرِ الْمَغْضُوبِ
عَلَيْهِمْ وَلَا الضَّالِّينَ. ءَامِين.

By the secret and the blessing of: In the name of Allah, All-Merciful,
the Most Merciful. Praise be to Allah, Lord of the worlds, the All-
Merciful, the Most Merciful, the King of the Day of Judgment. You
alone we worship, You alone we ask for help. Guide us on the Straight
Path, the Path of those whom You have blessed, not of those with anger
upon them, nor of the misguided. Amin.

سُبْحَانَ رَبِّكَ رَبِّ الْعِزَّةِ عَمَّا يَصِفُونَ. وَسَلَامٌ عَلَى الْمُرْسَلِينَ.
وَالْحَمْدُ لِلَّهِ رَبِّ الْعَٰلَمِينَ ○

Glory be to your Lord, the Lord of might, above all else that they
describe. And peace be upon the Messengers.
And praise belongs to Allah, the Lord of all the worlds.

ثم تدعو لنفسك ولوالديك ولمشائخك ولشيخ وقتك ولأمير المومنين خصوصا
ولكافة المسلمين عموما

*Then pray for yourself and your parents and for your shaykhs and for the Shaykh*
*of your age and for the Amir al-Muminin in particular*
*and for all the Muslims in general.*

اللَّهُمَّ صَلِّ عَلَى سَيِّدِنَا مُحَمَّدٍ وَعَلَىٓ ءَالِ سَيِّدِنَا مُحَمَّدٍ صَلَاةً تُنْجِينَا
بِهَا مِنْ جَمِيعِ الْأَهْوَالِ وَالْآفَاتِ. وَتَقْضِي لَنَا بِهَا جَمِيعَ الْحَاجَاتِ.
وَتُطَهِّرُنَا بِهَا مِنْ جَمِيعِ السَّيِّئَاتِ. وَتَرْفَعُنَا بِهَآ
أَعْلَا الدَّرَجَاتِ. وَتُبَلِّغُنَا بِهَآ أَقْصَى الْغَايَاتِ مِنْ جَمِيعِ الْخَيْرَاتِ
فِي الْحَيَاةِ وَبَعْدَ الْمَمَاتِ.

O Allah, bless our master Muhammad and the family of our master
Muhammad with a blessing by which You will save us from every fear
and harm, and by which You will supply us with all our needs, and by
which You will purify us from all evils, and by which You will raise
us to the highest degrees, and by which You will make us attain the
furthest goal of good in life and after death.

اَللّٰهُمَّ أَنْزِلْ عَلَيْنَا فِي هٰذِهِ السَّاعَةِ مِنْ خَيْرِكَ وَبَرَكَاتِكَ.

كَمَا أَنْزَلْتَ عَلَى أَوْلِيَائِكَ. وَخَصَّصْتَ بِهِ أَحِبَّائَكَ. وَأَذِقْنَا بَرْدَ

عَفْوِكَ وَحَلَاوَةَ مَغْفِرَتِكَ. وَانْشُرْ عَلَيْنَا رَحْمَتَكَ الَّتِي وَسِعَتْ كُلَّ

شَيْءٍ. وَارْزُقْنَا مِنْكَ مَحَبَّةً وَقَبُولًا. وَتَوْبَةً نَصُوحًا. وَإِجَابَةً وَمَغْفِرَةً

وَعَافِيَةً. تَعُمُّ الْحَاضِرِينَ وَالْغَائِبِينَ وَالْاحْيَاءَ وَالْمَيِّتِينَ. بِرَحْمَتِكَ

يَا أَرْحَمَ الرَّاحِمِينَ يَا أَرْحَمَ الرَّاحِمِينَ يَا أَرْحَمَ الرَّاحِمِينَ.

O Allah, in this hour send down some of Your good and Your baraka
on us as You sent it down on Your near ones, and singled it out for Your
lovers. Let us taste the coolness of Your pardon and the sweetness of
Your forgiveness. Spread over us Your compassion which encompasses
all things. Provide us with Your love and acceptance and sincere
turning to You, and Your response to our asking, forgiveness, and wellbeing that will encompass those present and absent,
the living and the dead, by Your mercy,
O Most Merciful of the merciful. (3)

اَللّٰهُمَّ لَا تُخَيِّبْنَا مِمَّا سَأَلْنَاكَ. وَلَا تَحْرِمْنَا مِمَّا رَجَوْنَاكَ. وَاحْفَظْنَا

وَاحْفَظْنَا وَاحْفَظْنَا فِي الْمَحْيَا وَالْمَمَاتِ.

إِنَّكَ مُجِيبُ الدَّعَوَاتِ.

O Allah, do not disappoint us in what we ask of You. Do not deny us
what we hope for from You. Protect us. Protect us. Protect us in life
and in death. You are the Answerer of prayers.

سُبْحَانَ رَبِّكَ رَبِّ الْعِزَّةِ عَمَّا يَصِفُونَ. وَسَلَامٌ عَلَى الْمُرْسَلِينَ.
وَالْحَمْدُ لِلَّهِ رَبِّ الْعَالَمِينَ.

Glory be to your Lord, the Lord of might, above all else that they
describe. And peace be upon the Messengers.
And praise belongs to Allah, the Lord of all the worlds.

اَللَّهُمَّ إِنِّي أَسْتَخِيرُكَ بِعِلْمِكَ. وَأَسْتَقْدِرُكَ بِقُدْرَتِكَ.
وَأَسْأَلُكَ مِنْ فَضْلِكَ الْعَظِيمِ الْاَعْظَمِ.

O Allah, I ask You to choose by Your knowledge. And I ask You to decree
by Your power. And I ask You for some of Your great and sublime bounty.

فَإِنَّكَ تَقْدِرُ وَلَا أَقْدِرُ. وَتَعْلَمُ وَلَا أَعْلَمُ. وَأَنْتَ عَلَّامُ الْغُيُوبِ.

For You have power and I do not. You know and I do not.
And You are the Knower of the Unseen.

اَللَّهُمَّ إِنْ كُنْتَ تَعْلَمُ أَنَّ هٰذَا الْاَمْرَ وَهُوَ جَمِيعُ حَرَكَاتِي وَسَكَنَاتِي
الظَّاهِرَةِ وَالْبَاطِنَةِ. مِنْ قَوْلٍ وَفِعْلٍ وَخُلُقٍ وَحَالٍ. عِبَادَةً وَعَادَةً.
فِي حَقِّي وَفِي حَقِّ غَيْرِي. فِي هٰذَا الْيَوْمِ وَفِيمَا بَعْدَهُ { أَوْ: فِي
هٰذِهِ اللَّيْلَةِ وَفِي مَا بَعْدَهَا } وَفِي بَقِيَّةِ عُمْرِي.

O Allah, if You know that this affair – all my movement and stillness,
apparent and hidden, in speech, deeds, character and state, in
spiritual work and daily life, as regards myself and others, in this day
(or night) and those after it, and all the rest of my life –

خَيْرٌ لِّي فِي دِينِي وَدُنْيَايَ وَمَعَاشِي وَمَعَادِي وَعَاقِبَةِ أَمْرِي وَعَاجِلِهِ وَءَاجِلِهِ. فَاقْدُرْهُ لِي وَيَسِّرْهُ لِي ثُمَّ بَارِكْ لِي فِيهِ.

is good for me in my Deen, and my worldly existence, in this life and my next life, and my final end, be it sooner or later, then destine it for me, make it easy for me and bless me in it.

وَإِنْ كُنْتَ تَعْلَمُ أَنَّ هَـٰذَا الأَمْرَ وَهُوَ جَمِيعُ حَرَكَاتِي وَسَكَنَاتِي الظَّاهِرَةِ وَالبَاطِنَةِ. مِنْ قَوْلٍ وَفِعْلٍ وَخُلُقٍ وَحَالٍ. عِبَادَةً وَعَادَةً. فِي حَقِّي وَفِي حَقِّ غَيْرِي. فِي هَـٰذَا اليَوْمِ وَفِيمَا بَعْدَهُ {أَوْ: فِي هَـٰذِهِ اللَّيْلَةِ وَفِي مَا بَعْدَهَا} وَفِي بَقِيَّةِ عُمْرِي.

But if You know that this affair — all my movement and stillness, apparent and hidden, in speech, deeds, character and state, in spiritual work and daily life, as regards myself and others, in this day (or night) and those after it, and all the rest of my life —

شَرٌّ لِّي فِي دِينِي وَدُنْيَايَ وَمَعَاشِي وَمَعَادِي وَعَاقِبَةِ أَمْرِي وَعَاجِلِهِ وَءَاجِلِهِ. فَاصْرِفْهُ عَنِّي وَاصْرِفْنِي عَنْهُ. وَاقْدُرْ لِي الخَيْرَ حَيْثُ كَانَ ثُمَّ رَضِّنِي بِهِ. إِنَّكَ عَلَىٰ كُلِّ شَيْءٍ قَدِيرٌ.

is evil for me in my Deen, and my worldly existence, in this life and my next life, and my final end, be it sooner or later, then divert it from me and divert me from it, and destine the good for me wherever it may be and make me pleased with it. You have power over all things.

اَللّٰهُمَّ اقْسِمْ لَنَا مِنْ خَشْيَتِكَ مَا تَحُولُ بِهِ بَيْنَنَا وَبَيْنَ مَعَاصِيكَ.

وَمِنْ طَاعَتِكَ مَا تُبَلِّغُنَا بِهِ جَنَّتَكَ.

وَمِنَ الْيَقِينِ مَا تُهَوِّنُ بِهِ عَلَيْنَا مَصَآئِبَ الدُّنْيَا.

O Allah, provision us with fear of You that may come between us and
acts of disobedience against You. And grant us obedience to You that
will bring us to Your Garden. And grant us certainty that will make the
misfortunes of this world easy for us.

اَللّٰهُمَّ مَتِّعْنَا بِأَسْمَاعِنَا وَأَبْصَارِنَا وَقُوَّتِنَا مَآ أَحْيَيْتَنَا. وَاجْعَلْهُ

الْوَارِثَ مِنَّا. وَاجْعَلْ ثَارَنَا عَلَىٰ مَنْ ظَلَمَنَا. وَانصُرْنَا عَلَىٰ مَنْ

عَادَانَا. وَلَا تَجْعَلْ مُصِيبَتَنَا فِي دِينِنَا. وَلَا تَجْعَلِ الدُّنْيَا أَكْبَرَ هَمِّنَا.

وَلَا مَبْلَغَ عِلْمِنَا. وَلَا غَايَةَ رَغْبَتِنَا. وَلَآ إِلَى النَّارِ مَصِيرَنَا. وَلَا

تُسَلِّطْ عَلَيْنَا بِذُنُوبِنَا مَنْ لَا يَرْحَمُنَا.

يَآ أَرْحَمَ الرَّاحِمِينَ. يَآ أَرْحَمَ الرَّاحِمِينَ. يَآ أَرْحَمَ الرَّاحِمِينَ.

O Allah, let us enjoy our hearing and vision and strength for as long as
You grant us life and make it our legacy. Avenge us on those who have
wronged us and give us victory over those who have attacked us, and
do not give us misfortune in our Deen. Do not let this world be the
greatest of our cares, nor the scope of our knowledge, nor the object
of our desire, and do not let our homecoming be the Fire. Do not place
over us because of our wrong actions those who will not show mercy to
us. O Most Merciful of the merciful. (3)

اَللّٰهُمَّ يَا رَبِّ بِجَاهِ نَبِيِّكَ الْمُصْطَفَىٰ. وَرَسُولِكَ الْمُرْتَضَىٰ. طَهِّرْ
قُلُوبَنَا مِنْ كُلِّ وَصْفٍ يُبَاعِدُنَا عَنْ مُشَاهَدَتِكَ وَمَحَبَّتِكَ. وَأَمِتْنَا
عَلَى السُّنَّةِ وَالْجَمَاعَةِ وَالشَّوْقِ إِلَىٰ لِقَائِكَ يَا ذَا الْجَلَالِ وَالْاِكْرَامِ.
يَا ذَا الْجَلَالِ وَالْاِكْرَامِ. يَا ذَا الْجَلَالِ وَالْاِكْرَامِ.

O Allah! O Lord, by the rank of Your chosen Prophet and approved
Messenger, purify our hearts of every attribute that might separate
us from Your contemplation and love. Let us die in the Sunna and the
Jama'a and in yearning for Your encounter.
O Lord of majesty and generosity. (3)

فَسُبْحَانَ اللهِ حِينَ تُمْسُونَ وَحِينَ تُصْبِحُونَ وَلَهُ الْحَمْدُ فِي السَّمٰوٰاتِ
وَالْاَرْضِ وَعَشِيًّا وَحِينَ تُظْهِرُونَ. يُخْرِجُ الْحَيَّ مِنَ الْمَيِّتِ وَيُخْرِجُ
الْمَيِّتَ مِنَ الْحَيِّ وَيُحْيِ الْاَرْضَ بَعْدَ مَوْتِهَا. وَكَذٰلِكَ تُخْرَجُونَ.

Glory be to Allah both in your evening hour and in your morning hour.
Praise belongs to Him in the heavens and the earth, alike at the setting
of the sun and in your noontide hour. He brings forth the living from
the dead and brings forth the dead from the living.
In that manner you shall be brought forth.

اَللّٰهُمَّ إِنَّا نَسْأَلُكَ رِضَاكَ وَالْجَنَّةَ.
وَمَا يُقَرِّبُ إِلَيْهِمَا مِنْ قَوْلٍ وَعَمَلٍ.

O Allah, we ask You for Your pleasure and the Garden,
and the speech and action that bring us near to them.

وَنَعُوذُ بِكَ مِنْ سَخَطِكَ وَالنَّارِ.

وَمَا يُقَرِّبُ إِلَيْهِمَا مِنْ قَوْلٍ وَعَمَلٍ.

And we take refuge with You from Your displeasure and the Fire,
and the speech and action that bring us near to them.

اَللَّهُمَّ يَا سَابِغَ النِّعَمِ. وَيَا دَافِعَ النِّقَمِ. وَيَا فَارِجَ الْغُمَمِ.

وَيَا كَاشِفَ الظُّلَمِ. وَيَآ أَعْدَلَ مَنْ حَكَمَ.

وَيَا حَسْبَ مَنْ ظُلِمَ. وَيَا وَلِيَّ مَنْ ظُلِمَ.

O Allah, O Abundant in blessing. O Repeller of adversities. O One
Who frees us from troubles. O One Who removes the darkness. O
Most Just of those who judge. O Reckoner of those who are unjust.
O Protector of those who are wronged!

يَآ أَوَّلًا بِلَا بِدَايَةٍ. يَآ ءَاخِرًا بِلَا نِهَايَةٍ. يَا مَنْ لَهُ إِسْمٌ بِلَا كُنْيَةٍ.

فَرِّجْ عَنَّا وَعَنْ جَمِيعِ الْمُسْلِمِينَ مَا هُمْ فِيهِ.

O First without beginning! O Last without end! O You Who have a name
without a kunya! Free us and all the muslims from the state they are in –

بِسِرِّ اسْمِكَ الْمَخْزُونِ الْمَكْنُونِ الْمُبَارَكِ الطَّاهِرِ الْمُطَهِّرِ الْمُقَدَّسِ.

إِنَّكَ عَلَى كُلِّ شَيْءٍ قَدِيرٌ. وَبِالْإِجَابَةِ جَدِيرٌ.

By the secret of Your Guarded, Hidden, Blessed, Pure, Purified,
Wholly Pure Name. You are able to do all things,
and disposed to answer our prayers.

سُبْحَانَ رَبِّكَ رَبِّ الْعِزَّةِ عَمَّا يَصِفُونَ. وَسَلَامٌ عَلَى الْمُرْسَلِينَ.
وَالْحَمْدُ لِلَّهِ رَبِّ الْعَالَمِينَ ﴿۝﴾

Glory be to your Lord, the Lord of might, above all else that they
describe. And peace be upon the Messengers.
And praise belongs to Allah, the Lord of all the worlds.

# The Wird of the Salat

أدعية دبر الصلوات

وَبَعْدَ كُلِّ فَرِيضَةٍ مِنَ الصَّلَوَاتِ الخَمْسِ تَقُولُ:

*After each of the fard prayers say:*

أَسْتَغْفِرُ اللهَ العَظِيمَ الَّذِي لَاۤ إِلَهَ إِلَّا هُوَ الحَيُّ القَيُّومُ
وَأَتُوبُ إِلَيْهِ. (ثلاثا)

I ask forgiveness of Allah the Vast. There is no god but He, the Living,
the Eternal: to Him I turn. (3)

اَللّٰهُمَّ مَغْفِرَتُكَ أَوْسَعُ مِنْ ذُنُوبِي
وَرَحْمَتُكَ أَرْجَىٰ عِنْدِي مِنْ عَمَلِي. (ثلاثا)

O Allah, Your forgiveness is vaster than my wrong actions
and Your mercy more hopeful for me than my behaviour. (3)

اَللّٰهُمَّ صَلِّ عَلَىٰ سَيِّدِنَا مُحَمَّدٍ عَبْدِكَ وَنَبِيِّكَ وَرَسُولِكَ النَّبِيِّ الأُمِّيِّ
وَعَلَىٰٓ ءَالِهِ وَصَحْبِهِ وَسَلِّمْ تَسْلِيمًا.
بِقَدْرِ عَظَمَةِ ذَاتِكَ فِي كُلِّ وَقْتٍ وَحِينٍ. (ثلاثا)

O Allah, bless our master Muhammad, Your slave, Prophet and

Messenger, the unlettered Prophet and his family and Companions, and grant them peace, as great in measure as Your essence, at all times and in every age. (3)

اَللَّهُمَّ إِنَّا نَسْأَلُكَ فِعْلَ الْخَيْرَاتِ وَتَرْكَ الْمُنْكَرَاتِ وَحُبَّ الْمَسَاكِينِ. وَإِذَآ أَرَدْتَ بِعِبَادِكَ فِتْنَةً فَاقْبِضْنَا إِلَيْكَ غَيْرَ مَفْتُونِينَ. (ثَلَاثًا) ءَامِين. ءَامِين. ءَامِين.

O Allah, we ask You that we should do good, leave what is objectionable and love the poor. If You will that there be schism among Your slaves, grant that You will take us to You uncorrupted. (3) Amin Amin. Amin.

سُبْحَانَ رَبِّكَ رَبِّ الْعِزَّةِ عَمَّا يَصِفُونَ. وَسَلَامٌ عَلَى الْمُرْسَلِينَ. وَالْحَمْدُ لِلَّهِ رَبِّ الْعَلَمِينَ.

Glory be to your Lord, the Lord of might, above all else that they describe. And peace be upon the Messengers.
And praise belongs to Allah, the Lord of all the worlds.

ثُمَّ تُسَبِّحُ اللهَ ثَلَاثًا وَثَلَاثِينَ وَتَحْمَدُهُ كَذَالِكَ وَتُكَبِّرُهُ كَذَالِكَ وَتَخْتِمُ الْمِائَةَ بِ:

*Then say:*

سُبْحَانَ اللهِ. (ثَلَاثًا وَثَلَاثِينَ)

Glory be to Allah. (33)

اَلْحَمْدُ لِلَّهِ. (ثَلَاثًا وَثَلَاثِينَ)

Praise belongs to Allah. (33)

$$\text{اَللَّهُ أَكْبَرُ. (ثَلَاثًا وَثَلَاثِينَ)}$$

Allah is greater. (33)

*Then seal the hundred with:*

$$\text{لَا إِلَهَ إِلَّا اللهُ وَحْدَهُ لَا شَرِيكَ لَهُ. لَهُ الْمُلْكُ وَلَهُ الْحَمْدُ.}$$

$$\text{وَهُوَ عَلَى كُلِّ شَيْءٍ قَدِيرٌ.}$$

There is no god except Allah, alone, without partner. The kingdom and
the praise belong to Him. And He has power over all things.

$$\text{ثُمَّ تَقُولُ:}$$

*Then say:*

$$\text{أَسْتَغْفِرُ اللهَ. ( ثَلَاثًا )}$$

I ask forgiveness of Allah. (3)

$$\text{الْحَمْدُ لِلَّهِ وَالشُّكْرُ لِلَّهِ. ( ثَلَاثًا )}$$

Praise be to Allah and thanks be to Allah. (3)

$$\text{لَا حَوْلَ وَلَا قُوَّةَ إِلَّا بِاللهِ.}$$

There is no power and no strength but through Allah.

$$\text{اَللَّهُمَّ إِنَّا نَسْتَوْدِعُكَ دِينَنَا وَإِيمَانَنَا فَاحْفَظْهُمَا عَلَيْنَا حِفْظًا مُحَمَّدِيًّا}$$

$$\text{فِي حَيَاتِنَا وَعِنْدَ مَمَاتِنَا وَبَعْدَ وَفَاتِنَا وَارْزُقْنَا كِلَاهُمَا بِمُتَابَعَتِهِ صَلَّى}$$

$$\text{اللهُ عَلَيْهِ وَسَلَّمَ فِي الْأَقْوَالِ وَالْأَفْعَالِ وَالْأَخْلَاقِ وَالْأَحْوَالِ}$$

مُرِيدِينَ بِذَٰلِكَ وَجْهَكَ الْكَرِيمَ.

يَآ أَكْرَمَ الاَكْرَمِينَ. ءَامِينَ.

O Allah, we commend our Deen and our Iman to You, so protect them for
us with a Muhammadan protection in our lives and at our deaths and after
our passing and perfect them by our following him, blessings of Allah be
upon him, in words, deeds, behaviour and states, seeking Your noble face,
O Most Noble of the noble. Amin.

بِسْمِ اللهِ الرَّحْمَٰنِ الرَّحِيمِ الْحَمْدُ لِلَّهِ رَبِّ الْعَٰلَمِينَ الرَّحْمَٰنِ الرَّحِيمِ
مَلِكِ يَوْمِ الدِّينِ. إِيَّاكَ نَعْبُدُ وَإِيَّاكَ نَسْتَعِينُ. اهْدِنَا الصِّرَاطَ
الْمُسْتَقِيمَ صِرَاطَ الَّذِينَ أَنْعَمْتَ عَلَيْهِمْ غَيْرِ الْمَغْضُوبِ عَلَيْهِمْ وَلَا
الضَّآلِّينَ. ءَامِينَ.

In the name of Allah, All-Merciful, the Most Merciful. Praise be to Allah,
Lord of the worlds, the All-Merciful, the Most Merciful, the King of
the Day of Judgment. You alone we worship, You alone we ask for help.
Guide us on the Straight Path, the Path of those whom You have blessed,
not of those with anger upon them, nor of the misguided. Amin.

سُبْحَانَ رَبِّكَ رَبِّ الْعِزَّةِ عَمَّا يَصِفُونَ. وَسَلَامٌ عَلَى الْمُرْسَلِينَ.
وَالْحَمْدُ لِلَّهِ رَبِّ الْعَٰلَمِينَ ○

Glory be to your Lord, the Lord of might, above all else that they
describe. And peace be upon the Messengers.
And praise belongs to Allah, the Lord of all the worlds.

ثُمَّ

*Then say:*

اَللَّهُ لَاۤ إِلَهَ إِلَّا هُوَ. الْحَىُّ الْقَيُّومُ. لَا تَأْخُذُهُ سِنَةٌ وَلَا نَوْمٌ. لَهُ مَا فِى السَّمَـٰوَٰتِ وَمَا فِى الْاَرْضِ. مَن ذَا الَّذِي يَشْفَعُ عِندَهُۤ إِلَّا بِإِذْنِهِۦ. يَعْلَمُ مَا بَيْنَ أَيْدِيهِمْ وَمَا خَلْفَهُمْ. وَلَا يُحِيطُونَ بِشَىْءٍ مِّنْ عِلْمِهِۦۤ إِلَّا بِمَا شَاۤءَ. وَسِعَ كُرْسِيُّهُ السَّمَـٰوَٰتِ وَالْاَرْضَ. وَلَا يَئُودُهُ حِفْظُهُمَا. وَهُوَ الْعَلِىُّ الْعَظِيمُ.

Allah! There is no god but Him. The Living, the Self-Sustaining. He
is not subject to drowsiness or sleep. Everything in the heavens and
the earth belongs to Him. Who can intercede with Him except by His
permission? He knows what is before them and what is behind them.
But they cannot grasp any of His knowledge save what He wills. His
Footstool encompasses the heavens and the earth and their preservation
does not tire Him. He is the Most High, the Magnificent.

ثُمَّ

*Then say:*

ءَامَنَ الرَّسُولُ بِمَاۤ أُنزِلَ إِلَيْهِ مِن رَّبِّهِۦ وَالْمُومِنُونَ. كُلٌّ ءَامَنَ بِاللَّهِ وَمَلَـٰۤئِكَتِهِۦ وَكُتُبِهِۦ وَرُسُلِهِۦ. لَا نُفَرِّقُ بَيْنَ أَحَدٍ مِّن رُّسُلِهِۦ. وَقَالُواْ سَمِعْنَا وَأَطَعْنَا. غُفْرَانَكَ رَبَّنَا. وَإِلَيْكَ الْمَصِيرُ.

The Messenger has Iman in what has been sent down to him from his

Lord, and so do the muminun. Each one has Iman in Allah and His angels, and His books and His messengers. We do not differentiate between any of His messengers. They say, 'We hear and we obey. Forgive us, our Lord! You are our journey's end.'

لَا يُكَلِّفُ اللّٰهُ نَفْسًا إِلَّا وُسْعَهَا. لَهَا مَا كَسَبَتْ. وَعَلَيْهَا مَا اكْتَسَبَتْ. رَبَّنَا لَا تُؤَاخِذْنَا إِن نَّسِينَا أَوْ أَخْطَأْنَا. رَبَّنَا وَلَا تَحْمِلْ عَلَيْنَا إِصْرًا كَمَا حَمَلْتَهُ عَلَى الَّذِينَ مِن قَبْلِنَا. رَبَّنَا وَلَا تُحَمِّلْنَا مَا لَا طَاقَةَ لَنَا بِهِۦ. وَاعْفُ عَنَّا. وَاغْفِرْ لَنَا. وَارْحَمْنَا. أَنتَ مَوْلَانَا فَانصُرْنَا عَلَى الْقَوْمِ الْكَافِرِينَ.

Allah does not impose on any self more than it can stand. For it is what it has earned; against it what it has merited. Our Lord, take us not to task if we forget or make a mistake! Our Lord, do not place on us a load like the one You placed on those before us! Our Lord, do not place on us a load we have not the strength to bear! And pardon us; and forgive us; and have mercy on us. You are our Master, so Help us against the people of the kafirun.

ثُمَّ

*Then say:*

شَهِدَ اللّٰهُ أَنَّهُۥ لَا إِلَٰهَ إِلَّا هُوَ وَالْمَلَائِكَةُ وَأُولُوا الْعِلْمِ قَائِمًا بِالْقِسْطِ. لَا إِلَٰهَ إِلَّا هُوَ. الْعَزِيزُ الْحَكِيمُ. إِنَّ الدِّينَ عِندَ اللّٰهِ الْإِسْلَامُ.

Allah bears witness that there is no god but Him, as do the angels and
the people of knowledge, upholding justice. There is no god but Him,
the Almighty, the All-Wise. The Deen with Allah is Islam.

ثُمَّ

*Then say:*

قُلِ اللّهُمَّ مَـٰلِكَ الْمُلْكِ تُوتِي الْمُلْكَ مَن تَشَاءُ وَتَنزِعُ الْمُلْكَ مِمَّن
تَشَاءُ وَتُعِزُّ مَن تَشَاءُ وَتُذِلُّ مَن تَشَاءُ بِيَدِكَ الْخَيْرُ. إِنَّكَ عَلَى كُلِّ
شَىْءٍ قَدِيرٌ.

Say: 'O Allah! Master of the kingdom! You give sovereignty to
whomever You will. You take sovereignty from whomever You will.
You exalt whomever You will. You abase whomever You will. All good
is in Your hands. You have power over all things.

تُولِجُ الَّيْلَ فِي النَّهَارِ وَتُولِجُ النَّهَارَ فِي الَّيْلِ وَتُخْرِجُ الْحَيَّ مِنَ الْمَيِّتِ
وَتُخْرِجُ الْمَيِّتَ مِنَ الْحَيِّ
وَتَرْزُقُ مَن تَشَاءُ بِغَيْرِ حِسَابٍ.

You merge the night into the day. You merge the day into the night. You
bring out the living from the dead. You bring out the dead from the
living. You provide for whomever You will without any reckoning.

لَقَدْ جَاءَكُمْ رَسُولٌ مِّنْ أَنفُسِكُمْ عَزِيزٌ عَلَيْهِ مَا عَنِتُّمْ. حَرِيصٌ
عَلَيْكُمْ. بِالْمُؤْمِنِينَ رَءُوفٌ رَّحِيمٌ.

A Messenger has come to you from among yourselves. Your suffering is
distressing to him; he is deeply concerned for you;

he is gentle and merciful to the muminun.

فَإِن تَوَلَّوْا فَقُلْ حَسْبِيَ اللَّهُ. لَآ إِلَهَ إِلَّا هُوَ. عَلَيْهِ تَوَكَّلْتُ.
وَهُوَ رَبُّ الْعَرْشِ الْعَظِيمِ.

But if they turn away, say, 'Allah is enough for me. There is no god but
Him. I have put my trust in Him. He is the Lord of the Mighty Throne.'

بِسْمِ اللَّهِ الرَّحْمَنِ الرَّحِيمِ قُلْ هُوَ اللَّهُ أَحَدٌ. اللَّهُ الصَّمَدُ.
لَمْ يَلِدْ وَلَمْ يُولَدْ. وَلَمْ يَكُن لَّهُ كُفُوًا أَحَدٌ.

In the name of Allah, All-Merciful, Most Merciful, Say: 'He is Allah,
Absolute Oneness. Allah, the Everlasting Sustainer of all. He has not
given birth and was not born. And no one is comparable to Him.'

بِسْمِ اللَّهِ الرَّحْمَنِ الرَّحِيمِ قُلْ أَعُوذُ بِرَبِّ الْفَلَقِ مِن شَرِّ مَا خَلَقَ
وَمِن شَرِّ غَاسِقٍ إِذَا وَقَبَ وَمِن شَرِّ النَّفَّاثَاتِ فِي الْعُقَدِ وَمِن شَرِّ
حَاسِدٍ إِذَا حَسَدَ.

In the name of Allah, All-Merciful, Most Merciful, Say: 'I seek refuge
with the Lord of Daybreak, from the evil of what He has created and
from the evil of darkness when it gathers and from the evil of women
who blow on knots and from the evil of an envier when he envies.'

بِسْمِ اللَّهِ الرَّحْمَنِ الرَّحِيمِ قُلْ أَعُوذُ بِرَبِّ النَّاسِ مَلِكِ النَّاسِ إِلَهِ

النَّاسِ مِن شَرِّ الْوَسْوَاسِ الْخَنَّاسِ الَّذِي يُوَسْوِسُ فِي صُدُورِ النَّاسِ مِنَ الْجِنَّةِ وَالنَّاسِ.

In the name of Allah, All-Merciful, Most Merciful, Say: 'I seek refuge with the Lord of mankind, the King of mankind, the God of mankind, from the evil of the insidious whisperer who whispers in people's breasts and comes from the jinn and from mankind.'

اللَّهُمَّ أَنْتَ رَبِّي لَآ إِلَهَ إِلَّآ أَنْتَ. خَلَقْتَنِي وَأَنَا عَبْدُكَ وَأَنَا عَلَى عَهْدِكَ وَوَعْدِكَ مَا اسْتَطَعْتُ. أَعُوذُ بِكَ مِنْ شَرِّ مَا صَنَعْتُ. أَبُوءُ لَكَ بِنِعْمَتِكَ عَلَيَّ وَأَبُوءُ بِذَنْبِي فَاغْفِرْ لِي فَإِنَّهُ لَا يَغْفِرُ الذُّنُوبَ إِلَّآ أَنْتَ.

O Allah, You are my Lord. There is no god but You. You created me and I am Your slave and I act according to Your covenant and Your promise as far as I am able. I take refuge with You from the evil of what I have done. I acknowledge to You Your blessings to me and I acknowledge my wrong action, so forgive me. None forgives wrong action but You.

رَبِّ اغْفِرْ لِي وَارْحَمْنِي وَتُبْ عَلَيَّ. إِنَّكَ أَنْتَ التَّوَّابُ الرَّحِيمُ.

O my Lord, forgive me and have mercy on me and turn towards me. You are the One Who Turns, the Compassionate.

بِسْمِ اللهِ الرَّحْمَنِ الرَّحِيمِ الْحَمْدُ لِلَّهِ رَبِّ الْعَالَمِينَ الرَّحْمَنِ الرَّحِيمِ مَلِكِ يَوْمِ الدِّينِ. إِيَّاكَ نَعْبُدُ وَإِيَّاكَ نَسْتَعِينُ. اِهْدِنَا الصِّرَاطَ

الْمُسْتَقِيمَ صِرَاطَ الَّذِينَ أَنْعَمْتَ عَلَيْهِمْ غَيْرِ الْمَغْضُوبِ عَلَيْهِمْ وَلَا الضَّآلِّينَ. ءَامِين.

In the name of Allah, All-Merciful, the Most Merciful. Praise be to Allah, Lord of the worlds, the All-Merciful, the Most Merciful, the King of the Day of Judgment. You alone we worship, You alone we ask for help. Guide us on the Straight Path, the Path of those whom You have blessed, not of those with anger upon them, nor of the misguided. Amin.

سُبْحَانَ رَبِّكَ رَبِّ الْعِزَّةِ عَمَّا يَصِفُونَ. وَسَلَامٌ عَلَى الْمُرْسَلِينَ. وَالْحَمْدُ لِلَّهِ رَبِّ الْعَٰلَمِينَ.

Glory be to your Lord, the Lord of might, above all else that they describe. And peace be upon the Messengers.
And praise belongs to Allah, the Lord of all the worlds.

بِسْمِ اللهِ الرَّحْمَٰنِ الرَّحِيمِ الْحَمْدُ لِلَّهِ الَّذِي خَلَقَ السَّمَٰوَٰتِ وَالْأَرْضَ وَجَعَلَ الظُّلُمَٰتِ وَالنُّورَ ثُمَّ الَّذِينَ كَفَرُواْ بِرَبِّهِم يَعْدِلُونَ.

In the name of Allah, All-Merciful, Most Merciful,
praise belongs to Allah, Who created the heavens and the earth
and appointed the shadows and the light,
then the ones who cover over ascribe equals to their Lord.

هُوَ الَّذِي خَلَقَكُم مِّن طِينٍ ثُمَّ قَضَىٰٓ أَجَلًا.

وَأَجَلٌ مُسَمًّى عِنْدَهُ، ثُمَّ أَنْتُمْ تَمْتَرُونَ.

It is He Who created you from clay, then determined a term. And a
term is stated with Him. Yet thereafter you doubt.

وَهُوَ اللّٰهُ، فِى السَّمٰوٰتِ وَفِي الْاَرْضِ
يَعْلَمُ سِرَّكُمْ وَجَهْرَكُمْ وَيَعْلَمُ مَا تَكْسِبُونَ.

He is Allah. In the heavens and in the earth He knows your secrets and
what you publish and He knows what you are earning.

اَلْحَمْدُ لِلّٰهِ الَّذِي هَدٰنَا لِهٰذَا وَمَا كُنَّا لِنَهْتَدِىَ لَوْلَا أَنْ هَدٰنَا اللّٰهُ،
لَقَدْ جَاءَتْ رُسُلُ رَبِّنَا بِالْحَقِّ. (ثلاثا)

Praise belongs to Allah Who guided us to this, and had Allah not
guided us we would surely never have been guided. Indeed our Lord's
messengers came with the truth.

وَبَعْدَ كُلِّ مَرَّةٍ تَقُولُ

*Then each time say:*

اَللّٰهُمَّ لَكَ الْحَمْدُ. (ثلاثا)

O Allah, praise belongs to You. (3)

ثُمَّ تَقُولُ

*Then say:*

اَللّٰهُمَّ مَآ أَنْعَمْتَ بِهِ فَمِنْكَ بِكَ لَكَ وَحْدَكَ لَا شَرِيكَ لَكَ.

لَا أُحْصِي ثَنَاءً عَلَيْكَ. أَنْتَ كَمَآ أَثْنَيْتَ عَلَى نَفْسِكَ.

O Allah, what You have bestowed on us of blessing is from You, by You
and Yours alone. There is no partner with You. I am unable to praise
You properly; You are as You praise Yourself. (3)

مَا شَآءَ اللّٰهُ. لَا قُوَّةَ إِلَّا بِاللّٰهِ. (ثلاثا) الْحَمْدُ لِلّٰهِ رَبِّ الْعَالَمِينَ.

It is as Allah wills. There is no strength but with Allah. (3)
Praise belongs to Allah, the Lord of the worlds.

ثُمَّ تَرْفَعُ يَدَيْكَ مُصَلِّيًا عَلَى النَّبِيِّ صَلَّى اللّٰهُ عَلَيْهِ وَسَلَّمَ دَاعِيًا لِآلِ الْبَيْتِ وَلِآلِ جَانِب
اللهِ وَالْمَشَايِخِ وَالْوَالِدَيْنِ وَالْإِخْوَانِ وَالْأَحْبَابِ وَلِكَافَّةِ الْمُسْلِمِينَ وَالْمُسْلِمَاتِ: تَقُولُ

*Then raise your hands and pray for the Prophet ﷺ and for the people of the house
and for the near-to-Allah and the Shaykhs, parents, brothers and loved ones, and
all the muslims, men and women. Then say:*

اَللّٰهُمَّ صَلِّ عَلَى سَيِّدِنَا مُحَمَّدٍ عَبْدِكَ وَرَسُولِكَ النَّبِيِّ الْأُمِّيِّ
وَعَلَى ءَالِهِ وَصَحْبِهِ وَسَلِّمْ. (ثلاثا)

O Allah, bless our master Muhammad, Your slave and Your Messenger,
the unlettered Prophet, and his family and Companions,
and grant them peace. (3)

وَتَزِيدُ بَعْدَ الثَّالِثَةِ: تَسْلِيمًا ثُمَّ تَقُولُ:

*Add "tasleema" after the third, and then say:*

اَللَّهُمَّ إِنَّا نَسْأَلُكَ إِيمَانًا دَائِمًا. وَنَسْأَلُكَ قَلْبًا خَاشِعًا. وَنَسْأَلُكَ عِلْمًا نَافِعًا. وَنَسْأَلُكَ يَقِينًا صَادِقًا. وَنَسْأَلُكَ دِينًا قَيِّمًا. وَنَسْأَلُكَ الْعَافِيَةَ مِنْ كُلِّ بَلِيَّةٍ. وَنَسْأَلُكَ تَمَامَ الْعَافِيَةِ. وَنَسْأَلُكَ دَوَامَ الْعَافِيَةِ. وَنَسْأَلُكَ الشُّكْرَ عَلَى الْعَافِيَةِ. وَنَسْأَلُكَ الْغِنَى عَنِ النَّاسِ.

Allah, we ask You for a constant Iman. We ask you for a humble heart. We ask You for useful knowledge. We ask You for genuine certainty. We ask You for correct Deen. We ask You for a safe outcome from every trial. We ask You for complete wellbeing. We ask You for enduring wellbeing. We ask You for gratitude for wellbeing. We ask You for freedom from need of people.

اَللَّهُمَّ أَحْسِنْ عَاقِبَتَنَا فِي الْأُمُورِ كُلِّهَا وَأَجِرْنَا مِنْ خِزْيِ الدُّنْيَا وَعَذَابِ الْآخِرَةِ.

Allah, make good the outcome of all our affairs,
and protect us from the shame of the world,
and from punishment in the world to come.

اَللَّهُمَّ يَا لَطِيفُ نَسْأَلُكَ اللُّطْفَ فِي مَا جَرَتْ بِهِ الْمَقَادِيرُ. (ثلاثا)

Allah, O Latif, we ask You for lutf in what the decrees entail. (3)

54

سُبْحَانَ رَبِّكَ رَبِّ الْعِزَّةِ عَمَّا يَصِفُونَ. وَسَلَامٌ عَلَى الْمُرْسَلِينَ.
وَالْحَمْدُ لِلَّهِ رَبِّ الْعَالَمِينَ ۝

Glory be to your Lord, the Lord of might, above all else that they
describe. And peace be upon the Messengers.

And praise belongs to Allah, the Lord of all the worlds.

# The Wird of Fajr
أذكار الفجر

وَيَنْبَغِي لِكُلِّ فَقِيرٍ أَنْ لَا يَتْرُكَ حَظَّهُ مِنْ رُكَيْعَاتٍ قُبَيْلَ الْفَجْرِ، ثُمَّ يُصَلِّي عَلَى النَّبِيِّ صَلَّى

اللَّهُ عَلَيْهِ وَسَلَّمَ بِالصَّلَاةِ الْمَشِيشِيَّةِ الْمَشْهُورَةِ ثُمَّ يَذْكُرُ مِنَ الْاِسْمِ الْمُفْرَدِ سِتَّمِائَةٍ وَسِتِّينَ مَرَّةً

*No faqeer should leave out his portion of rak'ats shortly before Fajr, then he*
*should ask for blessings on the Prophet ﷺ with the well known*
*Salat al-Mashishiyya. Then he should invoke the Singular Name*
*six hundred and sixty times.*

ثُمَّ تَقُولُ بَعْدَ رَغِيبَةِ الْفَجْرِ

*Then you say after the two sunna rak'ats of Fajr:*

يَا حَيُّ يَا قَيُّومُ لَا إِلَهَ إِلَّا أَنْتَ. (إِحْدَى وَأَرْبَعِينَ مَرَّةً)

O Living, O Self-subsistent! There is no god but You. (41)

ثُمَّ تَقُولُ

*Then say:*

سُبْحَانَ اللهِ وَبِحَمْدِهِ سُبْحَانَ اللهِ الْعَظِيمِ. أَسْتَغْفِرُ اللهَ. (عشرا)

Glory be to Allah by His praise, Glory be to Allah the Vast. I seek
forgiveness of Allah. (10)

ثُمَّ تَقُولُ

*Then say:*

اللهُ (سبعا)

Allah (7)

وَتَعْقِبُهُ بِالتَّهْلِيلِ وَالْإِبْتِهَالِ حَتَّى تُقَامَ صَلَاةُ الْفَرِيضَةِ.

*Follow that with La ilaha illa'llah and with supplication
until the iqama of the obligatory salat.*

# Commentary on the Wird

تَائِيَّةُ الْوِرْدِ الشَّرِيفِ

يَقُولُ عُبَيْدُ اللهِ أَعْنِي مُحَمَّدًا
هُوَ ابْنُ حَبِيبٍ قَاصِدًا لِلنَّصِيحَةِ

The lowly slave of Allah, Muhammad ibn al-Habib,
says intending counsel:

أَيَا صَاحِبِي عِشْ فِي هَنَاءٍ وَنِعْمَةٍ
إِذَا كُنْتَ فِينَا ذَا اعْتِقَادٍ وَنِيَّةٍ

O my companion! Live in joy and serenity
if you are among us as one with firm belief and intention,

وَأَخْلَصْتَ فِي الْوُدِّ الَّذِي هُوَ رُكْنُنَا
فِي سَيْرِ طَرِيقِ اللهِ مِنْ غَيْرِ مِرْيَةٍ

And if you are sincere in the love which is, without doubt,
our firm support while travelling on the Tariq of Allah,

وَكُنْتَ قَوِيَّ الْعَزْمِ فِي الْوِرْدِ حَاضِرًا

بِقَلْبٍ لِتَحْقِيقِ الْمَعَانِي الدَّقِيقَةِ

And if you have a strong resolve to recite the Wird, and are
present with an attentive heart to realise its subtle meanings,

وَأَحْضَرْتَ مَعْنَى الذِّكْرِ فِي كُلِّ مَرَّةٍ

تَكُونُ مُعَانًا فِي الْأُمُورِ بِسُرْعَةٍ

And if at all times you call to mind the meaning of the dhikr,
you will be quickly helped in your affairs.

فَمِفْتَاحُ وِرْدٍ قُلْ صَلَاةٌ تَعَوُّذٌ

وَبَسْمِلْ وَحَوْقِلْ تُكْفَ كُلَّ بَلِيَّةٍ

The key of the Wird is the prayer on the Prophet, the taking refuge,
the 'Bismillah', the 'no power' – and that is enough for every problem.

فَتَبْدَا بِالِاسْتِغْفَارِ أَوَّلَ وِرْدِنَا

تَحُوزُ بِهِ نَيْلًا لِكُلِّ فَضِيلَةٍ

You begin our Wird with the Istighfar,
and by it you will obtain every good quality.

وَمَعْنَاهُ سِتْرُ اللهِ لِلْعَبْدِ عَنْ ذَنْبٍ

فَيَحْفَظُهُ مِنْ كُلِّ هَوْلٍ وَفِتْنَةٍ

Its real meaning is Allah's veil over the wrong action of His slave,
and so it protects him from every terror and trial.

60

فَلَا هَمَّ يَبْقَىٰ مَعَ دَوَامِكَ ذِكْرَهُ

وَلَا رَيْبَ فِي تَسْهِيلِ رِزْقٍ بِكَثْرَةِ

No care can remain when you persevere in His dhikr,
and no doubt can remain when your needs are amply met.

وَبَعْدَ الْفَرَاغِ مِنْهُ صَلِّ عَلَى النَّبِي

صَلَاةَ مُحِبٍّ رَاسِخٍ فِي الْمَحَبَّةِ

After you finish this, ask for blessing on the Prophet
with the prayer of a lover firmly rooted in love –

وَمَعْنَاهَا رَحْمَةٌ تُنَاسِبُ قَدْرَهُ

وَقَدْرُهُ يَعْلُو قَدْرَ كُلِّ الْخَلِيقَةِ

Its true meaning is the mercy that befits his rank,
and his rank is above the rank of every person.

وَشَخِّصْهُ فِي مِرْآةِ قَلْبِكَ دَائِمًا

وَعَوِّلْ عَلَيْهِ فِي الْوُصُولِ لِحَضْرَةِ

Constantly see him in the mirror of your heart
and rely on him for attainment of the Presence.

وَهَيْلِلَةٌ بَعْدَ الصَّلَاةِ عَلَى النَّبِي

فَتَنْفِي بِهَا وَهْمًا عَنْ عَيْنِ الْبَصِيرَةِ

After the prayer on the Prophet, recite 'La ilaha illa'llah'.
By it you will expel illusion from the inner eye.

وَتُسْرِعُ فِي نَفْيِ السِّوَىٰ وَهْوَ قَاطِعُ

لِقَوْمٍ طَرِيقِ الْحَقِّ مِنْ غَيْرِ مِرْيَةِ

And you will be swift to negate otherness for there is no doubt
that it is a screen to the people on the Tariq al-Haqq.

وَتَشْهَدُ رَبًّا قَدْ تَجَلَّتْ صِفَاتُهُ

بِأَسْرَارِ أَكْوَانٍ وَأَنْوَارِ جَنَّةِ

And you will witness a Lord Whose Attributes have been manifested
by the secrets of phenomena and the lights of the Garden.

وَتُدْرِكُ سِرًّا لَيْسَ يَعْرِفُ قَدْرَهُ

سِوَىٰ عَارِفٍ بِاللهِ صَاحِبِ نَظْرَةِ

And you will grasp a secret whose true value is only known
by an 'arif bi'llah who possesses vision.

وَسَبِّحْ بِتَسْبِيحِ الالَهِ فِي كُتْبِهِ

وَإِيَّاكَ تَنْزِيهًا بِعَقْلٍ وَفِكْرَةِ

Glorify Him with Allah's glorification that is in His Book,
but take care not to perform tanzih with reason and thinking.

وَنَزِّهْ بِمَا قَدْ نَزَّهَ الْحَقُّ نَفْسَهُ

وَفَوِّضْ وَنَزِّهْ عَنْ حُدُوثٍ وَشِرْكَةِ

And do it in the way that the Haqq has purified Himself —
entrust yourself to Him, and free Him from being-in-time and shirk.

وَكُنْ حَامِدًا مُسْتَحْضِرَ الْعَجْزِ فِي الثَّنَا
كَمَا جَاءَ وَارِدًا عَنْ خَيْرِ الْخَلِيقَةِ

Give praise while you bear in mind your inability to praise
as it was reported by the Best of Creation.

وَحَسْبَلَةٌ بَعْدَ الْفَرَاغِ مِنَ الْوِرْدِ
فَتَذْكُرُ مِنْهَا عَدَّ سِجِّي بِنِيَّةٍ

After finishing the Wird say 'Hasbuna'llah'
and say it with firm intention seventy-three times.

وَقَدْ وَعَدَ الْحَقُّ الْجَلِيلُ كِفَايَةً
لِذَاكِرِهَا مِنْ غَيْرِ قَيْدٍ بِحَالَةٍ

The Majestic Truth has promised the dhakir who recites it
that he will have what he needs, not limited to any state.

فَقَدْ طَفِئَتْ نَارُ الْخَلِيلِ بِسِرِّهَا
وَنَالَ الْحَبِيبُ مِنْهَا كُلَّ فَضِيلَةٍ

It extinguished the fire of the Khalil (Ibrahim) by its secret,
and from it the Habib (Muhammad) was given every gift.

فَفِي وَقْتِنَا هَذَا يُرَجَّحُ ذِكْرُهَا
عَلَى الذِّكْرِ بِالاَحْزَابِ أَوْ بِوَظِيفَةٍ

In this time of ours, its dhikr and invocation
take preference over Hizbs or Wazifas.

وَإِنْ شِئْتَ إِسْرَاعًا لِفَهْمِ الْحَقِيقَةِ

فَوَاظِبْ عَلَى الاِسْمِ الْعَظِيمِ بِهِمَّةِ

If you wish to hasten understanding of the Haqiqa,
then with Himma persevere in repeating the Tremendous Name.

وَشَخِّصْ حُرُوفَ الاِسْمِ فِي الْقَلْبِ دَائِمًا

وَرَاجِعْهُ فِي النِّسْيَانِ فِي كُلِّ مَرَّةِ

Always mirror the letters of the Name in your heart,
and bring it back every time you forget.

وَلَا تَلْتَفِتْ لِلْغَيْرِ إِنَّهُ قَاطِعُ

وَلَوْ كَانَ مَحْمُودًا فَأَحْرَىٰ لِظُلْمَةِ

Do not turn to otherness – it is indeed a barrier.
Even when praiseworthy, it is still more suited to darkness.

فَذِكْرُهُ عِنْدَ الْقَوْمِ يُغْنِي عَنْ غَيْرِهِ

وَلَا عَكْسَ ع إِنْ كُنْتَ صَاحِبَ هِمَّةِ

To the People, His dhikr frees from what is other-than-Him,
and there is no opposite to Allah; pay attention if you possess himma.

وَرَاقِبْهُ عِنْدَ الذِّكْرِ وَافْنَ عَنْ غَيْرِهِ

وَلَا غَيْرَ إِلَّا مِنْ تَوَهُّمِ كَثْرَةِ

Watch for Him in the dhikr and be annihilated to other-than-Him,
and there is no other except for the illusion of multiplicity.

وَمَا هِيَ إِلَّا وَحْدَةٌ قَدْ تَكَثَّرَتْ

بِمُقْتَضَىٰ أَسْمَاءٍ وَءَاثَارِ قُدْرَةٍ

Multiplicity is only oneness multiplied in accordance
with the Names and the traces of Divine Power.

وَمَظْهَرُهَا الْاَعْلَى الرَّسُولُ مُحَمَّدٌ

عَلَيْهِ صَلَاةُ اللهِ فِي كُلِّ لَحْظَةٍ

Its highest place of manifestation is the Messenger Muhammad,
may the blessings of Allah be upon him at every instant,

وَءَالِهِ وَالْاَصْحَابِ مَا حَنَّ ذَاكِرٌ

لِذِكْرِ إِلَهِ الْعَرْشِ فِي كُلِّ حَالَةٍ

and on his family and Companions as long as there is a dhakir
who yearns to do the dhikr of the God of the Throne in every state.

طَرِيقَتُنَا تَعْلُو الطَّرَائِقَ كُلَّهَا

لِتَحْرِيرِنَا الْمَقْصُودَ أَوَّلَ مَرَّةٍ

Our Tariqa greatly surpasses all other paths –
because we obtain the goal we desire, first time.

وَلِلْجَمْعِ بَيْنَ الْمَشْهَدَيْنِ بِلَا رَيْبٍ

فَمَشْهَدُ حَقٍّ ثُمَّ مَشْهَدُ شِرْعَةٍ

And it unites the two aspects without any doubt –
the aspect of the Haqiqa and the aspect of the Shari'a.

وَأَسْأَلُ رَبِّ اللهَ فَتْحًا إِلَهِيًّا

لِكُلِّ مُرِيدٍ صَادِقٍ فِي الطَّرِيقَة

I ask Allah, my Lord, to grant a Divine opening
to each and every sincere murid on the Tariqa,

وَأَنْ يُرْشِدَ الاِخْوَانَ لِلْجَمْعِ دَائِمًا

عَلَىٰ كُلِّ مَا يُرْضِي إِلَهَ الْبَرِيَّة

And that He always guide the brotherhood to stay together,
holding to what is pleasing to the God of creation.

وَأُهْدِي سَلَامِي لِلَّذِينَ تَعَلَّقُوا

بِأَذْكَارِ خَيْرِ الْخَلْقِ مِنْ كُلِّ فِرْقَة

I convey my greetings of peace to those of every group
devoted to the dhikrs of the Best of Creation.

فَتَابِعْهُ إِنْ كُنْتَ الْمُحِبَّ لِرَبِّنَا

يُثِبْكَ عَلَىٰ ذَاكَ الاِلَهُ بِنَظْرَة

Follow him if you are a lover of our Lord,
and Allah will reward you with a glance from Him.

فَقَدْ كُمِّلَتْ مُسْتَغْفِرًا مِنْ تَوَهُّمِ

لِغَيْرِ وُجُودِ الْحَقِّ فِي كُلِّ لَمْحَة ۞

The song is complete and I seek forgiveness for any illusion
of other than the existence of the Haqq in every glance.

# The Greater Qasida

وله رضي الله عنه القصيدة المسماة
بالتائية الكبرى

فَإِنْ شِئْتَ أَنْ تَرَقَّ رُقِيَ الاَحِبَّةِ
فَعَرِّجْ عَلَى لَيْلَى بِصِدْقِ الْمَوَدَّةِ

If you wish to ascend as the lovers ascend,
turn to Layla with complete sincerity in love.

وَكُلَّ عَذُولٍ فِي مَحبتِهَا انْبُذَنْ
وَسَافِرْ إِلَى الاَحْبَابِ فِي كُلِّ بَلْدَةِ

Dismiss all who criticise Her love,
and travel to the lovers in every land.

وَلَوْ أَنَّ صِدْقَ الْحُبِّ فِيكَ حَقِيقَةً
رَأَيْتَ بِهَا الاَحْبَابَ مِنْ غَيْرِ رِحْلَةِ

If your sincerity in love were real, by it
you would see the lovers without journeying.

67

وَلَوْ أَنَّ عَيْنَ الْقَلْبِ مِنْكَ تَطَهَّرَتْ
لَأَبْصَرَتِ الْأَنْوَارَ مِنْهَا تَجَلَّتِ

If your heart's eye had been purified
you would see the lights manifested from Her.

فَكُنْ عَبْدَهَا شُكْرًا بِلَا رُؤْيَةِ السَّوَا
وَمَا بِكَ مِنْ نُعْمَى فَمِنْهَا تَبَدَّتْ

Be Her slave gratefully without seeing otherness.
Every aspect of your happiness has come from Her.

وَإِيَّاكَ تَلْبِيسَ الْخَوَاطِرِ إِنَّهَا
تَمُوهُ نُصْحًا وَهْوَ أَعْظَمُ فِرْيَةٍ

Beware of the deceptions of thoughts which arise.
They weaken good counsel and they are the greatest lies.

فَخَالِلْ أَخَا صِدْقٍ يُمَيِّزُ بَيْنَهَا
وَيُذْهِبُ عَنْكَ مَا أَتَاكَ بِشُبْهَةٍ

Take a sincere brother as your intimate who can distinguish
between them and dispel any doubts you have.

وَهَيْلَلَةٌ تَنْفِي جَمِيعَ الْوَسَاوِسِ
بِتَلْقِينِ شَيْخٍ عَارِفٍ بِالْحَقِيقَةِ

'La ilaha illa'llah' banishes all whisperings
with the instruction of a Shaykh who knows the Haqiqa.

وَءَايَاتُهُ نُورٌ يَلُوحُ بِظَاهِرٍ
وَسِرٌّ بَدَا مِنْ بَاطِنٍ مَعَ هِمَّةٍ

His signs are a light which shines, appearing outwardly
and a secret which appears inwardly with himma.

وَتَرْقِيَةٌ بِاللَّحْظِ قَبْلَ تَلَفُّظٍ
فَإِنْ كَانَ مِنْهُ اللَّفْظُ جَاءَ بِحُلَّةٍ

He elevates you with a glance even before he speaks,
and if he speaks it brings a Robe of Honour.

وَأَعْنِي بِهَا الْأَنْوَارَ تَسْرِي بِسُرْعَةٍ
لِقَلْبِ مُرِيدِ الْحَقِّ مِنْ غَيْرِ شِرْكَةٍ

By that I mean the lights which flow rapidly
into the heart of the murid seeking the truth without shirk.

وَزُهْدُهُ فِي الْأَكْوَانِ عُمْدَةُ سَيْرِهِ
وَشُغْلٌ بِإِفْرَادِ الْحَبِيبِ بِرُؤْيَةِ

His zuhd among people is the staff of his journey
and his occupation with seeking the Beloved alone in vision.

وَتَصْرِيحُهُ بِالْإِذْنِ مِنْ خَيْرِ أُمَّةٍ
عَلَيْهِ اعْتِمَادُ الصَّادِقِينَ الْأَجِلَّةِ

His speech is by Idhn from the Best of the Umma
upon whom the glorious truthful ones depend.

فَإِنْ حَصَلَ الْمَقْصُودُ مِمَّا ذَكَرْتهُ

فَبَادِرْ وَأَعْطِ النَّفْسَ مِنْ غَيْرِ مُهْلَةِ

If you attain the goal of finding someone like this,
then set out and offer up the self without delay.

وَلَا تَعْتَبِرْ شَيْئًا سِوَىٰ مَا رَسَمْتهُ

فَفِيهِ الَّذِي يُغْنِي وَكُلُّ الْمَسَرَّةِ

Consider nothing except what I have described here,
for it is enough, and it contains every happiness.

فَإِنْ لَمْ تَجِدْ مِمَّا ذَكَرْتُ فَإِنَّنِي

سَأَشْرَحُ نَهْجَ الْحَقِّ مِنْ غَيْرِ مِرْيَةِ

If you have not found such a man,
then let me describe to you the certain path of truth.

فَأَوَّلُ فِعْلِ الْمَرْءِ فِي بَدْءِ سَيْرِهِ

مُجَانَبَةُ الْأَشْرَارِ مِنْ كُلِّ فِرْقَةِ

At the beginning of his journey a man's first act
is to avoid the evil people of every group.

وَشُغْلٌ بِذِكْرِ اللهِ جَلَّ جَلَالُهُ

فَفِيهِ الدَّوَا مِنْ كُلِّ عَيْبٍ وَعِلَّةِ

He should busy himself with dhikr of Allah, may He be glorified,
for in that lies the remedy for every fault and ill.

وَخِدْمَةُ خَيْرِ الْخَلْقِ أَعْظَمُ قُرْبَةٍ

فَفِيهِ مِنَ الْخَيْرَاتِ أَعْلَا مَزِيَّةَ

The greatest offering is to serve the Best of Creation.
Therein lies the highest excellence in good deeds.

فَشَاهِدْهُ فِي الْاَكْوَانِ قَدْ عَمَّ نُورُهُ

وَمِنْهُ أَتَى الْإِمْدَادُ فِي كُلِّ لَحْظَةٍ

Witness him in created forms where his light has spread.
Help is coming from him in every instant.

وَحَكِّمْهُ فِي التَّشْرِيعِ دُونَ تَكَاسُلٍ

وَجَانِبْ مُرَادَ النَّفْسِ أَصْلَ الْبَلِيَّةَ

Make him the arbiter in following the Shari'a without laziness,
and avoid the will of the self, the source of grief.

وَغَلِّبْ جَنَابَ الْحَقِّ عِنْدَ نِزَاعِهَا

وَلَا تَغْتَرِرْ بِالْعِلْمِ إِلَّا بِخَشْيَةَ

Let the truth take over in the struggle with the self.
Do not be deceived by knowledge without fear of Allah.

وَأَعْظَمُ ذَنْبِ الْعَبْدِ رُؤْيَةُ نَفْسِهِ

فَفِيهَا مِنَ الْاَخْبَاثِ كُلُّ شَنِيعَةَ

The worst thing the slave can do is look at his self.
It contains every dreadful and atrocious thing!

وَوَحْدَةُ فِعْلِ اللهِ تَنْفِي رُسُومَهَا

وَتَطْوِي جَمِيعَ الْكَوْنِ عَنْهَا فِي لَحْظَةِ

In one instant the unity of the Act of Allah
wipes out every trace of the self and engulfs all creation.

فَعَوِّلْ عَلَى التَّوْحِيدِ وَاتْرُكْ شُكُوكَهَا

تَفُزْ بِالَّذِي قَدْ فَازَ كُلُّ الاَجِلَّةِ

Rely on Tawhid and leave behind the doubts of the self
and you will achieve what all the noble ones have achieved.

فَإِنْ تَصْدُرِ الاَعْمَالُ مِنْهُمْ كَآلَةِ

تُحَرِّكُهَا الاَقْدَارُ مِنْ غَيْرِ رِيبَةِ

When they make any action there is no question
but that they are just like instruments moved by Divine decrees,

فَتَوْبَتُهُمْ لِلَّهِ بِاللهِ مُطْلَقًا

وَخَوْفُهُمْ تَعْظِيمُ عِزٍّ وَهِيبَةِ

And their tawba is to Allah by Allah absolutely.
Their khawf is in feeling His immense might and awesomeness.

رَجَاؤُهُمْ حُسْنُ الْيَقِينِ بِوَعْدِه

وَشِدَّةُ إِتْعَابِ الْجُسُومِ فِي خِدْمَةِ

Their raja' is complete certainty in His promise
and the hardship and fatigue of their bodies in His service.

وَشُكْرُهُمْ شُغْلٌ بِرُؤْيَةِ مُنْعِمٍ

وَغِيبَتُهُمْ عَنْ كُلِّ ضِيقٍ وَنِعْمَةِ

Their shukr is in being occupied in seeing the Bestower of blessings,
and in being detached from both constriction and blessing.

وَصَبْرُهُمْ حُسْنُ الرِّضَىٰ بِمَقَادِرٍ

وَلَيْسَ لَهُمْ تَدْبِيرُ سُقْمٍ وَصِحَّةٍ

Their sabr is complete contentment with events.
They seek no control over either sickness or good health.

تَوَكُّلُهُمْ تَفْوِيضُ كُلِّ أُمُورِهِمْ

لِمَنْ هُوَ أَدْرَىٰ بِالْأُمُورِ الْخَفِيَّةِ

Their tawakkul consists in handing over all their affairs
to the One Who has the best knowledge of hidden matters.

وَزُهْدُهُمْ يَأْسٌ مِمَّا لَمْ يَكُنْ لَهُمْ

بِسَابِقِ عِلْمِ اللَّهِ مِنْ بَرْمِ قِسْمَةِ

Their zuhd is to renounce everything except
what Allah has decreed for them in His fore-knowledge.

مَحَبَّتُهُمْ سُكْرٌ بِحُسْنِ جَمَالِهِ

وَفِيهَا مَقَامُ الْأُنْسِ أَشْرَفُ حِلْيَةِ

Their love is intoxication with the perfection of His beauty.
This love contains the Maqam al-Uns, the noblest adornment.

وَبَسْطٌ وَإِدْلَالٌ وَتَكْلِيمُ حِبِّهِمْ

وَأَسْرَارُهَا تَسْرِي إِلَىٰ غَيْرِ غَايَةِ

And bast, liberation, and speaking with their Beloved
– the secrets of love endlessly flow on and on.

فَنَافِسْهُمْ فِيهَا بِحُسْنِ تَأَدُّبِ

وَأَحْسِنْ لِأَحْبَابِ الْحَبِيبِ بِفَضْلَةِ

Outdo them in actions with the best adab.
Be generous and treat the lovers of the Beloved well.

فَلَوْ عَرَفَ الْإِنْسَانُ قِيمَةَ قَلْبِهِ

لَأَنْفَقَ كُلَّ الْكُلِّ مِنْ غَيْرِ قَتَرَةِ

For a man would unceasingly spend all he had –
if he only understood the secret of his own heart.

وَلَوْ أَدْرَكَ الْإِنْسَانُ لَذَّةَ سِرِّهِ

لَقَارَنَ أَنْفَاسَ الْخُرُوجِ بِعَبْرَةِ

If a man could but grasp the bliss of his secret
he would shed a tear with every breath he breathed.

وَطَارَ مِنَ الْجِسْمِ الَّذِي صَارَ قَفْصَهُ

بِأَجْنِحَةِ الْأَفْكَارِ مُنْتَهَىٰ سِدْرَةِ

Then, his body become his cage, he would fly from it
with the wings of contemplation to the Furthest Lote-Tree.

74

وَجَالَ نَوَاحِي الْعَرْشِ وَالْكُرْسِيِّ الَّذِي
تَضَاءَلَتِ الاَجْرَامُ عَنْهُ كَخَلْقَة

He would freely roam around the Throne and the Footstool
which make the heavenly bodies appear like a small ring.

وَشَاهَدَ أَفْلَاكًا وَسِرَّ بُرُوجِهَا
وَشِدَّةَ إِفْرَاطِ الْمُرُورِ بِسُرْعَة

He would see the spheres and the secrets of their constellations
and the meaning of their tremendously rapid movement.

وَزَالَ حِجَابُ اللَّوْحِ عَنْ طَيِّ سِرِّهِ
فَفَاحَتْ عُلُومُ الْكَشْفِ مِنْ غَيْرِ سُتْرَة

The veil of the Tablet of Forms would be lifted from his secret
and so the hidden knowledges would emerge uncovered.

فَلَوْ كَانَتِ الاَشْجَارُ أَقْلَامَ كَتْبِهَا
وَمِدَادُهَا الْبَحْرُ الْمُحِيطُ لَجَفَّتِ

Had the trees been the pens to write it and their ink
the oceans, they would have dried up.

وَزَارَ مِنَ الْمَعْمُورِ أَمْلَاكَهُ الَّتِي
تَنُوفُ عَلَى الاَعْدَادِ مِنْ غَيْرِ غَايَة

And he would visit the Frequented House
with its countless myriad angels.

75

وَوَافَىٰ دُخُولَ حَضْرَةِ الْقُدْسِ طَالِبًا

لِتَطْهِيرِ سِرِّ السِّرِّ مِنْ كُلِّ وَقْفَةِ

And, in his quest to purify the secret of his secret from every way-stage
he finally comes to the door to the pure Presence.

فَهَذَا مَحَطُّ الْقَوْمِ عِنْدَ سَرَائِهِمْ

بِأَرْوَاحِهِمْ مَحَلُّ كَتْمٍ وَحِيرَةِ

Now, this Station of the People in the journey of their spirits
is the Station of concealment and bewilderment.

وَمِنْ بَعْدِهَا الْعِلْمُ الَّذِي لَا يَبِثُّهُ

سِوَىٰ مَنْ لَهُ الْإِذْنُ الصَّرِيحُ بِرُؤْيَةِ

After it comes knowledge – which may not be divulged
except by the one who in vision has received a clear Idhn.

وَفِي الْأَرْضِ ءَايَاتٌ لِكُلِّ مُفَكِّرٍ

عَجَائِبُهَا تَمْضِي إِلَىٰ أَعْلَا عِبْرَةِ

The earth is full of signs for all who look and reflect.
Its marvels can take one to the highest teaching –

فَأَسْمَاءُ رَبِّ الْعَرْشِ قَدْ عَمَّ نُورُهَا

بِأَجْزَائِهَا مَا بَيْنَ خَافٍ وَشُهْرَةِ

For the light of the Names of the Lord of the Throne
extends throughout all its known and hidden parts.

فَلَوْ جُلْتَ فِي الْمِيَاهِ مَعْ أَصْلِ نَشْئِهَا

وَتَرْبِيَةِ الأَشْيَاءِ مِنْهَا بِحِكْمَةِ

If you were to reflect on the oceans and their origin,
and how things were fostered from out of them with wisdom,

حَكَمْتَ بِعَجْزِ الْكُلِّ عَنْ دَرْكِ سِرِّهَا

وَبُحْتَ بِتَخْصِيصِ الإِلَهِ بِقُدْرَةِ

then you would know that no one is capable of grasping their secret
and you would affirm that power belongs to Allah alone.

وَأَطْلِقْ عِنَانَ الْفِكْرِ عِنْدَ جِبَالِهَا

تَجِدْهَا هِيَ الأَوْتَادُ مِنْ غَيْرِ مِرْيَةِ

Let your thoughts flow freely regarding its mountains
and you will find that they are the pegs without doubt.

وَمَا حَوَتِ الأَزْهَارُ مِنْ حُسْنِ مَنْظَرِ

وَكَثْرَةِ تَنْوِيعِ الثِّمَارِ الْبَدِيعَةِ

Look at the beauty of the appearance of the flowers,
and the marvellous variety of different fruits.

وَمَا أَظْهَرَتْ مِنْ كُلِّ شَيْءٍ يُرَىٰ بِهَا

وَكُلُّ أَتَىٰ مِنْ عَيْنِ عِزٍّ وَسَطْوَةِ

Look at every visible manifestation!
It all gushes from the fount of energy and power.

فَشَاهِدْ جَمَالَ الْحَقِّ عِنْدَ لِحَاظِهَا

وَإِيَّاكَ تَنْكِيفًا عَلَى أَدْنَى ذَرَّةٍ

Consider all this and then see the beauty of the truth.
Take care – you cannot despise even the lowest atom.

فَمَا قَامَتِ الاَشْيَاءُ إِلَّا بِرِبِّهَا

فَيَا حَيُّ يَا قَيُّومُ أَبْلَغُ حُجَّةٍ

Things have no existence except through their Lord.
O Living! O Eternal! Your own most eloquent proof!

فَفِي النَّفْسِ ءَايَاتٌ لِكُلِّ مُفَكِّرٍ

فَفِيهَا انطَوَى الْكَوْنُ الْكَبِيرُ بِرُمَّةٍ

There are signs in the self for any who ponders it
because the entire universe is contained in it.

وَزَادَتْ بِوُسْعِ الْحَقِّ عِنْدَ تَطَهُّرٍ

وَذَا قُلْ بِلَا كَيْفٍ وَأَيْنَ وَشُبْهَةٍ

In purification the self expands by the power of the Haqq.
Now do not wonder and ask 'How?' or 'Where?' or 'What?'

وَزَادَتْ بِتَحْمِيلِ الالَهِ أَمَانَةً

عَلَيْهَا فَمَا حَدُّ الالَهِ تَعَدَّتِ

It expands by Allah's bestowal of the trust upon it
– and godhood has no limitation whatsoever.

وَقَدْ عَجَزَتْ عَنْهَا الْعِظَامُ مِنَ الْوَرَىٰ

وَقَامَ بِهَا الإِنْسَانُ أَرْفَعَ قَوْمَةِ

Even great men have proved unable to bear this trust,
yet still man has to take it on, and this is the highest task.

فَيَا سَعْدَ مَنْ أَضْحَىٰ يُتَابِعُ سَيِّدًا

رَسُولًا لَهُ أَعْلَا الْمَزَايَا وَرُتْبَةِ

How fulfilled is the one who has begun to follow a master,
a Messenger who has the highest rank and merit,

فَفَازَ مِنَ الْخَيْرَاتِ فَوْقَ نِهَايَةِ

وَأُمَّتُهُ أُرْبَتْ عَلَىٰ كُلِّ أُمَّةِ

For he will gain benefits without end or limit,
and his Community is above every other.

فَلَا أَحَدٌ يَرْقَىٰ لِرُتْبَةِ قُرْبِهِ

وَذَاكَ بِتَخْصِيصِ الإِلَهِ بِعَطْفَةِ

No one may rise to the rank of His nearness which he enjoys,
since that is a special mark of favour from Allah.

فَلَا كَسْبَ لِلْإِنْسَانِ فِي دَرْكِ غَايَةِ

لِمَا خَصَّهُ الرَّحْمَٰنُ فِي أَصْلِ نَشْأَةِ

There is nothing to be gained by a man trying to reach a place
set aside for the Prophet from the beginning of creation.

عَلَيْهِ صَلَاةُ اللهِ مَا جَاءَ وَارِدُ

يُبيِّنُ طُرُقَ الْحَقِّ مَعَ سَوْقِ مِنْحَةٍ

May Allah's blessings be upon him as long as someone comes
to make clear the paths of truth and bringing gifts,

وَءَالِهِ وَالْاَصْحَابِ مَعَ كُلِّ مُرْشِدٍ

دَعَا لِطَرِيقِ اللهِ فِي كُلِّ حَالَةٍ

and on his family and Companions, and every Murshid
who calls to the Path of Allah in every situation.

وَأَسْأَلُ رَبِّ اللهَ إِلْقَاءَ سِرِّهِ

عَلَيَّ مَعَ الْاِخْوَانِ فِي كُلِّ وِجْهَةٍ

I ask my Lord Allah to bestow His secret on me
and on my brothers in every way.

قَدْ وَافَقَتِ الْاِسْمَ الْعَظِيمَ جَلَالَةً

بَعْدٌ فَنَفِّسْ فِي افْتِتَاحٍ وَخَتْمَةٍ ۞

All this is in harmony with the majesty of the Supreme Name,
and numerically, so pay attention to its beginning and its end.

# Lesser Qasida

وله رضي الله عنه ورزقنا في الدارين رضاه آمين

التائية الوسطى

شَرِبْنَـا مِنَ الأَنْوَارِ فِي حَـانِ حَضْرَةٍ

شَرَابًـا أَزَالَ اللَّبْسَ مِنْ غَيْرِ مِرْيَةِ

In the tavern of the Presence we drank a wine
of the lights that totally dispelled the darkness.

فَأَدْرَكْنَـا أَنَّ الْفِعْلَ فِي كُلِّ ذَرَّةٍ

بِخَـالِقِهَـا الْمَعْبُودِ فِي كُلِّ وِجْهَةِ

Through it we grasped that the act is in every atom
through its Creator Who is worshipped everywhere.

وَحَقَّقْنَـا أَنَّ اللهَ فِي الْكُلِّ ظَـاهِرٌ

بِأَسْمَـائِهِ الْحُسْنَىٰ وَأَسْرَارِ قُدْرَةِ

We realised that Allah is manifest in everything
through His most Beautiful Names and the secrets of power.

81

وَلَكِنَّ أَحْوَالَ الْوُجُودِ كَثِيرَةٌ

بِهَا وَقَعَ الْحُجُبُ الْعَظِيمُ لِحِكْمَةٍ

However, the states of existence are numerous,
and because of this, great veils have fallen over wisdom.

لِذَا أَرْسَلَ الرَّحْمَنُ خِيرَةَ خَلْقِهِ

بَشِيرًا نَذِيرًا دَاعِيًا بِالْبَصِيرَةِ

Thus the Merciful has sent the flower of His creation
bringing good news and warning, inviting with inner sight.

فَإِنْ شِئْتَ أَنْ تَحْظَى بِنَيْلِ سَعَادَةٍ

فَحَكِّمْهُ تَحْكِيمًا عَلَى كُلِّ خَطْرَةٍ

If you wish to obtain the gift of happiness
then make him the guide of your every thought and move.

وَقُلْ لِحُظُوظِ النَّفْسِ لَا تَذْهَبِي مَعِي

وَلَا تَقْطَعِي سَيْرِي لِرَبِّ الْبَرِيَّةِ

Tell the impulses of the self: 'Do not come with me.
Do not cut off my path to the Lord of creation.'

فَمَنْ كَانَ ذَا ذِكْرٍ وَفِكْرٍ وَهِمَّةٍ

تَرَقَّى عَنِ الْأَغْيَارِ فِي كُلِّ لَحْظَةٍ

Whoever has got dhikr, fikr and himma
will in every moment transcend otherness.

وَحَـازَ مِنَ الْعِرْفَانِ فَوْقَ مُرَادِهِ

وَحَقَّقَ أَسْرَارَ الْوُجُودِ بِسُرْعَةِ

He will attain gnosis beyond his desires
and fast realise the secrets of existence.

وَشَـاهَدَ أَنَّ الْفَرْقَ مَحْضُ شَرِيعَةٍ

وَهِيَ عَلَى التَّحْقِيقِ عَيْنُ الْحَقِيقَةِ

He will see that separation is the pure Shari'a,
which, properly speaking, is the source of Haqiqa.

لِذَا أَمَرَ الْقُرْءَانُ بِالْفِكْرِ فِي الْوَرَىٰ

وَجَـاءَ بِتَوْحِيدٍ مُزِيلٍ لِرِيبَةٍ

This is why the Qur'an commands reflection on mankind
which brings a Tawhid that eliminates any doubt.

وَلَيْسَ يُرَى الرَّحْمَـٰنُ إِلَّا فِي مَظْهَرٍ

كَعَرْشٍ وَكُرْسِيٍّ وَلَوْحٍ وَسِدْرَةِ

The Merciful is only to be seen in manifestations
like the Throne, the Footstool, the Tablet, or the Lote-Tree.

وَكُنْهُ صِفَـاتِ الرَّبِّ لَيْسَ النُّهَىٰ تَفِي

بِتَحْقِيقِهَـا كَشْفًا فَأَحْرَى الْمَهِيَّةِ

The intellect cannot grasp the nature of the Attributes of the Lord
through unveiling, let alone the Essence.

83

فَكِّرْ عَلَىٰ أَوْصَافِ نَفْسِكَ فَامْحُهَا

تُمَدُّ بِأَنْوَارِ الصِّفَاتِ الْقَدِيمَةِ

So attack the attributes of the self and efface them,
and you will be helped by the lights of the eternal Attributes.

لِذَاكَ تَرَى الْعُشَّاقَ قَدْ ثَمِلُوا بِهَا

وَأَحْسَنُهُمْ سُكْرًا مَلِيكُ الْاِبَاحَةِ

Thus you will see lovers who have become intoxicated by the lights,
and the drunkest lover is the one who is given special licence.

وَلَيْسَ عَلَى الْمَغْلُوبِ مِنْ حَرَجٍ وَلَا

عَلَىٰ أَهْلِ الْاِذْنِ مِنْ وُضُوجِ الْاِشَارَةِ

There is no restriction on the clear ishara those utterly overwhelmed
by Allah may make, nor on the people of Idhn.

فَدُونَكَ قَوْمًا قَدْ أَذَابُوا نُفُوسَهُمْ

نَفَاضُوا بِحَارَ الْحُبِّ فِي كُلِّ لُجَّةِ

Here are ones who have obliterated their selves
and plumbed every depth in the oceans of love.

فَسَلِّمْ لَهُمْ فِيمَا تَرَىٰ مِنْ صَبَابَةٍ

وَرَقْصٍ عَلَىٰ ذِكْرِ الْحَبِيبِ بِنَغْمَةِ

So submit to them for what you see of their ardent love,
and the dancing and singing in their dhikr of the Beloved.

فَلَوْ ذُقْتَ شَيْئًا مِنْ مَعَانِي كَلَامِنَا

لَكُنْتَ مِنَ السُّبَّاقِ فِي كُلِّ حَالَةِ

If you had but tasted something of the meaning of our words,
you would have been one of the foremost in every circumstance.

وَأَغْضَيْتَ يَا أَخِي الْجُفُونَ عَنِ الْقَذَا

ومزَّقْتَ أَثْوَابَ الْحَيَا وَالْمَهَابَةِ

And, my brother, you would have borne your troubles patiently,
and you would have rent the robes of shame and self-importance.

وَقُلْتَ لِحَادِي الْقَوْمِ حَبِّنَا فِي اسْمِهِ

فَلَا عَارَ فِي ذَاكَ الْحِدَا وَالصَّبَابَةِ

You would have said to the leader of the people, 'Make us love His name!
There is no shame in that song, nor in that love!'

وَلَكِنَّ مَنْ قَدْ صَارَ مِلْكًا لِنَفْسِهِ

تَقَاعَدَ عَنْ أَسْرَارِ تِلْكَ الطَّرِيقَةِ

Unfortunately, whoever becomes subject to his own self
is cut off from the secrets of this path.

فَأَعْدَا عَدُوٍّ فِي الْوَرَىٰ نَفْسُكَ الَّتِي

تُعَطِّلُ عَنْ تَحْقِيقِ فَهْمِ الْحَقِيقَةِ

The most hostile enemy of man is his self,
which hinders him from real understanding of the Haqiqa.

فَكَبِّرْ عَلَى الأَكْوَانِ إِنْ شِئْتَ وَصْلَهُ

وَإِيَّاكَ أَنْ تَرْضَىٰ بِنَيْلِ الكَرَامَة

So become greater than the common people if you desire to reach Him,
and do not be satisfied with a mere reputation of nobility.

فَيَا فَوْزَ قَوْمٍ قَدْ أَجَابُوا حَبِيبَهُمْ

لِدَعْوَتِهِ الْعُظْمَىٰ فَفَازُوا بِجَنَّة

Oh the triumph of a people who have answered
the great call of the Beloved, and so obtained the Garden!

وَأَعْنِي بِهِ الْعِرْفَانَ فِي حَضْرَةِ الدُّنَا

وَجَنَّةَ أَنْهَارٍ وَحُورٍ وَلَذَّةِ

By that I mean both 'irfan in the presence of nearness
and the garden of rivers, houris, and delight.

عَلَىٰ نَفْسِهِ فَلْيَبْكِ مَنْ صَارَ قَلْبُهُ

خَرَابًا مِنَ الْعِرْفَانِ فِي كُلِّ فِكْرَة

Let the one whose heart has become devoid and empty
of 'irfan in every thought weep over himself.

وَمَا لَذَّةُ الْعَيْشِ السَّلِيمِ مِنَ النَّغْصِ

وَرَبِّي إِلَّا فِي تَحَقُّقِ وُصْلَة

The joy of life without trouble, by my Lord,
is only found in the realisation of reunion.

عَسَىٰ نَظْرَةٌ تَشْفِي السَّقِيمَ مِنَ الضَّنَا

فَقَدْ عَزَّ إِدْرَاكٌ لِكُنْهِ الْحَقِيقَةِ

Perhaps a glance will cure the sick man of his sickness,
for the perception of the essence of Haqiqa is mighty.

فَأَطْيَبُ أَوْقَاتِي اتِّصَافِي بِذِلَّةٍ

وَعَجْزٍ وَفَقْرٍ وَانْسِلَابِ إِرَادَةٍ

My best time is when I am characterised by humility,
incapacity, poverty, and negation of the will.

فَتِلْكَ أُصُولٌ فِي طَرِيقَتِنَا الْمُثْلَىٰ

فَكُنْهُ وَجِنْبْ عَنْ عُلُوٍّ وَرِفْعَةٍ

For these are the foundations of our perfect path.
So follow it and avoid reputation and self-importance.

وَكُلُّ صِفَاتِ الرَّبِّ فَاهْرُبْ لِضِدِّهَا

تَكُونُ بِفَضْلِ اللهِ أَغْنَى الْبَرِيَّةِ

Flee to the opposite of the Attributes of the Lord,
then by Allah's favour, you will be the richest of creation.

فَأَوْصَافُهُ الْعِلْمُ الْمُحِيطُ وَقُدْرَةٌ

وَأَوْصَافُنَا جَهْلٌ وَعَجْزٌ عَنْ ذَرَّةٍ

His Attributes are encompassing knowledge, and power over everything,
and our attributes are ignorance and less power than a particle of dust.

وَإِنْ شِئْتَ قَصْدَ الْعَارِفِينَ بِأَسْرِهِمْ

نْخُذْهُ وَكُنْ يَا صَاحِ صَاحِبَ هِمَّة

If you desire to reach the goal of all the 'Arifeen,
then take it, O my companion, and have himma.

عُبُودِيَّةٌ لِلَّهِ صَادِقَةً وَمَعْ

قِيَامٍ بِحَقِّ الرَّبِّ فِي كُلِّ لَحْظَة

Being a slave of Allah is sincere when it goes
along with undertaking the rights of the Lord at every moment.

وَأَعْنِي بِهَا التَّجْرِيدَ مِنْ كُلِّ قُوَّةٍ

وَحَوْلٍ وَأَسْبَابٍ وَنَيْلِ الْمَزِيَّة

By slavehood I mean *tajrid* from every power and strength
and any means, and even getting things for yourself.

لِأَنَّ بِهَا يَصْفُو الْفُؤَادُ مِنَ الْعَمَىٰ

وَيَمْلَأُ بِالْأَنْوَارِ فِي كُلِّ فِكْرَة

Because in this way the heart is purified of blindness
and is filled with lights in every thought.

فَقَدْ كَمُلَتْ وَالْحَمْدُ فِي الْبَدْءِ وَانْخَتَمْ

عَلَىٰ نِعْمَةِ الْإِمْدَادِ مِنْ خَيْرِ أُمَّة

The song is over. Praise is due at the beginning and the end
for the gift of help from the Best of the Community.

عَلَيْهِ صَلَاةُ اللهِ فِي كُلِّ لَحْظَةٍ

وَءَالِهِ وَالاَصْحَابِ أَهْلِ الْعِنَايَةِ

May the blessings of Allah be upon him at every instant
and his family, and his Companions, the people in Allah's care.

وَنَاظِمُهَا الْمَعْرُوفُ أَعْنِي مُحَمَّدًا

هُوَ ابْنُ حَبِيبٍ طَالِبًا لِلْعُبُودَةِ

Its well-known writer, I mean Muhammad
ibn al-Habib, seeks perfect slavehood.

فَبَلِّغْهُ يَا ذَا الْفَضْلِ مِنْكَ بِنَفْحَةٍ

تَسُحُّ عَلَى الاَكْوَانِ فَيْضَ الْحَقِيقَةِ ۞

So convey him a fragrance from You, O Master of Generosity,
that will spread the effulgence of Haqiqa over all creation.

# Minor Qasida

وتليهَا

التَّائِيَة الصغرى

سَقَـانِي حِبّي مِنْ صَفَـاءٍ مَحبَّةٍ
فَأَصْبَحْتُ مَحبُوبًـا لَدَىٰ كُلِّ نِسْبَةٍ

My Beloved gave me a drink of the purest love,
so I became beloved in every way.

وغَيبِنِي عَنِّي فَلَمْ أَرَ غَيرَه
ونَعَّمَ سِرِّي فِي مَظَـاهِرِ حَضْرَةٍ

He blinded me to myself so that I saw only Him,
and dissolved my secret in the manifestations of the Presence.

فَفَرَّقْتُ فِي جَمْعِي وَجَمَعتُ مَفْرُوقِي
وَحَقَّقْتُ تَوْحِيدِي بِإِفْرَادِ وَحْدَةٍ

I separated what was gathered in me and gathered what was separate;
by the isolation of unity I realised my Tawhid.

وَنِلْتُ مُرَادِي مِنْ شُهُودِ كَمَالِهِ

وَحَقَّقْتُهُ فِي كُلِّ مَعْنًى وَصُورَةٍ

I attained my desire – directly to see His perfection
and to experience it in every meaning and form.

وَمَزَّقْتُ وَهْمِي وَهْوَ أَعْظَمُ قَـاطِعٍ

فَأَلْفَيْتُهُ قَيُّومًا فِي كُلِّ ذَرَّةٍ

I tore down my illusion, which is the greatest screen,
and then I found Him, timeless, in every atom.

وَحَكَّمْتُ شَرْعِي فِي تَجَلِّي صِفَـاتِهِ

فَأَطْلَعَنِي رَبِّي عَلَىٰ سِرِّ حِكْمَتِي

I made the Shari'a my guide in taking on His Attributes,
and my Lord revealed to me the secret of my wisdom.

فَطَوْرًا أَرَى الْاكْوَانَ مَظْهَرَ أَحْمَدٍ

وَطَوْرًا أَرَاهَـا مِنْ مَظَـاهِرِ عِزَّةٍ

Sometimes I see creatures as a manifestation of Ahmad,
and sometimes I see them as manifestations of divine Power.

وَطَوْرًا يَفْنَىٰ فِعْلِي بِرُؤْيَةِ فِعْلِهِ

وَطَوْرًا أَرَى الْاوْصَافَ مِنْهُ تَبَدَّتْ

Sometimes my action is obliterated by the sight of His action,
and sometimes I see the Attributes appearing from Him.

وَطَوْرًا أَغِيبُ عَنْ وُجُودٍ مَجَازِيٍّ

فِي وَحْدَةِ حَقٍّ لَا تُشَابُ بِشِرْكَةِ

And sometimes I withdraw from metaphorical existence
into the unity of a Truth unmarked by shirk.

وَمَا الْخَلْقُ إِلَّا كَالْهَبَا فِي الْهَوَى لِمَنْ

تَغَيَّبَ فِي أَنْوَارِ ذِكْرِ الْحَقِيقَةِ

To anyone who withdraws into the lights of the dhikr of the Truth,
creation is nothing more than particles of dust in the air.

فَفِي ذِكْرِهَا الْفَتْحُ الْمُبِينُ لِتَائِبِ

تَجَلَّى بِصَبْرٍ مَعَ تَحَقُّقِ نِعْمَةِ

The dhikr of the Truth contains the clear opening for the man of tawba
who has adorned himself with patience and the realisation of benefits.

فَقَامَ بِشُكْرِ اللهِ لِكُلِّ نِعْمَةٍ

تَجَلَّى بِهَا الْوَهَّابُ فِي كُلِّ حَالَةِ

He has thus undertaken to show gratitude to Allah in every state
for every gift by which the Giver manifests Himself.

فَأَوْرَثَهُ حُبُّ التَّفَرُّدِ دَائِمًا

تَحَقُّقَ إِمْدَادٍ أَتَتْ بِسَكِينَةِ

The love of isolation grants him continual realisation
of aid which comes with the Sakina.

فَصَارَ يُحِبُّ اللهَ حَقًّا بِلَا رَيْبِ

لِرُؤْيَتِهِ الإِحْسَانَ فِي كُلِّ لَحْظَةِ

He will begin to love Allah truly, without doubt,
since he witnesses Ihsan at every instant.

فَكُلُّ مَقَامَاتِ الْيَقِينِ قَدِ انْطَوَتْ

فِي صَبْرٍ وَحُبٍّ خَالِصٍ مِنْ مَشُوبَةِ

Firm patience and untarnished, pure love
indeed contain all the Stations of Certainty.

وَلَا بُدَّ فِي ذَا مِنْ إِمَامٍ لِسَالِكٍ

يَدُلُّ عَلَىٰ بِرٍّ وَتَقْوَىٰ وَسُنَّةِ

To obtain these the Salik must have an Imam
to guide him in right action, taqwa and Sunna.

وَدَعْ عَنْكَ مَحْجُوبًا غَفُولًا عَنْ رَبِّهِ

جَهُولًا بِطُرْقِ اللهِ مِنْ فَرْطِ ظُلْمَةِ

Leave alone the one who is veiled, unaware of his Lord,
and in his deep inner darkness utterly ignorant of the Paths of Allah.

وَإِيَّاكَ أَنْ تَرْضَىٰ بِصُحْبَةِ فِرْقَةِ

تَمَكَّنَ مِنْهَا الشَّرُّ فِي كُلِّ قَوْلَةِ

Beware of ending up satisfied to be in the company
of a sect whom evil masters in their every word,

يَقُولُونَ بِالْأَفْوَاهِ مَا لَيْسَ فِي الْحَشَا

وَيَاتُونَ مِنْ أَفْعَالٍ كُلَّ قَبِيحَةِ

Saying with their mouths what is not in their hearts,
while at the same time doing every revolting act.

نَصَحْتُكَ بَعْدَ الْبَحْثِ إِنْ كُنْتَ سَامِعًا

فَمَا الدِّينُ إِلَّا نُصْحُ كُلِّ الْخَلِيقَةِ

I have counselled you after investigation if you will only listen,
for the Deen is only giving every person good counsel.

فَكَمْ قَدْ أَزَاغُوا مِنْ عُقُولٍ بَسِيطَةِ

خَلَتْ عَنْ تَوْفِيقِ نُورِ رَبِّ الْبَرِيَّةِ

How many simple minds have got lost because they lacked
the guidance of the light of the Lord of creation?

وَقَدْ صَارَتِ الْأَعْرَاضُ فِي هَتْكِهَا لَهُمْ

قَبَائِحُ أَغْرَاضٍ هِيَ شَرُّ فِتْنَةِ

Their original good name has been debased and disgraced
falling into the worst temptation, ugly deeds of shame.

وَقَدْ أَمَرَ الشَّرْعُ الْمُبِينُ بِتَعْظِيمِ

لِمَنْ كَانَ ذَا نَفْعٍ بِإِرْشَادِ أُمَّةِ

The clear Shari'a commands that we honour and esteem,
whoever has the best guidance for the Community.

وَطُوبَىٰ لِمَشْغُولٍ بِتَهْذِيبِ نَفْسِهِ
يُجَاهِدُهَا بِالذِّكْرِ فِي كُلِّ حَالَةِ

Bliss belongs to the one occupied with correction of the self,
who struggles against it with dhikr in every State,

وَيَتْلُو كِتَابَ اللهِ بِالْجِدِّ دَائِمًا
وَيَقْتَبِسُ الأَنْوَارَ مِنْ كُلِّ ءَايَةِ

who constantly reads the Book of Allah with gravity,
and who seeks the knowledge of lights from every ayat,

يُحَكِّمُهُ فِي كُلِّ مَا هُوَ فَاعِلٌ
وَيَتْبَعُ أَخْلَاقًا لِخَيْرِ الْخَلِيقَةِ

taking it as his judgment in all that he does,
and following the behaviour of the Best of the Community.

فَهُوَ الصِّرَاطُ الْمُسْتَقِيمُ لِمَنْ دَرَا
وَهُوَ الَّذِي أَتَىٰ بِأَفْضَلِ مِلَّةِ

He is the Straight Path for those who understand,
and he is the one who has brought the fullest of spiritual teachings.

عَلَيْهِ صَلَاةُ اللهِ مَعْ ءَالِهِ وَمَنْ
تَلَاهُمْ بِإِحْسَانٍ إِلَىٰ يَوْمِ بِعْثَةِ ۝

May Allah's blessings always be upon him and his family
and whoever follows them with Ihsan until the Day of Rising.

# Doctrines of Tawhid

ويليها رجز

عقائد التوحيد

يَقُولُ عَبْدُ رَبِّهِ مُحَمَّدُ

إِبْنُ الْحَبِيبِ رَبُّهُ يُوَحِّدُ

The slave of his Lord, Muhammad ibn al-Habib,
says, declaring the absolute oneness of his Lord:

بِاسْمِ الإِلَهِ فِي الأُمُورِ أَشْرَعُ

إِلَيْهِ بَدْؤُهَا كَذَاكَ الْمَرْجَعُ

I begin all things with the 'Bismillah' –
to Him belong their beginning as well as their returning.

مَعْنَى الإِلَهِ الْغَنِي عَنْ سِوَاهُ

وَلَهُ يَفْتَقِرُ مَا عَدَاهُ

The meaning of 'god' is That which has no need of other-than-Him,
while anything other has need of Him.

لِلِاسْتِغْنَىٰ عَنْ كُلِّ مَا سِوَاهُ

يَجِّ مِنَ الْاَوْصَافِ لَا تَنْسَاهُ

This 'That' which has no need of other-than-Him
possesses thirteen Attributes, do not forget it!

وُجُودُ ثُمَّ قِدَمُ ثُمَّ الْبَقَا

مُخَالَفَهْ ثُمَّ غِنَاهُ مُطْلَقَا

Existence, then pre-existence, then going-on,
being different from creation, then His absolute independence.

وَالسَّمْعُ وَالْبَصَرُ وَالْكَلَامُ

وَالْكَوْنُ لَازِمُ لَهَا أَحْكَامُ

Hearing, sight and speech
and the fact that there are rulings inherent in them.

وَعَدَمُ الْاَغْرَاضِ فِي الْاَفْعَالِ

كَذَ'كَ فِي الْاَحْكَامِ رُدَّ الْبَالِ

Acts devoid of motive or need,
and similarly judgments; pay attention.

جَوَازُ فِعْلٍ ثُمَّ تَرْكِ أَلْحَقَا

بِمَا ذَكَرْنَاهُ وَكُنْ مُحَقِّقَا

Total freedom of action and of non-action
– connect to what we have told you and realise it!

وَلِافْتِقَارِ كُلِّ مَا عَدَاهُ

يَبّ مِنَ الْأَوْصَافِ مُنْتَهَاهُ

The poverty of all that is other-than-Him
has in the end twelve attributes:

اَلْعِلْمُ وَالْقُدْرَةُ وَالْاِرَادَهْ

ثُمَّ الْحَيَاةُ حَقِّقِ الْاِفَادَهْ

Knowledge, power, and will,
then life – grasp the lesson intended here!

زِدْ قَادِرًا وَمُرِيدًا وَعَالِمْ

حَيًّا فَلَا تَكْتَفِي بِاللَّوَازِمْ

In addition He is Capable, Willing, Knowing
Living – but do not be content with the inherent attributes.

وَحْدَةُ فِعْلٍ وَكَذَا وَصْفٍ وَذَاتْ

بِنَفْيِ كَمِّ فَاسْئَلَنْ عَنْهَا الثِّقَاتْ

Unity of action, attribute and essence
with rejection of quantity – ask trustworthy ones about it.

حُدُوثُ عَالَمٍ وَنَفْيُ تَأْثِيرِ

بِطَبْعٍ أَوْ بِقُوَّةٍ فَاعْتَبِرِ

The originated nature of the universe and the negation
of effect either by nature or by a faculty – so take note.

فَتِلْكَ خَمْسَةٌ وَعِشْرُونَ صِفَهْ

وَالضِّدُّ مِثْلُهَا فَفَصِّلْ عَدَدَهْ

These are twenty-five attributes.
Their opposites are the same in number – count them.

وَلِلإِيمَانِ بِالرَّسُولِ عَشَرَهْ

وَسِتَّةٌ مِنَ الصِّفَاتِ تَابَعَهْ

Belief in the Messenger
has sixteen attributes which are:

اَلصِّدْقُ وَالتَّبْلِيغُ وَالأَمَانَهْ

وَجَوَازُ الأَعْرَاضِ لِلإِفَادَهْ

Truthfulness, conveyance of the message and trustworthiness,
the conceivability of being subject to accidents that have meaning.

وَإِيمَانٌ بِكُتُبٍ وَأَنْبِيَا

وَرُسُلٍ وَأَمْلاكٍ يَا ذَكِيَا

Belief in the Books and the Prophets,
and the Messengers, and the Angels, O man of intellect!

وَإِيمَانٌ بِيَوْمِ الآخِرِ فَعْ

أَضْدَادَهَا وَكُنْ لِنَفْيِهَا سَاعِي

And belief that the Last Day must come.
Be aware of their opposites and struggle to reject them.

فَتِلْكَ سِتَّةٌ وَسِتُّونَ صِفَه

تَدْخُلُ فِي الْكَلِمَةِ الْمُشَرَّفَه

These are sixty-six Attributes
which are contained in the noble phrase.

فَاشْغَلْ بِهَا الْأَوْقَاتَ بِالْحُضُورِ

تَرْقَىٰ إِلَى الْمَعْنَىٰ مَعَ السُّرُورِ

So occupy your Awqat with them in the Presence,
and joyfully you will rise to their meaning.

دَلِيلُهَا النَّظَرُ فِي الْقُرْءَانِ

وَجَوَلَانُ الْعَقْلِ فِي الْأَكْوَانِ

Their proof lies in contemplation of the Qur'an
and in reflecting on created beings with the intellect.

يَا رَبَّنَا صَلِّ عَلَىٰ مُحَمَّد

وَءَالِهِ وَكُلِّ عَبْدٍ مُقْتَدِى

O our Lord, bless Muhammad, and his family
and every slave of Allah who copies him.

وَانْفَعْ بِهَا يَا رَبِّ كُلَّ مَنْ قَرَا

وَسَامِعٍ وَأُمِّيٍّ وَمَنْ دَرَىٰ

And, O Lord, let the educated and the unlettered,
whoever reads or hears this, benefit from these attributes.

وَانْصُرْ أَمِيرَنَا بِخَرْقِ الْعَادَه

وَاحْفَظْ أَنْجَالَهُ وَكُلَّ الْعَائِلَه

And help our Amir with the breaking of norms
and preserve his descendants and all of his family.

وَاجْعَلْهُ عَيْنًا مِنْ عُيُونِ اللهِ

يَنْفَعُ فِي كُلِّ بِلَادِ اللهِ

And make him one of the springs of Allah
who will bring benefit in all the lands of Allah.

وَوَالِ مَنْ وَلَاهُ بِالْإِحْسَانِ

وَمَنْ أَعَانَهُ بِلَا خِذْلَانِ

And befriend whoever befriends him with Ihsan
and whoever helps him without forsaking him.

وَاجْعَلْ لَهُ مِنْ عُلَمَاءِ الْأُمَّه

مَنْ يُخْلِصُ النُّصْحَ لَهُ وَالنِّيَّه

And appoint for him of the 'ulama of the Community
those who are sincere in counsel and intention towards him.

وَوَفِّقِ الْوُلَاةَ لِلْمُسَاعَدَه

لِكُلِّ مَا فِيهِ صَلَاحُ الْعَمَلَه

Grant success to the leaders who help
in everything in which there is good for the people.

وَاخْتِمْ لَنَا يَا رَبِّ بِالسَّعَادَهْ

وَارْفُقْ بِنَا عِنْدَ قِيَامِ السَّاعَهْ ﴿ ﴾

And grant us a seal, O Lord, of serenity
— and be kind to us when the Hour arrives.

# Buraq of the Tariq

ويليه رجز
براق الطريق

يَقُولُ أَفْقَرُ الْوَرَىٰ مُحَمَّدُ
إِبْنُ الْحَبِيبِ قَوْلَهُ مُسَدَّدُ

The poorest of mankind, Muhammad
ibn al-Habib, speaking plainly, says:

اَلْحَمْدُ لِلَّهِ الَّذِي بِخَيْرِهِ
عَمَّ الْوَرَىٰ فِي بَرِّهِ وَبَحْرِهِ

Praise belongs to Allah through Whose generosity
mankind has spread over land and sea.

وَأَرْسَلَ الرُّسُلَ بِالشَّرَائِعْ
وَمُعْجِزَاتٍ مَا لَهَا مِنْ دَافِعْ

He sent the Messengers, each with a Shari‘a
and miracles which cannot be refuted.

فَلُبُّهَا تَصَوُّفٌ مُحَرَّرُ

عَلَى كِتَابٍ سُنَّةٍ مُقَرَّرُ

And its core is Sufism based exactly
and established on the Book and the Sunna.

فَهَاكَ مِنْهَا نُبْذَةً تُقَرِّبُ

طَرِيقَهُ وَسَيْرَهُ تُحَبِّبُ

Here is a fragment of it which will bring His path close
and make its journeying precious and dear to you.

سَمَّيْتُهَا بِبُرَاقِ الطَّرِيقِ

تُسْرِعُ بِالْمُرِيدِ لِلتَّحْقِيقِ

I have named it 'The Buraq of the Tariq'
for it will bring the murid swiftly to realisation.

فَإِنْ تُرِدْ سُلُوكَكَ الطَّرِيقَا

فَاعْتَمِدِ اللهَ وَسَلْ تَوْفِيقَا

If you wish to take Suluk on the Path,
then rely on Allah and ask Him for success.

وَأَرِحِ النَّفْسَ مِنَ التَّدْبِيرِ

فَإِنَّ ذَا يَجْلُبُ لِلتَّنْوِيرِ

Relieve the self of management,
for that will bring enlightenment.

إِيَّاكَ أَنْ تَهْتَمَّ بِالْأَرْزَاقِ

لِأَنَّهَا فِي ضَمَانِ الْخَلَّاقِ

Beware of anxiety about your means of living,
for that is the responsibility of the Creator.

وَخَصْلَتَانِ لَيْسَ شَيْءٌ يُوجَدُ

فَوْقَهُمَا مِنَ الْخَيْرَاتِ يُحْمَدُ

The highest and most praiseworthy qualities
are contained in these two good practices:

حُسْنُ ظَنٍّ بِاللهِ ثُمَّ بِالْعِبَادْ

فَكُنْ هُمَا وَجَنِّبَنَّ لِلْعِنَادْ

Think the best of Allah and then think the best of His slaves.
Hold to these two things and avoid being wilful.

وَأَقْرَبُ الطُّرُقِ عِنْدَ اللهِ

أَنْ تُكْثِرَ الذِّكْرَ بِإِسْمِ اللهِ

The closest path which leads to Allah
is frequent dhikr of the Name of Allah,

لِأَنَّهُ الاِسْمُ الْعَظِيمُ الأَعْظَمُ

عَلَى الاَصَحِّ مِنْ خِلَافٍ يُعْلَمُ

Because it is the sublime and Supreme Name,
according to the most sound of the different points of view.

وَفَرِّغِ الْقَلْبَ مِنَ الْأَغْيَارِ
عِنْدَ التَّوَجُّهِ لِذِكْرِ الْبَارِي

Completely free the heart of all otherness
when you turn to the dhikr of the Creator.

وَانْظُرْ لِأَسْرَارِ الْحَكِيمِ وَاعْتَبِرْ
وَجَنِّبِ الْخَوْضَ وَلَا تَكُنْ تُصِرُّ

Look at the secrets of the All-Wise and take note.
Avoid plunging into them. Do not persist.

بَلْ عَقِّبِ الذَّنْبَ بِالِاسْتِغْفَارِ
وَبِالتَّضَرُّعِ وَالِانْكِسَارِ

Rather, after your wrong action you must ask forgiveness
with contrite entreaty and regret.

وَانْظُرْ لِمَا مَنَّ بِهِ عَلَيْكَا
مِنْ كُلِّ طَاعَةٍ سَعَتْ إِلَيْكَا

Look to Him and grasp that every act in which you obey Him
is, in fact, a gift which He gave to you.

وَاحْمَدْهُ فِي السَّرَّاءِ وَالضَّرَّاءِ
لِأَنَّهُ الْفَاعِلُ فِي الْأَشْيَاءِ

Praise Him whether things go well or go badly,
because He is the Actor in everything.

106

وَحَرِّكِ الْهِمَّةَ بِـالأَشْوَاقِ

وَلَا تَكُنْ تَرْضَىٰ بِدُونِ الْبَاقِي

Awaken your himma with yearning and longing,
and do not be content with less than the Ever-Continuing.

وَلَا تَقِفْ مَعَ الْبَوَارِقِ وَلَا

مَعْ غَيْرِهَا مِنْ كُلِّ شَيْءٍ حَصَلَا

Do not stop just at the first gleams,
nor with anything else you may experience at this stage.

وَاسْأَلْهُ أَنْ يَطْوِي لَكَ الطَّرِيقَا

حَتَّىٰ تَذُوقَ ذَٰلِكَ التَّحْقِيقَـا

Ask Him to let you cover the path with speed
until you fully taste that realisation.

فَـاللهُ يَجْتَبِي مِنَ الْعَبِيدِ

مَنْ شَـاءَهُ لِحَضْرَةِ التَّفْرِيدِ

Allah chooses whomever He wants from among His slaves
for the Presence of Isolation.

إِيَّـاكَ أَنْ تَسْتَبْعِدَ الطَّرِيقَـا

فَإِنَّ ذَا يُكْسِبُكَ التَّعْوِيقَـا

Take care you do not consider the path too long,
since that will just become an obstruction for you.

وَاسْلُكْ بِنَفْسِكَ سَبِيلَ الرِّفْقِ

لِكَيْ يَكُونَ سَيْرُهَا بِالشَّوْقِ

Travel with your nafs the way of gentleness
so that you may travel the path with yearning.

فَإِنَّ رَكْعَتَيْنِ مِنْ مُحِبٍّ

أَفْضَلُ مِنْ أَلْفٍ مِنْ غَيْرِ حُبِّ

Indeed, two rak'ats from a lover are more excellent
than a thousand performed without love.

وَالْأَدَبَ اجْعَلْنَهُ رَفِيقًا

فِي أَخْذِكَ التَّشْرِيعَ وَالتَّحْقِيقَا

Make adab your companion as you follow the Shari'a,
and as you recognise the Haqiqa.

فَمَثَلُ الْأَدَبِ فِي الْأُمُورِ

كَخَلْطِكَ الْحَدِيدَ بِالْإِكْسِيرِ

The mithal of adab in these matters
is like mixing iron with elixir.

أَمَا تَرَاهُ يَقْلِبُ الْحَدِيدَا

فِي لَحْظَةٍ بِذَهَبٍ جَدِيدَا

Do you not see how it turns the iron
in an instant to new gold?

كَذَٰلِكَ الْاَدَبُ لِلْقُلُوبِ

يَنْقُلُهَا لِحَضْرَةِ الْغِيُوبِ

In the same way adab acts on the heart
and carries it to the Presence of the Unseen.

فَكَمْ مُجِدٍّ عَمَلًا قَدْ وَكَّلَهُ

لِنَفْسِهِ وَكَمْ أَدِيبٍ قَرَّبَهُ

How many a man of earnest right actions He has left to himself,
and how many men of adab He has brought near.

فَأَدَبُ النَّظَرِ فِي الْاَكْوَانِ

شُهُودُ بَارِيهَا بِغَيْرِ ثَانِ

The adab of looking at created beings
is that you see the Creator – no second!

فَتُبْصِرُ الْخَالِقَ فِي الْمَخْلُوقِ

وَتُبْصِرُ الرَّازِقَ فِي الْمَرْزُوقِ

Thus you discern the Creator in the created
and the Provider in the provision.

وَالْحَقُّ لَا يُرَىٰ فِي غَيْرِ مَظْهَرِ

لِأَحَدٍ مِنْ مَلَكٍ أَوْ بَشَرِ

The Haqq can only be seen in manifestation,
whether by an angel or a mortal man.

فَالْمَظْهَرُ الاَوَّلُ نُورُ أَحْمَدَا

عَلَيْهِ أَفْضَلُ الصَّلَاةِ سَرْمَدَا

The first manifestation is the light of Ahmad,
may the most excellent of blessings be upon him eternally.

قَدْ مَلَأَ الْحَقُّ بِهِ الاَكْوَانَا

وَكُلَّ مَا يَكُونُ أَوْ قَدْ كَانَا

By him the Haqq has filled every living creature
as well as all that is or was.

فَاشْهَدْهُ فِي النَّفْسِ وَفِي الآفَاقِ

وَامْزِجْ بِذَلِكَ رُؤْيَةَ الْخَلَّاقِ

So see him in the self and on the horizon,
and join to that perception of the Creator.

تُكْفَى بِذَا الشُّهُودِ كُلَّ عَيْبٍ

فِي النَّفْسِ وَالْقَلْبِ وَغَيْبِ الْغَيْبِ

And that seeing will compensate for every defect
in the self, the heart, and the unseen of the unseen.

وَذَكِّرِ النَّفْسَ بِحُسْنِ نِيَّةٍ

وَاقْرِنْهَا بِالسُّكُونِ وَالْحَرَكَةِ

Remind the self by having a good niyyat,
and bind it to that in stillness and in movement.

110

وَنَمِّهَا تَنْمِيَةً وَكَثِّرَا

لَهَا تَحُوزُ فَضْلَهَا بِلَا مِرَا

Foster its growth a great deal,
and you will undoubtedly gain a great gift for it.

وَاخْتَصِرِ الطَّرِيقَ بِالتَّعْظِيمِ

لِكُلِّ مَا شُرِعَ مِنْ مَرْسُومِ

Shorten the Tariqa by showing honour and respect
for all that is laid down as the Shari'a.

وَلَا تَكُنْ تَحْقِرْ مِنَ الْاَعْمَالِ

شَيْئًا أَتَىٰ وَلَا مِنَ الْاقْوَالِ

Make sure you do not scorn any deeds or words
that have been passed down to us.

طَرِيقَةُ الْابْدَالِ جُوعٌ سَهَرٌ

صَمْنٌ وَعُزْلَةٌ وَذِكْرٌ حَرَّرُوا

The Tariqa of the Abdal is hunger, sleeplessness,
silence, withdrawal and dhikr. They give freedom.

قَدِ انْتَهَتْ نُبْذَةُ ذَا التَّصَوُّفِ

وَالْحَمْدُ لِلَّهِ عَلَى التَّعَرُّفِ

This fragment of Sufism is ended
and praise belongs to Allah for the knowledge of it.

وَأُصَلِّي عَلَى النَّبِيِّ الْمُمِدّ
صَلاةَ رَبِّنَا بِغَيْرِ حَدّ

I ask for the limitless blessings of our Lord
on the Prophet, the Helper.

وَءَالِهِ وَصَحْبِهِ الثِّقَاتِ
اَلسَّالِكِينَ سُبُلَ النَّجَاةِ

And on his family and trustworthy Companions,
the wayfarers who trod the paths of safety.

وَأَسْأَلُ اللهَ صَلَاحَ الْحَالِ
لَنَا وَلِلاَحْبَابِ فِي الْمَئَآلِ

I ask Allah to give us and our loved ones
a sound state in the future.

وَأَنْ يُزِيلَ عَنَّا كُلَّ رَيْبٍ
بِجَاهِ كُلِّ عَارِفٍ مُرَبِّي

And that He remove every doubt from us,
by the rank of every teaching 'Arif.

وَالْحَمْدُ لِلَّهِ عَلَى التَّمَامِ
وَالشُّكْرُ لِلَّهِ عَلَى انْخِتَامِ ۞

Praise is to due to Allah for its completion
and thanks is due to Allah for its seal.

# Miracles of the Way

وَيَلِيهِ رَجَزٌ

خَوَارِقُ الطَّرِيقِ

اَلْحَمْدُ لِلَّهِ وَصَلَّى اللهُ

عَلَى النَّبِيِّ مُحَمَّدُ الاوَّاهُ

Praise belongs to Allah. May Allah bless
the Prophet Muhammad, the Shelter.

قَالَ أَبُو حَامِدٍ الصُّوفِيُّ

حُجَّةُ الاِسْلَامِ هُوَ الطُّوسِيِّ

Abu Hamid at-Tusi, the Sufi
and proof of Islam, said:

كَرَامَةُ الدَّاخِلِ فِي الطَّرِيقِ

عِشْرُونَ فِي الدُّنْيَا عَلَى التَّحْقِيقِ

The marks of honour for the one who enters
the Tariq are twenty in number:

أَوَّلُهَا يَذْكُرُهُ الالَهُ

كَمَا يَلِيقُ بِهِ يَا بُشْرَاهُ

The first of them is that Allah remembers him
as is fitting. Oh what good news that is!

ثَانِيهَا تَعْظِيمُهُ بَيْنَ الانَامْ

وَالثَّالِثُ الْحُبُّ لَهُ بِلَا مَلَامْ

The second sign is that he is exalted among people,
and the third is a love which finds no reproach.

وَكُلُّ مَنْ أَحَبَّهُ الالَهُ

أَحَبَّهُ الْخَلْقُ فَيَا سَعْدَاهُ

And everyone Allah loves, is loved by the creation
— what good fortune he gains!

رَابِعُهَا يُدَبِّرُ الامُورَا

لَهُ فَيَبْقَى دَائِمًا مَسْرُورَا

The fourth is that Allah directs all his affairs,
so he remains constantly full of joy.

خَامِسُهَا تَسْهِيلُهُ الرِّزْقَ لَهُ

بِلَا مَشَقَّةٍ فِيهِ تَلْحَقُهُ

The fifth is that Allah makes his food easy to get,
and he does not have to struggle to get it.

سَادِسُهَا يَنْصُرُهُ عَلَى الْعِدَا

بِخَرْقِ عَادَةٍ مَعْ حِفْظٍ أَبَدَا

The sixth is that He helps him against his enemies
by miracles, with constant protection.

سَابِعُهَا يَكُونُ أُنْسَهُ فَلَا

وَحْشَةَ تَأْتِيهِ مِنْ شَيْءٍ نَزَلَا

The seventh is intimacy with Allah,
so he is never lonely whatever happens.

ثَامِنُهَا الْعِزُّ لَهُ فِي النَّفْسِ

فَالْكَوْنُ يَخْدِمُهُ دُونَ لَبْسِ

The eighth is his nobility of self,
so that creation serves him without confusion.

تَاسِعُهَا الرَّفْعُ لِهِمَّةٍ لَهُ

عَنْ كُلِّ شَيْءٍ فَاتِنٍ يَشْغَلُهُ

The ninth is the elevation of his Himma
above every temptation that might obsess him.

عَاشِرُهَا الْغِنَى لِقَلْبِهِ مَعَ

تَسْهِيلِ أَمْرِهِ الَّذِي فِيهِ سَعَى

The tenth sign is his heart's freedom from need,
along with every matter he strives for being made easy.

وَهَاكَ بَاقِيًا مَعَ اخْتِصَارِ

بِعَطْفِ بَعْضِهَا نَخُذْ يَا قَارِي

Here briefly follow the rest of them,
stressing only some of them, so attend, O reader!

تَنْوِيرُ قَلْبٍ يَهْتَدِي بِنُورِهِ

لِفَهْمِ أَسْرَارٍ بِفَضْلِ رَبِّهِ

Enlightenment of the heart by whose light he is guided
to an understanding of secrets through the gift of his Lord.

وَشَرْحُ صَدْرِهِ فَلَا يَهْتَمُّ

بِكُلِّ مِحْنَةٍ بِهِ تَلَمُّ

And the expansion of his breast so that
he is undisturbed by whatever trouble befalls him.

مَهَابَةٌ لَهُ وَحُسْنُ مَوْقِعِ

فِي نُفُوسِ النَّاسِ بِغَيْرِ دَافِعِ

He possesses dignity as well as unquestioned
good standing in the hearts of people.

تَحْبِيبُهُ لِكُلِّ خَلْقٍ فِي الْوَرَىٰ

بِوَعْدِ رَبِّنَا لَهُ بِلَا مِرَا

He is made beloved to every single human creature
through the undoubted promise he has from our Lord.

116

تَبرُّكٌ بِهِ مَعَ الآدَابِ

مَعَهُ وَلَوْ نُقِلَ لِلتُّرَابِ

People seek baraka from him along with proper adab
towards him, even after he has turned to dust.

تَسْخِيرُهُ الأَرْضَ لَهُ فَيَذْهَبُ

حَيْثُ يَشَا بِسُرْعَةٍ لَا يَرْهَبُ

The earth is subjected to him so that he may go
with speed and without fear wherever he wishes.

وَالبَرُّ وَالبَحْرُ مَعَ الْهَوَاءِ

خَادِمَةٌ لَهُ بِلَا امْتِرَاءِ

The land, the sea and the air
are his servants without doubt.

وُحُوشٌ ثُمَّ سِبَاعٌ مَعَ الْهَوَامْ

سَخَّرَهَا الرَّبُّ لَهُ عَلَى الدَّوَامْ

The wild animals, the beasts of prey and the reptiles
have all been subjugated to him by the Lord forever.

مَفَاتِيحُ الكُنُوزِ وَالْمَعَادِنْ

تَطْلُبُهُ وَهُوَ عَنْهَا بَائِنْ

And the keys of treasures and mines
offer themselves to him, but he has no need.

$$\text{تَوَسُّلُ النَّاسِ بِجَاهِهِ إِلَى}$$

$$\text{إِلَهِهِ فِي كُلِّ شَيْءٍ نَزَلَا}$$

By means of his rank, people seek to draw nearer to Allah
in everything that happens.

$$\text{فَيَقْضِيهِ الرَّبُّ بِلَا تَعْسِيرِ}$$

$$\text{بِفَضْلِهِ الْمَصْحُوبِ بِالتَّيْسِيرِ}$$

So the Lord accomplishes that without hardship
by His bounty accompanied by ease.

$$\text{وَذَاكَ مَوْكُولٌ إِلَى إِخْتِيَارِ}$$

$$\text{إِلَهِهِ فِي سَابِقِ الْأَقْدَارِ}$$

That has been left to the choice of his God
in His previously ordained decrees.

$$\text{فَلَا تَقُلْ دَعَوْتُه فَلَمْ يُجِبْ}$$

$$\text{فَذَاكَ شَأْنُ كُلِّ غَافِلٍ مُرِيبْ}$$

So do not say, 'I called on Him and He did not respond.'
That is the condition of the doubters and the heedless.

$$\text{أَمَّا الْكَرَامَةُ لَهُ فِي الْآخِرَةْ}$$

$$\text{عِشْرُونَ أَيْضًا هَاكَهَا مُتَّبِعَهْ}$$

As for the marks of honour which he has in the Akhira,
they are also twenty in number and they follow here.

تَسْهِيلُ مَوْتِهِ مَعَ انْخِتَامِ

عَلَى الايمَانِ فَازَ بِالْمَرَامِ

Ease of death when the seal is set with Iman
so that he will get what he wants.

تَبْشِيرُهُ بِالرَّوْجِ وَالرَّيْحَانِ

وَالامْنِ مِنْ خَوْفٍ مَعَ الرِّضْوَانِ

The good news of cool refreshment, sweet basil,
acceptance, and safety from fear,

كَذَا انْخُلُودُ فِي الْجِنَانِ أَبَدًا

فِي جِوَارِ الرَّحْمَٰنِ دَأْبًا سَرْمَدَا

and abiding in the Gardens forever,
near to the All-Merciful, perpetually without end.

لِرُوحِهِ الْعُرُوجُ وَالاِكْرَامُ

مِنَ الْمَلَائِكَةِ وَالانْعَامُ

His ruh enjoys ascent and honour
and tribute from the angels and bliss.

وَالنَّاسُ تَزْدَحِمُ لِلصَّلَاةِ

عَلَيْهِ إِذْ كَانَ مِنَ الثِّقَاتِ

People will crowd around to pray over him
as had been among those worthy of trust.

119

يُلَقَّنُ الصَّوَابَ فِي السُّؤَالِ

فَلَا يَخَافُ شِدَّةَ الاَهْوَالِ

He will be taught what is correct when asked,
so that he will not fear the severe terrors.

تَوْسِعَةُ القَبْرِ لَهُ فِي رَوْضَةٍ

يَكُونُ فِيهَا ءَامِنًا مِنْ فِتْنَةٍ

The expanse of his grave is in a meadow,
where he will be safe from every trial.

وَإِينَاسٌ لِرُوحِهِ وَجِسْمِهِ

إِذْ تَأْتِيهِ البُشْرَىٰ لَهُ مِنْ رَبِّهِ

When the good news comes to him from his Lord
both his ruh and his body will enjoy intimacy.

تَحْمِلُهُ الطُّيُورُ فِي أَجْوَافِهَا

فِي جَنَّةٍ حَيْثُ يَشَا فِي عَرْضِهَا

Birds will carry him within them
wherever he wishes to roam in the Garden.

وَالْحَشْرُ فِي الْعِزِّ مَعَ الْكَرَامَهْ

وَالتَّاجِ وَالْحُلَلِ وَالشَّفَاعَهْ

On the Day of Gathering, he will be glorified
with honour, a crown, robes of honour and intercession.

بَيَـاضُ وَجْهِهِ وَنُورُهُ ظَهَرْ

لِكُلِّ مَنْ بِمَوْقِفٍ قَدِ انْتَشَرْ

His face will be radiantly white and its light
will be manifest to all those gathered at the place of standing.

وَهَوْلُ مَوْقِفٍ فَلَا يَرَاهُ

وَالآخِذُ الْكُتْبَ لَهُ يُمْنَـاهُ

He will not see the terror of the place where they stand,
and he will receive his book in his right hand.

فَلَا يُحَاسَبُ حِسَابَ عُنْفٍ

بَلْ يَبْتَدَىٰ بِجَمِيلٍ وَلُطْفٍ

It will not be with severity that he is called to account
but rather it will begin with kindness and gentleness.

أَعْمَـالُهُ تَثْقُلُ عِنْدَ الْوَزْنِ

وَالشُّرْبُ مِنْ حَوْضِ نَبِيٍّ يُغْنِي

His deeds will weigh heavily in the balance
and he will drink from the basin of a Prophet who satisfies every thirst.

جَوَازُهُ الصِّرَاطَ بِالإسْرَاعِ

لِجَنَّةِ الْخُلْدِ بِلَا نِزَاعِ

He will cross the Sirat swiftly without struggle
to reach the Garden of timelessness.

121

فَلَا يُحَـاسَبُ وَلَا يُلَامُ

فِي مَوْقِفِ الْمِيزَانِ لَا يُضَـامُ

He will not be called to account for his actions or rebuked,
and in the place of weighing them he will not be harmed.

يَشْفَعُ فِي الاَهْلِ وَفِي الاِخْوَانِ

وَيُكْتَسَىٰ مِنْ حُلَلِ الرِّضْوَانِ

He will intercede for his family and the brothers,
and he will be clothed in the robes of serene contentment.

ثُمَّ لِقَـاءُ اللهِ بِالْمَعَـايَنَهْ

مِنْ غَيْرِ تَكْيِيفٍ وَلَا مُشَـابَهَهْ

Then he will meet Allah with actual vision
and without qualification or resemblance.

وَهِيَ أَجَلُّ مِنْ دُخُولِ الْجَنَّهْ

كَمَا أَتَىٰ فِي كِتَـابٍ وَسُنَّهْ

That will be more glorious than entering the Garden,
as it says in the Book and the Sunna.

وَشَرْطُ مَنْ يَمْنَحُهُ الاِلَـهُ

بِهَذِهِ انْخَلَعَ لَا تَنْسَـاهُ

Take care not to forget that Allah's granting
of these robes of honour is conditional —

122

اَلْعِلْمُ وَالْعَمَلُ مَعَ إِخْلَاصٍ
وَالذِّكْرُ يُؤْذِنُ بِالاِخْتِصَاصِ

On knowledge, actions of Ikhlas
and the dhikr which indicates his special place.

فَغَـايَةُ الطَّرِيقِ فِي اسْتِغْرَاقِ
فِي شُهُودٍ لِمَـالِكٍ خَلَّاقِ

The end of the Path consists of total absorption
in the direct witnessing of the Owner, the Creator.

إِيَّاكَ أَنْ تَصْغَىٰ لِطَاعِنٍ فِيهَـا
لِجَهْلِهِ بِعِلْمِهَـا وَفَضْلِهَـا

Beware of listening to someone who might deny it
through his ignorance of its knowledge and excellence.

فَسَهِّلَنْ يَا رَبِّ لِلاِخْوَانِ
سُلُوكَهَـا فَضْلاً بِلَا تَوَانِ

O Lord! Out of Your bounty
make its journey easy for the brotherhood without flagging.

قَدِ انْتَهَتْ خَوَارِقُ الطَّرِيقِ
لِمَنْ مَشَىٰ فِيهَـا عَلَى التَّحْقِيقِ

This ends the Miracles of the Way
for the one who walks it gaining realisation.

فَارْحَمْ مُفِيدَهَا وَجَامِعًا لَهَا

وَمَنْ تَصَدَّىٰ مَعَنَا لِنَشْرِهَا

So have mercy on the one who related it, the one who collected it,
and whoever helps us to spread it.

نَاظِمُهَا مُحَمَّدُ ابْنُ الْحَبِيبْ

يَطْلُبُ لِلأُمَّةِ فَتْحًا فِي الْقَرِيبْ

The one who set it to verse, Muhammad ibn al-Habib,
asks Allah for an opening for the community soon,

وَنُصْرَةً لِظِلِّنَا الْمَحْبُوبْ

تُظْفِرُهُ بِجَمِيعِ الْمَرْغُوبْ

and for a victory for our beloved shelter
which will give him all his desires.

ثُمَّ صَلاَةُ اللهِ تَتْرَىٰ أَبَدًا

عَلَىٰ مُحَمَّدٍ وَمَنْ بِهِ اقْتَدَىٰ

May the blessings of Allah fall one after another eternally
on Muhammad and whoever copies him,

كَذَٰلِكَ الآلِ مَعَ الصِّحَابْ

اَلسَّالِكِينَ سُبُلَ الصَّوَابْ ۞

And also on his family and Companions,
the Salikeen who trod the paths of right action.

# Virtues of the Ism al-A'dham

وتليه دالية في
فضائل الاسم الاعظم

تَجَرَّدْ عَنِ الاغْيَارِ تَحْظَىٰ بِقُرْبِهِ
وَتَرْقَىٰ مَرَاقِي الْقَوْمِ فِي كُلِّ مَشْهَدِ

Free yourself from all that is other and you will attain His nearness,
and you will rise to the ranks of the People of every assembly.

وَعَمِّرْ بِذِكْرِ اللهِ أَنْفَاسَكَ الَّتِي
تُحَاسَبُ عَنْهَا يَوْمَ حَشْرٍ وَمَوْعِدِ

Fill your every breath with dhikr of Allah, because each breath
has to be accounted for on the Day of Gathering and promise.

وَعَظِّمْ جَمِيعَ الْكَوْنِ مِنْ حَيْثُ إِنَّهُ
تَكَوَّنَ مِنْ نُورِ النَّبِيِّ مُحَمَّدِ

Exalt all phenomena because they are formed
from the light of the Prophet Muhammad.

وَلَاحِظْهُ أَنْوَارًا لِأَسْمَاءِ رَبِّنَا

وَغِبْ عَنْ كَثَافَةٍ وَعَنْ قَوْلِ مُلْحِدِ

Regard them as lights from the Names of our Lord
and withdraw from being unresponsive and speaking from opinion.

وَأَحْبِبْ بِحُبِّ اللهِ وَابْغَضْ بِبُغْضِهِ

فَذَاكَ مِنَ التَّشْرِيعِ فَاحْفَظْهُ سَيِّدِي

Love with the love of Allah and hate with His hate.
This is the Shari'a so guard it, my friend!

وَكُنْ بَرْزَخَ الْبَحْرَيْنِ حَقٍّ وَشِرْعَةٍ

تَحُزْ رُتْبَةَ التَّعْرِيفِ فِي كُلِّ مَقْعَدِ

Be an isthmus between the two seas – the Haqiqa and the Shari'a,
and you will attain the rank of recognition in every assembly.

وَدُلَّ عِبَادَ اللهِ بِاللهِ مُعْلِنًا

بِتَحْسِينِ طُرْقِ اللهِ فِي كُلِّ مَسْجِدِ

In every mosque, guide the slaves of Allah by Allah
openly, by showing the beauty of the paths of Allah.

وَإِنْ شِئْتَ إِسْرَاعًا لِحَضْرَةِ رَبِّنَا

فَحَسِّنْ بِخَلْقِ اللهِ ظَنًّا وَمَجِّدِ

And if you wish to go swiftly into the presence of our Lord,
then have a good opinion of Allah's creation and praise Him.

وَوَاظِبْ عَلَى الاسْمِ الْعَظِيمِ الْمُعَظَّمِ

بِحُسْنِ سَرِيرَةٍ وَصِدْقٍ وَمَقْصِدِ

Persevere with the sublime Ism al-'Adhim
in your secret, with sincerity and concentration.

وَشَاهِدْ جَمَالَ الذَّاتِ فِي كُلِّ مَظْهَرٍ

فَلَوْ لَا هَا لَمْ يَثْبُتْ وُجُودُ لِمُوجَدِ

Witness the beauty of the Essence in every manifestation. Were it not for it –
the existence of the Existent would not have been established.

وَكُلُّ صِفَاتِ النَّفْسِ تَفْنَىٰ بِذِكْرِهِ

وَيَبْقَىٰ نَعِيمُ الْقَلْبِ أَحْلَىٰ مِنَ الشُّهْدِ

All the attributes of the self have fana' by His dhikr,
and the bliss of the heart remains, sweeter than honey.

وَكُلُّ تَجَلٍّ بِالْمَقَامَاتِ نَاشِئٌ

عَنِ الذِّكْرِ بِالاسْمِ الْعَظِيمِ مَعَ الْجَدِّ

Every station is acquired through the dhikr
of the Ism al-'Adhim done with gravity.

فَمِنْهُ يَكُونُ الْفَتْحُ لِكُلِّ سَالِكِ

وَمِنْهُ يَكُونُ الْفَيْضُ لِكُلِّ مُرْشِدِ

From it comes the Opening for every Salik,
and from it comes the overflowing for every Murshid.

وَعَنْهُ تَكُونُ حَالَةُ السُّكْرِ وَالْفَنَا

وَعَنْهُ تَكُونُ حَالَةُ الصَّحْوِ وَالْوَجْد

From it come the States of intoxication and fana',
and from it, too, the States of sobriety and ecstasy.

وَمَا نَالَ عِزًّا غَيْرُ مُنْفَرِدٍ بِهِ

تَحَلَّى بِمَا يُرْضِيهِ مَعْ كَثْرَةِ الْحَمْد

High rank is only given to the one isolated with Him,
who takes on what pleases Him along with much praise.

فَمَا زَالَ يَرْقَى فِي مَهَامَةِ ذَاتِهِ

وَيَفْنَى فَنَاءً لَيْسَ فِيهِ سِوَى الْفَقْد

Thus he will rise, crossing the deserts of His Essence, until
his fana' enters a fana' that has nothing in it but loss.

فَإِنْ رُدَّ لِلْآثَارِ جَاءَ بِحُلَّةٍ

تُنَادِي عَلَيْهِ بِالْوِلَايَةِ وَالْمَجْد

If he returns to the traces of existence, he brings
a Robe of Honour which proclaims his Wilaya and glory.

فَكُنْ خَادِمًا عَبْدًا لِمَنْ هَذَا وَصْفُهُ

وَوَفِّ بِعَهْدِ اللهِ يَأْتِكَ بِالْوَعْد

So be a servant and slave to the one whose description this is, and fulfil
the contract of Allah, and He will give you what He has promised.

وَأَعْظَمُ خَلْقِ اللهِ فِي ذَاكَ رُسْلُهُ

وَأَكْمَلُهُمْ فِيهِ النَّبِيُّ مُحَمَّدِ

The greatest of Allah's creation in this matter are His Messengers,
and the most perfect of them in it is the Prophet Muhammad.

فَظَاهِرُهُ نُورٌ وَبَاطِنُهُ سِرٌّ

كَمَالَاتُهُ لَيْسَتْ تُحَصَّلُ بِالْعَدِّ

His outward is a light and his inward is a secret.
His perfections are beyond numbering.

عَلَيْهِ صَلَاةُ اللهِ وَالآلِ وَالصَّحْبِ

وَدَارِكْنَا بِالألْطَافِ مِنْ غَيْرِ مَا حَدِّ ۞

May the blessings of Allah be upon him and his family and
Companions, and give us limitless and uninterrupted kindness.

# Praise

وتليه رائية

الحمد

لَكَ الْحَمْدُ يَا ذَا الْحِلْمِ وَالْعَفْوِ وَالسِّتْرِ

وَحَمْدِيَ مِن نُّعْمَاكَ يَا وَاسِعَ الْبِرِّ

Praise is due to You the Possessor of forbearance,
forgiveness and veiling of our actions.
My praise is one of Your greatest blessings, O Abundant Goodness.

لَكَ الْحَمْدُ عَدَّ الْقَطْرِ وَالرَّمْلِ وَالْحَصَىٰ

وَعَدَّ نَبَاتِ الاَرْضِ وَالْحُوتِ فِي الْبَحْرِ

Praise is due to You in number as great as the drops of rain,
grains of sand, pebbles, plants of the earth and fish in the sea.

لَكَ الْحَمْدُ عَدَّ النَّمْلِ وَالْجِنِّ وَالاِنْسِ

وَمِلْءَ السَّمَا وَالْعَرْشِ وَالْكَوْكَبِ الدُّرِّ

Praise is due to You in number as great as the ants, jinn and men,
in quantity as great as the sky, the Throne and the pearly stars.

وَمِلْءَ الْفَضَا وَاللَّوْحِ وَالْكُرْسِي وَالثَّرَىٰ

وَعَدَّ جَمِيعِ الْكَـائِـنَـاتِ إِلَى الْحَشْرِ

In quantity as great as space itself, the Tablet of Forms, the Footstool,
the moist earth, and the number of all living things on the Day of Gathering.

لَكَ الْحَمْدُ يَـا رَبِّي كَمَا أَنْتَ أَهْلُهُ

فَإِنِّي لَا أُحْصِي الثَّـنَـاءَ مَدَى الدَّهْرِ

Praise is due to You, O my Lord, as much You deserve,
for I cannot praise You fittingly to the full extent of time.

لَكَ الْحَمْدُ يَـا مُعْطِي الْمَوَاهِبِ بِالْفَضْلِ

وَمَـانِحَ أَهْلِ اللهِ بِالْفَتْحِ وَالنَّصْرِ

Praise is due to You, O endless Giver of gifts,
the One Who grants opening and triumph to the people of Allah.

لَكَ الْحَمْدُ بِالانْفَـاسِ وَالْجِسْمِ وَالْقَلْبِ

تَفَضَّلْ عَلَىٰ عَبْدٍ تَحَيَّرَ فِي الْأَمْرِ

Praise is due to You with every breath, with the body and the heart.
Look kindly on a slave who is perplexed by affairs.

فَإِنِّي وَإِنْ كَـانَتْ ذُنُوبِي تَعُوقُنِي

فَلِي فِيكَ حُسْنُ الظَّنِّ يَجْبُرُ لِي كَسْرِي

If my wrong actions weigh me down,
I still have a good opinion of You that mends my broken spirit.

فَمُنَّ عَلَيْنَا يَا غَفُورُ بِتَوْبَةٍ

تَجُبُّ الَّذِي قَدْ كَانَ فِي سَالِفِ الْعُمْرِ

O Forgiving! Give us tawba that will undo
what happened in our early years.

وَزِدْنَا مِنَ النَّعْمَاءِ وَالنُّورِ وَالْكَشْفِ

وَمَكِّنَّا فِي الِارْشَادِ بِالِاذْنِ وَالسِّرِّ

Increase us in blessing, light and unveiling,
and strengthen us in guidance, with Idhn and the Secret.

وَأَيِّدْنَا فِي أَقْوَالِنَا وَفِعَالِنَا

وَيَسِّرْ لَنَا الْارْزَاقَ مِنْ حَيْثُ لَا نَدْرِي

Support us in our words and deeds,
and make our provision easy for us – from where we know not.

فَهَا نَحْنُ فِي بَابِ التَّفَضُّلِ وَاقِفٌ

وَمُنْتَظِرٌ عَطْفَ الْحَبِيبِ بِلَا عُسْرٍ

Here we are standing at the door of favour,
waiting without hardship for the kindness of the Beloved.

فَأَنْعِمْ عَلَيْنَا يَا مُجِيبُ بِسُرْعَةٍ

فَإِنَّكَ أَهْلُ الْجُودِ وَالْمَنِّ وَالْخَيْرِ

Swiftly send us Your favour, O Answerer, for You are
the Possessor of generosity, liberality and goodness.

فَفَضْلُكَ مَوْجُودٌ بِغَيْرِ وُجُودِنَا

وَجُودُكَ مَسْدُولٌ عَلَيْنَا بِلَا نُكْرٍ

Your bounty exists without our existence,
and undeniably it is Your Generosity that pours down on us.

فَوَفِّقْنَا لِلشُّكْرِ الَّذِي هُوَ لَازِمٌ

عَلَيْنَا وَيَسْتَدْعِي الْمَزِيدَ بِلَا خُسْرٍ

Give us success in the thankfulness which is our duty
and which itself calls for increase from You without loss to us.

وَأَخْرِجْنَا مِنْ سِجْنِ الْجُسُومِ وَرَقِّنَا

لِحَضْرَةِ أَرْوَاحٍ ثَوَابًا عَلَى الشُّكْرِ

Free us from the prison of our bodies and raise us
up to the presence of the spirits as a reward for our gratitude.

وَأَشْهِدْنَا مَعْنَى الذَّاتِ فِي كُلِّ مَظْهَرٍ

لِيَقْوَىٰ شُهُودِي فِي الشَّدَائِدِ وَالْيَسْرِ

Let us see the meaning of the Essence in every manifestation
in order to strengthen our witnessing both in times of ease and trouble.

وَأَفْنِنَا عَنَّا وَأَبْقِنَا بِكَ دَائِمًا

لِنَلْحَقَ أَهْلَ الْإِرْثِ مِنْ حَضْرَةِ السِّرِّ

Annihilate us from ourselves and give us going-on in You always,
so that we may join the people who have inherited the presence of the secret.

فَأَمْرُكَ لِلاَشْيَاءِ فِي قَوْلِ كُنْ تَكُنْ

فَكَوِّنْ لَنَا الاَشْيَاءَ عَزْمًا بِلاَ مَكْرِ

Your command to things is in the word 'Be, and it is.'
So shape things for us with firm intention and without deception.

وَصَلِّ بِأَنْوَاعِ الْكَمَالاَتِ كُلِّهَا

عَلَىٰ أَحْمَدَ الْهَادِي إِلَىٰ حَضْرَةِ الطُّهْرِ

Bless Ahmad, the guide to the Presence of purity,
with all the forms of perfection.

وَءَالِهِ وَالصَّحْبِ الْكِرَامِ وَمَنْ دَعَا

لِنَاظِمِ هٰذَا النَّظْمِ بِالشَّرْحِ فِي الْقَبْرِ

And his family and noble Companions and whoever prays
for expansion of the grave for the composer of these verses.

وَيَا رَبِّ بِالْهَادِي الرَّؤُوفِ مُحَمَّدٍ

أَنِلْنَا عُلُومًا تَنْفَعُنَا يَوْمَ النَّشْرِ

And O Lord! Through the compassionate guide, Muhammad,
grant us knowledges that will benefit us on the Day of Rising.

وَقَوِّنَا بِالآنْوَارِ فِي كُلِّ لَحْظَةٍ

وَثَبِّتْنَا عِنْدَ الْخَتْمِ وَالنَّزْعِ وَالْقَبْرِ ۞

Strengthen us with lights at every instant, and make us
firm at the sealing, the agony of death, and the grave.

# Stimulation of Desire for the Act of Dhikr

وتليه رائية

الترغيب في الذكر

أَيَـا مَنْ يُرِدْ قُرْبًـا مِنَ اللهِ عَنْ فَوْرِ
عَلَيْكَ بِذِكْرِ اللهِ فِي السِّرِّ وَالْجَهْرِ

O you who desire nearness to Allah immediately
– you must perform dhikr of Allah openly and secretly.

وَعَمِّرْ بِهِ الأَوْقَاتَ تَسْمُو بِسُرْعَةٍ
إِلَىٰ ذِرْوَةِ الْعِرْفَانِ مَعْ خَـالِصِ الْفِكْرِ

Fill the moments with it and you will swiftly
ascend to the pinnacle of gnosis with pure reflection.

لِتَصْقِيلِ مِرْءَا الْقَلْبِ يَنْكَشِفُ الْغِطَـا
وَتَبْدُو لَهُ الأَنْوَارُ مِنْ خَـالِصِ الذِّكْرِ

Through polishing the mirror of the heart, the veil is removed,
and lights appear to it from the purity of the dhikr.

بِذِكْرِ إِلَهِ الْعَرْشِ تَزْهَدُ فِي الْوَرَىٰ
وَتَفْنَىٰ عَنِ النَّفْسِ الْمُعَطِّلَةِ السَّيْرِ

By dhikr of the God of the Throne you will come to do without people,
and you will be annihilated from the self, which delays you on the journey.

وَتَضْحَىٰ جَلِيسَ اللهِ مِنْ غَيْرِ كُلْفَةٍ
وَتَسْلَمُ مِنْ شَكٍّ وَشِرْكٍ وَمِنْ غَيْرِ

You will become one who sits with Allah, without ceremony,
and you will be safe from doubt, shirk and otherness.

وَتَرْحَلُ عَنْ كَوْنٍ إِلَىٰ حَضْرَةِ الصَّفَا
وَتَشْهَدُ فِعْلَ اللهِ فِي الْخَلْقِ وَالْأَمْرِ

You will journey from the cosmos to the presence of Purity,
and you will witness the act of Allah in the creation and in affairs.

وَتَرْقَىٰ إِلَى الْأَسْمَاءِ تُسْقَىٰ بِنُورِهَا
فَتَبْدُو لَكَ الْأَوْصَافُ مِنْ غَيْرِ مَا سِتْرِ

You will rise to the Names and drink of their light,
and the Attributes will appear to you without a veil.

وَيَظْهَرُ مَعْنَى الذَّاتِ مِنْ كَامِلِ الْفَنَا
فَتَبْقَىٰ غَنِيًّا بِالْإِلَهِ مَدَى الْعُمْرِ

The meaning of the Essence will emerge from the perfection of Fana',
and you will go on, rich with Allah for the rest of your life.

فَإِنْ عَبَقَتْ فِي الْغَرْبِ أَنْفَاسُ ذِكْرِهِ

وَفِي الشَّرْقِ مَعْلُولٌ تَعَافَىٰ مِنَ الضَّرِّ

If the breath of His dhikr were to fill the west and there was a sick man
in the east, that man would be cured of his affliction.

عَلَيْهِ مَدَارُ الدِّينِ فِي كُلِّ قُرْبَةٍ

وَلَا سِيَّمَا ذِكْرُ الْجَلَالَةِ مِنْ حُرِّ

In every drawing near, it is the pivot of the Deen,
especially the dhikr of Majesty by one who is free.

فَمَا مِنْ وَلِيٍّ إِلَّا هَامَ بِذِكْرِهِ

عَلَىٰ عَدَدِ الْأَنْفَاسِ بِالرُّوحِ وَالسِّرِّ

There is no Wali who is not infatuated with His dhikr,
with his ruh and his secret, in every breath.

فَقَدْ كَانَ ذَاكِرًا وَأَصْبَحَ مَذْكُورًا

يَتِيهُ عَلَى الْأَكْوَانِ مِنْ غَيْرِ مَا فَخْرٍ

He was a rememberer and he became remembered,
and this gave him superiority over creatures, without boasting.

وَمَا الْفَخْرُ إِلَّا بِالْعُبُودِيَّةِ الَّتِي

تَخَلَّصَتْ مِنْ حَوْلٍ وَقُوَىٰ وَمِنْ مَكْرِ

There is no boasting except in slavedom,
freed from strength, power and self-deception.

137

نَتَائِجُ ذِكْرِ اللهِ لَيْسَ لَهَا حَصْرُ
فَوَاظِبْ أَخِي وَلَوْ عَشِيًّا وَبِالْفَجْرِ

The results of dhikr of Allah are without limit,
so, my brother, persevere even if only in the evening and at Fajr.

لَقَدْ وَرَدَ الاِكْثَارُ مِنْهُ بِلَا حَدٍّ
تَصَفَّحْ كِتَابَ اللهِ مَعْ سُنَّةٍ تَدْرِي

Doing a lot of it without limit is transmitted;
study the Book of Allah along with the Sunna and you will understand.

وَقَدْ وَعَدَ الْجَلِيلُ بِذِكْرِ مَنْ غَدَا
لَهُ ذَاكِرًا يَا فَوْزَ مَنْ خُصَّ بِالذِّكْرِ

The Glorious has promised to remember whoever remembers Him –
Oh the victory of someone who is singled out by dhikr!

وَمَنْ يَعْشُ عَنْ ذِكْرِ الاِلَهِ يَكُنْ لَهُ
قَرِينٌ مِنَ الشَّيْطَانِ يُفْتِنُ عَنْ سَيْرِ

Whoever turns away from dhikr of God has a companion
allotted to him from Shaytan to tempt him from the journey.

فَلَا يَطْمَئِنُّ الْقَلْبُ إِلَّا بِذِكْرِهِ
فَيَسْكُنَ عَنْ خَوْفِ الْخَلِيقَةِ وَالْفَقْرِ

The heart is only made tranquil by His dhikr,
and it is calmed from fear of creation and poverty.

$$\text{وَلَا تُبْسَطُ الْاَرْزَاقُ إِلَّا لِمَنْ غَدَا}$$

$$\text{يُرَدِّدُهُ حَتَّى يَغِيبَ فِي الْوِتْرِ}$$

Provision is only assured for the one who goes forth in the morning
repeating it until he absents himself in the One.

$$\text{وَهَذَا رَسُولُ اللهِ يَذْكُرُ دَائِمًا}$$

$$\text{عَلَى كُلِّ أَحْيَانٍ يُشَرِّعُ لِلْغَيْرِ}$$

The Messenger of Allah did dhikr constantly at all times,
laying down the road for others.

$$\text{وَقَالَ اذْكُرُوا حَتَّى يَقُولُونَ إِنَّهُ}$$

$$\text{يُرَاءِي بِذِكْرِ اللهِ حِرْصًا عَلَى الْخَيْرِ}$$

He said, 'Do dhikr until they say, "He is showing off
with dhikr of Allah"' out of eagerness for the blessing.

$$\text{عَلَيْكَ بِهِ فَالْقَوْمُ قَدْ سَكِرُوا بِهِ}$$

$$\text{وَأَفْنَوْا فِيهِ الْاَرْوَاحَ يَالَهُ مِنْ ذُخْرٍ}$$

You must do it, for the People have become intoxicated by it,
and they have annihilated their spirits in it – what a treasure for them!

$$\text{فَكُلُّ مَقَامَاتِ الرِّجَالِ قَدِ انْطَوَتْ}$$

$$\text{فِي حُبٍّ وَذِكْرِ اللهِ بِالْفَمِ وَالصَّدْرِ}$$

All the stations of the Men are contained
in love and dhikr of Allah with mouth and heart.

وَلَا تَكْتَفِي بِالْوَارِدَاتِ عَنِ الْوِرْدِ
وَلَا تَطْلُبَنْ إِلَّا رِضَاهُ مَعَ السِّتْرِ

Do not be satisfied with lights that descend on the heart from the Wird;
only ask for His approval along with veiling of wrong actions.

فَيَا رَبِّ وَفِّقْنَا لِصِدْقِ تَوَجُّهٍ
بِجَاهِ الَّذِي قَدْ جَاءَ بِالْفَتْحِ وَالنَّصْرِ

So, O Lord, give us success in sincere turning to you,
by the rank of the one who brought an opening and a triumph.

مُحَمَّدُ أَصْلُ الْمَوْجُودَاتِ وَسِرُّهَا
وَخَاتَمُ رُسْلِ اللهِ وَالْأَنْبِيَا الْغُرِّ

Muhammad is the source and secret of existent beings,
and the seal of the Messengers of Allah and the glorious Prophets.

عَلَيْهِ صَلَاةُ اللهِ مَا هَامَ ذَاكِرٌ
بِذِكْرِ مَوْلَاهُ فِي الشَّدَائِدِ وَالْيُسْرِ

May the blessings of Allah be upon him as long as there is someone
in love with the remembrance of his Lord in times of trial and ease –

وَءَالِهِ وَالْأَصْحَابِ مَعَ كُلِّ مُقْتَفٍ
مُتَابَعَةَ الْمُخْتَارِ فِي النَّهْيِ وَالْأَمْرِ ۞

– and on his family and Companions and every follower
who follows the Chosen One in prohibition and command.

# Reflection

وتليه رائية
التفكر

تَفَكَّرْ جَمِيلَ الصُّنْعِ فِي الْبَرِّ وَالْبَحْرِ
وَجُلْ فِي صِفَـاتِ اللهِ فِي السِّرِّ وَالْجَهْرِ

Reflect upon the beauty of the way in which both the land and sea are made,
and contemplate the Attributes of Allah openly and secretly.

وَفِي النَّفْسِ وَالآفَـاقِ أَعْظَمُ شَـاهِدٍ
عَلَىٰ كَمَـالَاتِ اللهِ مِنْ غَيْرِ مَا حَصْرِ

The greatest evidence of the limitless perfections of Allah
can be found both deep within the self and on the distant horizon.

فَلَوْ جُلْتَ فِي الاَجْسَامِ مَعْ حُسْنِ شَكْلِهَا
وَتَنْظِيمِهَـا تَنْظِيمَ خَيْطٍ مِنَ الدُّرِّ

If you were to reflect on physical bodies and their marvellous forms
and how they are arranged with great precision, like a string of pearls;

وَجُلْتَ فِي أَسْرَارِ اللِّسَانِ وَنُطْقِهِ
وَتَعْبِيرِهِ عَمَّا تُكِنُّهُ فِي الصَّدْرِ

and if you were to reflect on the secrets of the tongue and its speech,
and how it articulates and conveys what you conceal in your breast;

وَجُلْتَ فِي أَسْرَارِ الْجَوَارِحِ كُلِّهَا
وَتَسْخِيرِهَا لِلْقَلْبِ مِنْ غَيْرِ مَا عُسْرِ

and if you were to reflect on the secrets of all the limbs
and how easily they are subject to the heart's command;

وَجُلْتَ فِي تَقْلِيبِ الْقُلُوبِ لِطَاعَةٍ
وَفِي بَعْضِ أَحْيَانٍ لِمَعْصِيَةٍ تَسْرِي

and if you were to reflect on how the hearts are moved to obey Allah
and how sometimes they move to disobedience;

وَجُلْتَ فِي أَرْضٍ مَعَ تَنَوُّعِ نَبْتِهَا
وَكَثْرَةِ مَا فِيهَا مِنَ السَّهْلِ وَالْوَعْرِ

and if you were to reflect on the earth and the diversity of its plants
and the great varieties of plains and rugged mountains in it;

وَجُلْتَ فِي أَسْرَارِ الْبِحَارِ وَحُوتِهَا
وَكَثْرَةِ أَمْوَاجٍ لَهَا حَاجِزٌ قَهْرِ

and if you were to reflect on the secrets of the oceans and all their fish,
and their endless waves held back by an unconquerable barrier;

وَجُلْتَ فِي أَسْرَارِ الرِّيَـاحِ وَجَلْبِهَـا
لِغَيمٍ وَسُحْبٍ قَدْ أَسَالَتْ مِنَ الْقَطْرِ

and if you were to reflect on the secrets of the many winds
and how they bring the mist, fog and clouds which release the rain;

وَجُلْتَ فِي أَسْرَارِ السَّمَـٰوَٰتِ كُلِّهَـا
وَعَرْشٍ وَكُرْسِيّ وَرُوحٍ مِنَ الأَمْرِ

and if you were to reflect on all the secrets of the heavens –
the Throne, the Footstool and the spirit which is Allah's Affair –

عَقَدْتَ عَلَى التَّوْحِيدِ عَقْدَ مُصَمِّمٍ
وَحُلْتَ عَنِ الأَوْهَـامِ وَالشَّكِّ وَالْغَيْرِ

then you would accept the reality of Tawhid with all your being,
and you would turn away from illusions, uncertainty and otherness;

وَقُلْتَ إِلَـٰهِي أَنْتَ سُؤْلِي وَمَطْلَبِي
وَحِصْنِي مِنَ الأَسْوَاءِ وَالضَّيْمِ وَالْمَكْرِ

and you would say, 'My God, You are my desire, my goal
and my impregnable fortress against evil, injustice, and deceit.

وَأَنْتَ رَجَـائِي فِي قَضَـاءِ حَوَائِجِي
وَأَنْتَ الَّذِي تُنْجِي مِنَ السُّوءِ وَالشَّرِّ

'You are the One I hope will provide for all my needs,
and You are the One Who rescues us from all evil and wickedness.

وَأَنْتَ الرَّحِيمُ الْمُسْتَجِيبُ لِمَنْ دَعَاكَ

وَأَنْتَ الَّذِي تُغْنِي الْفَقِيرَ عَنِ الْفَقْرِ

'You are the Compassionate, the One Who answers all who call on You.
And You are the One Who frees the needy of their need.

إِلَيْكَ رَفَعْتُ يَا رَفِيعُ مَطَالِبِي

فَعَجِّلْ بِفَتْحٍ يَا إِلَهِي مَعَ السِّرِّ

'It is to You, O Exalted, that I have raised all my requests,
so swiftly bring me the Opening along with the Secret, O my God.'

بِجَاهِ الَّذِي يُرْجَى يَوْمَ الْكَرْبِ وَالْعَنَا

وَيَوْمَ وُرُودِ النَّاسِ لِلْمَوْقِفِ الْحَشْرِ

By the rank of the one who is hoped for on the day of distress and grief,
and the day when people come to the Place of Gathering,

عَلَيْهِ صَلَاةُ اللهِ مَا جَالَ عَارِفٌ

فِي أَنْوَارِ ذَاتِهِ لَدَىْ كُلِّ مَظْهَرِ

may Allah's blessings be upon him as long as there is a gnostic
who reflects on the lights of His Essence in every manifestation,

وَءَالِهِ وَالأَصْحَابِ مَعَ كُلِّ تَابِعٍ

لِسُنَّتِهِ الْغَرَّاءِ فِي النَّهْيِ وَالأَمْرِ ۞

and upon his family and Companions and everyone who follows
his excellent Sunna in prohibition and command.

# Robe of Nearness

وتليه رائية

حلة التقريب

قَدْ كَسَانَا ذِكْرُ الْحَبِيبِ جَمَـالًا

وَبَهَـاءً وَرِفْعَةً وَسُرُورًا

Remembrance of the Beloved clothed us
in beauty, radiance, exaltation and joy.

وَخَلَعْنَـا الْعِذَارَ عِنْدَ التَّدَانِي

وَجَهَرْنَـا بِمَنْ نُحِبُّ افْتِخَـارَا

In drawing near we cast aside every restraint
and openly proclaimed the One we love, glorying in Him.

وَسَقَـانَا الْحَبِيبُ شَرْبَةَ حُبٍّ

قَدْ أَزَالَتْ سِوَى الْحَبِيبِ اضْطِرَارَا

The Beloved gave us a draught of pure love to drink
which forced all but the Beloved to disappear.

وَشَهِدْنَا الأَكْوَانَ مَحْضَ هَبَاءٍ
وَرَأَيْنَا الأَنْوَارَ تَبْدُو جِهَارَا

We witnessed beings as pure specks of dust;
we saw the lights appear openly.

وَرَجَعْنَا لِلْخَلْقِ بَعْدَ انْمِحَاقٍ
وَفَنَاءٍ فِي خَمْرَةٍ تُعْطِي نُورَا

After having been obliterated and annihilated
in a light-giving wine, we returned to creation.

فَبِفَضْلٍ مِنَ الالَهِ بَقِينَا
وَكَتَمْنَا الَّذِي نُحِبُّ اصْطِبَارَا

By a pure gift from God we were given Baqa,
and so, with patience, we concealed the One we love.

كَمْ نَظَرْنَا فِي سَالِكٍ فَتَرَقَّى
لِمَقَامِ الَّذِينَ خَاضُوا الْبِحَارَا

How often have we looked on a wayfarer who has then risen
to the stations of those who have plunged into the seas!

وَشَفَيْنَا الْقُلُوبَ مِمَّا عَرَاهَا
بِلَطِيفِ الْعُلُومِ ذَوْقًا فَطَارَا

We have healed hearts of what had befallen them
through knowledges of subtle taste, and they have soared.

146

وَهَمَمْنَا بِالشَّيْءِ سِرًّا فَكَانَا
وَأَتَانَا الَّذِي نُحِبُّ اخْتِيَارَا

We concerned ourselves with something secretly, so that it came about,
and the One we have chosen to love has come to us.

وَسَمِعْنَا مِنْ حَضْرَةِ الْغَيْبِ سِرًّا
أَنْتَ مَحْبُوبٌ عِنْدَنَا كُنْ شَكُورَا

We heard a secret from the presence of the Unseen
'In Our sight you are beloved so be grateful.'

وَأُذِنَّا بِسَقْيِ مَنْ جَاءَ شَوْقًا
لِلِقَانَا وَلَمْ يَكُنْ ذَا اخْتِبَارَا

We were granted Idhn to quench the thirst of whoever comes longing
to meet us, and not just researching.

وَإِذَا كَانَتِ الْمَوَاهِبِ فَضْلًا
فَتَعَرَّضْ لَهَا وَكُنْ ذَا افْتِقَارَا

If gifts are abundant,
expose yourself to them, and be a needy person.

وَتَذَلَّلْ لِأَهْلِهَا تَسْقَىٰ مِنْهُم
وَتَقَرَّبْ لَهُمْ وَلَا تَخْشَ عَارَا

Humble yourselves to their people – they will satisfy your thirst.
Draw near to them and have no fear of disgrace.

وَتَجَرَّدْ مِنْ كُلِّ عِلْمٍ وَفَهْمٍ
لِتَنَالَ الَّذِي نَالُوهُ الْكِبَارَا

Strip yourselves of all knowledge and understanding
so that you may obtain what the great have obtained.

وَابْذُلِ النَّفْسَ يَا مُحِبَّ الْوِصَالِ
وَاتْبِع الشَّيْخَ فِي الَّذِي قَدْ أَشَارَا

Freely offer up your self, you who desire arrival,
and follow the Shaykh in whatever he indicates.

وَاشْهَدِ الْحَقَّ فِيهِ ذَاتًا وَقَلْبًا
وَافْنَ فِيهِ تَكُنْ بِهِ ذَا انْتِصَارَا

Witness the truth in him, in both your essence and your heart,
annihilate yourself in him; by him you will gain victory.

فَهْوَ نُورُ الرَّسُولِ مِنْ كُلِّ وَجْهٍ
وَهْوَ طِبُّ الْقُلُوبِ سِرًّا وَجَهْرَا

He is the light of the Messenger in every aspect,
and the medicine of hearts, both openly and secretly.

فَالْحَظْنَهُ وَعَظِّمَنْهُ كَثِيرًا
وَاذْهَبَنْ عِنْدَهُ وَكُنْ ذَا انْكِسَارَا

Pay attention to him and show him great esteem.
Go into his presence in a broken condition.

وَصَلَاةٌ عَلَى النَّبِيّ وَءَالٍ

وَصِحَابٍ وَمَنْ لَهُ قَدْ أَشَارَا

Blessings be upon the Prophet and all his family
and Companions and all who direct people to him,

وَسَلَامٌ بِكُلِّ مِسْكٍ وَطِيبٍ

وَجَمَالٍ وَرِفْعَةٍ لَا تُجَارَا ۝

and peace, fragrant with musk and every scent,
beauty and unrivalled sublimity.

# Qasida Written Before the Prophet

وَتَلِيهَا اللامِيَّةُ الَّتِي أنشَأَهَا تُجَاه
النَّبِي صَلَّى الله عَلَيهِ وسلم

نَحْنُ فِي رَوْضَةِ الرَّسُولِ حُضُورُ
طَـالِبِينَ الرِّضَىٰ وَحُسْنَ قَبُولِ

We are present in the Rawda of the Messenger,
hoping for acceptance and welcome.

جِئْنَـا يَـا خَيْرَ مَنْ إِلَيْهِ الْمَلَاذُ
بِانْكِسَـارٍ وَذِلَّةٍ وَذُهُولِ

We have come, O best of refuges! –
broken, humbled and confused.

فَاسْأَلِ اللهَ فِينَـا كُلَّ عِنَـايَهْ
لِنَنَـالَ الْمُنَىٰ فِي وَقْتِ الْحُلُولِ

Ask Allah to show every concern for us,
so that our hopes will be fulfilled at the time debts fall due.

لَكَ قَدْرُ عَظِيمٌ لَيْسَ يُضَاهَى
وَرِسَالَهْ تَفُوقُ كُلَّ رَسُولِ

You have a vast power which is beyond compare,
and a message greater than every Messenger's.

أَنْتَ بَابُ الالَهِ فِي كُلِّ خَيْرٍ
مَنْ أَتَى فَازَ بِالرِّضَىٰ وَالْوُصُولِ

You are the door to God in every good thing,
whoever comes to you gains acceptance and union.

كُلُّ سِرٍّ فِي الانْبِيَا قَدْ أَتَاهُمْ
مِنْ عَلَاكُمْ مُؤَيَّدًا بِنَقُولِ

Every secret which came to the Prophets
is from your sublimity, confirmed through transmission.

قَدْ تَشَفَّعْتُ فِي أُمُورِي إِلَاهِي
بِالنَّبِيِّ الْمُشَفَّعِ الْمَقْبُولِ

I have looked to the Prophet to intercede with God in my affair,
for he is the accepted intercessor.

كُلُّ مَنْ حَطَّ رَحْلَهُ بِكَرِيمٍ
نَالَ أَقْصَى الْمُنَىٰ وَكُلَّ السُّؤْلِ

All of those whose journey ends at the house of a generous host,
get everything they ask for, even their most extreme wish.

قَدْ شَكَرْنَا الإِلَهَ فِي كُلِّ وَقْتٍ

حَيْثُ مَنَّ مِنْ بِزَوْرَةٍ لِرَسُولِ

We have given thanks to God for every time that He
has given us the gift of a visit to the Messenger –

وَكَذَاكَ لِكُلِّ مَنْ فِي بَقِيعٍ

مِنْ صِحَابٍ كَذَاكَ نَسْلُ الْبَتُولِ

and a visit to the Companions
and the offspring of Fatimah Batul in Baqi';

وَكَذَاكَ لِكُلِّ زَوْجٍ وَبِنْتٍ

وَابْنِ مُنْجِي الأَنَامِ يَوْمَ الْحُلُولِ

and a visit to every wife, daughter and son of the
deliverer of mankind on the day debts fall due;

وَكَذَاكَ لِكُلِّ مَنْ فِي أُحُدٍ

مِنْ شَهِيدٍ كَذَاكَ عَمُّ الرَّسُولِ

and a visit to every Shahid in Uhud,
and the uncle of the Messenger.

قَدْ طَلَبْنَا بِهِمْ تَمَامَ السَّلَامَهْ

فِي مَسِيرٍ لِأَرْضِنَا وَالدُّخُولِ

We have sought, by them, perfect safety for us on our
homeward journey and on our arrival.

وَطَلَبْنَا النَّجَاةَ فِي يَوْمِ حَشْرٍ

وَسَلَامًا مِنْ كُلِّ فَظٍّ جَهُولِ

We have sought rescue on the Day of Gathering
and safety from every ignorant, coarse person.

رَبِّ صَلِّ عَلَى النَّبِيِّ وَءَالٍ

وَصِحَابٍ وَتَابِعٍ بِشُمُولِ ۞

Our Lord, bless the Prophet and his family
and Companions and all the followers.

# Withdrawal into the Perception of the Essence

وتليه رائية

الغيبة في شهود الذات

قَدْ بَدَا وَجْهُ الْحَبِيبِ
لَاحَ فِي وَقْتِ السَّحَرْ

The Face of the Beloved appeared
and shone in the pre-dawn.

نُورُهُ قَدْ عَمَّ قَلْبِي
فَسَجَدْتُ بِانْكِسَارْ

His light pervaded my heart,
so I prostrated myself in awe.

قَالَ لِي ارْفَعْ وَاسْأَلَنِّي
فَلَكُمْ كُلُّ وَطَرْ

He said to me, 'Rise! – ask of Me!
You will have whatever you desire.'

قُلْتُ أَنْتَ أَنْتَ حَسْبِي

لَيْسَ لِي عَنْكَ اصْطِبَارْ

I replied, 'You. You are enough for me!
Away from You I cannot live!'

قَالَ عَبْدِي لَكَ بُشْرَىٰ

فَتَنَعَّمْ بِالنَّظَرْ

He said, 'My slave, there is good news for you,
so enjoy the vision.

أَنْتَ كَنْزٌ لِعِبَادِي

أَنْتَ ذِكْرَىٰ لِلْبَشَرْ

'You are a treasure for My slaves
and you are a reminder for mankind.

كُلُّ حُسْنٍ وَجَمَالٍ

فِي الْوَرَىٰ مِنِّي انْتَشَرْ

'Every good and every beauty in mankind
has spread from Me.

بَطَنَتْ أَوْصَافُ ذَاتِي

وَتَجَلَّتْ فِي الْأَثَرْ

'The Attributes of My Essence were hidden,
and they manifested themselves in creation.

إِنَّمَا الْكَوْنُ مَعَانٍ
قَائِمَاتٌ بِـالصُّوَرْ

'Created beings are only meanings
projected in forms.

كُلُّ مَنْ يُدْرِكُ هٰذَا
كَـانَ مِنْ أَهْلِ الْعِبَــرْ

'All who grasp this
are among the people of discrimination.

لَمْ يَذُقْ لَذَّةَ عَيْشٍ
اَلَّذِي عَنَّا انْحَصَــرْ

'The one who is prevented from reaching Us
has not tasted the sweetness of life.'

رَبَّنَـا صَلِّ عَلَىٰ مَنْ
نُورُهُ عَمَّ الْبَشَرْ

O Lord, bless the one whose light has spread
through all mankind,

وَءَالٍ مَعَ صِحَابٍ
مَا لَاحَ نُورُ الْقَمَرْ ۞

and the family and Companions
as long as the light of the moon shines.

# The Qualities of Muhammad

وتليه لامية

الشمائل

مُحَمَّد مَنْشَؤُ الانَّوَارِ وَالظِّلَلِ

وَأَصْلُ تَكْوِينِهَا مِنْ حَضْرَةِ الازَلِ

Muhammad is the fountain-head of lights and darkness and
the source of their emergence from the presence of before-time.

فَنُورُهُ أَوَّلُ الانَّوَارِ لَمَّا قَضَىٰ

إِظْهَارَ أَسْمَائِهِ فِي الْعَالَمِ الاوَّلِ

His light was the first of lights when He determined
the manifestation of His Names in the first world.

مِنْهُ اكْتَسَتْ سَائِرُ الاشْيَاءِ إِيجَادَهَا

وَمِنْهُ إِمْدَادُهَا مِنْ غَيْرِ مَا خَلَلِ

From him all things were clothed in their origination in existence,
and their continuance comes from him without interruption.

تَقَـاطَرَ الاَنْبِيَـا وَالرُّسْلُ مِنْهُ كَمَا

تَقَـاطَرَتْ سَـائِرُ الاَمْلَاكِ وَالْحَلَلِ

The Prophets and Messengers have come from him one by one,
as well as all the angels and all the creatures.

فَنِسْبَةُ الْخَتْمِ وَالاَقْطَـابِ مِنْ نُورِهِ

كَنُقْطَةٍ مِنْ بُحُورِ النُّورِ وَالْبَلَلِ

The relationship of the Seal and the Poles to his light
is that of a drop to oceans of light and refreshment.

وَالشَّمْسُ وَالْبَدْرُ وَالنَّجُومُ مِنْهُ بَدَتْ

كَالْعَرْشِ وَاللَّوْحِ وَالْكُرْسِيِّ وَالدُّوَلِ

The sun, moon and stars have appeared from him,
as have the Throne, Tablet, Footstool, and the dynasties.

فَشَـاهِدِ النُّورَ قَدْ عَمَّ الْوُجُودَ وَلَا

تَكُنْ تَرَىٰ غَيْرَهُ تَصِلْ عَلَىٰ عَجَلِ

Witness the light which has spread through existence
and do not see other-than-it, and you will soon arrive.

لِأَنَّهُ الْمَظْهَرُ الاَعْلَىٰ لِأَسْمَـائِهِ

وَسِرُّ أَوْصَـافِهِ مِنْ غَيْرِ مَـا عِلَلِ

For he is the highest manifestation of Allah's Names
and the perfect unfaulted secret of His Attributes.

فَاللهُ إِخْتَارَهُ فِي عِلْمِهِ الْقَدِيمِ
لِلْخَلْقِ أَرْسَلَهُ طُرًّا وَلِلرُّسُلِ

Allah chose him in His timeless knowledge
and sent him to all of creation and to the other Messengers.

أَسْرَىٰ بِهِ اللهُ لَيْلًا بَعْدَ مَبْعَثِهِ
لِقَابِ قَوْسَيْنِ حَتَّىٰ فَازَ بِالْأَمَلِ

After sending him as a Messenger, Allah conveyed him one night
to the distance of two bow-spans until he achieved his desire.

وَاسْتَبْشَرَ الْعَالَمُ الْعُلْوِيُّ لَمَّا رَقَىٰ
وَالْعَرْشُ قَدْ حَصَّلَ الْأَمَانَ مِنْ وَجَلٍ

The higher world rejoiced when he ascended,
and the Throne gave him security from fear.

وَاخْتَرَقَ الْحُجْبَ وَالْأَنْوَارَ حَتَّىٰ دَنَا
وَنُودِيَ ادْنُ حَبِيبِي وَاسْكُنْ مِنْ خَجَلِ

He passed through the veils and lights until he drew near,
and he was summoned, 'Draw near, Beloved, and set aside your shyness.'

وَمَتِّعِ اللَّحْظَ فِي أَنْوَارِنَا وَاطْلُبَنْ
كُلَّ الَّذِي شِئْتَهُ تُعْطَ بِلَا مَلَلِ

'Rejoice in the sight of Our lights and demand all you want
and it will be given to you without delay.'

159

فَأُرْجِعَ الْمُصْطَفَىٰ بِكُلِّ مَكْرُمَةٍ
وَأَخْبَرَ النَّاسَ بِالاَقْصَا وَبِالسُّبُلِ

Then the Chosen One was returned with every noble quality
and he informed the people about al-Aqsa and the roads to it.

فَلُذْ بِهِ يَا أَخِي فِي كُلِّ مُعْضِلَةٍ
يَضْحَىٰ حَدِيثُكَ بَيْنَ النَّاسِ كَالْعَسَلِ

Take refuge with him in every dilemma, O my brother,
and your speech among the people will become like honey.

وَلَذِّذِ السَّمْعَ بِالاَخْلاقِ وَالشِّيَمِ
وَاذْكُرْ شَمَائِلَهُ وَاحْذَرْ مِنَ الزَّلَلِ

Delight in hearing of his good character and qualities,
and evoke his virtues, and remain on guard against mistakes.

فَكَمْ خَوَارِقَ قَدْ جَاءَتْ عَلَىٰ يَدِهِ
فَأَعْجَزَتْ سَائِرَ الْحُسَّادِ وَالْمِلَلِ

How many miracles have come from his hand,
leaving the envious and all other religions powerless!

وَإِنَّ أَعْظَمَ خَارِقٍ لَهُ ظَهَرَا
هٰذَا الْكِتَابُ الَّذِي قَدْ جَاءَ بِالْعَمَلِ

The greatest of the miracles which were manifested for him
is this Book which brought us action.

فِي كُلِّ جَـارِحَةٍ مِنْهُ فَوَائِدُ لَا

يُحْصِيهَـا عَدُّ وَلَا تُدْرِكْهَـا بِالْمُقَلِ

In every act from it there are innumerable benefits,
which are not perceptible to the eyes.

وَقَدْ أَحَـاطَ كِتَـابُ اللهِ مِنْهَـا بِمَـا

يُبْرِئُ كُلَّ سَقِيمِ الْقَلْبِ مِنْ عِلَلِ

The Book of Allah contains some of these benefits
by which every one who is sick of heart is healed of his sickness.

وَلَيْسَ يَقْدِرُ قَدْرَهُ الْعَظِيمَ فَتَى

فَالْعَجْزُ عَنْ مَدْحِهِ مِنْ أَحْسَنِ السُّبُلِ

No hero is capable of attaining his mighty rank,
so the inability to praise him is the best of ways.

وَقَدْ تَشَبَّهْتُ فِي مَدْحِي وَجِئْتُ إِلَى

رُحْمَاكَ مُسْتَشْفِعًا لِلَّهِ تَشْفَعُ لِي

I have copied you in my praise and I have come to your compassion
seeking intercession with Allah, so intercede on my behalf!

يَـا أَعْظَمَ الْخَلْقِ عِنْدَ اللهِ مَنْزِلَةً

اعْطِفْ عَلَيْنَـا بِمَـا نَرْجُوهُ يَـا أَمَلِي

O greatest of creation with Allah in rank,
be kind to us with what we hope for, O my desire!

مَنْ يَحْتَمِي بِكَ يَضْحَى الْكَوْنُ يَخْدُمه

لِأَجْلِ جَاهِكَ يَا مُمِدَّ كُلِّ وَلِي

By your rank, created beings serve whoever
seeks shelter with you, O Protector of every Wali.

بِكَ احْتَمَيْتُ فَلَا تَكِلْنِي يَا سَنَدِي

لِلنَّفْسِ وَالْجِنْسِ وَاجْبُرْنَا مِنَ الْخَلَلِ

O my support! I have sought shelter with you,
so do not leave me to my self and my humanness, but mend our faults.

وَلَيْسَ يَلْحَقُ عَبْدٌ أَنْتَ نَاصِرُهُ

فَأَنْتَ لِي عُمْدَةٌ فِي السَّهْلِ وَالْجَبَلِ

Nothing befalls the slave if you are his helper.
You are my staff on the level land and on the mountains.

وَقَدْ تَحَيَّرْتُ فِي أَمْرِي فَخُذْ بِيَدِي

فَلَا تَحَوُّلَ لِي عَنْ نُورِكَ الْأَوَّلِ

I have become confused about myself, so take me by the hand.
For me there is no turning away from your first light.

صَلَّى عَلَيْكَ إِلَهُ الْعَرْشِ مَا ظَهَرَتْ

شَمْسُ الْحَقِيقَةِ بِالْأَسْمَاءِ وَالْفِعَالِ

May the God of the Throne bless you as long
as the sun of the reality is manifested by the Names and the Acts.

كَذَاكَ ءَالُكَ وَالاَصْحَابُ مَا نَبَتَتْ

عُشْبٌ وَمَا سَحَّتِ السَّمَاءُ مِنْ بَلَلِ

As well as your family and Companions as long as the grass grows
and the sky pours down abundant rain.

ثُمَّ الرِّضَىٰ عَنْ رِجَالِ اللهِ كُلِّهِمِ

مَا سَبَّحَ الْكَوْنُ مَنْ يَجِلُّ عَنْ مَثَلِ

Then I ask for Your good pleasure for all the Men of Allah
as long as beings glorify the One Who is above identification with forms.

وَابْسُطْ لِإِخْوَانِنَا الْخَيْرَاتِ أَجْمَعَهَا

دُنْيًا وَأُخْرَىٰ وَلَا تَكِلْنَا لِلْعَمَلِ

And unfold all blessings on our brothers, in this world and the next,
and do not leave us to our actions.

وَاغْفِرْ لِوَالِدِينَا الزَّلَّاتِ أَجْمَعَهَا

وَالْمُسْلِمِينَ بِفَضْلٍ مِنْكَ يَا أَزَلِي ۞

Forgive our parents all their mistakes, and the Muslims,
by an outpouring from You – O Before-endless-time!

163

# Forgiveness

وتليها لامية
الاستغفار

أَسْتَغْفِرُ اللّٰهَ إِنَّ اللّٰهَ ذُو كَرَمٍ
وَرَحْمَةٍ لِلَّذِي قَدْ تَابَ مِنْ زَلَلِ

I ask forgiveness of Allah! Allah possesses generosity
and mercy for the one who turns away from his error.

أَسْتَغْفِرُ اللّٰهَ مِنْ ذَنْبٍ وَمِنْ زَلَلٍ
وَمِنْ خَطَايَا وَمِنْ وَهْمٍ وَمِنْ أَمَلِ

I ask forgiveness of Allah for wrong actions and mistakes,
and for my errors, delusion and wishful thinking.

أَسْتَغْفِرُ اللّٰهَ مِنْ كِبْرٍ وَمِنْ حَسَدٍ
وَمِنْ رِيَاءٍ لِأَهْلِ الْمَالِ بِالْعَمَلِ

I ask forgiveness of Allah for any pride and envy,
and for hypocritical behaviour towards the rich.

أَسْتَغْفِرُ اللّٰهَ مِنْ ظَنٍّ قَبِيحٍ بَدَا

مِنْ رُؤْيَةِ النَّفْسِ عُجْبًا مِنْهَا بِالْحُلَلِ

I ask forgiveness of Allah for ugly thoughts which
emerge from seeing the self and admiring its form.

أَسْتَغْفِرُ اللّٰهَ مِنْ غِلٍّ وَحِقْدٍ وَمَا

أَضْمَرْتُ فِي سَالِفِ الْاَعْمَارِ مِنْ عِلَلٍ

I ask forgiveness of Allah for all malice and spite
and for the faults I concealed in my earlier years.

أَسْتَغْفِرُ اللّٰهَ مِنْ نُطْقٍ بِفَاحِشَةٍ

وَمِنْ سُكُوتٍ عَنْ غِيبَةٍ وَعَنْ خَلَلِ

I ask forgiveness of Allah for saying dreadful things
and for being silent in the face of slander and injury to others.

أَسْتَغْفِرُ اللّٰهَ مِنْ زُورٍ وَمِنْ كَذِبٍ

وَمِنْ غُرُورٍ يَجُرُّ النَّفْسَ لِلْكَسَلِ

I ask forgiveness of Allah for dishonesty and lying
and for self-delusion which leads the self to indolence.

أَسْتَغْفِرُ اللّٰهَ مِنْ ذَنْبٍ بِجَارِحَةٍ

وَمِنْ حُقُوقٍ أَتَتْ لِلنَّاسِ مِنْ قِبَلِي

I ask forgiveness of Allah for wrong actions done with the limbs,
and for rights owed to people.

أَسْتَغْفِرُ اللهَ مِنْ عِلْمٍ أَزِيغُ بِهِ

عَنِ الصِّرَاطِ الْقَوِيمِ الْمُفْضِي لِلْوَجَلِ

I ask forgiveness of Allah for any knowledge by which I deviate
from the straight path that leads to fear.

أَسْتَغْفِرُ اللهَ مِنْ حَـالٍ أُصُولُ بِهِ

وَمِنْ مَقَـامٍ أَدَّىٰ لِلْخَوْفِ وَانْجَلِ

I ask forgiveness of Allah for any state which I rush into,
and for any station that leads to fear and confusion.

أَسْتَغْفِرُ اللهَ مِنْ فِعْلٍ بِلَا نِيَّةٍ

وَمِنْ ذُهُولٍ أَتَىٰ لِلْقَلْبِ عَنْ عَجَلِ

I ask forgiveness of Allah for any act done without intention
and for distraction which quickly overwhelms the heart.

أَسْتَغْفِرُ اللهَ مِنْ دَعْوَى الْحُلُولِ وَمِنْ

دَعْوَى اتِّحَـادٍ أَدَّىٰ لِلزَّيْغِ وَالْفَشَلِ

I ask forgiveness of Allah for claiming incarnation
and for claiming fusion, as these claims lead to deviation and failure.

أَسْتَغْفِرُ اللهَ مِنْ دَعْوَى الْوُجُودِ وَمِنْ

إِثْبَاتِ شَيْءٍ سِوَى الْمَوْجُودِ فِي الْأَزَلِ

I ask forgiveness of Allah for claiming existence,
and for affirming anything other than the Existent in before-time.

166

أَسْتَغْفِرُ اللهَ مِنْ عَقَائِدٍ طَرَأَتْ

قَدْ خَـالَفَتْ مِنْهَـاجَ الْمُخْتَارِ وَالرُّسُلِ

I ask forgiveness of Allah for beliefs that occur which are
contrary to the path of the Chosen One and the Messengers.

أَسْتَغْفِرُ اللهَ مِنْ جَهْلٍ وَمِنْ سَفَهٍ

وَمِنْ فُتُورٍ أَتَىٰ لِلنَّفْسِ عَنْ مَلَلِ

I ask forgiveness of Allah for ignorance and folly
and for the languor that comes to the self from boredom.

أَسْتَغْفِرُ اللهَ مِنْ فِكْرٍ أَجُولُ بِهِ

بِلَا اعْتِبَـارٍ جَرَىٰ فِي الْعُلْوِيِّ وَالسُّفُلِ

I ask forgiveness of Allah for any thought, be it high or low,
that has occupied me without taking a reminder from it.

أَسْتَغْفِرُ اللهَ مِقْدَارَ الْعَوَالِمِ مِنْ

عَرْشٍ وَلَوْحٍ وَعُمْرِ سَـائِرِ الدُّوَلِ

I ask forgiveness of Allah by the measure of the worlds of the Throne,
the Tablet of forms and the duration of every dynasty.

أَسْتَغْفِرُ اللهَ وَهَّـابَ الْعَطَـايَا لِمَنْ

قَدِ اتَّقَـاهُ بِلَا حَوْلٍ وَلَا حِيَلِ

I ask forgiveness of Allah, the Ceaseless Giver of gifts to all
who fear Him, being themselves unreservedly powerless.

أَسْتَغْفِرُ اللَّهَ مُعْطِي مَنْ يَلُوذُ بِهِ

مَعَارِفًا بِطُرُوقِ الْعِلْمِ وَالنِّحَلِ

I ask forgiveness of Allah Who grants gnoses in the paths of knowledge
and gifts, to whoever takes refuge with Him.

أَسْتَغْفِرُ اللهَ رَحْمَنَ الْخَلَائِقِ مِنْ

جِنٍّ وَإِنْسٍ وَأَمْلَاكٍ وَكُلِّ عَالِي

I ask forgiveness of Allah Who has compassion on all creatures:
jinn, men, angels, and every exalted one.

رَبِّ بِأَحْمَدَ كُنْ لِأَمْرِنَا وَلِيًّا

وَمُرْشِدًا لِاتِّبَاعِ أَقْوَمِ السُّبُلِ

My Lord, by Ahmad, be the Master of our affair
and the Guide in following the straightest of paths.

عَلَيْهِ أَزْكَىٰ صَلَاةِ اللهِ مَا هَطَلَتْ

غَيْثٌ وَمَا قَدْ سَرَىٰ فِي الْأَرْضِ مِنْ بَلَلِ

May the purest of Allah's blessings be upon him
as long as rain pours down and waters flow in the earth.

كَذَاكَ آلَكَ وَالصَّحْبُ الْكِرَامُ وَمَنْ

قَدِ اقْتَفَىٰ إِثْرَهُمْ مِنْ مُتَّقٍ وَوَلِي ۞

And upon your family and noble Companions and all
who follow in their footsteps who have fear of Allah, and every Wali.

# Departure of Illusion

تليها لامية

ارتحال الوهم

كَـانَ لِي وَهْمٌ فَلَمَّـا أَنْ رَحَلْ
أَشْرَفَ الْقَلْبُ عَلَىٰ نُورِ الازَلْ

I had an illusion. When it departed,
the heart looked upon the light of before-time.

رَكِبَ الشَّوْقَ الَّذِي طَـارَ بِهِ
فَدَنَـا مِنْ حِبِّهِ حَتَّى اتَّصَـلْ

It rode on longing, which flew with it,
so the heart drew near to its Beloved until it was united.

شَـاهَدَ الْكَوْنَ خَيَـالًا زَائِلًا
وَانْمَحَىٰ رَسْمُ الْوُجُودِ وَأَفَــلْ

It saw created beings as an imagination that faded,
and the form of existence was obliterated and vanished.

ثُمَّ رُدَّ لِلْبَقَاءِ مُثْبِتًا
جَمِيعَ الْكَوْنِ الَّذِي عَنْهُ انْعَزَلْ

Then it was returned to going-on, confirming
all the beings from which it had withdrawn.

جَمَعَ الضِّدَّيْنِ فِي مَشْهَدِهِ
وَحَّدَ اللهَ وَقَامَ بِالْعَمَلْ

It joined the two opposites in witnessing Him;
it unified Allah and took on action.

حَازَ سِرًّا وَصِرَاطًا سَوِيًّا
قَلَّ مَنْ ذَاقَهُ مِنْ أَهْلِ الْكَمَالْ

It gained a secret and a level path;
how few of the people of perfection taste it.

رَبَّنَا صَلِّ عَلَى النُّورِ الَّذِي
كُلُّ عَبْدٍ أَمَّهُ حَازَ الْأَمَلْ

Our Lord, bless the light.
Every slave who reaches him gains his desire.

وَارْضَ عَنْ ءَالِهِ هُمْ أَهْلُ النُّهَى
وَصِحَابٍ مَعَ قُطْبٍ وَبَدَلْ ۞

Be pleased with his family, they are the people of understanding;
and the Companions, the Qutb and the Abdal.

# Eyewitnessing

وتليه نونية

الشهود والعيان

يَـا مَنْ يُرِدْ حَضْرَةَ الْعِيَـانِ
إِرْقَ عَنِ الرُّوحِ وَالاَوَانِي

O you who desire the presence of eyewitnessing,
ascend and rise above the spirit and the forms.

وَالْعَدَمَ الاَصْلِيَّ الْزَمَنْهُ
وَكُنْ كَأَنْ لَمْ تَكُنْ يَـا فَانِي

And you must cling to the original void –
and be as if you were not, O annihilated!

تَرَىٰ بِسِرٍّ وُجُودًا حَقًّـا
سَرَتْ مَعَـانِيهْ فِي كُلِّ ءَانِ

Indeed you will see existence truly
by a secret whose meanings have spread in every age.

فَلَمْ يُعَدِّدْ ذَا الْفِعْلِ شَيْءٌ
مِنْ صُوَرِ الْفِعْلِ وَالْكِيَانِ

None of the many images of action and entity
multiply the Actor in any way.

فَمَنْ تَرَقَّى عَنْ كُلِّ فَانٍ
رَءَا وُجُودًا بِغَيْرِ ثَانٍ

So whoever rises above every vanishing thing
will see existence without any second.

يَا فَوْزَ مَنْ قَدْ غَدَا يُشَاهِدْ
رَبًّا عَطُوفًا حَلِيمًا دَانِي

Oh the victory of one who has come to witness
a Lord Who is compassionate, forbearing and near.

يَقْبَلُ مَنْ قَدْ أَتَى فَقِيرًا
قَدْ تَابَ مِنْ حَالِهِ الظَّلْمَانِي

He accepts whoever comes in need,
who has turned away from his own dark state.

فَتَوْبَةُ الْعَبْدِ تَصْطَفِيهِ
لِحَضْرَةِ الْحُبِّ وَالتَّدَانِي

The slave's turning away from wrong action
purifies him for the presence of love and drawing-near.

172

$$\text{وَذِكْرُهُ مَعْ شُهُودِ فَضْلٍ}$$
$$\text{يُحَصِّلُ الْوَارِدَ النُّورَانِي}$$

Dhikr of Allah while witnessing His overflowing
obtains for him a luminous awakening.

$$\text{مَنْ كَانَ مِنْ نَفْسِهِ فِي أَمْنٍ}$$
$$\text{كَانَ مِنَ الْخَلْقِ فِي أَمَانِ}$$

Whoever is safe from his own self
is also safe from the creation.

$$\text{نُخَالِفِ النَّفْسَ فِي هَوَاهَا}$$
$$\text{وَصَاحِبَنْ عَارِفًا رَبَّانِي}$$

So oppose the self in its desires
and seek the company of a gnostic of Allah.

$$\text{يُرِيكَ مِنْ عَيْبِهَا الْخَفِي}$$
$$\text{يُعَالِجَنْ بِالدَّوَا الرُّوحَانِي}$$

He will point out to you your hidden faults
and will treat you with a spiritual remedy.

$$\text{يَسْلُكُ بِالرِّفْقِ فِي الْمَسِيرِ}$$
$$\text{يَرْحَمُ أَهْلَ الْبَلَا وَالْجَانِي}$$

He acts gently towards you on the journey
with compassion for the people of trial and the delinquent.

يُفْنِيكَ بِالذِّكْرِ فِي الْحَقِيقَه
يُذَكِّرُ الْقَلْبَ بِالْقُرْءَان

He annihilates you through dhikr in the reality;
he reminds the heart through the Qur'an.

يُرَوِّحُ الرُّوحَ بِالاِشَارَه
فَتَنْجَلِي عِنْدَهَا الْمَعَانِي

He refreshes the spirit through indications
so at that the meanings disclose themselves.

يَا رَبِّ صَلِّ عَلَى النَّبِيِّ
مَا تُلِيَتْ سُورَةُ الْمَثَانِي

O Lord, bless the Prophet
as long as Surat al-Mathani is recited,

وَءَالِهِ وَالصِّحَابِ طُرًّا
مَا رَبِحَ النَّاسُ بِالاِيمَانِ

And his family and all of the Companions
as long as people profit by Iman.

وَأَطْلُبُ الْحَقَّ فِي السَّعَادَه
لِكُلِّ مَنْ ضَمَّهُ زَمَانِي ۝

I ask the Truly Real for bliss
for all whom my age comprises.

# The Oneness of Action and Existence

وله رضي الله عنه رائية

وحدة الفعل والوجود

سَأَلْتُ قَلْبِي عَنْ قُرْبِ رَبِّي

فَقَالَ لَا شَكَّ هُوَ حَاضِرْ

I asked my heart about the nearness of my Lord,
so it said, 'There is no doubt that He is present.'

فَقُلْتُ مَا لِيَ لَا أَرَاهُ

فَقَالَ لِي هُوَ فِيكَ ظَاهِرْ

I said, 'What is wrong with me that I do not see Him?'
And it said to me, 'He is manifest in you.'

فَقُلْتُ هَٰذَا الْأَمْرُ عَجِيبْ

فَكَيْفَ يَخْفَىٰ وَالنُّورُ بَاهِرْ

I said, 'This is truly astonishing –
how can He be hidden when light is brilliant?'

فَقَـالَ وَهْمٌ هُوَ الْحِجَـابُ

وَهْوَ لِكُلِّ الْأَنَـامِ قَـاهِرْ

So it said, 'It is illusion that is the veil:
and it overpowers each and every one.'

لَكِنَّ مَنْ كَـانَ ذَا اجْتِبَـاءِ

غَـابَ عَنِ الْوَهْمِ بِالسَّرَائِرْ

'However, the one who is chosen
withdraws from illusion through his secrets.

وَصَـارَ رُوحًـا بِغَيْرِ جِسْمٍ

وَشَـاهَدَ الرَّبَّ بِالْبَصَـائِرْ

'And he becomes a spirit without body
and directly sees the Lord with inner sight.'

فَغَـايَةُ الْفَتْحِ فِي الشُّهُودِ

لِحَضْرَةٍ مَا لَهَا مِنْ سَـاتِرْ

So the goal of opening in vision
is a Presence that has no veil.

فَلَيْسَ فِعْلٌ وَلَا وُجُودُ

لِغَيْرِ رَبِّي عِنْدَ الْأَكَـابِرْ

For the great there is neither action
nor existence from other than my Lord.

فَكُلُّ مَنْ بَاحَ بِاخْتِيَارٍ

مِنْ غَيْرِ إِذْنٍ لَهُ الزَّوَاجِرْ

Whoever divulges the Secret by choice,
without Idhn, has restrictions placed on him.

يَا رَبِّ إِفْتَحْ لَنَا الْبَصَائِرْ

وَنَوِّرِ الْقَلْبَ وَالسَّرَائِرْ

O Lord, open our inner sight for us
and illumine our heart and our secret.

ثُمَّ الصَّلَاةُ عَلَى النَّبِيِّ

مَا جَدَّ حِبٌّ وَسَارَ سَائِرْ

Then bless the Prophet as long as there is a lover
serious in his love and a wayfarer journeying.

وَءَالِهِ وَالصِّحَابِ جَمْعًا

مَا طَارَ شَوْقًا لِلَّهِ طَائِرْ ۝

And his family and Companions altogether,
as long as there is one who flies to Allah with longing.

# Counsel

وتليه عينية
النصح

سَلَامٌ عَلَى الاِخْوَانِ فِي كُلِّ مَوْضِعِ
سَلَامًا يَعُمُّ الْكُلَّ فِي كُلِّ مَجْمَعِ

Peace be upon the brothers in every place
— a peace that embraces all in every assembly.

وَإِنِّي أُرِيدُ النُّصْحَ لِلْكُلِّ رَاجِيًا
بُلُوغَ الْمُنَى وَالْعِزِّ وَالْفَتْحِ وَالْوُسْعِ

I wish to give good counsel to all, hoping
to obtain desire, might, the opening and strength.

فَأَوَّلُ نُصْحِي لِلَّذِي حَرَّرَ التَّقْوَىٰ
مُصَاحَبَةُ الاَخْيَارِ فِي الْجَلْبِ وَالدَّفْعِ

My first counsel for those dedicated to Taqwa
is to accompany the best in attracting and repulsing.

فَهَذَا أَسَاسُ الْخَيْرِ إِنْ كُنْتَ عَاقِلًا

فَعَوِّلْ عَلَيْهِ مَعْ مُرَاعَاةٍ لِلشَّرْعِ

For this is the basis of all good if you are intelligent;
so rely on it, along with being mindful of the Shari'a.

وَكُلُّ الَّذِي قَدْ نَالَ عِلْمًا وَسُؤْدَدَا

فَمَا نَالَهُ إِلَّا بِصُحْبَةِ خَاشِعِ

All those who have obtained knowledge and mastery
have only obtained them by accompanying a humble man.

وَأَعْنِي بِهِ الشَّيْخَ الَّذِي فَاضَ نُورُه

وَجَاءَ بِأَسْرَارٍ وَخَيْرٍ مُتَابِعِ

By him I mean the Shaykh whose light has overflowed,
and who has brought secrets and uninterrupted good with him.

فَإِنْ شِئْتَ أَنْوَارًا وَفَتْحَ بَصِيرَةٍ

فَقَلِّدْهُ تَعْظِيمًا وَعُجْ عَنْ مُنَازِعِ

If you desire lights and the opening of inner sight,
then copy him in exalting Allah and turn from people of conflict.

وَوَاظِبْ عَلَى الذِّكْرِ الْمُلَقَّنِ بِالْإِذْنِ

وَلَا تَغْفُلَنْ فِي حَالَةِ الضِّيقِ وَالْوُسْعِ

And persevere in the dhikr taught through Idhn
and neglect it neither in constriction nor expansion.

وَزِنْ وَارِدَاتِ الذِّكْرِ بِالشَّرْعِ حَاكِيًا

لِشَيْخِكَ كُلَّ مَا أَتَاكَ وَسَارِعِ

Weigh the luminous openings of the dhikr with the Shari'a,
telling your Shaykh quickly all that happens to you.

فَسَلْبُ اخْتِيَارٍ ثُمَّ كُلِّ إِرَادَةٍ

هُوَ الْمَوْرِدُ الْاَصْفَىٰ فَهَلْ أَنْتَ سَامِعِ

So the negation of choice, and then all will,
is the purest of springs, if you are able to hear.

وَهَاكَ مَقَامَاتِ الْيَقِينِ فَبَادِرَنْ

بِتَوْبَةِ زُهْدٍ ثُمَّ خَوْفٍ بِوَازِعِ

These are the Stations of Certainty – hasten to tawba,
doing-without, and then fear which brings restraint.

رَجَاءٍ وَشُكْرٍ ثُمَّ صَبْرٍ تَوَكُّلٍ

كَذَاكَ الرِّضَىٰ وَالْحُبُّ لِلْكُلِّ جَامِعِ

Hope, gratitude, then patience and putting your trust in Allah,
similarly contentment, and love unites them all.

وَأَسْبَابُهُ الْفِكْرُ الصَّفِيُّ فِي نِعْمَةٍ

وَحُسْنِ صِفَاتٍ ثُمَّ فِي النُّورِ اللَّامِعِ

Its causes are the pure contemplation of blessing and of
the perfection of the Attributes, then of the dazzling light.

وَأَعْنِي بِهِ ذَاكَ الرَّسُولَ مُحَمَّدًا

عَلَيْهِ صَلَاةٌ عَدَّ وِتْرٍ مَعَ الشَّفْعِ

By it, I mean that Messenger Muhammad,
may blessings be upon him in quantity as great as all that is even or odd,

وَءَالِهِ وَالْاَصْحَابِ مَعْ كُلِّ عَارِفٍ

دَعَا لِطَرِيقِ اللهِ فِي كُلِّ مَجْمَعِ ۞

And on his family and Companions and every gnostic,
calling to the path of Allah in every assembly.

# Annihilation in Allah

وتليه هائية

الفناء في الله

يَا طَالِبَ الْفَنَا فِي اللهْ

قُلْ دَائِمًا اَللهْ اَللهْ

O seeker of annihilation in Allah,
say constantly, 'Allah! Allah!'

وَغِبْ فِيهِ عَنْ سِوَاهْ

وَاشْهَدْ بِقَلْبِكَ اَللهْ

And withdraw into Him from other-than-Him,
and with your heart – witness Allah.

وَاجْمَعْ هُمُومَكَ فِيهِ

تُكْفَىٰ بِهِ عَنْ غَيْرِ اللهْ

Gather your concerns in Him and He will be
enough in place of other-than-Allah.

وَكُنْ عَبْدًا صِرْفًا لَهُ

تَكُنْ حُرًّا عَنْ غَيْرِ اللهْ

Be a pure slave to Him and
you will be free from other-than-Allah.

وَاخْضَعْ لَهُ وَتَذَلَّلْ

تَفُزْ بِسِرٍّ مِنَ اللهْ

Submit to Him and humble yourself
and you will win a secret from Allah.

وَاذْكُرْ بِجِدٍّ وَصِدْقٍ

بَيْنَ يَدَيْ عَبِيدِ اللهْ

Do dhikr with intensity and sincerity in the
presence of the slaves of Allah.

وَاكْتُمْ إِذَا تَجَلَّى لَكْ

بِأَنْوَارٍ مِنْ ذَاتِ اللهْ

Conceal it when He manifests Himself to you
with lights from the Essence of Allah.

فَالْغَيْرُ عِنْدَنَا مُحَالْ

فَالْوُجُودُ الْحَقُّ لِلَّهْ

With us, other is impossible,
for true existence belongs to Allah.

183

وَوَهْمَكَ اقْطَعْ دَائِمًا

بِتَوْحِيدٍ صِرْفٍ لِلَّه

Constantly cut through your illusion
with a Tawhid that is purely for Allah.

فَوَحْدَةُ الْفِعْلِ تَبْدُو

فِي أَوَّلِ الذِّكْرِ لِلَّه

The oneness of action appears
at the beginning of dhikr of Allah.

وَوَحْدَةُ الْوَصْفِ لَه

تَأتِي مِنَ الْحُبِّ فِي الله

And the oneness of His attributes
comes from love for the sake of Allah.

وَوَحْدَةُ الذَّاتِ لَه

تُورِّثُ الْبَقَا بِالله

And the oneness of His Essence
gives going-on by Allah.

فَهَنِيئًا لِمَنْ مَشَى

فِي طَرِيقِ الذِّكْرِ لِلَّه

Joy to the one who walks
on the path of dhikr for the sake of Allah,

مُعْتَقِدًا شَيْخًا حَيًّا

يَكُونُ عَارِفًا بِاللهْ

believing in a living Shaykh
who is a gnostic of Allah.

وَلَازَمَ الْحُبَّ لَهُ

وَبَـاعَ نَفْسَهُ لِلَّهْ

He holds constantly to His love
and sells his self to Allah.

وَقَـامَ فِي اللَّيْلِ يَتْلُو

كَلَامَهُ شَوْقًا لِلَّهْ

He rises in the night to recite His word,
longing for Allah.

فَنَـالَ مَا يَطْلُبُه

مِنْ قُوَّةِ الْعِلْمِ بِاللهْ

He gets what he seeks of the power
of knowledge of Allah.

وَفَيْضُنَـا مِنْ نَبِيّ

سَيِّدُ مَخْلُوقَاتِ اللهْ

Our gifts are from a Prophet who is the
master of the creatures of Allah.

عَلَيْهِ أَزْكَىٰ صَلَاةٍ

عَدَدَ مَعْلُومَاتِ اللّٰهِ

May the purest of blessings be upon him
in quantity as great as the things known to Allah.

وَءَالِهِ وَصَحْبِهِ

وَكُلِّ دَاعٍ إِلَى اللّٰهِ ۞

And his family and Companions,
And everyone who calls to Allah.

# Withdrawal from Other Than Allah

وتليه هائية

الغيبة عما سوى الله

رُوحِي تُحَدِّثُنِي بِأَنَّ حَقِيقَتِي

نُورُ الاِلَهِ فَلَا تَرَىٰ إِلَّاهُ

My spirit tells me, "My reality is the light of Allah,
so see no one but Him."

لَوْ لَمْ أَكُنْ نُورًا لَكُنْتُ سِوَاءَهُ

إِنَّ السِّوَا عَدَمٌ فَلَا تَرْضَاهُ

If I were not a light I would be other-than-Him.
Indeed otherness is nothingness, so do not be content with it.

وَإِذَا نَظَرْتَ بِعَيْنِ سِرِّكَ لَمْ تَجِدْ

غَيْرَ الاِلَهِ فِي أَرْضِهِ وَسَمَاهُ

If you look with the eye of your Secret you will not find
a trace of other-than-Allah in either His earth or His heaven.

لَكِنْ تَوَهُّمُ غَيْرِهِ يُخْفِىٰ بِهِ

فَانْبُذْ هَوَاكَ إِذَا أَرَدْتَ تَرَاهُ

But the illusion of other-than-Him hides Him.
So combat your desires if you wish to see Him.

وَارْكَبْ سَفِينَةَ سُنَّةٍ تَنْجُو بِهَـا

وَاسْلُكْ سَبِيلَ رَئِيسِهَا فِي هَوَاهُ

Board the ship of the Sunna and you will be rescued by it,
and travel the path of its captain in his love.

وَصِلِ الشَّرَابَ بِكَأْسِهَا وَافْنَىٰ بِهِ

تَحُزِ الْبَقَـاءَ بِسِرِّهِ وَعُلَاهُ

Unite the wine with the goblet and be annihilated by it,
and you will obtain going-on by His secret and sublimity.

وَاشْهَدْ بِعَيْنِ بَصِيرَةٍ تَوْحِيدَهُ

وَالْفَرْقُ شِرْعَتُهُ فَلَا تَنْسَـاهُ

See His Tawhid with the eye of inner sight,
but separation is His Shari‘a so do not forget it!

وَاجْعَلْ هُمُومَكَ وَاحِدًا تُكْفَىٰ بِهِ

كُلَّ الْهُمُومِ وَتَدْخُلَنْ فِي حِمَـاهُ

Make your concerns one, and by Him all your needs
will be met, and you will enter into His protection.

وَانْزِلْ أُمُورَكَ بِالَّذِي أَدْرَىٰ بِهَا

فَهُوَ الْخَبِيرُ بِقَلْبِنَا وَمُنَاهُ

Hand over your affairs to the One Who knows them best,
for He is the Aware Who knows our hearts and their desires.

يَـا رَبِّ صَلِّ عَلَى النَّبِيِّ مُحَمَّدٍ

سِرِّ الْوُجُودِ وَأَصْلِهِ وَسَنَاهُ ﴿﴾

O Lord, bless the Prophet Muhammad,
the secret of existence and its source and splendour.

# Manifestation of the Essence

وتليه هائية

التجلي

أَشَمْسٌ بَدَا مِنْ عَالَمِ الْغَيْبِ ضَوْؤُهَا

أَمِ انْكَشَفَتْ عَنْ ذَاتِ لَيْلَىٰ سُتُورُهَا

Has the light of the sun appeared from the world of the Unseen,
or have the veils of Layla been lifted from Her essence?

نَعَمْ تِلْكَ لَيْلَىٰ قَدْ أَبَاحَتْ بِحُبِّهَا

لِخِلٍّ لَهَا لَمَّا تَزَايَدَ شَوْقُهَا

Yes, Layla revealed Her love
for Her intimate friend when Her longing grew.

فَأَضْحَىٰ أَسِيرًا فِي مُرَادِ غَرَامِهَا

وَنَادَتْ لَهُ الاشْوَاقُ هَذِي كُؤُوسُهَا

He became a captive of Her ardent desire
and the longings which are Her goblets called out to him.

فَمَا بَرِحَتْ حَتَّى سَقَتْهُ بِكَأْسِهَا

فَلَا لَوْمَ فَاشْرَبْ فَالشَّرَابُ حَدِيثُهَا

She did not leave until She had given him a drink from Her goblet.
There is no blame. Drink – for the wine is Her speech.

وَمَا هِيَ إِلَّا حَضْرَةُ الْحَقِّ وَحْدَهَا

تَجَلَّتْ بِأَشْكَالٍ تَلَوَّنَ نُورُهَا

She is none but the Presence of the Truth alone,
Who manifests Herself with forms whose every light is different.

فَأَبْدَتْ بَدِيعَ الصُّنْعِ فِي طَيِّ كَوْنِهَا

فَلَاحِظْ صِفَاتِ الْحِبِّ فِيكَ ظُهُورُهَا

In folding up Her cosmos, She showed the Originator of the design,
so look how the Attributes of the Beloved are manifest within you.

فَوَاللهِ مَا حَازَ السَّعَادَةَ كُلَّهَا

سِوَى مَنْ بَدَا عَبْدًا ذَلِيلًا يَؤُمُّهَا

By Allah, no one ever obtains complete bliss
except one who becomes a humble slave and seeks Her out.

فَغَطَّتْ قَبِيحَ الْوَصْفِ مِنْهُ بِوَصْفِهَا

وَلَاحَتْ لَهُ الْأَنْوَارُ يَبْدُو شُعَاعُهَا

She covered the ugliness of his attributes with the beauty of Hers,
and lights shone from him, their rays appearing.

فَغَابَ عَنِ الْحِسِّ الَّذِي كَانَ قَاطِعًا
وَعَانَقَ مَعْنًى لَا يَحِلُّ فِرَاقُهَا

He withdrew from the sensory which is a barrier
and embraced a meaning from which it is unlawful to be separated.

لِخُرِّرْ أَخِي قَصْدًا وَأَعْرِضْ عَنِ السِّوَى
يَهُبُّ عَلَى الْأَحْبَابِ مِنْكَ نَسِيمُهَا

Let your goal be to commit yourself, brother, and avoid otherness,
and Her breeze will waft over the lovers from you.

وَتَفْتَحُ سَمْعًا لِلْفُؤَادِ مِنْ سَالِكٍ
لِأَنَّ لَطِيفَ الْعِلْمِ مِنْهَا دَلِيلُهَا

You will open the hearing of the wayfarer's heart because
the all-pervading nature of the knowledge from Her is proof of Her.

فَمُنَّ عَلَيْنَا دَائِمًا بِوِصَالِهَا
وَغَيِّبْنَا عَنْ حِسِّ الْمَوْجُودَاتِ كُلِّهَا ۞

Bestow on us always the blessing of union with Her
and make us withdraw from every existent thing.

# Purification

وتليها واوية

التطهير

فَإِنْ شِئْتَ تَطْهِيرًا مِنَ الشِّرْكِ وَالدَّعْوَىٰ
وَتَشْرَبَ مِنْ تَسْنِيمٍ وَصْلٍ حَتَّىٰ تَرْوَىٰ

If you wish purification from shirk and the claim that you exist,
and to drink from the nectar of union until you are quenched –

فَمَنْطِقْ بِصَبْرٍ ثُمَّ عِمِّمْ بِتَوْبَةٍ
وَلَازِمْ قَمِيصَ الزُّهْدِ وَابْذُلْ فِيهِ قُوَىٰ

– then wrap yourself in patience and wind on the turban of Tawba.
Wear the shirt of doing-without and in it exhaust your strength.

وَلَا بُدَّ مِنْ نَعْلَيْنِ خَوْفٍ مَعَ الرَّجَىٰ
وَعُكَّازِ إِيقَانٍ وَزَادٍ مِنَ التَّقْوَىٰ

The twin sandals of fear and hope are indispensable.
Take the staff of certainty and a store of Taqwa.

وَقَائِدُ عِلْمٍ مَعْ مَطِيَّةِ هِمَّةٍ
وَصُحْبَةِ حِفْظٍ لِلْجَوَارِحِ مِنْ بَلْوَى

Take the bridle of knowledge for the horse of Himma, and the
protection of companions who will guard the limbs from trials.

بُجِدَّ وَأَسْرِعْ فِي الْمَسِيرِ وَلَا تَقِفْ
بِفِكْرٍ عَلَى كَوْنٍ فَتُحْجَبَ عَنْ مَأْوَى

Struggle seriously and travel quickly on the journey.
Do not stop to think about the universe, and so be barred from refuge.

وَفِكْرٍ فِي إِحْسَانٍ وَأَخْلِصْ فِي شُكْرِهِ
وَقُمْ سَحَرًا وَاخْضَعْ وَبُثَّ لَهُ الشَّكْوَى

Rather reflect on Ihsan and be sincere in gratitude to Him,
and get up before dawn, submit, and hand over your complaint to Him.

وَصَلِّ عَلَى قُطْبِ الْوُجُودِ وَحِزْبِهِ
صَلَاةً تَعُمُّ السِّرَّ مِنَّا مَعَ النَّجْوَى ۞

Bless the Qutb of existence and his group with a blessing
that will spread the Secret from us.

# Counsel on Death

نصيحة

للشيخ سيدي محمد ابن الحبيب

تَزَوَّدْ أَخِي لِلْمَوْتِ إِنَّهُ نَـازِلُ

وَلَا تُطِلِ الآمَـالَ يَقْسُوا لَكَ الْقَلْبُ

Prepare yourself for death, O my brother, for it will descend.
Do not draw out your hopes, in case your heart becomes hard.

وَوَاظِبْ عَلَى الْفِكْرِ الْمُعِينِ عَلَى الْجِدِّ

وَسَـارِعْ إِلَى الاَعْمَـالِ فَالْعُمْرُ يَذْهَبُ

Persevere in reflection which will make you aware
and move you to do good works, for life will soon depart.

وَفَكِّرْ فِي أَحْوَالِ الْقِيَـامَة دَائِمًـا

كَبَعْثٍ وَنَشْرٍ وَالْمَوازِينُ تُنصَبُ

Constantly reflect on the states of the Last Hour, the Rising,
the Gathering and the Balance of actions which is set up.

وَكَالصِّرَاطِ الَّذِي لَهُ عَقَبَاتُهُ
تَطُولُ عَلَى الْعَاصِي وَمَشيهِ يَصْعُبُ

Then there is the Bridge which has its steep and difficult ascents;
it will be lengthy for the disobedient and walking on it will be hard,

وَمَنْ كَانَ طَائِعًا وَلِلَّهِ مُخْلِصًا
يَمُرُّ كَبَرْقٍ أَوْ كَرِيحٍ فَيَذْهَبُ

while whoever was obedient and sincere towards Allah
will pass over it like lightning or a wind and will go on.

وَإِنْ شِئْتَ أَنْ تُسْقَى مِنَ الْحَوْضِ فِي الْحَشْرِ
فَلَازِمْ حُبَّ النَّبِي وَمَنْ لَهُ يَنْسَبُ

If you wish to be given a drink from the Basin on the Day of Gathering,
you must love the Prophet and his descendants.

وَصَلِّ عَلَى الْهَادِي الْمُشَفَّع فِي الْوَرَى
فَهُوَ الَّذِي لَهَا إِذَا الْخَلْقُ يَرْهَبُ

And bless the Guide whose intercession for mankind is accepted,
for he is the one who intercedes when people are terrified.

عَلَيْهِ صَلَاةُ اللهِ فِي كُلِّ مَوْطِنٍ
وَءَالٍ وَأَصْحَابٍ وَمَنْ يَتَحَبَّبُ

May the blessings of Allah be upon him in every land,
and on his family and Companions and those who show love for him.

وَأَسْأَلُ رَبِّ اللهَ نَيْلَ سَعَـادَةٍ

لِي وَلِلْأَحْبَابِ وَمَنْ يَتَقَرَّبُ ﴿۝﴾

I ask my Lord, Allah, for the gift of true happiness
for me and the beloved ones and those who draw near.

# Another Song

وله أيضا

رضي الله عنه

أَهِيمُ وَحْدِي بِذِكْرِ رَبِّي
فَذِكْرُ رَبِّي هُوَ الشِّفَاءُ

I am ecstatic, alone, in the dhikr of my Lord,
for the dhikr of my Lord – it is the cure.

أَحْبَبْتُ رَبًّا هُوَ اعْتِمَادِي
لِكُلِّ شَيْءٍ هُوَ يَشَاءُ

I have loved a Lord – on Whom I rely;
in each single thing – it is He Who wills it.

وَكُلُّ حُبٍّ لِغَيْرِ رَبِّي
فِيهِ الْعَذَابُ فِيهِ الشَّقَاءُ

In every love for other than my Lord
there is torment and grief.

يَـا فَوْزَ فَانٍ عَنِ الْفَنَـاءِ

لَهُ الْحَيَـاةُ لَهُ الْبَقَـاءُ

Oh the victory of the one annihilated to annihilation,
he will have life and going on.

يَـا رَبِّ صَلِّ عَلَىٰ مُحَمَّدْ

مِنْ ذَاتِهِ النُّورُ وَالضِّيَـاءُ

O my Lord, bless Muhammad.
From his essence there is light and radiance.

وَءَالِهِ وَالصَّحْبِ الْكِرَامِ

لَهُمْ عُهُودٌ لَهُمْ وَفَـاءُ ۝

And bless his family and noble Companions.
They have covenants; they fulfil them.

# Song on Departure

قصيدة تذكر عند ختام
كل جلسة من جلسات الفقراء

كَمْ لَكَ مِنْ نِعْمَةٍ عَلَيَّ
وَلَمْ تَزَلْ مُحْسِنًا إِلَيَّ

How many blessings You grant me
and You are continually good to me.

غَدَّيْتَنِي فِي الْحَشَا جَنِينًا
وَكُنْتَ لِي قَبْلَ وَالِدَيَّ

You fed me as an embryo in the womb
and You were mine before my parents.

خَلَقْتَنِي مُسْلِمًا وَلَوْ لَا
فَضْلُكَ لَمْ أَعْرِفِ النَّبِيَّ

You created me Muslim and had it not been for Your gift,
I would not have known the Prophet.

أَسْجُدُ حَقًّا عَلَىٰ جَبِينِي

نَعَمْ وَخَدَّيْ وَنَاظِرَيَّا

In truth I prostrate on my forehead –
yes, and on my cheeks and eyes.

يَا رَبِّ صَلِّ عَلَى النَّبِيِّ

مَا تُلِيَتْ سُورَةُ الْمَثَانِي

O Lord, bless the Prophet
as long as the Surat al-Mathani is recited.

وَءَالِهِ وَالصَّحَابِ طُرًّا

مَا رَبِحَ النَّاسُ بِالإِيمَانِ

And his family and all the Companions,
as long as people profit by Iman.

وَأَطْلُبُ الْحَقَّ فِي السَّعَادَهْ

لِكُلِّ مَنْ ضَمَّهُ زَمَانِي ۞

I ask of the Real good fortune
for all whom my age comprises.

# The Final Song

وهذا ما دَعَت الحاجَةُ لذكْرِه،

وأمّا الأَمْداحُ في جَنابِ هذا الهَيْكل الصَّمَدانى العَلَّامَة الرَّبّاني

فلا تُعَدُّ ولا تُحْصَى كَثْرَة اه

سَلَامٌ عَلَىٰ أَهْلِ الْحِمَىٰ حَيْثُمَـا حَلُّوا
هَنِيئًا لَهُمْ يَـا حَبَّذَا مَـا بِهِ حَلُّوا

Peace be upon the People of the sanctuary wherever they alight.
May they enjoy it! How excellent the place where they stay.

لَهُمْ أَظْهَرَ الْمَوْلَىٰ شُمُوسَ بَهَـائِه
فَيَـا لَيْتَ خَدِّي فِي التُّرَابِ لَهُمْ نَعْلُ

For them, the Lord has manifested the suns of His splendour.
Would that my cheek were a sandal for them in the dust!

مَتَىٰ يَـا عُرَيْبَ الْحَيِّ يَاتِي بَشِيرُكُمْ
فَتَبْتَهِجَ الدُّنْيَـا وَيَجْتَمِعَ الشَّمْلُ

When, dear brothers, will the herald bring good news of you
so that the world can celebrate and be reunited?

202

صِلُونِي عَلَى مَا بِي فَإِنِّي لِوَصْلِكُمْ

إِذَا لَمْ أَكُنْ أَهْلًا فَأَنْتُمْ لَهُ أَهْلُ

Make our bond of love close in spite of what is inside me,
for if I do not deserve it, you are worthy of it.

سَلَامٌ عَلَيْكُمْ شَرَّفَ اللهُ قَدْرَكُمْ

وَدَامَتْ عَلَيْكُمْ نِعْمَةٌ وَسُرُورُهَا

Peace be upon you, may Allah exalt your rank,
and may the joy of blessings be upon you always.

فَمَا طَابَتِ الأَيَّامُ إِلَّا بِذِكْرِكُمْ

فَأَنْتُمْ ضِيَاءُ الْعَيْنِ حَقًّا وَنُورُهَا

The days are joyless without your dhikr,
for truly you are the illumination of the eye and its light.

إِذَا نَظَرَتْ عَيْنِي وُجُوهَ أَحِبَّتِي

فَتِلْكَ صَلَاتِي فِي اللَّيَالِي الرَّغَائِبِ

When my eye looks on the faces of my beloved friends
that is my prayer during the longed-for nights.

وُجُوهٌ إِذَا مَا أَسْفَرَتْ عَنْ جَمَالِهَا

أَضَاءَتْ لَهَا الأَكْوَانُ مِنْ كُلِّ جَانِبٍ ۞

They are such faces that when they shine, from their beauty
they light up the whole world.

# Takhmis
# Commentaries on Qasidas

# The Takhmis on
# 'The Qualities of Muhammad'

by the Perfect Gnostic Teaching Shaykh of the Tariqa,

Shaykh Muhammad ibn al-Habib

تخميس للقصيدة المحمدية للشيخ العارف المربي الكامل

شيخ الطريقة الحبيبية سيدي محمد بن الحبيب

إِنْ شِئْتَ نَيْلَ الْمُنَى وَالسُّولِ وَالامَلِ

فَانْشِدْ مَدَائِحَ نُورِ الْعَقْلِ وَالْمُقَلِ

مَلَاذُ هَذَا الْوَرَى آتٍ وَمُنْتَقِلِ

مُحَمَّدٌ مَنْشَأُ الانْوَارِ وَالظِّلَلِ

وَأَصْلُ تَكْوِينِهَا مِنْ حَضْرَةِ الازَلِ

If you desire your wishes to be granted,
your prayers and hopes to be answered,
then sing the praises of the light of the intellect and eyes,
the refuge of mankind, future and past.
*Muhammad is the fountain-head of lights and darkness and
the source of their emergence from the presence of before-time.*

قَدْ كَانَ رَبُّ الْوَرَىٰ فِي الْكَوْنِ قَبْلُ قَضَا

ءِ الْكَائِنَاتِ وَحِيداً ثُمَّ بَعْدُ اقْتَضَىٰ

خَلْقًا لِقَبْضَةِ نُورِ الْمُصْطَفَى الْمُرْتَضَىٰ

فَنُورُهُ أَوَّلُ الأَنْوَارِ لَمَّا قَضَى

إِظْهَارَ أَسْمَائِهِ فِي الْعَالَمِ الأَوَّلِ

The Lord of mankind was alone in Being
before He determined beings.
Then He decreed an outer form
for the 'handful of light', for the Approved Chosen one –
*His light was the first of lights when He determined*
*the manifestation of His Names in the first world.*

كَـانَتْ جَمِيعُ الْوَرَىٰ مِنْ قَبْلِ إِبْرَازِهَا

فِي ظُلْمَةِ الْعُدْمِ تَشْتَكِي لِخَـالِقِهَـا

فَأَشْرَقَتْ مِنْ ظَلَامِ الْعُدْمِ أَنْوَارُهَـا

مِنْهُ اكْتَسَتْ سَائِرُ الأَشْيَاءِ إِيجَادَهَا

وَمِنْهُ إِمْدَادُهَا مِنْ غَيْرِ مَا خَلَلِ

Before being caused to emerge, all mankind
were in the darkness of nothingness, complaining to their Creator.
Then their lights arose
shining from the darkness of the void –
*From him all things were clothed in their origination in existence,*
*and their continuance comes from him without interruption.*

هُوَ الْمَلْجَأُ الَّذِي لَهُ الْوُجُودُ انْتَمَى

هُوَ الْمَلَاذُ غَدًا بِهِ الْجَمِيعُ احْتَمَى

مِنْهُ الْوُجُودُ بَدَا مِنْ أَرْضِنَا وَسَمَا

تَقَاطَرَ الأَنْبِيَا وَالرُّسْلُ مِنْهُ كَمَا

قَاطَرَتْ سَائِرُ الأَمْلَاكِ وَالْحُلَلَ

He is the shelter upon which existence depends,
and he is the refuge to which all come
tomorrow to seek for protection. From him
existence in our earth and heaven appeared –
*The Prophets and Messengers have come from him one by one,*
*as well as all the angels and all the creatures.*

قَدِ اصْطَفَاهُ إِلَهُ الْعَرْشِ مِنْ خَلْقِهِ

هَلْ يُرَى أَحَدٌ يَحْظَى بِمَنْصِبِهِ

فَالْخَتْمُ وَالْقُطْبُ وَالأَفْرَادُ مِنْ جُودِهِ

فَنِسْبَتُ الْخَتْمِ وَالأَقْطَابِ مِنْ نُورِهِ

كَقُطْطَةٍ مِنْ بُحُورِ النُّورِ وَالْبَلَلِ

The Lord of the Throne chose him from His creation.
Is any to be seen who has obtained his rank?
The Seal, the Pole, and the unique ones
come from his munificent generosity –
*The relationship of the Seal and the Poles to his light*
*is that of a drop to oceans of light and refreshment.*

209

ذَاتُ الْعُلُومِ لَهُ مِنْ بَحْرِهِ طُلِبَتْ

مِنْهُ تَفَتَّقَتِ الْعِرْفَانُ وَانْسَحَبَتْ

غَيْمُ الْجَهَالَةِ حِينَ شَمْسُهُ طَلَعَتْ

وَالشَّمْسُ وَالْبَدْرُ وَالنُّجُومُ مِنْهُ بَدَتْ

كَالْعَرْشِ وَاللَّوْحِ وَالْكُرْسِيِّ وَالدُّوَلِ

The essence of knowledge is his and is sought from his sea:
from him gnosis emerged and been brought to light.
When his sun rises
the mists of ignorance melt away –
*The sun, moon and stars have appeared from him,*
*as have the Throne, Tablet, Footstool, and the dynasties.*

لَاحَتْ شَوَاهِدُ هَذَا النُّورِ مِنْهُ عَلَى

طَوَالِعِ الْكَوْنِ مِمَّا قَدْ دَنَا وَعَلَا

يَطْوِي الطَّرِيقَ لِعَيْنِ الْحَقِّ مُنْتَقِلاً

فَشَاهِدِ النُّورَ قَدْ عَمَّ الْوُجُودَ وَلَا

تَكُنْ تَرَى غَيْرَهُ تَصِلْ عَلَى عَجَلِ

The evidences of this light appear from him
glimmering over the ascendant stars of the cosmos,
both low and high. It folds up the Path
that goes to the fount of the Real –
*Witness the light which has spread through existence*
*and do not see other-than-it, and you will soon arrive.*

هُوَ الدَّلِيلُ دَلِيلُ اللهِ مِنْ خَلْقِهِ

هُوَ الْحِجَابُ الْعَظِيمُ الْقَدْرِ مِنْ بَابِهِ

يَرْقَى الْمُرِيدُ مِنَ الْوَرَى لِحَضْرَتِهِ

لِأَنَّهُ الْمَظْهَرُ الأَعْلَى لِأَسْمَائِهِ

وَسِرُّ أَوْصَافِهِ مِنْ غَيْرِ مَا عِلَلِ

He is the proof: the proof of Allah from His creation.
He is the immense veil of might and power
from whose door the murid
ascends from mankind to His presence –
*For he is the highest manifestation of Allah's Names*
*and the perfect unfaulted secret of His Attributes.*

عَمَّتْ رِسَالَتُهُ فِي الْعُرْبِ وَالْعَجَمِ

وَالرُّسْلُ نَائِبَةٌ عَنْهُ عَلَى الأُمَمِ

بَدَتْ فَضَائِلُهُ وَالْخَلْقُ فِي الْعَدَمِ

فَاللهُ إِخْتَارَهُ فِي عِلْمِهِ الْقَدَمِ

لِلْخَلْقِ أَرْسَلَهُ طُرًّا وَلِلرُّسُلِ

His message embraces Arabs and non-Arabs.
The Messengers were delegates
from and to different nations. His qualities appeared
when creation still was in the void –
*Allah chose him in His Timeless knowledge*
*and sent him to all of creation and to the other Messengers.*

لَا زَالَ مُنْتَقِلاً ذَخْرًا لِأُمَّتِهِ

فِي الطَّيِّبِينَ مِنْ الاَصْلاَبِ ءَابَائِهِ

حَتَّى إِذَا أُسْعِدَ الْوَرَىٰ بِبِعْثَتِهِ

أَسْرَى بِهِ اللَّهُ لَيْلاً بَعْدَ مَبْعَثِهِ

لِقَابِ قَوْسَيْنِ حَتَّى فَازَ بِالاَمَلِ

He was constantly moving,
a treasure stored-up for his community
in the loins of his noble ancestor
until mankind rejoiced in his selection –
*After sending him as a Messenger, Allah conveyed him one night*
*to the distance of two bow-spans until he achieved his desire.*

أَسْمَاهُ رَبُّهُ عَلَىٰ كُلِّ الْوَرَىٰ فَارْتَقَى

إِلَىٰ السَّمَاوَاتِ بِالاَمِينِ مُرْتَفِقًا

فَاسْتَنْشَقَ الْمَلَكُوتُ الطَّيِّبَ إِذْ عَبِقَا

وَاسْتَبْشَرَ الْعَالَمُ الْعُلْوِيُّ لَمَّا رَقَى

وَالْعَرْشُ قَدْ حَصَّلَ الاَمَانَ مِنْ خَجَلِ

His Lord nominated him above all mankind
so he ascended to the heavens accompanied by the trusty (Jibril.
So the malakut inhaled sweet scents
when it was exhaled – and
*The higher world rejoiced when he ascended,*
*and the Throne gave him security from fear.*

لَا زَالَ يَسْمُو إِلَىٰ أَنْ نَالَ أَعْلَا مُنَىٰ

وَنِيلَ مِنْهُ الْمُنَىٰ وَبُشِّرَتْ بِالْهَنَا

أُهِيْلَ ذَاكَ الْفَنَا وَلَاحَ مِنْهُ السَّنَا

وَاخْتَرَقَ الْحُجُبَ وَالْأَنْوَارَ حَتَّى دَنَا

وَنُودِيَ ادْنُ حَبِيبِي وَاسْكُنْ مِنْ خَجَل

He continued to ascend until he attained the highest of desires,
and through him desires were realised
and the good news of congratulation was announced.
That annihilation poured forth and radiance shone from him –
*He passed through the veils and lights until he drew near,*
*and he was summoned, 'Draw near, Beloved, and set aside your shyness.'*

يَا خَيْرَ مَنْ حَلَّ بِالْأُفْقِ الْمُبِينِ وَمَنْ

يَحْظَىٰ بِرُؤْيَتِنَا دُونَ الْوَرَىٰ فَاشْكُرَنْ

وَاسْكُنْ فُؤَادًا وَطِبْ نَفْسًا وَلَا تَجْزَعَنْ

وَمَتِّعِ اللَّحْظَ فِي أَنْوَارِنَا وَاطْلُبَنْ

كُلَّ الَّذِي شِئْتَهُ تُعْطَ بِلَا مَلَل

'How excellent is he who alights at the clear horizon.
He is favoured with the vision of Us, beyond mankind!
So give thanks and still your heart,
be happy and joyful, and do not grieve –
*'Rejoice in the sight of Our lights and demand all you want*
*and it will be given to you without delay.'*

وَسَلْ مَا شِئْتَ تَفُزْ بِكُلِّ مَسْئَلَةٍ

فَنَالَ أَقْصَى الْمُنَى وَكُلَّ مَنْقَبَةٍ

سَمَتْ بِأُمَّتِهِ عَنْ كُلِّ مَا أُمَّةٍ

فَأُرْجِعَ الْمُصْطَفَى بِكُلِّ مَكْرُمَةٍ

وَأَخْبَرَ النَّاسَ بِالْأَقْصَى وَبِالسُّبُلِ

'Ask for whatever you want,
you will receive every request.'
So he achieved the ultimate desires and every attainment,
He raised his community above all communities.
*Then the Chosen One was returned with every noble quality*
*and he informed the people about al-Aqsa and the roads to it.*

بَحْرُ الْفَضَائِلِ مِنْ عِلْمٍ وَمَعْرِفَةٍ

كَهْفُ الضِّعَافِ مَلَاذُ كُلِّ ذَائِبَةٍ

مَنْ أَمَّ سَاحَتَهُ حَاشَاهُ مِنْ خَيْبَةٍ

فَلُذْ بِهِ يَا أَخِي فِي كُلِّ مُعْضَلَةٍ

يَضْحَى حَدِيثُكَ بَيْنَ النَّاسِ كَالْعَسَلِ

He is the sea of virtues in knowledge and gnosis.
He is the cave of the weak, the refuge of every one of the elect.
Whoever is gathered in his courtyard
is far from disappointment.
*Take refuge with him in every dilemma, O my brother,*
*and your speech among the people will become like honey.*

وَاسْبَحْ بِفِكْرِكَ فِي بَحْرِ النَّدَىٰ الْعِمَمِ

تُلْقِ الْمُنَىٰ فَوْقَ مَا تَرْجُو مِنَ الْكَرَمِ

كَذَاكَ هِمَّته أَرْبَتْ عَلَىٰ الْهِمَمِ

وَلَذِّذ السَّمْعَ بِالْأَخْلَاقِ وَالشِّيَمِ

وَاذْكُرْ شَمَائِلَهُ وَاحْذَرْ مِنَ الزَّلَلِ

Swim with your contemplation in the sea
of his pervading dew of generosity,
you will discover blessings of giving beyond your wildest hopes.
In the same way his himma increases the himma of others –
*Delight in hearing of his good character and qualities,*
*and evoke his virtues, and remain on guard against mistakes.*

أَعْيَى الْوَرَىٰ فَهْمُ مَعْنَىٰ بَعْضِ مَنْصِبِهِ

حَدِّثْ عَنِ الْبَحْرِ هَلْ تَأْتِي بِإِحْصَائِهِ

وَاقْنَعْ بِمَا طِقْتَ مِنْ مَكْنُونِ جَوْهَرِهِ

فَكَمْ خَوَارِقَ قَدْ جَاءَتْ عَلَى يَدِهِ

فَأَعْجَزَتْ سَائِرَ الْحُسَّادِ وَالْمِلَلِ

The attempt to understand the meaning
of a part of his place exhausts mankind.
Better to speak of the ocean – can you encompass it?
Be content then with what you can for his essence is hidden –
*How many miracles have come from his hand,*
*leaving the envious and all other religions powerless!*

215

قَدْ حَنَّ جِذْعٌ لَهُ كَذَا دَعَا الشَّجَرَا

فَأَقْبَلَتْ وَأَرَتْ مِنْ مَشْيِهَا أَثَرَا

بَيْنَ الاَصَابِع عَذْبُ الْمَاءِ مِنْهُ جَرَى

وَإِنَّ أَعْظَمَ خَارِقٍ لَهُ ظَهَرَا

هَذَا الْكِتَابُ الَّذِي قَدْ جَاءَ بِالْعَمَل

The very tree trunks yearned for him,
and he called the trees, so they approached
and traces of their movement were seen,
and sweet water sprang from between his fingers –
*The greatest of the miracles which were manifested for him*
*is this Book which brought us action.*

وَأَشْبَعَ الالَفَ صَاعٌ مِنْهُ قَدْ كَمَلَا

تَشْفَعَ الظَّبْيُ جَهْراً مِمَّا قَدْ نَزَلَا

وَالْبَدْرُ شُقَّ وَغَيْثُ الْمَحْلِ قَدْ هَطَلَا

فِي كُلِّ جَارِحَةٍ مِنْهُ فَوَائِدُ لَا

يُحْصِيهَا عَدٌّ وَلَا تُدْرِكُهَا بِالْمُقَل

A full measure of his fills up a thousand measures.
The gazelle intercedes openly about what happened.
The full moon was split
and the barren clouds pour down rain –
*In every act from it there are innumerable benefits,*
*which are not perceptible to the eyes.*

كَمْ أَطْنَبَ الْأُمَمُ الْمَاضُونَ وَالْعُلَمَا

مَا جَاءَ بِالْبَعْضِ مِنْهَا النُّبْلُ وَالنُّظَمَا

مَنْ حَاوَلَ الشَّأْ وَنَالَ النَّصْبَ وَالنَّدَمَا

وَقَدْ أَحَاطَ كِتَابُ اللهِ مِنْهَا بِمَا

يُبْرِئُ كُلَّ سَقِيمِ الْقَلْبِ مِنْ عِلَلِ

How often past nations and scholars boasted
when their nobles and poets brought them a fragrance of his insight!
How many tried to obtain it
and only became exhausted and remorseful! –
*The Book of Allah contains some of these benefits*
*by which every one who is sick of heart is healed of his sickness.*

أَعْيَى الْوَرَىٰ مَدْحُهُ مِمَّا مَضَىٰ وَأَتَىٰ

فِي الذِّكْرِ أَثْنَىٰ عَلَيْهِ اللهُ قُلْ لِي مَتَىٰ

يُحْصِي مَزَايَاهُ هَذَا الْخَلْقُ قُلْ لِي مَتَىٰ

وَلَيْسَ يَقْدُرُ قَدْرَهُ الْعَظِيمُ فَتَى

فَالْعَجْزُ عَنْ مَدْحِهِ مِنْ أَحْسَنِ السُّبُلِ

Men in the past have grown weary, failing in their attempts
to praise him through the dhikr with which Allah praised him.
Tell me when will this creation
enumerate his blessings – O tell me, when? –
*No hero is capable of attaining his mighty rank,*
*so the inability to praise him is the best of ways.*

مَا مَدْحُ مِثْلِي جَنَابَكُمْ خَلَا الأَمَلَا

حَاشَا يُخِيبُ الَّذِي بِرَبْعِكُمْ نَزَلَا

فَقَدْ وَقَفْتُ بِبَابِ فَضْلِكُمْ عَائِلَا

وَقَدْ تَشَبَّهْتُ فِي مَدْحِي وَجِئْتُ إِلَى

رُحْمَاكَ مُسْتَشْفِعًا لِلَّهِ تَشْفَعْ لِي

The praising of you by one such as me is empty of hope
(yet none is disappointed who alights at his abode,
So I have stood at the door
of your bounty indigent and in need –
*I have copied you in my praise and I have come to your compassion*
*seeking intercession with Allah, so intercede on my behalf!*

أَرْضَاكَ رَبُّكَ فِي التَّنْزِيلِ تَرْضِيَّةً

وَفِي الْقِيَامَةِ فُقْتَ الْكُلَّ مَكْرُمَةً

أَنْتَ الشَّفِيعُ لِكُلِّ الْخَلْقِ قَاطِبَةً

يَا أَعْظَمَ الْخَلْقِ عِنْدَ اللهِ مَنْزِلَةً

إِعْطِفْ عَلَيْنَا بِمَا نَرْجُوهُ يَا أَمَلِي

May your Lord grant you satisfaction in revelation
and may you be honoured above all
on the Day of Resurrection.
You are the one who intercedes for all creation –
*O greatest of creation with Allah in rank,*
*be kind to us with what we hope for, O my desire!*

وَاشْفَعْ لَنَا فِي وُرُودِ الْحَوْضِ نَشْرَبُهْ

كَذَا الصِّرَاطُ كَمِثْلِ الْبَرْقِ نَسْلُكُهْ

أَنْتَ الْمَلَاذُ وَبَابُ اللهِ نُخْبَتُهْ

مَنْ يَحْتَمِي بِكَ يَضْحَى الْكَوْنُ يَخْدُمُهْ

لِأَجْلِ جَاهِكَ يَا مُمَدَّ كُلِّ وَلِي

Intercede for us when we come to the fountain
that we may drink from it, and at the bridge
that we may pass over it like a flash of lightning.
You are the refuge and the door of Allah for the elect —
*By your rank, created beings serve whoever*
*seeks shelter with you, O Protector of every Wali.*

إِنِّي غَرِيقٌ بِحَارِ الْوِزْرِ فِي كَبَدِ

وَلَيْسَ لِي مُنْجِدٌ سِوَاكَ مِنْ أَحَدِ

أَنْتَ الْغِيَاثُ وَأَنْتَ خَيْرُ مُعْتَمَدِ

بِكَ احْتَمَيْتُ فَلَا تَكِلْنِي يَا سَنَدِي

لِلنَّفْسِ وَالْجِنْسِ وَاجْبُرْنَا مِنَ الْخَلَلِ

I am worn out,
drowning in oceans of wrong actions
and there is no one to aid me except you.
You are our aid and the best of supports —
*O my support! I have sought shelter with you,*
*so do not leave me to my self and my humanness, but mend our faults.*

عُبَيْدُكُمْ ضَاقَ بِالْعِصْيَانِ مَذْهَبُهُ

وَالنَّفْسُ أَمَّارَةٌ وَالذَّنْبُ يَحْجُبُهُ

فَكُنْ نَصِيرًا لَهُ وَاللهُ يَرْحَمُهُ

وَلَيْسَ يُلْحَقُ عَبْدٌ أَنْتَ نَاصِرُهُ

فَأَنْتَ لِي عُمْدَةٌ فِي السَّهْلِ وَالْجَبَلِ

The path of your slave has been narrow through rebellion.
The self is in control and wrong actions veil him.
Be his helper and Allah may have mercy on him, for —
*Nothing befalls the slave if you are his helper.*
*You are my staff on the level land and on the mountains.*

قَدْ ضَاعَ عُمْرِي وَزَادَ الذَّنْبُ فِي الْعَدَدِ

وَقَدْ غَدَوْتُ شَغِيلَ الْعَقْلِ وَانْخَلَدِ

وَلَيْسَ لِي عَمَلٌ أَنْجُو بِهِ فِي غَدِ

وَقَدْ تَحَيَّرْتُ فِي أَمْرِي فَخُذْ بِيَدِي

فَلَا تَحَوَّلْ لِي عَنْ نُورِكَ الْأَوَّلِ

My life was lost and my wrong actions increased in number.
My heart and intellect had become preoccupied.
Now I do not possess an act which can save me tomorrow.
*I have become confused about myself, so take me by the hand.*
*For me there is no turning away from your first light.*

يَا خَيْرَةَ الْخَلْقِ يَا شَمْسًا إِذَا بَزَغَتْ

بَدَا الْوُجُودُ وَغَابَ الْكُلُّ إِنْ حُجِبَتْ

يَا مَنْ بِمَبْعَثِهِ الْاَكْوَانُ قَدْ حَظِيَتْ

صَلَّى عَلَيْكَ إِلَهُ الْعَرْشِ مَا ظَهَرَتْ

شَمْسُ الْحَقِيقَةِ بِالْاَسْمَاءِ وَالْفِعَالِ

O Best of Creation! O Sun! which when it rises,
existence appears, but everything disappears if it is veiled.
O he who through his mission beings have found favour –
*May the God of the Throne bless you as long*
*as the sun of the reality is manifested by the Names and the Acts.*

ثُمَّ الصَّلَاةُ عَلَى الْمُخْتَارِ مَا سَجَعَتْ

وُرْقٌ وَهَبَّ نَسِيمُ الرَّوْضِ وَانْتَشَرَتْ

بَسْطُ الْاَزَاهِرِ مِنْ أَكْمَامِهَا انْفَتَحَتْ

كَذَاكَ ءَالُكَ وَالْاَصْحَابُ مَا بَتَتْ

عُشْبٌ وَمَا سَحَّتِ السَّمَاءُ مِنْ بَلَلِ

Blessing upon the Chosen One as long as doves coo,
the gentle breeze of the meadow blows,
and the scents of flowers are diffused from their open petals –
*As well as your family and Companions as long as the grass grows*
*and the sky pours down abundant rain.*

وَالتَّابِعُونَ ذَوُوا الْعَلْيَا مِنَ الْهِمَمِ

الْحَامِلُو رَايَةِ الاِسْلاَمِ وَالْعَلَمِ

أَهْلُ الْوَفَا وَالتُّقَى وَالْجُودِ وَالْكَرَمِ

ثُمَّ الرِّضَى عَنْ رِجَالِ اللَّهِ كُلِّهِمِ

مَا سَبَّحَ الْكَوْنُ مَنْ يُجَلُّ عَنْ مَثَلِ

And blessing upon the Followers
who had outstanding himma,
bearing the banner and standards of Islam,
people of fidelity and piety, generosity and nobility –
*Then I ask for Your good pleasure for all the Men of Allah*
*as long as beings glorify the One Who is above identification with forms.*

وَاحْفَظْ لِرَايَةِ دِينِ الْحَقِّ حَامِلَهَا

وَارْدُدْ لِسُنَّةِ هَذَا الدِّينَ عِزَّتَهَا

وَانْصُرْ لِأُمَّةِ خَيْرِ الرُّسْلِ قَادَتَهَا

وَابْسُطْ لِإِخْوَانِنَا الْخَيْرَاتِ أَجْمَعَهَا

دُنْيَا وَأَخْرَى وَلاَ تَكِلْنَا لِلْعَمَلِ

Protect the standard-bearer of the Deen of the Truth,
and restore the Sunna of this Deen to its position of might.
Grant victory to the Community led by the best of the Messengers –
*And unfold all blessings on our brothers, in this world and the next,*
*and do not leave us to our actions.*

وَأَيِّدَنْ لِطَرِيقِ الْقَوْمِ أَنْصَارَهَا

وَأَلْحِقَنْ بِدُعَاةِ الْخَيْرِ أَتْبَاعَهَا

وَاجْعَلْ أَوَاخِرَ ذِي الْأَيَّامِ أَسْعَدَهَا

وَاغْفِرْ لِوَالِدِينَا الزَّلَّاتِ أَجْمَعَهَا

وَالْمُسْلِمِينَ بِفَضْلٍ مِنْكَ يَا أَزَلِي ﴿﴾

Support the supporters of the Tariq of the people,
and connect its followers to those who call to the best,
and make the last of our days the happiest –
*Forgive our parents all their mistakes, and the Muslims,*
*by an outpouring from You — O Before-endless-time!*

وهذه تخميسات على بعض قصائد الأستاذ المذكور
لبعض تلامذته أولها :

The following Takhmisat are on some of the Qasidas of the Shaykh

by some of his pupils, the first being:

# The Takhmis in *Lam* on 'The Departure of Illusion'

by the needy slave Abu Hafs 'Umar

تخميس لاميَّة ارتحال الوهم

للعُبَيْد المفتقر أبي حفص عمر

بَعْدَ عِلْمٍ بِإِخْلَاصٍ مَعْ وَجَلْ

وَابْتِهَالٍ لِلَّهِ عَزَّ وَجَلْ

قَالَ حِبٌّ حِينَ التَّجَلِّي حَصَلْ

كَانَ لِي وَهْمٌ فَلَمَّا أَنْ رَحَلْ

أَشْرَفَ الْقَلْبُ عَلَى نُورِ الْازَلْ

After knowledge coupled with sincerity and fear,
and humble entreaty to Allah, the Mighty and Exalted,
when the manifestation occurred, a lover said:
*I had an illusion. When it departed,*
*the heart looked upon the light of before-time.*

لَمَّا رَامَ الْوَصْلَ بِمَحْبُوبِهِ

طَارَ مَوْلَّى مَشُوقًا بِهِ

عِلْمًا بِأَنَّ الْفَوْزَ فِي قُرْبِهِ

رَكِبَ الشَّوْقَ الَّذِي طَارَ بِهِ

فَدَنَا مِنْ حِبِّهِ حَتَّى اتَّصَلْ

When he desired to reach his Beloved,
he took flight with passion and yearning,
knowing that success lies in nearness to Him.
*It rode on longing, which flew with it,*
*so the heart drew near to its Beloved until it was united.*

فِي فَنَاءٍ عَنْ فَنَاهُ وَاهِلاً

لَا الْمَلَا يَبْقَى لَدَيْهِ وَالْمَلَا

لَمْ يَرَ مِنْ شَيْءٍ سِوَى ذِي الْكِلَا

شَاهَدَ الْكَوْنَ خَيَالاً زَائِلاً

وَانْمَحَى رَسْمُ الْوُجُودِ وَأَفَلْ

Weakening in annihilation to his annihilation,
and no assembly nor anything else remained with him,
he did not see anything except the One with shelter.
*It saw created beings as an imagination that faded,*
*and the form of existence was obliterated and vanished.*

لَمْ يَرَ نَاطِقًا وَلَا صَامِتًا

بَلْ وَلَا خَائِفًا وَلَا قَانِتًا

لَا غَفُولًا إِذًا وَلَا مُخْبِتًا

ثُمَّ رُدَّ لِلْبَقَاءِ مُثْبِتًا

جَمِيعَ الْكَوْنِ الَّذِي عَنْهُ انْعَزَلْ

He did not see anyone speaking or silent,
nor fearful nor obedient,
nor heedless then nor humble.
*Then if was returned to going-on, confirming*
*all the beings from which it had withdrawn.*

حَكَّمَ شَرْعَهُ فِي تَوْحِيدِهِ

لَنْ يُجَاوِزْنَهُ فِي تَحْدِيدِهِ

أَزِمَّةُ النَّجْدَيْنِ فِي يَدِهِ

جَمَعَ الضِّدَّيْنِ فِي مَشْهَدِهِ

وَحَّدَ اللَّهَ وَقَامَ بِالْعَمَلْ

He judged by His Shari'a in His Tawhid
and did not exceed it in defining Him.
The reins of the two paths are in His hand.
*It joined the two opposites in witnessing Him;*
*it unified Allah and took on action.*

عَلَى كِلْتَا لَمْ يَزَلْ مُسْتَوِيًا

كِلَا بَحْرَيْهِ لَنْ يُرَى بَاغِيًا

صَارَ فَرْدًا أَعْنِي مُحَمَّدِيًّا

حَازَ سِرًّا وَصِرَاطًا سَوِيًّا

قَلَّ مَنْ ذَاقَهُ مِنْ أَهْلِ الكَمَالُ

He remained straight in both.
You do not see him wronging either of His seas.
He became the Muhammadan individual.
*It gained a secret and a level path;*
*how few of the people of perfection taste it.*

كَرَمَاتٌ مِنَ الْمُهَيْمِنِ ذِي

سَلِّمَنْ تَسْلَمَنْ وَدَعِ الْبَذِي

إِنْ تُرِدْ عِزَّةً فَقُلْ مُحْتَذِي

رَبَّنَا صَلِّ عَلَى النُّورِ الَّذِي

كُلُّ عَبْدٍ أَمَّهُ حَازَ الأَمَلُ

Miracles from the Protector.
Grant peace, grant peace and abandon what is foul.
If you desire might, then say in imitation:
*Our Lord, bless the Light.*
*Every slave who reaches him gains his desire.*

كَرِّرْنَهَا دَوْمًا وَكُنْ وَالِهًا

تَحُزِ الْفَضْلَ وَالرِّضَىٰ وَالْبَهَا

عَاطِفًا زِدْ وَقُلْ بِغَيْرِ انْتِهَا

وَأَرْضَ عَنْ ءَالِه هُمْ أَهْلُ النُّهَى

وَصِحَابٍ مَعَ قُطْبٍ وَبَدَلْ ۞

Repeat it constantly and be fearful.
You will obtain excellence, contentment and radiance.
And also say without end:
*Be pleased with his family, they are the people of understanding;*
*and the Companions, the Qutb and the Abdal.*

# The Takhmis in *Ha* on
# 'The Manifestation of the Essence'

by Abu Hafs 'Umar

تَخْمِيسُ هَائِيَّةُ التَّجَلِّي

لأبي حفص عمر

إِذَا مَا لَيَالِي الْوَهْمِ زَالَ ظَلَامُهَا

أُقِيمَتْ لِأَرْبَابِ الْقُلُوبِ صَلَاتُهَا

فَلَمَّا كَسَاهَا النُّورُ قَالَ إِمَامُهَا

أَشَمْسٌ بَدَا مِنْ عَالَمِ الْغَيْبِ ضَوْؤُهَا

أَم انْكَشَفَتْ عَنْ ذَاتِ لَيْلَى سُتُورُهَا

When the darkness of the nights of illusion departed,
the prayer of the lords of the hearts was established for them.
When light clothed them, their imam said:
*Has the light of the sun appeared from the world of the Unseen,*
*or have the veils of Layla been lifted from Her essence?*

229

أَمِ الاَنْجُمُ الزُّهْرُ الْمُضَاءُ بِنُورِهَا

أَمِ الْبَدْرُ عَمَّ الاَفْقَ مِنْ بَعْدِ غَيْمِهَا

أَمِ الْهَجْرُ أَبْدَلَتْهُ سَلْمَى بِوَصْلِهَا

نَعَمْ تِلْكَ لَيْلَى قَدْ أَبَاحَتْ بِحُبِّهَا

لِخِلٍّ لَهَا لَمَّا تَزَايَدَ شَوْقُهَا

Or have the brilliant stars been illuminated by Her light,
or the full moon enveloped the horizon after the clouds have lifted,
or has Salma replaced estrangement with union?
*Yes, Layla revealed Her love*
*for Her intimate friend when Her longing grew.*

تَرَاءَتْ بِمِرْءَاةِ الصَّفَا لِصَفِيِّهَا

وَفَاحَ شَذَاهَا مِنْ وَرَاءِ حِجَابِهَا

وَطَارَ قُلَيْبُ الْحِبِّ عِنْدَ بُدُوِّهَا

فَأَضْحَى أَسِيرًا فِي مُرَادِ غَرَامِهَا

وَنَادَتْ لَهُ الاَشْوَاقُ هَذِي كُؤُوسُهَا

She appeared in the mirror of purity to Her dear friend.
Her fragrance diffused from behind Her veil.
And the heart of the lover took flight at Her appearance.
*He became a captive of Her ardent desire*
*and the longings which are Her goblets called out to him.*

تَحَلَّتْ بِحَلْي الْعِزِّ وَسْطِ خَانِهَا

وَبَثَّتْ فِرَاشَ الْمَجْدِ حَوْلَ خِيَامِهَا

وَجَاءَتْ بِأَكْوَابِ الطَّلَا لِشَرَابِهَا

فَمَا بَرِحَتْ حَتَّى سَقَتْهُ بِكَأْسِهَا

فَلَا لَوْمَ فَاشْرَبْ فَالشَّرَابُ حَدِيثُهَا

She adorned herself in the robe of might in the midst of Her tavern,
and spread out the carpet of glory around Her tents
and brought goblets of sweet wine to drink.
*She did not leave until She had given him a drink from Her goblet.*
*There is no blame. Drink — for the wine is Her speech.*

فَمَا سَلْمَى مَنْ تُهْوَى وَلَمْ أَهْوَ غَيْرَهَا

وَلَيْسَ الْمُرَادُ حَلْيهَا وَجَمَالَهَا

وَلَمْ تَطْلُبِ الْعُشَّاقُ لَيْلَى وَشُرْبَهَا

وَمَا هِيَ إِلَّا حَضْرَةُ الْحَقِّ وَحْدَهَا

تَجَلَّتْ بِأَشْكَالٍ تَلَوَّنَ نُورُهَا

Salma is not the one who is desired and I do not desire other than Her.
What is desired is not Her robes and beauty.
The passionate lovers did not seek Layla and Her drink.
*She is none but the Presence of the Truth alone,*
*Who manifests Herself with forms whose every light is different.*

تَلَاشَىٰ عُقَيْلُ الخِلِّ وَقْتَ بُرُوزِهَا

وَأَدْهَشَهُ إِذْ ذَاكَ بَاهِرُ حُسْنِهَا

وَعَمَّ جَمِيعَ الْكَوْنِ حُسْنُ جَمَالِهَا

فَأُبْدَتْ بَدِيعَ الصُّنْعِ فِي طَيِّ كَوْنِهَا

فَلَاحِظْ صِفَاتِ الْحِبِّ فِيكَ ظُهُورُهَا

The consciousness of the lover disappeared at the moment She appeared
and at that the splendour of Her beauty dazzled him.
The splendour of Her beauty enveloped the entire cosmos.
*In folding up Her cosmos, She showed the Originator of the design,*
*so look how the Attributes of the Beloved are manifest within you.*

فَقُلْ لِلَّذِي يَهْوَىٰ وَيَطْلُبُ حُسْنَهَا

وَيَنْهَىٰ لِأَرْبَابِ الْمَقَامَاتِ وَالنُّهَىٰ

تَوَجَّهْ بِدُونِ حَظِّ نَفْسِكَ نَحْوَهَا

فَوَاللَّهِ مَا حَازَ السَّعَادَةَ كُلَّهَا

سِوَى مَنْ بَدَا عَبْدًا ذَلِيلًا يَؤُمُّهَا

Tell the one who desires and seeks Her beauty
and inform the masters of stations and understanding:
Direct yourselves towards Her without any portion for your self.
*By Allah, none ever obtains complete bliss*
*except the one who becomes a humble slave and seeks Her out.*

فَالْكَوْنُ فِي ظُلَمِ الْفَنَا فَأَنَارَهُ

نُورُ الإِلَهِ فَلَاحِظَنْ ءَاثَارَهُ

إِنِّي أُرَانِي نُورَهُ وَسَنَاءَهُ

لَوْ لَمْ أَكُنْ نُورًا لَكُنْتُ سِوَاءَهُ

إِنَّ السِّوَى عَدَمٌ فَلَا تَرْضَاهُ

Being is in the darkness of annihilation,
then the light of God illuminated it, so look at His traces.
I saw myself as His light and radiance.
*If I were not a light I would be other-than-Him.*
*Indeed otherness is nothingness, so do not be content with it.*

طَهِّرْ بِمَاءِ الذِّكْرِ قَلْبَكَ وَاجْتَهِدْ

أَلَّا تُشَاهِدَ غَيْرَ حَقٍّ مُنْفَرِدْ

فَالْغَيْرُ وَهْمٌ قَاطِعٌ عَمَّا تُرِيدْ

وَإِذَا نَظَرْتَ بِعَيْنِ سِرِّكَ لَمْ تَجِدْ

غَيْرَ الإِلَهِ فِي أَرْضِهِ وَسَمَاهُ

Purify your heart with the water of dhikr and strive
not to witness other than the Truth alone.
Other is illusion which cuts you off from what you desire.
*If you look with the eye of your Secret you will not find*
*a trace of other-than-Allah in either His earth or His heaven.*

فَالْكُلُّ مِرْآةٌ لِبَاهِرِ حُسْنِهِ

فَافْنَ عَنِ الْأَكْوَانِ تَحْظَ بِقُرْبِهِ

لَا يَخْتَفِي قِدْمًا بَدَا فِي خَلْقِهِ

لَكِنْ تَوَهُّمُ غَيْرِهِ يَخْفَى بِهِ

فَابْذُ هَوَاكَ إِذَا أَرَدْتَ تَرَاهُ

All is a mirror for the radiance of His beauty.
Be annihilated to phenomenal beings and you will obtain His nearness.
He is eternally unconcealed and manifest in His creation.
*But the illusion of other-than-Him hides Him.*
*So combat your desires if you wish to see Him.*

لَا تَشْرَبَنْ صِرْفَ الْحَقِيقَةِ وَحْدَهَا

وَامْزُجْ بِمَاءِ شَرِيعَةٍ صَهْبَاءَهَا

وَانْظُرْ بِعَيْنِ الْحَقِّ ثُمَّ بِعَيْنِهَا

وَارْكَبْ سَفِينَةَ سُنَّةٍ تَنْجُو بِهَا

وَاسْلُكْ سَبِيلَ رَئِيسِهَا فِي هَوَاهُ

Do not drink the pure wine of the Reality alone.
Mix its red wine with the water of the Shari'a.
Look with the eye of the Real and then with the eye of the Shari'a.
*Board the ship of the Sunna and you will be rescued by it,*
*and travel the path of its captain in his love.*

فَهِيَ الصِّرَاطُ الْمُسْتَقِيمِ بِنَهْجِه

تَرْقَىٰ ذُرَى الْعِرْفَانِ جَدَّ لِسَيْرِه

لَا تَعْدِلَنْ عَنْ شُرْبِهَا مِنْ عَيْنِه

وَصِلِ الشَّرَابَ بِكَأْسِهَا وَافْنَ بِه

تَحْزِ الْبَقَاءَ بِسِرِّه وَعُلَاه

It is the Straight Path of His Road.
You will rise to the peak of gnosis, striving in travelling it.
Do not refrain from drinking it from His source.
*Unite the wine with the goblet and be annihilated by it,*
*and you will obtain going-on by His secret and sublimity.*

وَانْظُرْهُ فِي كُلِّ الْمَظَاهِرِ إِنَّه

سِرُّ الْوَرَىٰ وَالْغَيْرُ إِنْ حَقَّقْتَه

كَأْسٌ إِذَا مَا شِئْتَ خَمْرَه

وَاشْهَدْ بِعَيْنِ بَصِيرَةٍ تَوْحِيدَه

وَالْفَرْقُ شِرْعَتُه فَلَا تَنْسَاه

See Him in all manifestations, He is
the secret of mankind, and Other, if you have achieved realisation,
is a glass, if you wish His wine!
*See His Tawhid with the eye of inner sight,*
*but separation is His Shari'a so do not forget it!*

239

لَا تَحْتَجِبْ بِالْكَوْنِ عِنْدَ وُرُودِه

عَنْ غَايَةٍ وَاقْطَعْ مَسَافَةَ وَهْمِه

وَارْفَعْ أُخَيَّ الْهِمَّةَ عَنْ غَيْرِه

وَاجْعَلْ هُمُومَكَ وَاحِدًا تُكْفَى بِه

كُلَّ الْهُمُومِ وَتَدْخُلَنْ فِي حِمَاه

Do not let the arrival of phenomenal being veil you
to the End. Cut through its intervening illusion.
And, my brother, raise your himma above other-than-Him.
*Make your concerns one, and by Him all your needs*
*will be met, and you will enter into His protection.*

قَامَتْ لَنَا كُلُّ الْأُمُورِ بِرَبِّهَا

لَا نَفْعَ حَقًّا لِلْخَلِيقَةِ كُلِّهَا

فَلْتَيْئَسَنْ طُولَ الْمَدَى مِنْ نَفْعِهَا

وَانْزِلْ أُمُورَكَ بِالَّذِي أَدْرَى بِهَا

فَهُوَ الْخَبِيرُ بِقَلْبِنَا وَمُنَاه

For us all matters are established by their Lord.
All creatures truly are of no benefit at all,
so despair of ever having any benefit from them.
*Hand over your affairs to the One Who knows them best,*
*for He is the Aware Who knows our hearts and their desires.*

وَالْجَأْ إِلَى الرُّكْنِ الْعَظِيمِ الأَحْمَدِي

فَهُوَ الْوَسِيلَةُ لِلاِنَامِ الأَوْحَدِ

وَهُوْ لَنَا ذُخْرٌ لِيَوْمِ الْمَوْعِدِ

يَا رَبِّ صَلِّ عَلَى النَّبِيِّ مُحَمَّدِ

سِرِّ الْوُجُودِ وَأَصْلِهِ وَسَنَاهُ ﴿٢٦﴾

Seek shelter in the great Ahmadi pillar.
He is the only means of access for mankind.
He is a treasure for us for the promised day.
*O Lord, bless the Prophet Muhammad,*
*the secret of existence and its source and splendour.*

# The Takhmis in *Waw* on 'Purification'

by Sayyidi Fudul al-Huwari

تَخْمِيسٌ وَاوِيَّة
التَّطْهِير
لِسيدي فضول الْهَوَّاري

أَمَنْ رَامَ أَنْ يَرْقَىٰ لِحَضْرَةِ مَنْ يَهْوَىٰ

إِلَى أَنْ يُهَيَّأَ لِلْمَوَاهِبِ وَالنَّجْوَىٰ

وَيَصْفُو مِنْ تَكْدِيرِ نَفْسٍ وَمَا تَهْوَىٰ

فَإِنْ شِئْتَ تَطْهِيرًا مِنَ الشِّرْكِ وَالدَّعْوَى

وَتَشْرَبَ مِنْ تَسْنِيمِ وَصْلٍ حَتَّى تُرْوَى

Does someone desire to rise to the presence of the One he loves?
He should prepare for gifts and intimate conversation
And be purified of the turbidity of the nafs and what it desires.
*If you wish purification from shirk and the claim that you exist,*
*and to drink from the nectar of union until you are quenched —*

فَهَيْهَاتَ مَا طُرْقُ الْكَمَالِ بِسَهْلَةٍ

إِذَا مَا جَعَلْتَ الْعَزْمَ خَيْرَ مَطِيَّةٍ

وَإِنْ شِئْتَ وَصْلَ الْعَارِفِينَ لِحَضْرَةٍ

فَمَنْطِقْ بِصَبْرٍ ثُمَّ عَمِّمْ بِتَوْبَةٍ

وَلَازِمْ قَمِيصَ الزُّهْدِ وَابْذُلْ فِيهِ قُوَى

How unlikely it is that the paths of perfection will be easy!
Make firm resolve the best of mounts,
and if you wish to join the gnostics of the Presence,
— then wrap yourself in patience and wind on the turban of Tawba.
Wear the shirt of doing-without and in it exhaust your strength.

وَكُنْ ذَاكِرًا دَأْبَ النَّهَارِ وَفِي الدُّجَا

لِيَضْحَىٰ بِنُورِ الذِّكْرِ قَلْبُكَ مُسْرَجَا

وَلَا تَيْأَسَنْ فِي السَّيْرِ فَالْفَضْلُ يُرْتَجَى

وَلَا بُدَّ مِنْ نَعْلَيْنِ خَوْفٍ مَعَ الرَّجَى

وَعُكَّازِ إِيقَانٍ وَزَادٍ مِنَ التَّقْوَى

Do dhikr all day long and when it is dark
to illuminate your heart with the light of dhikr.
Do not despair in the journey. Favour is hoped for.
*The twin sandals of fear and hope are indispensable.*
*Take the staff of certainty and a store of Taqwa.*

وَلَا تَذْهَبَنْ فِي السَّيْرِ مِنْ غَيْرِ رُفْقَةٍ

مِنَ الصَّادِقِينَ الْمُخْلِصِينَ لِصُحْبَةٍ

تُصَانُ بِهِمْ مِنْ كُلِّ ضَعْفٍ وَفَتْرَةٍ

وَقَائِدُ عِلْمٍ مَعْ مَطِيَّةِ هِمَّةٍ

وَصُحْبَةِ حِفْظٍ لِلْجَوَارِحِ مِنْ بَلْوَى

Do not set out travelling without taking comrades
for companionship from among those who are truthful and sincere.
By them you are protected against every weakness and lassitude.
*Take the bridle of knowledge for the horse of Himma, and the*
*protection of companions who will guard the limbs from trials.*

وَإِنْ رُمْتَ أَنْ تَفْنَى فَنَاءً وَتَنْحَذِفْ

وَبِاللهِ أَنْ تَبْقَى بِوَصْفِكَ فَاعْتَرِفْ

وَإِنْ مَا بَدَا كَوْنٌ لِيُلْهِيكَ فَانْصَرِفْ

وَجِدَّ وَأَسْرِعْ فِي الْمَسِيرِ وَلَا تَقِفْ

بِفِكْرٍ عَلَى كَوْنٍ فَتُحْجَبَ عَنْ مَأْوَى

If you want to be annihilated and cut off,
and go on with your description by Allah, then acknowledge.
If a phenomenal being appears to you to excite you, then depart.
*Struggle seriously and travel quickly on the journey.*
*Do not stop to think about the universe, and so be barred from refuge.*

وَكُنْ حَامِدًا عَبْدًا شَكُورًا لِرَبِّهِ

وَمُسْتَحْضِرًا عَجْزَ الثَّنَاءِ فِي حَمْدِهِ

لِأَنَّهُ يَهْدِي مَنْ يَشَاءُ بِفَضْلِهِ

وَفَكِّرْ فِي إِحْسَانٍ وَأَخْلِصْ فِي شُكْرِهِ

وَقُمْ سَحَرًا وَاخْضَعْ وَبُثَّ لَهُ الشَّكْوَى

Praise a slave who was thankful to his Lord
And remember one's inability to praise Him
because He guides whomever He wills by His bounty.
*Rather reflect on Ihsan and be sincere in gratitude to Him,*
*and get up before dawn, submit, and hand over your complaint to Him.*

وَلَا تَدَّعِ حُبَّ الْإِلَهِ وَحِبِّهِ

مِنْ غَيْرِ اقْتِفَا إِثْرِ الرَّسُولِ وَصَحْبِهِ

عَلَامَةُ حُبِّ اللهِ حُبُّ حَبِيبِهِ

وَصَلِّ عَلَى قُطْبِ الْوُجُودِ وَحِزْبِهِ

صَلَاةً تَعُمُّ السِّرَّ مِنَّا مَعَ النَّجْوَى ۞

Do not abandon love of Allah and His beloved
or fail to follow the tracks of the Messenger and his Companions.
The sign of love of Allah is love for the one He loves.
*Bless the Qutb of existence and his group with a blessing*
*that will spread the Secret from us.*

# The Takhmis in *Ha* on
# 'Withdrawal from all that is other than Allah'

### by the faqih Sayyidi Hammoud ibn al-Bashir

تَخْمِيسٌ هَائِيَّة

الْغَيْبَة عَمَّا سِوَى الله

للفقيه سيدي حَمُّود بن الْبَشِير

كُلُّ الْوُجُودِ مِنْ مَرَاتِبِ حِكْمَةٍ

لَوْحُ الْمُرِيدِ فِي مُشَاهِدِ وَحْدَةٍ

فَانْظُرْ بِمَا صَرَّحَ الْمَكِينُ فِي قُرْبَةٍ

رُوحِي تُحَدِّثُنِي بِأَنَّ حَقِيقَتِي

نُورُ الالَه فَلَا تَرَى إِلاَّهُ

All existence comes from the ranks of wisdom.
The tablet of the murid is witnessing Him alone,
So look at what the one who is firm in nearness clearly states:
*My spirit tells me, "My reality is the light of Allah,*
*so see no one but Him."*

وَحَيْثُ سِرُّ السِّرِ يَنْشُرُ وَصْفَه

يَفْنَى الْعَلِيلُ بِوَصْفِهِ وَعُلَاه

يَبْقَى الْعَدِيمُ صَارِخًا وَقَوْلُه

لَوْ لَمْ أَكُنْ نُورًا لَكُنْتُ سِوَاءَه

إِنَّ السِّوَا عَدَمٌ فَلَا تَرْضَاه

When the attribute of the secret of the secret spreads out,
the sick one is annihilated by His description and sublimity,
And the non-existent remains shouting. His words are:
*If I were not a light I would be other-than-Him.*
*Indeed otherness is nothingness, so do not be content with it.*

مَنْ كَانَ لِلَّهِ فِي الْمَشَاهِدِ مُقْتَصِد

فَيُفَارِقُ طَوْرًا وَطَوْرًا يَتَّحَد

وَلِذَا تَرَاهُ يَجُودُ بِالْقَوْلِ فَاسْتَفِد

وَإِذَا نَظَرْتَ بِعَيْنِ سِرِّكَ لَمْ تَجِد

غَيْرَ الالَهَ فِي أَرْضِهِ وَسَمَاه

Whoever aims for Allah in what he witnesses,
and leaves stage after stage will be unified.
That is why you see him generous with words, so learn!
*If you look with the eye of your Secret you will not find*
*a trace of other-than-Allah in either His earth or His heaven.*

أَحَدٌ أَفَاضَ شُؤُونَهُ فِي وِتْرِهِ

فَاسْلُكْ طَرِيقَ الْقَوْمِ تَحْظَ بِوَصْلِهِ

فَافْنِ الطَّبِيعَةَ وَالنَّاسُوتَ فِي نَعْتِهِ

لَكِنْ تَوَهُّمُ غَيْرِهِ يَخْفَى بِهِ

فَانْبُذْ هَوَاكَ إِذَا أَرَدْتَ تَرَاهُ

One pours forth his affairs in his Witr.
So travel the paths of the people and you will win arrival to Him.
Annihilate Nature and human nature in His attribute.
*But the illusion of other-than-Him hides Him.*
*So combat your desires if you wish to see Him.*

فَالْزَمِ الشَّرِيعَةَ وَالْحَقِيقَةَ إِثْرَهَا

بِعَوْنِ حِبْرٍ مُسْتَقِيمٍ لِسَقْيِهَا

وَاسْتَسْلِمِ الْأَحْوَالَ طَوْعًا بِحُبِّهَا

وَارْكَبْ سَفِينَةَ سُنَّةٍ تَنْجُو بِهَا

وَاسْلُكْ سَبِيلَ رَئِيسِهَا فِي هَوَاهُ

Cling to the Shari'a, and the Haqiqa as well
with help of an upright scholar to gain its drink.
Submit all states willingly for love of it.
*Board the ship of the Sunna and you will be rescued by it,*
*and travel the path of its captain in his love.*

وَانْسُجْ لِقَلْبِكَ مَنَاسِجَ فَوْرِهِ

وَاعْلَقْ بِسِرِّكَ فِي امْتِزَاجِ سِرِّهِ

مَزْجَ الاَشِعَّةِ فِي شُرُوقِ شَمْسِهِ

وَصِلِ الشَّرَابَ بِكَأْسِهَا وَافْنَ بِهِ

تَحْزِ الْبَقَاءَ بِسِرِّهِ وَعُلَاهُ

Weave for your heart the carpets of its diffusion
And join your secret to the mixture of His secret.
Mix the rays in the rising of its sun.
*Unite the wine with the goblet and be annihilated by it,*
*and you will obtain going-on by His secret and sublimity.*

وَالْزَمْ صَنِيعَ الْبِرِّ طَوْرًا إِنَّهُ

يُدْنِي الْمُرِيدَ لِعِزِّهِ وَعُلَاهُ

وَكُنْ كَسِيرَ الْقَلْبِ وَارْعَ ضَبْطَهُ

وَاشْهَدْ بِعَيْنِ بَصِيرَةٍ تَوْحِيدَهُ

وَالْفَرْقُ شِرْعَتُهُ فَلَا تَنْسَاهُ

Cling to the doing of good deeds at times.
It will bring the murid near to His might and sublimity.
Have a broken heart and keep it in order.
*See His Tawhid with the eye of inner sight,*
*but separation is His Shari'a so do not forget it!*

249

وَاقْطَعْ بِظَنِّكَ فِي إِنَالَةِ فَيْضِهِ

وَاسْكُنْ بِقَلْبِكَ فِي حَضِيرَةِ قُرْبِهِ

وَاشْرَبْ بِسِرِّكَ مَا حَلَا مِنْ عَطْفِهِ

وَاجْعَلْ هُمُومَكَ وَاحِدًا تُكْفَى بِهِ

كُلَّ الْهُمُومِ وَتَدْخُلَنْ فِي حِمَاهُ

Concentrate your thought on obtaining His overflowing abundance,
and reside with your heart among the people of His nearness.
Drink with your secret the sweetness of His kindness.
*Make your concerns one, and by Him all your needs*
*will be met, and you will enter into His protection.*

وَاتْرُكْ مُرَادَكَ لِلْإِرَادَةِ وَحْدَهَا

وَافْزَعْ بِنَفْسِكَ لِلْمُدَبِّرِ أَمْرَهَا

وَقَيِّدَنْ أَهْوَاءَكَ بِقُيُودِهَا

وَانْزِلْ أُمُورَكَ بِالَّذِي أَدْرَى بِهَا

فَهُوَ الْخَبِيرُ بِقَلْبِنَا وَمُنَاهُ

Leave your will to the Will alone,
and seek aid your self from the Manager of its affairs.
Limit your desires with its bonds.
*Hand over your affairs to the One Who knows them best,*
*for He is the Aware Who knows our hearts and their desires.*

وَاسْبَحْ بِحُبِّكَ لِلشَّفِيعِ مُحَمَّدٍ

فَهُوَ الْمُحَامِي وَالاِمَامُ السَّيِّدِ

وَهُوَ الشَّفِيقُ عَلَى كِلاَءَةِ حِزْبِهِ

يَا رَبِّ صَلِّ عَلَى النَّبِيِّ مُحَمَّدٍ وَءَالِهِ

سِرِّ الْوُجُودِ وَأَصْلِهِ وَسَنَاهُ ﴿٢٠﴾

Be swift with your love and go to the intercessor Muhammad.
He is the protector and the Imam, the Master.
He has compassionate concern for the safekeeping of his party.
*O Lord, bless the Prophet Muhammad,*
*the secret of existence and its source and splendour.*

# A Qasida

by Sayyidi Fudul ibn Muhammad al-Huwari

قصيدة

لسيدي فضول بن محمد الهواري

يَـا كَوْكَبًـا عَمَّنَـا نُورًا بِأَحْيَـانَـا
شَرْقًا وَأَوْسَطَ وَالادْنَىٰ وَأَقْصَـانَـا

O star whose light enveloped those of us alive,
both in the east and middle, far and near!

بَدَا يَشُقُّ سَحَابَ الجَهْلِ مُقْتَحِمًا
لَغْبَ الهِدَايَةِ مَاسِكًا بِيْنَـانَـا

He split apart the clouds of ignorance, quickly piercing through them,
showing the path of guidance while holding our right hands.

مَـا أَمَّ نَـاحِيَةً إِلَّا وَمَعْشَرُهَا
بَيْنَ القُرَىٰ أَخْصَبَت عَيْشًا وَإِيمَـانَـا

He did not go to a region but that its towns
flourished with abundant livelihood and faith.

252

أَلَا تَرَاهُ مُغَـادِرًا لِمَنْزِلِهِمْ

تَبْكِي الدِّيَـارُ أَسًى عَلَيْهِ مُذْ بَـانَـا

Do you not see that when he leaves their homes
the houses weep for him after he has left?

وَفِي الْوَدَاعِ تَرَىٰ وَفْدًا يُرَادِفُهُ

وَفْدٌ مُشَـاتًـا عَلَىٰ بُعْدٍ وَرُكْبَـانَـا

When he takes his leave you see a delegation following him,
walking and riding from afar

حَتَّىٰ نَئَىٰ مُتَجَـافِيًـا وَقَدْ مُلِئَتْ

قُلُوبِهِمْ مِنْ جَوَى الْفِرَاقِ أَشْجَـانَـا

Until he is distant and out of sight while their hearts
are full of the sorrow of separation.

كَمْ مِنْ مَعَـاهِدَ قَدْ سَمَتْ بِمَوْرِدِهِ

قَدْ أَمْطَرَتْهَـا سَنَـا الْعِرْفَانِ هَتَّـانَـا

Until he is distant and out of sight while their hearts
are full of the sorrow of separation.

يَدعُو لِسُنَّةِ خَيْرِ الْخَلْقِ كُلِّهِمِ

غَنٍ بِرَبِّهِ لَا يَصْبُو لِدُنْيَـانَـا

He called people to the Sunna of the best of all creation,
Enriched by his Lord, not hankering after this world.

مِنْ نُورِ نِبْرَاسِنَا الاعْلَى وَدَوْحَتِهِ
قَدِ اسْتَمَدَّ سُلَالَةً وَعِرْفَـانَـا

The purest wine and gnosis are sought
From the most sublime light of our lanterns and its tree.

أَعْظِمْ بِهِمَّتِه الْعَلْيَـا وَأَخْلَاقِه
الْعُظْمَى وَشِيمَتِه بِرًّا وَإِحْسَـانَـا

Exalt his sublime *himma* and splendid character
and nature in righteousness and *ihsan*,

مُبْدٍ بِشَـاشَتِه مُسْدٍ نَصِيحَتِه
مُلْقٍ مَوَاعِظَه سِرًّا وَإِعْلَانَـا

Displaying a smile, offering good advice,
giving his admonitions both secretly and openly.

فَالْحِلْمُ حِلْيَتِه وَالْجِدُّ عُدّتِه
وَالنُّصْحُ خِدْمَتِه وَالذِّكْرُ دَيْدَانَـا

Forbearance is his adornment and earnestness is his tool,
Advice is his work and dhikr his practice

دَوْمًا تَرَى بِرْزَخَ الْبَحْرَيْنِ مَشْرَبَه
وَالْحَقُّ مَشْهَدُه وَالْخَلْقَ عُنْوَانَـا

Constantly. You see that he drinks from the barzakh of the two seas.
The Real is his witnessing and creation his sign.

تُحْيى بِتَذْكِيرِهِ مَوْتَى الْقُلُوبِ كَمَا
تُجْلَى الْكُرُوبُ وَيَضْحَى الْقَلْبُ جَذْلَانَا

His reminding revives those whose hearts are dead
as cares are removed and the heart becomes exuberant.

عَمَّ الْوَقَارُ مَجَالِسًا شَرُفْنَ بِهِ
مَعَ السَّكِينَةِ تَعْظِيمًا وَإِذْعَانَا

Gravity fills the assemblies honoured by him,
along with tranquillity, out of respect and submission,

مُطَهَّرُ الْقَوْلِ وَالْافَعَالِ مَجْلِسُهُ
فَالذِّكْرُ يَمْلَأُهُ وَالْوَعْظُ أَحْيَانَا

His gathering is purified in words and deeds,
and dhikr fills it, as well as admonition at times.

حَازَ الْفَضَائِلَ وَالْاحْوَالَ شَاهِدَةً
بِالْكَدِّ فِي صَالِحِ الْاعْمَالِ عِيَانَا

Virtues and witnessed states are seen
to be obtained by exertion in righteous actions.

إِنَّ الْفَضَائِلَ عَنْ كَدٍّ وَعَنْ كَبَدٍ
نَتَائِجُ أَثْبَتَتْ لِلْحَقِّ بُرْهَانَا

Virtues come from exertion and from toil,
results which confirm the evidence of the Truth.

أَكْرِمْ بِمَنْ سَادَ أَخْلَاقًا وَمَكْرُمَةً
ءَاسِي الْقُلُوبِ إِذَا مَا دُنِّسَتْ رَانَا

Honour the one who has mastered character and honour.
He treats the hearts when they are soiled with rust.

هُوَ الْحَبِيبُ الَّذِي نَفْدِيهِ بِالْمُهَجِ
وَابْنُ الْحَبِيبِ غَدَا لِلْعَيْنِ إِنْسَانَا

He is the Beloved whom we would ransom with our lifeblood.
Ibn al-Habib, who became a fount for human beings.

فَاصْحَبْهُ بِالنَّصْرِ وَالتَّأْيِيدِ وَالْمَدَدِ
وَاحْفَظْهُ يَا رَبَّنَا وَزِدْهُ إِيقَانَا

Accompany him with help, support and aid.
Preserve him, our Lord, and increase him in certainty.

وَاسْدُلْ عَلَيْنَا جَمِيلَ السِّتْرِ قَاطِبَةً
وَكُنْ لَنَا وَلِيًّا دُنْيًا وَأُخْرَانَا

Drop over all of us a beautiful veil
And be our protector in this world and the Next,

بِقُطْبِ دَائِرَةِ الْأَكْوَانِ أَحْمَدَ مَنْ
عَمَّتْ رِسَالَتُهُ جِنًّا وَإِنْسَانَا

By the Qutb, the axis of beings, Ahmad,
whose Message embraces both jinn and human beings.

256

عَلَيْهِ أَوْفَىٰ صَلَاةِ اللهِ مَا جُعِلَتْ

أَوْقَاتُ أَهْلِ الْحِجَىٰ لِلذِّكْرِ مَيْدَانَا

On him be the most ample blessing of Allah as long as
the people of intelligence assign times as arenas for dhikr,

وَءَالِهِ الْغُرِّ وَالاَصْحَابِ أَجْمَعِهِمْ

وَاجْعَلْ بِفَضْلِكَ فِي الْفِرْدَوْسِ مَأْوَانَا ۝

And on his glorious family and all his Companions
and make Paradise our resting place, by Your bounty.

# Another Qasida

by Sayyidi Fudul ibn Muhammad al-Huwari

قصيدة أخرى

لسيدي فضول بن محمد الهواري

رَائِدُ الِاخْوَانِ ذَا الْاَمْرُ عَجِيبْ

حَـانَ وَقْتُ السَّيْرِ وَالنَّهْجِ رَسِيبْ

Scout of the brothers, the business is extraordinary!
The time of the journey is near and the path is firm.

ضَـاعَ هَذَا الْعُمْرُ فِي غَيِّ الصِّبَـا

وَانْقَضَىٰ حَتَّىٰ بَدَا مِنِّي الْمَشِيبْ

This life was squandered in the error of youth,
which ended when our white hair appeared.

ذَهَبَ الرِّفَـاقُ حَيْثُ الْمُلْتَقَىٰ

بِتُقَى الزَّادِ وَزَادِي مِنْ لَعِبْ

Companions left at the meeting place
with taqwa for provision, while my provision was merely games.

أَيْنَ إِلْفٌ أَيْنَ أُمٌّ وَأَبُّ

أَيْنَ حِبٌّ وَالْعِدَىٰ أَيْنَ الْقَرِيبُ

Where is friendship? Where are one's mother and father?
Where are lovers and enemies? Where are relatives?

أَشْهَرَ الْمَوْتُ عَلِيهِمْ حَرْبَهُ

فَغَدَوْا أَسْرَىٰ لِرَمْسٍ وَقَلِيبُ

Death declared war on them,
and they were captured by the tombs and ditches.

شَمْسُ كُلٍّ عَنْ يَقِينٍ وَجَبَتْ

وَشُمُوسِي عَنْ قَرِيبٍ سَتَجِبُ

The sun of everyone is necessary by certainty,
and my suns are necessary by proximity.

أَيْنَ أَحْلَامُ الصِّبَا كَمْ لَعِبَتْ

بِعُقُولٍ تَدَّعِي الْفَهْمَ الْمُصِيبُ

Where are the dreams of youth? How often they toyed
with minds which claimed to have sound understanding!

مَا هَذِهِ الْغَفْلَةُ يَا صَاحِ وَمَا

هَذِهِ الْقَسْوَةُ بِاللهِ أُجِبُ

What is this headlessness, friend?
What is this hardness with which I answer Allah?

وَنَذِيرُ الْوَعْظِ يَدْعُو مُزْعِجًا

هَلْ إِلَى اللهِ سَمِيعٌ أَوْ مُجِيبْ

The warner with admonitions summons and unsettles.
Is there anyone who listens to or answers Allah?

هُبَّ مِنْ نَوْمٍ قَسَا الْقَلْبُ بِهِ

وَاغْتَنَمْ عُمْرًا كَكَلْمٍ مِنْ كَذِبْ

The heart was propelled from a sleep by which the heart became hard
and which captured its life, like a dream of lies.

خَالِفِ النَّفْسَ وَتُبْ ثُمَّ أَجِبْ

دَاعِيَ اللهِ تَحُزْ أَعْلَا نَصِيبْ

Oppose the nafs and turn in tawba. Then respond to
the one who calls to Allah and you will win the highest share.

دَاعِي اللهِ وَبِاللهِ عَلَى

صِدْفِ قَصْدٍ قَصْدُهُ لَيْسَ يَخِيبْ

He calls to Allah and by Allah
with sincere intention. His aim does not fail.

بَحْرُ عِلْمٍ وَنَدًى مَنْ أَمَّهُ

نَالَ عِرْفَانًا وَمَعْرُوفًا خَصِيبْ

A sea of knowledge and dew. The one who goes to him
obtains gnosis and ample kindness.

هُوَ فِي الْعِرْفَانِ بَحْرٌ زَاخِرٌ
وَهْوَ فِي الْمَعْرُوفِ كَالْغَيْثِ الصَّبِيبْ

He is a sea abounding in gnosis,
and in kindness he is like the abundant rain.

يَبْذُلُ النُّصْحَ جِهَارًا مِثْلَمَا
يُطْعِمُ الدَّانِي وَالْقَصِي الْغَرِيبْ

He gives counsel publicly as
he feeds both the near and distant stranger.

يُحَطِّمُ الدَّاءَ بِوَعْظٍ لَيِّنٍ
حَيْثُ يَسْرِي مِثْلَ مَاءٍ فِي الْقَضِيبْ

The illness is shattered by gentle admonition
which flows like water in the stalk.

شَيْخُ عِلْمٍ وَطَرِيقٍ طَهُرَتْ
بَرْزَخُ الْبَحْرَيْنِ لِلَّهِ مُنِيبْ

A shaykh of knowledge and a purified Path,
the barzakh of the two seas, turning to Allah.

وَرِثَ الْأَسْرَارَ مِنْ عُنْصُرِهْ
خَيْرِ رُسْلِ اللهِ أَزْكَاهُمْ نَصِيبْ

He inherits secrets from his line,
from the best of the Messenger of Allah with the purest portion.

هُوَ فِي التَّحْقِيقِ عَنْهُ نَائِبُ
يَنْشُرُ السُّنَّةَ بِالسِّرِّ الْعَجِيبْ

He represents him in realisation,
spreading the Sunna by the wondrous secret.

مِنْ حَبِيبٍ مُسْتَمِدٌ وَاسْمُه
كَإِسْمِهِ لَكِنَّ هَذَا ابْنُ الْحَبِيبْ

From a beloved whose help is sought.
His name is the same as his, but this is Ibn al-Habib.

مَا أُحَيْلَا مَجْلِسًا حَلَّ بِهِ
وَهُوَ يُمْلِي وَعْظُهُ سَهْمٌ مُصِيبْ

How sweet is his gathering,
when he gives his admonition straight as an arrow.

كَمْ تَرَقَّى سَالِكٌ مِنْ نَظْرَةٍ
جَاءَ شَوْقًا لِهَوَى النَّفْسِ سَلِيبْ

How often a wayfarer rose by a single glance
when he came in yearning, dispossessed by the passion of the nafs.

سَلْ وُفُودًا كَمْ أَتَتْ مُشْتَاقَةً
نَائِيَّاتِ الْحَيِّ دَعْوَاهُ تُجِيبْ

Ask those who come. How many came from distant lands
in yearning to answer his call!

يَشْرَبُونَ الْعَذْبَ مِنْ عِرْفَانِهِ

حَسَبَ اسْتِعْدَادِ هَذَا الْمُنْتَسِبْ

They drink sweet water from His gnosis,
according to the predisposition of those affiliated to him.

كُلُّ عَامٍ مِنْ رَبِيعٍ يَا لَهَا

مِنْ وُفُودٍ تَقْصِدُ الرَّبْعَ الرَّحِيبْ

Every year in Rabi‘
how many delegations make for his ample house,

قَصْدَ إِحْيَاءٍ لِذِكْرَى الْمُصْطَفَى

مَنْبَعِ الآنْوَارِ شَرْقًا وَمَغِيبْ

Intending to be revived by the remembrance of the Chosen,
the fount of lights, both east and west.

فَاسْتَنَارَ الْكَوْنُ مِنْ مَوْلِدِهِ

فَاحَ مِنْ عَرْفِ الشَّذَا مِسْكًا وَطِيبْ

Existence was illuminated from his birth,
diffusing the musk and perfume of the fragrance of the wine.

خَرَّ صَرْحُ الْكُفْرِ مِنْ هَيْبَتِهِ

وَبَدَا مِنْهُ عَوِيلٌ وَنَحِيبْ

The lofty tower of kufr fell out of awe of him,
and wailing and lament appeared from it.

مَلأَ الْكَوْنَ سَنَاءً وَسَنَىٰ
وَمَحَتْ شَمْسُ الْهُدَىٰ غَيْمَ الصَّلِيبْ

He filled all existence with radiance and splendour,
and the sun of guidance obliterated the cloud of the cross.

كُلُّ فَضْلٍ حَازَ مِنْهُ الْمُنْتَهَىٰ
كَيْفَ يُحْصِيهِ مَدِيحٌ أَوْ أَدِيبْ

The utmost of every virtue is obtained from him,
so how can an eulogiser or writer enumerate them?

صَلِّ يَا رَبِّ عَلَى الدَّاعِي إِلَىٰ
حَضْرَةِ الْقُدْسِ ذَوِي الْقَلْبِ الْمُنِيبْ

O Lord, bless the one who calls those with repentant hearts
to the Presence of Purity.

ثُمَّ آلٍ وَصِحَابٍ عَدَّ مَا
حَنَّ مُشْتَاقٌ وَغَنَّى الْعَنْدَلِيبْ

And on his family and Companions
as long as anyone has yearning and the nightingale sings.

وَاحْفَظِ الْإِخْوَانَ وَالْإِسْلَامَ مِنْ
نَكَبَاتِ الدَّهْرِ نِعْمَ الْمُسْتَجِيبْ

Preserve the brothers and Islam from the misfortunes of time,
You are the best Answerer.

يَا أُهَيْلَ الْفَضْلِ لِلْفَضْلِ أَتَا

كُمْ فُضُولٍ عَسَى أَنْ لَا يَخِيبْ

O You worthy of favour, show favour to Fudul who has come to You,
hopefully he will not be disappointed.

لِي ذُنُوبٌ مَالَهَا مِنْ عَدَدٍ

إِنَّنِي مِنْهَا حَزِينٌ وَكَئِيبْ

I have wrong actions beyond number, and
I am sorrowful and grieved by them.

أَبْتَغِي الْخَتْمَ بِحُسْنَى وَالنَّجَا

ةَ غَدًا مِنْ حَرِّ نَارٍ وَلَهِيبْ ۞

I desire for my seal to be the best
and to obtain salvation tomorrow from the heat and flames of a Fire.

# A Qasida

by Sayyidi Muhammad ibn al-Habib ad-Dar'i

قصيدة

لسيدي محمد بن الحبيب الدَّرعيّ

حُيِّيتَ يَا بَحْرَ شِرعَةٍ ومَعْفِرَةٍ

وَلَمْ تَزَلْ لِلْعُلَا تَعْلُو مَعَالِيكَا

You revived, O sea of the Shari'a and gnosis,
and your fine qualities continue to ascend to the heights.

أُسْدِيتَ سِرًّا سَرَىٰ في الْكَوْنِ مَقْبِسُهُ

يُهْدَى بِهِ مَنْ نَئَىٰ ومَنْ يُدَانِيكَا

You conferred a secret whose torch flows in existence,
by which those who are far and those near are guided to you.

يَا مُفْرَدًا عِلْمًا أَشَيْخَ تَرْبِيَةٍ

أَقُطْبَ عَصْرٍ أَفُوزَ مَنْ يُوَالِيكَا

O unique in knowledge, Shaykh of teaching,
Qutb of the age! Those who befriend you win!

266

كُنْتَ الْمُرَبِّيَ لِلْأَرْوَاحِ نِعْمَ فَتَى

رَبَّىٰ وَرُبِّيَ قَدْ جَلَّتْ مَسَاعِيكَا

You were tending to the spirits while still an excellent youth,
both teaching and taught, with noble efforts.

يَا سَيِّدِي يَا أَبَا عَبْدِ الْإِلَهِ الَّذِي

طَابَتْ عَنَاصِرُهُ تُكْفَى أَعَادِيكَا

O Master, O slave of Allah whose origins
are excellent and defend against enemies:

نَجْلُ الشَّرِيفِ الْمُحَبَّبِ الْحَبِيبِ السَّرِي

مِنْ فَضْلِهِ فِي الْوَرَىٰ أَنْ كَانَ مُبْقِيكَا

The scion of the beloved sharif al-Habib.
It is part of His favour to mankind if He makes you remain.

أَفْرَعَ أَمْغَارِهِمْ أَيْ نَجْلَ إِدْرِيسَ مَنْ

يُعْزَىٰ إِلَى الْمُصْطَفَى الْمُخْتَارِ نَاهِيكَا

A branch of Amghar, i.e. the descendent of Idris.
It is enough to say that your lineage goes back to the Chosen one.

كَأَنَّ دَوْحَتَكُمْ عِقْدُ اللَّآلِي عَلَى

هَامِ الْمُلُوكِ وَقَدْ فَاقَ الْمَمَالِيكَا

It is as if your family tree were a necklace of pearls
on the head of kings, but it is far above kingdoms.

هَاكَ الْبَرَاهِينَ فَاقْرَأْهَا وَأَصْغِ لَهَا
تَصَدُقُ لَطَائِفَ مَا كُنْتُ أُهَادِيكَا

Here are proofs, so read them and listen to them.
They tell about the subtleties to which I guide you.

قَدْ جَاءَ إِدْرِيسُ مَنْجَاةً لِمَغْرِبِنَا
فَنَجْلُهُ الْفَذُّ وهو غَيْرُ خَافِيكَا

Idris came as salvation to our Maghrib,
His descendant is unique and he is not hidden from you.

وهكَذَا وَالْجَمِيعُ فِي التَّوَارِيخِ قَدْ
ذَاعَتْ مَآثِرُهُ دَامَتْ مَرَاقِيكَا

It is like that with all those in history
whose feats are known, as long as your ascent continues.

وَمِنْكُمُ الْقُطْبُ عَبْدُ اللهِ نَجْلُ حُسَيْ
نِ الَّذِي سِرُّهُ يَحْكِي مَعَانِيكَا

They include the Qutb 'Abdullah, an excellent son
whose secret conveys your meanings.

وَالْفَرْدُ إِبْرَاهِيمُ ءَايَاتُهُ اشْتَهَرَتْ
تِرْيَاقُ تُرْبَتِهِ عَنْهَا سَلَاكِيكَا

The signs of the unique individual Ibrahim are famous
The antidote of his earth is your coat of mail.

وَهَكَذَا فِي طِوَالِ الدَّهْرِ لَسْتَ تَرَىٰ

إِلَّا هُمَامًا بِنُورِهِ يُفَاجِيكَا

Similarly, for all time, you will not see
other than a gallant one whose light overwhelms you.

تِلْكَ الْعُهُودُ تَوَارَثَتْ مَكَارِمَهَا

اِبْنَا مِنْ آبَائِهِمْ بُشْرَىٰ بِهَاتِيكَا

Those times have passed down their noble qualities.
A son conveys the good news of that from their fathers.

هَذَا وَفَضْلُ الالَهِ لَيْسَ مُنْحَصِرًا

يَخْتَصُّ مَنْ شَاءَ فَاحْمَدَنَّ هَادِيكَا

Furthermore, the favour of Allah is unconfined,
He singles out for it whomever He wishes, so praise Allah, your Guide.

سَلَامُ مَوْلَى الْمَوَالِي مَعْ رَوَادِفِهِ

عَلَيْكَ وَالْمُنْتَمِينَ مَعْ أَهَالِيكَا

May the Master of masters and His viceregents
grant peace to you, your descendants and your family.

يَا مَنْ لَهُ جُمِعَتْ مَعَارِفُ فُرِّقَتْ

وَهَلْ يُرَىٰ جَمْعُهَا فِي غَيْرِ نَادِيكَا

O you for whom gnoses were joined which had been separated!
Is their joining seen in other than your circle?

أَحْيَ بِكَ اللهُ طُرْقًا لِلْهُدَىَ دَرَسَتْ
لَاكِنْ أَزِمَّتَهَا طَوْعُ أَيَادِيكَا

By you Allah revived paths of guidance which had been effaced,
But their reins are subject to you.

سُبْحَانَ مَنْ نَالَهُ عِلْمًا لَهُ لَدُنِي
فِي عَصْرِهِ فُهْ بِذَا فَمَنْ يُبَارِيكَا

Glory be to Allah who gave him laduni knowledge,
in his time. Say that, and who will vie with you?

يَا مَنْ لَهُ فِي النَّدَا بَاعٌ طَوِيلٌ وَفِي
مَرْضَاةِ رَبِّ الْوَرَىَ كُلُّ تَفَانِيكَا

You have great strength in the call and in pleasing
the Lord of mankind with total dedication!

وَرِجْلُهُ رَسَخَتْ فِي عِلْمِ شِرْعَتِنَا
مَا رُمْتَ مِنْهَا بِهِ فَوْرًا يُوَافِيكَا

His foot is firm in the knowledge of our Shari'a.
and he immediately satisfies you with what you desire of it.

وَفِكْرُهُ دَارِسٌ طَرْقَ الْحَقِيقَةِ مَا
مِنْ خَبْرِهَا شِئْتَهُ إِلَّا وَيَأْتِيكَا

His reflection treads the paths of the Reality –
by report, if you wish, unless he comes to you.

خُلْقُ التَّوَاضُعِ مَعَ حِلْمٍ لَهُ حُلَلٌ

وَهَيْبَةٌ عَنْ أَذًى فَلَا يُجَازِيكَا

He is robed in the qualities of humility and forbearance,
too awesome for harm, and so he does not punish you

إِلَّا إِذَا انْتُهِكَتْ حُرْمَةُ رَبِّ الْعُلَا

فَلَا يُرَى أَحَدٌ مِنْهُ يُفَادِيكَا

Unless the sanctity of the Lord of the High is violated.
Then there is no one who can ransom you from him.

أَقْدَامُهُ إِثْرَ خُطْوَةِ الرَّسُولِ فَمَا

كَانَتْ طَرِيقَتُهُ إِلَّا عَلَى تِيكَا

His feet follow in the tracks of the steps of the Messenger.
His Path only follows that.

يُحْيِ اللَّيَالِي فِي الاَذْكَارِ مَعَ كَرَمٍ

وَإِنْ حَضَرْتَ النَّهَارَ اللَّيْلَ يُنْسِيكَا

He brings the nights to life with dhikr and generosity,
and if you recall the day in the night, it makes you forget.

فَهَكَذَا هَكَذَا شُيُوخُ تَرْبِيَةٍ

فَدَعْ دُعَاةً عَلَى الْعُلْيَا مَرَاهِيكَا

That is how it is with the shaykhs of teaching.
So summon callers on your fine swift mounts.

وَإِنْ يُقَدَّرْ بِأَنْ أَبْصَرْتَ مُشْبِهَهُ

لَا تَعْدُ هَذَا الْمُعَلَّى فَهْوَ كَافِيكَا

If it is decreed that you see someone like him,
do not miss this exalted one. He is enough for you.

سَلِّمْ لِسَلْمَى وَلَا تَرْكَنْ لِمُعْتَرِضٍ

فَذَا اعْتِرَاضُ عُضَالٌ لَا يُعَادِيكَا

Greet Salma and do not place any trust in an opponent.
That is an inveterate opposition which will not drive you away.

مَا كُلُّ مَنْ جَا الْحِمَى لَاقَى أَحَاسِنَهُ

وَلَا جَمِيعُ الْحُلَى صَارَتْ دَرَانِيكَا

Not all who come to the sanctuary discover its beauties.
Not all of its finery becomes your stubble.

لَا تَقْتَرِبْ لِحَظَائِرِ الْخُصُوصِ سِوَى

أَنْ تُحْسِنَ الظَّنَّ طُرًّا فِي تَدَانِيكَا

Do not approach the preserves of the elite except
always with a good opinion when you approach.

يَا مَنْ يَرُومُ أَمَانِيًّا وَمَعْرِفَةً

بَادِرْ لِزَوْرَتِهِ مَعْ مَنْ يُوَاتِيكَا

O you who desire hopes and gnosis,
Set out to visit him with those who agree with you.

وَلَا تَقَـاعَسْ فَزَوْرُ الْعَـارِفِينَ شِفَـ
اءُ دَاءِ قَلْبِكَ مُرْغِمٌ لِقَالِيكَـا

Do not hold back. Visiting the gnostics contains healing
for the illness of your heart, despite those who hate you.

إِنْ جِئْتَهُ فَاغْرِفَنْ مِنْ بَحْرِ حِكْمَتِهِ
وَاقِلِ الْعَوَائِقَ وَلْتَصْدُدْ تَوَانِيكَـا

If you come to him, then take a handful from the sea of his wisdom,
and remove attachments and confront your lassitude.

تَأَدَّبَنْ إِنْ لَقِيتَهُ وَكُنْ خَـاضِعًـا
إِيَّـاكَ أَنْ يُجْتَلَى لَهُ تَعَـالِيكَـا

Show adab if you meet him and be humble.
Take care lest your lack of respect be disclosed to him.

وَاخْفِضْ لَهُ الصَّوْتَ وَاقْصِرِ الْكَلَامَ فَلَا
تَنْطِقْ بِمَا كَـانَ هُوَ غَيْرَ بَـادِيكَـا

Lower your voice before him and speak little.
Do not speak about what he does not start.

وَاغْضُضْ لِحَاظَكَ فِي غَيْرِ عُبُوسٍ وَكُنْ
مُسْتَقْبِلاً وَجْهَهُ وَانْفِ تَـافِيكَـا

Lower your glance without a frown,
face him and banish your contrariety.

وَدَعْ وَسَاوِسَ مَا تَدْعُو النُّفُوسُ لَهُ
فَرُبَّمَا كُشِفَتْ لَهُ خَوَافِيكَا

Abandon the whisperings to which the selves call.
Often your secrets will be disclosed to him.

لَا تَنْخَدِعْ إِنْ يَبِنْ إِغْضَا فَكَمْ مِحَنٍ
فِي ذَاكَ وَالْجَأْ لِرَبِّي فَهْوَ وَاقِيكَا

Do not be deceived if you are overlooked. How many afflictions
lie in that! Seek refuge in my Lord. He will protect you.

وَلَا تَكُنْ مُنْكِرًا مَا أَنْتَ تَجْهَلُهُ
وَانْسُبْ إِلَيْكَ الْقُصُورَ مَعْ تَغَاضِيكَا

Do not deny that of which you are ignorant.
Ascribe shortcoming to yourself if he seems not to notice you.

يَا أَيُّهَا الْفَخْمُ يَا أَجَلَّ مَنْ نُشِرَتْ
أَمْدَاحُهُ فَابْشِرَنْ وَاشْكُرْ مَوَالِيكَا

O splendour! How excellent is the one whose praises are unfolded,
so give good news and thank your Master.

أَمَمْتُكُمْ عَلِنِي أَحْظَى بِرُؤْيَتِكُمْ
وَدَعْوَةٍ نَوَّرَتْ قَلْبِي لِآتِيكَا

I went to you hoping to manage to see you
and by a call which inspired my heart to come to you,

حَتَّىٰ يُرَىٰ مِلْؤُهُ عِلْمًا وَمَعْرِفَةً

وَيَنْمَحِي الرَّانُ مَعْ مَا كَانَ تَافِيكَا

Until it is seen filled with knowledge and gnosis
and its rust is removed along with what is trivial.

وَيَحْسُنُ الْخَتْمُ وَالرِّضْوَانُ يَصْحَبُهُ

وَالْغُفْرُ إِذْ فَارَقَ الرُّوحُ الْحَرَاكِيكَا

And I hope for a good seal accompanied by divine pleasure,
And forgiveness when ruh departs from life,

وَأَنْ أُظَلَّ بِظِلِّ اللهِ مِمَّنْ نَجَوْا

مِنَ الْحِسَابِ وَمَوْلَانَا يُجَازِيكَا

And to be shaded in the shade of Allah among those who are saved
from the reckoning – may our Master repay you –

وَأَنْ أُرَىٰ فِي الْفَرَادِيسِ مَعْ

أَحِبَّتِي كُلِّهِمْ رَاقَتْ مَعَالِيكَا

And for I and my family to be in Paradise
with all my beloveds. You are greatly exalted.

مُسْتَشْفِعًا سَيِّدِي بِفَيْضِكُمْ وَبِمَنْ

يُنْمَىٰ لِحَضْرَتِكُمْ وَمَن حَوَالِيكَا

Seeking intercession, my master, by your generosity and by
those ascribed to your presence and those around you.

كُلٌّ يُقَدِّمُ مَا فِي الطَّوْقِ مِنْ تُحَفٍ

فَتُحْفَتِي لَكُمُ أُنْشُودَتِي فِيكَا

Every one offers whatever gifts he can.
My gifts to you are my songs about you.

وَلْتَغْضِ عَنْ خَطَلِي فِي مِدْحَتِي إِذْ أَتَتْ

بِقَدْرِ مُهْدٍ لَهَا جَلَّتْ أَيَادِيكَا

Overlook my prattle in my praise when it occurs
by the decree of the One Who guided to it. Your authority is sublime.

أَطَالَ رَبُّ الْوَرَىٰ فِي حُسْنِ طَاعَتِهِ

حَيَاتَكُمْ وَوَقَاكُمُ الدَّاءَالِيكَا

May the Lord of mankind prolong excellent obedience to Him
in your life and protect you from illness.

وَلَا تَزَلْ فِي رُقِيٍّ لَا انْتِهَاءَ لَهُ

وَلَمْ تَرَ أَبَدًا سُوءًا يُحَاذِيكَا

You continue to rise constantly without end
and you do not ever see any evil to counter it.

بِالْمُصْطَفَىٰ خَيْرِ مَنْ بِهِ تَشَفَّعَ مَنْ

يَرْجُو وَيُخْشَىٰ وَخَيْرِ مِنْ بِهِ عِيكَا

The Chosen is the best person who can intercede
for someone who hopes and fears, and the best to whom one can resort.

صَلَّى عَلَيْهِ وَسَلَّمَ الإِلَهُ وَءَآ

لِهِ وَصَحْبِهِ مَا فِي مَدْحِهِ حِيكَا ۞

May Allah bless him and grant him peace, and his family
and Companions as long as his praises are composed.

# A Qasida

by Sayyidi 'Abdullah ibn al-Habib ad-Dar'i

قصيدة

لسيدي عبد الله بن الحبيب الدَّرعِي

جَمْعُنَا هَذَا يُبَاهِي

كُلَّ جَمْعٍ فِي الْمَلَا

This group of ours vies
with every group in its gathering

بِوُجُودِ الْغَوْثِ فِيهِ

شَيْخُنَا قُطْبُ الْعُلَا

Because of the existence of the Ghawth,
our shaykh, the Qutb of the high.

جَمْعُنَا سَادَ الْجُمُوعَا

وَغَدَا لِلرُّشْدِ مَرْعَىٰ

Our gathering is the chief of all gatherings,
and has become a pasture for guidance.

حَبَّذَا مَنْ جَاءَ يَسْعَىٰ

هُنَا حِصْنُ النَّاسِ جَمْعَا

How excellent is the one who came running:
here is the fortress of protection for all people.

مَعْشَرَ الاِخْوَانِ بُشْرَىٰ

هَذَا غَوْثُ النَّاسِ طُرًّا

Company of brothers, good news!
This is the Ghawth of all people,

مَلْجَا كُلِّ مَنْ أَتَاهُ

بِهِ جَمْعُ الخَيْرِ يُدْرَىٰ

The refuge of all who come to him,
and by him all good is perceived.

شَيْخُنَا هَذَا حَلِيمٌ

وَكَرِيمٌ وَجَوَادٌ

This Shaykh of ours
is forbearing, noble and generous.

رَبَّنَا زِدْهُ عُلُوًّا

وَسَنَا فِي كُلِّ نَادْ

Our Lord, increase him
in sublimity and radiance in every circle!

وَابْقِهِ لِلنَّاسِ نَفْعَا

وَاهْدِنَا لِلْخَيْرِ جَمْعَا

Make him endure for the benefit of people
and guide us to all good.

وَارْضَ عَنْهُ كُلَّ الرِّضَىٰ

وَاسْتَجِبْ مِنَّا الدُّعَا

Be completely pleased with him,
and grant our supplication.

شَيْخُنَا يَعْسُوبُ قَوْمٍ

لِلْمَعَالِي قَدْ أَوَوْا

Our Shaykh is the prince of a people
who sought refuge in the heights,

وَبِهِ فِي كُلِّ سِرٍّ

اقْتَدَوْا ثُمَّ اقْتَفَوْا

And who follow him in every secret,
and imitate him.

وَبِهِ فِي بَحْرِ وِزْرٍ

امْتَطَوْا فُلْكَ النَّجَا

And who board the ship of salvation
in the sea of the burdens of sin.

قَطَعُوا تِلْكَ الْفَيَـافِي
وَصَلُوا مَأْوَى الرَّجَا

They crossed those deserts
and reached the refuge of hope.

وَبِهِ سَـادُوا وَعَـادُوا
لِلْهُدَى بَعْدَ الرَّدَى

By him they became masters
and returned to guidance after ruin.

وَاسْتَفَـادُوا كُلَّ خَيْرٍ
وَوُقُوا شَرَّ الْعِدَا

They profited from every good,
and are protected from the evil of the enemy.

فَلْتَقِفْ مَدْحِي فَهَذَا
بَحْرُ سِرٍّ قَدْ بَدَا

So understand my praise.
This is a sea of a secret which has appeared.

لَا تَرُمْ حَصْرَ اللَّـالِي
فِيهِ دَوْمًا سَرْمَدَا

Do not desire to restrict
the pearls in it constantly and forever.

رَبَّنَا زِدْهُ سَنَاءً
وَنَفَارًا وَهُدَىٰ

Our Lord, increase him
in radiance, glory and guidance,

وَبَقَاءً وَنَمَاءً
وَقِهِ شَرَّ الْعِدَا

And going on and expansion,
and protect him from the evil of enemies!

رَبَّنَا بَوِّأْنَا مِنْهُ
كُلَّ عِزٍّ وَرِضَا

Our Lord, provide us
with every might and pleasure from him.

وَاجْعَلِ الأَفْعَالَ مِنَّا
تَجْتَبِي مَا يُرْتَضَىٰ

Make our actions
bear pleasing fruit.

جَمْعُنَا جَمْعُ إِخَاءٍ
وَوِدَادٍ وَصَلَاحْ

Our gathering is one of brotherhood,
love and righteousness,

وَوَقَارٍ وَحَيَاءٍ
وَنَجَاحٍ وَفَلَاحْ

And gravity, modesty,
victory and success.

رَبَّنَا زِدْهُ وِءَامًا
وَجَلَالاً يُجْتَلَى

Our Lord, increase him
in harmony and majesty which is unmistakable,

وَكَمَالًا وَعُلُوًّا
وَاهْتِدَاءً لِلْعُلَا

And perfection and sublimity,
and guidance for the noble-minded.

رَبَّنَا صَلِّ وَسَلِّمْ
عَلَى مَنْ جَاءَ لَنَا

Our Lord, bless and grant peace
on the one who came to us

بِسَنَا الاِسْلَامِ سُدْنَا
وَبِهِ لِلْخَيْرِ عُدْنَا

With the radiance of Islam; we became leaders
and by it we returned to good.

وَعَلَى الآلِ وَصَحْبِ
كُلَّ حِينٍ بِاتِّصَالْ

And bless his family and Companions
in every time as well,

وَعَلَى مَنْ غَدَا يَقْفُو
أَثَرَهُمْ فِي كُلِّ حَالْ ۝

And those who will follow tomorrow
in our footsteps in every state.

# THE HAFIDHA

# The Hafidha

*This is the Wazifa known as the Hafidha which the Master, may Allah be pleased with him, recited every morning and evening, as do the elite of the mightiest of the fuqara in every place: and in it are secrets beyond number.*

In the name of Allah, All-Merciful, Most Merciful:

O Allah bless our master Muhammad and his family.

O Allah bless our master Muhammad, your slave and Messenger, the unlettered Prophet, and his family and companions, and grant them peace according to the number of Your creation and Your pleasure and the weight of Your Throne and the ink of Your words.

I take refuge with Allah, the All-Hearing, the Knowing, from the accursed shaytan. In the name of Allah, All-Merciful, Most Merciful, there is no power and no strength except with Allah the Exalted, the Great. Praise belongs to Allah Who has put away all sorrow from us.

Surely our Lord is All-Forgiving, All-Thankful.

In the name of Allah, All-Merciful, Most Merciful: Praise belongs to Allah Who created the heavens and the earth and appointed darkness and light. Then those who are kafir make others equal to their Lord!

# الْحَفِيظَةُ

وهذه الوظيفة المشهورة بالحفيظة التي يقرؤها الأستاذ رضي الله عنه وأرضاه صباحًا ومساءً ،
وكذلك خواص الأقوياء من الفقراء في كلِّ ناحيةٍ وفيها من الأسرار ما لا يدخل تحت حصر

بِسْمِ اللهِ الرَّحْمٰنِ الرَّحِيمِ. وصلَّى اللهُ على سَيِّدِنَا مُحَمَّدٍ وءَالِهِ.
اَللّٰهُمَّ صَلِّ على سَيِّدِنَا مُحَمَّدٍ عَبْدِكَ ورَسُولِكَ النَّبِيِّ الأُمِّيِّ وعلى
ءَالِهِ وَصَحْبِهِ وَسَلِّمْ تَسْلِيمًا. عَدَدَ خَلْقِكَ ورِضا نَفْسِكَ
وزِنَةَ عَرْشِكَ ومِدَادَ كَلِمَاتِكَ.

أَعُوذُ بِاللهِ السَّمِيعِ العَلِيمِ مِنَ الشَّيْطَانِ الرَّجِيمِ. بِسْمِ اللهِ الرَّحْمٰنِ
الرَّحِيمِ. وَلَا حَوْلَ وَلَا قُوَّةَ إِلَّا بِاللهِ العَلِيِّ العَظِيمِ. الْحَمْدُ لِلَّهِ الَّذِي
أَذْهَبَ عَنَّا الْحَزَنَ إِنَّ رَبَّنَا لَغَفُورٌ شَكُورٌ.

بِسْمِ اللهِ الرَّحْمٰنِ الرَّحِيمِ الْحَمْدُ لِلَّهِ الَّذِي خَلَقَ السَّمٰوَاتِ
وَالأَرْضَ وَجَعَلَ الظُّلُمَاتِ وَالنُّورَ
ثُمَّ الَّذِينَ كَفَرُوا بِرَبِّهِمْ يَعْدِلُونَ.

It is He Who created you from clay and then decreed a fixed term, and another fixed term is specified with Him. Yet you still have doubts! He is Allah in the heavens and in the earth. He knows what you keep secret and what you make public and He knows what you earn.

I have put my nafs and my iman and all that I owe to Allah in the protection of Allah which is the best protection possible, and in the proximity of Allah which cannot be overlooked, and in the invincibility of Allah which cannot be perceived, and in the veil of Allah which cannot be torn, and in the invincible troops of Allah and in the trusts of Allah which cannot be lost. The proximity of Allah is protected, and whoever clings to Allah is inviolable. The majesty of Allah is exalted and there is no place which is empty of Allah. May Allah permit every eye which looks on me with evil to be humbled.

Glory be to Allah and praise belongs to Allah, and there is no god except Allah, and there is no power and no strength except with Allah. Allah is enough for you against them.
He is the All-Hearing, the Knowing.

Allah is enough for me in everything. Allah overcomes all and nothing can stop the command of Allah. Allah is the Conqueror, the Victor, the Abaser of every stubborn tyrant, the Protector of the truth where it is. He has all power and strength.
It is only one shout and then they are silent.

May Allah bless our lord and master Muhammad and his family and Companions and grant them peace.

هُوَ الَّذِي خَلَقَكُمْ مِنْ طِينٍ ثُمَّ قَضَىٰ أَجَلًا. وَأَجَلٌ مُسَمًّى عِنْدَهُ. ثُمَّ أَنْتُمْ تَمْتَرُونَ. وَهُوَ اللَّهُ. فِي السَّمَوَاتِ وَفِي الْأَرْضِ يَعْلَمُ سِرَّكُمْ وَجَهْرَكُمْ وَيَعْلَمُ مَا تَكْسِبُونَ.

جَعَلْتُ نَفْسِي وَإِيمَانِي وَجَمِيعَ مَا لِلَّهِ عَلَيَّ فِي حِمَى اللَّهِ الَّذِي لَا يُرَامُ. وَفِي جِوَارِ اللَّهِ الَّذِي لَا يُخْفَرُ. وَفِي مَنَعَةِ اللَّهِ الَّتِي لَا تُدْرَكُ. وَفِي سِتْرِ اللَّهِ الَّذِي لَا يُهْتَكُ. وَفِي جُنْدِ اللَّهِ الْمَنِيعِ. وَفِي وَدَائِعِ اللَّهِ الَّتِي لَا تَضِيعُ. وَجِوَارُ اللَّهِ مَحْفُوظٌ. وَمَنْ يَعْتَصِمْ بِاللَّهِ مَعْصُومٌ. وَجَلَّ جَلَالُ اللَّهِ. وَلَا يَخْلُو مَكَانٌ مِنَ اللَّهِ. وَذَلَّتْ كُلُّ عَيْنٍ نَظَرَتْنِي بِسُوءٍ بِإِذْنِ اللَّهِ.

وَسُبْحَانَ اللَّهِ وَالْحَمْدُ لِلَّهِ. وَلَا إِلَهَ إِلَّا اللَّهُ. وَلَا حَوْلَ وَلَا قُوَّةَ إِلَّا بِاللَّهِ. فَسَيَكْفِيكَهُمُ اللَّهُ. وَهُوَ السَّمِيعُ الْعَلِيمُ.

حَسْبِيَ اللَّهُ مِنْ كُلِّ شَيْءٍ. اللَّهُ يَغْلِبُ كُلَّ شَيْءٍ. وَلَا يَقِفُ لِأَمْرِ اللَّهِ شَيْءٌ. اللَّهُ الْغَالِبُ الْقَاهِرُ مُذِلُّ كُلِّ جَبَّارٍ عَنِيدٍ. نَاصِرُ الْحَقِّ حَيْثُ كَانَ. بِهِ الْحَوْلُ وَالْقُوَّةُ. إِنْ كَانَتْ إِلَّا صَيْحَةً وَاحِدَةً فَإِذَا هُمْ خَامِدُونَ.

وَصَلَّى اللَّهُ عَلَى سَيِّدِنَا وَمَوْلَانَا مُحَمَّدٍ وَءَالِهِ وَصَحْبِهِ وَسَلَّمَ تَسْلِيمًا.

O Allah praise belongs to You with everything You look
to be praised with, for everything which You love to
be praised for. O Allah – thanks belongs to You with
everything You love to be thanked by, and for everything
You love to be thanked for, everlasting praise and thanks
as You are everlasting, in quantity as great as what You
know and the capacity of what You know and the ink of
Your words, and many times more than that. (3)

O Allah, praise and thanks belong to You for all these. O
Allah, praise and thanks be to You
for Your gathered gifts. (3)

O Lord, lead me in with a just ingoing and lead me out
with a just outgoing: grant me authority from You
to help me. (3)

There is no god but You! Glory be to You!
Truly I have been one of the wrongdoers. Allah is greater.
Allah is greater. Allah is greater. Bismillah on my nafs
and my Deen. Bismillah over what I possess and my
household. Bismillah over everything which my Lord has
given me. In the Name of Allah, the best of names.

In the Name of Allah, the Lord of the earth and heaven.
In the Name of Allah with whose name
nothing is harmed.

اَللّٰهُمَّ لَكَ الْحَمْدُ بِكُلِّ شَيْءٍ تُحِبُّ أَنْ تُحْمَدَ بِهِ.
عَلَى كُلِّ شَيْءٍ تُحِبُّ أَنْ تُحْمَدَ عَلَيْهِ. اَللّٰهُمَّ لَكَ الشُّكْرُ بِكُلِّ شَيْءٍ
تُحِبُّ أَنْ تُشْكَرَ بِهِ. عَلَى كُلِّ شَيْءٍ تُحِبُّ أَنْ تُشْكَرَ عَلَيْهِ. حَمْدًا
وَشُكْرًا دَآئِمَيْنِ بِدَوَامِكَ عَدَدَ مَا عَلِمْتَ وَزِنَةَ مَا عَلِمْتَ وَمِلْءَ مَا
عَلِمْتَ وَمِدَادَ كَلِمَاتِكَ وَأَضْعَافَ أَضْعَافِ ذٰلِكَ. (ثلاثًا)

اَللّٰهُمَّ لَكَ الْحَمْدُ وَلَكَ الشُّكْرُ عَلَى ذٰلِكَ كَذٰلِكَ. اَللّٰهُمَّ لَكَ الْحَمْدُ
وَلَكَ الشُّكْرُ عَلَى جَمِيعِ إِحْسَانِكَ. (ثلاثًا)

رَبِّ أَدْخِلْنِي مُدْخَلَ صِدْقٍ وَأَخْرِجْنِي مُخْرَجَ صِدْقٍ
وَاجْعَلْ لِّي مِنْ لَدُنْكَ سُلْطَانًا نَصِيرًا. (ثلاثًا)

لَآ إِلٰهَ إِلَّآ أَنْتَ سُبْحَانَكَ إِنِّي كُنْتُ مِنَ الظَّالِمِينَ. اللهُ أَكْبَرُ اللهُ
أَكْبَرُ اللهُ أَكْبَرُ. بِسْمِ اللهِ عَلَى نَفْسِي وَدِينِي. بِسْمِ اللهِ عَلَى مَالِي
وَأَهْلِي. بِسْمِ اللهِ عَلَى كُلِّ شَيْءٍ أَعْطَانِيهِ رَبِّي.
بِسْمِ اللهِ خَيْرِ الْاَسْمَاءِ.

بِسْمِ اللهِ رَبِّ الْاَرْضِ وَالسَّمَآءِ.
بِسْمِ اللهِ الَّذِي لَا يَضُرُّ مَعَ اسْمِهِ شَيْءٌ.

In the Name of Allah I have begun and in Allah I have put my
trust. Allah! Allah is my Lord I associate none with Him.

O Allah, from Your blessing I have asked for Your
blessing which none but You can give. Mighty is the one
in Your nearness and exalted is Your praise,
and there is no god except You.

O Allah, place me in Your sanctuary and Your protection
from every evil and from the accursed shaytan.

O Allah, I seek refuge with You from everything which
You have created, that I may be on my guard against it
through You. Before me I offer: In the Name of Allah, the
Merciful, the Compassionate: Say: 'He is Allah, Absolute
Oneness, Allah, the Everlasting Sustainer of all. He has not
given birth and was not born.
And no one is comparable to Him.'

Behind me I offer: In the Name of Allah, the Merciful,
the Compassionate: Say: 'He is Allah, Absolute Oneness,
Allah, the Everlasting Sustainer of all. He has not given
birth and was not born.
And no one is comparable to Him.'

To my right I offer: In the Name of Allah, the Merciful,
the Compassionate: Say: 'He is Allah, Absolute Oneness,
Allah, the Everlasting Sustainer of all. He has not given
birth and was not born.
And no one is comparable to Him.'

بِسْمِ اللهِ افْتَتَحْتُ وَعَلَى اللهِ تَوَكَّلْتُ.

أَللّٰهُ أَللّٰهُ رَبِّي لَاۤ أُشْرِكُ بِهِ أَحَدا.

أَسْأَلُكَ اللّٰهُمَّ خَيْرَكَ مِنْ خَيْرِكَ الَّذِي لَا يُعْطِيهِ غَيْرُكَ

عَزَّ جَارُكَ وَجَلَّ ثَنَاؤُكَ وَلَاۤ إِلٰهَ إِلَّاۤ أَنْتَ.

اَللّٰهُمَّ اجْعَلْنِي فِي عِيَاذِكَ وَجِوَارِكَ مِنْ كُلِّ سُوءٍ

وَمِنَ الشَّيْطَانِ الرَّجِيمِ.

اَللّٰهُمَّ إِنِّي أَسْتَجِيرُكَ مِنْ كُلِّ شَيْءٍ خَلَقْتهُ وَأَحْتَرِزُ بِكَ مِنْهُ وَأُقَدِّمُ

بَيْنَ يَدَيَّ بِسْمِ اللهِ الرَّحْمٰنِ الرَّحِيمِ قُلْ هُوَ اللهُ أَحَدٌ.

اللهُ الصَّمَدُ. لَمْ يَلِدْ وَلَمْ يُولَدْ. وَلَمْ يَكُنْ لَهُ كُفُوًا أَحَدٌ.

وَمِنْ خَلْفِي بِسْمِ اللهِ الرَّحْمٰنِ الرَّحِيمِ قُلْ هُوَ اللهُ أَحَدٌ.

اللهُ الصَّمَدُ. لَمْ يَلِدْ وَلَمْ يُولَدْ. وَلَمْ يَكُنْ لَهُ كُفُوًا أَحَدٌ.

وَعَنْ يَمِينِي بِسْمِ اللهِ الرَّحْمٰنِ الرَّحِيمِ قُلْ هُوَ اللهُ أَحَدٌ.

اللهُ الصَّمَدُ. لَمْ يَلِدْ وَلَمْ يُولَدْ. وَلَمْ يَكُنْ لَهُ كُفُوًا أَحَدٌ.

To my left I offer: In the Name of Allah, the Merciful,
the Compassionate: Say: 'He is Allah, Absolute Oneness,
Allah, the Everlasting Sustainer of all. He has not given
birth and was not born.
And no one is comparable to Him.'

Above me I offer: In the Name of Allah, the Merciful,
the Compassionate: Say: 'He is Allah, Absolute Oneness,
Allah, the Everlasting Sustainer of all. He has not given
birth and was not born.
And no one is comparable to Him.'

Underneath me I offer: In the Name of Allah, the
Merciful, the Compassionate: Say: 'He is Allah, Absolute
Oneness, Allah, the Everlasting Sustainer of all. He has
not given birth and was not born.
And no one is comparable to Him.'

O Allah, make me content with Your decree and make
me firm in what You have decreed for me so that I do not
wish to bring forward what You have held back nor to
hold back what You have brought forward.

O Allah, I seek refuge with You from the evil of my nafs
and from the evil of others and from the evil
of all that crawls on the earth.
You are my Lord Who takes them by the forelock.
Straight is the path of my Lord.

O Allah, O You Who give profit and You Who harm —
O Expander! O With-holder! O Shielder! O Exalter!
O Abaser! O Advancer! O Deferrer! O Reckoner! O
Reviver! Bring life to our essences through the light of
Your Gnosis and illumine our secrets with the inspiration
of Your Wilayat, and let us taste the signs of Your Tawhid
until we recognise only You, O most Merciful of the
Merciful, O Lord of the worlds,
O Lord of Majesty and Generosity.

وَعَنْ شَمَالِي بِسْمِ اللهِ الرَّحْمَنِ الرَّحِيمِ قُلْ هُوَ اللهُ أَحَدُ.

اللهُ الصَّمَدُ. لَمْ يَلِدْ وَلَمْ يُولَدْ. وَلَمْ يَكُنْ لَهُ كُفُؤًا أَحَدُ.

وَمِنْ فَوْقِي بِسْمِ اللهِ الرَّحْمَنِ الرَّحِيمِ قُلْ هُوَ اللهُ أَحَدُ.

اللهُ الصَّمَدُ. لَمْ يَلِدْ وَلَمْ يُولَدْ. وَلَمْ يَكُنْ لَهُ كُفُؤًا أَحَدُ.

وَمِنْ تَحْتِي بِسْمِ اللهِ الرَّحْمَنِ الرَّحِيمِ قُلْ هُوَ اللهُ أَحَدُ.

اللهُ الصَّمَدُ. لَمْ يَلِدْ وَلَمْ يُولَدْ. وَلَمْ يَكُنْ لَهُ كُفُؤًا أَحَدُ.

اللَّهُمَّ رَضِّنِي بِقَضَائِكَ وَبَارِكْ لِي فِيمَا قَدَّرْتَ لِي حَتَّى لَا أُحِبَّ تَعْجِيلَ مَا أَخَّرْتَ وَلَا تَأْخِيرَ مَا عَجَّلْتَ.

اللَّهُمَّ إِنِّي أَعُوذُ بِكَ مِنْ شَرِّ نَفْسِي وَمِنْ شَرِّ غَيْرِي وَمِنْ شَرِّ كُلِّ دَابَّةٍ أَنْتَ رَبِّي آخِذٌ بِنَاصِيَتِهَا.

إِنَّ رَبِّي عَلَى صِرَاطٍ مُسْتَقِيمٍ.

اللَّهُمَّ يَا نَافِعُ يَا دَافِعُ يَا بَاسِطُ يَا قَابِضُ يَا مَانِعُ يَا مُعِزُّ يَا مُذِلُّ يَا مُقَدِّمُ يَا مُؤَخِّرُ يَا حَسِيبُ يَا مُحْيِي أَحْيِ ذَوَاتِنَا بِنُورِ مَعْرِفَتِكَ وَنَوِّرْ سَرَائِرَنَا بِإِلْهَامِ وِلَايَتِكَ وَأَذِقْنَا مَذَاقَ مَعَالِمِ تَوْحِيدِكَ حَتَّى لَا نَعْرِفَ سِوَاكَ يَا أَرْحَمَ الرَّاحِمِينَ يَا رَبَّ الْعَالَمِينَ يَا ذَا الْجَلَالِ وَالْإِكْرَامِ.

295

O Allah let us be constantly with You and acting through You and let us return to You with health. O Lord of the worlds.

O Allah, bestow on us a mercy from You which will make us forget the remembrance of other-than-You, and a gift which will cut us off from other-than-You, and a gnosis of Yours by which we may witness only You, surrounded with loving care from trials and temptations in every state.

Place the sweetness of Your intimacy in our hearts, O most Generous of the Generous! O most Merciful of the Merciful, O Lord of the worlds.

O Allah, illumine my heart with knowledge and make my body obedient to You and purify my secret of temptations and occupy my thoughts with Your worth and protect us from the whisperings of shaytan and give me shelter from him, O Merciful, so that he may have no power over me.

I seek refuge with the perfect words of Allah from His wrath, His punishment, the evil of His slaves, and the insinuations of the shayateen and from their presence.

I take refuge with Allah, the Generous, for there is nothing greater than Him, and with the most perfect words of Allah which neither the awed nor the shameless can surpass, and with all His most beautiful names —

اَللّٰهُمَّ اجْعَلْنَا عِنْدَكَ دَائِمِينَ وَبِكَ عَامِلِينَ وَرُدَّنَا إِلَيْكَ بِالْعَافِيَةِ. يَا رَبَّ الْعَٰلَمِينَ.

اَللّٰهُمَّ امْنُنْ عَلَيْنَا بِرَحْمَةٍ مِنْكَ تُنْسِينَا ذِكْرَ مَنْ سِوَاكَ وَمِنَّةٍ تَقْطَعُنَا عَنْ مَنْ عَدَاكَ وَمَعْرِفَةٍ بِكَ لَا نَشْهَدُ بِهَآ إِلَّآ إِيَّاكَ مَحْفُوفِينَ بِالْعِنَايَةِ مِنَ الْمِحَنِ وَالْفِتَنِ فِي كُلِّ حَالٍ.

وَاجْعَلْ فِي قُلُوبِنَا حَلَاوَةَ أُنْسِكَ يَآ أَكْرَمَ الْاَكْرَمِينَ يَآ أَرْحَمَ الرَّاحِمِينَ يَا رَبَّ الْعَٰلَمِينَ.

اَللّٰهُمَّ نَوِّرْ بِالْعِلْمِ قَلْبِي وَاسْتَعْمِلْ بِطَاعَتِكَ بَدَنِي وَخَلِّصْ مِنَ الْفِتَنِ سِرِّي وَاشْغَلْ بِالِاعْتِبَارِ فِكْرِي وَقِنَا شَرَّ وَسَاوِسَ الشَّيْطَانِ وَأَجِرْنِي مِنْهُ يَا رَحْمٰنُ حَتَّى لَا يَكُونَ لَهُ عَلَيَّ سُلْطَانٌ.

أَعُوذُ بِكَلِمَاتِ اللهِ التَّآمَّاتِ مِنْ غَضَبِهِ وَعِقَابِهِ وَشَرِّ عِبَادِهِ وَمِنْ هَمَزَاتِ الشَّيَاطِينِ وَأَنْ يَحْضُرُونِ.

أَعُوذُ بِاللهِ الْكَرِيمِ الَّذِي لَيْسَ شَيْءٌ أَعْظَمَ مِنْهُ وَبِكَلِمَاتِ اللهِ التَّآمَّاتِ الَّتِي لَا يُجَاوِزُهُنَّ بَرٌّ وَلَا فَاجِرٌ. وَبِجَمِيعِ أَسْمَائِهِ الْحُسْنَىٰ

those which I know and those which I do not know
– from the evil of what He has created and originated
and made to multiply, and from the evil of what He
has created in the earth and what He has brought out
from it, and from the evils of what descends from
the heaven and rises to it, and from the evils of the
temptations of the night and day and the disasters of
the night and day – except for what knocks at my door
with good, O Merciful!

O Allah, provide us with fear of You that may come
between us and wrongful acts of disobedience against
You, and grant us obedience to You that will bring us to
Your Garden, and grant us certainty that will make the
misfortunes of this world easy for us.

O Allah, let us enjoy our hearing and vision and vigour
for as long as You grant us life, and let it be our legacy.
Avenge us on those who have wronged us and give us
victory over those who have attacked us.

Do not let this world be the greatest of our cares, nor the
scope of our knowledge, nor the object of our desire, and
do not allow us to take the path to the Fire. Do not place over
us because of our wrong actions those who have no fear of
You and will not show mercy to us – O most Merciful of the
Merciful, O Lord of the worlds. (3)

I take refuge with Allah, the All-Hearing, the Knowing
from the accursed shaytan. In the Name of Allah, the
Merciful, the Compassionate, and there is no power and

no strength except with Allah the Exalted, the Great.

مَا عَلِمْتُ مِنْهَا وَمَا لَمْ أَعْلَمْ. مِنْ شَرِّ مَا خَلَقَ وَبَرَأَ وَذَرَأَ وَمِنْ شَرِّ

مَا ذَرَأَ فِي الْأَرْضِ وَمَا يَخْرُجُ مِنْهَا وَمِنْ شَرِّ مَا يَنْزِلُ مِنَ السَّمَاءِ

وَمَا يَعْرُجُ فِيهَا وَمِنْ شَرِّ فِتَنِ اللَّيْلِ وَالنَّهَارِ وَطَوَارِقِ اللَّيْلِ وَالنَّهَارِ إِلَّا

طَارِقًا يَطْرُقُ بِخَيْرٍ يَا رَحْمٰنُ.

اَللّٰهُمَّ ارْزُقْنَا مِنْ خَشْيَتِكَ مَا تَحُولُ بِهِ بَيْنَنَا وَبَيْنَ مَعَاصِيكَ. وَمِنْ

طَاعَتِكَ مَا تُبَلِّغُنَا بِهِ جَنَّتَكَ.

وَمِنَ الْيَقِينِ مَا تُهَوِّنُ بِهِ عَلَيْنَا مَصَائِبَ الدُّنْيَا.

اَللّٰهُمَّ مَتِّعْنَا بِأَسْمَاعِنَا وَأَبْصَارِنَا وَقُوَّتِنَا مَا أَحْيَيْتَنَا. وَاجْعَلْهُ الْوَارِثَ

مِنَّا. وَاجْعَلْ ثَأْرَنَا عَلَى مَنْ ظَلَمَنَا. وَانْصُرْنَا عَلَى مَنْ عَادَانَا.

وَلَا تَجْعَلْ مُصِيبَتَنَا فِي دِينِنَا. وَلَا تَجْعَلِ الدُّنْيَا أَكْبَرَ هَمِّنَا وَلَا مَبْلَغَ

عِلْمِنَا وَلَا غَايَةَ رَغْبَتِنَا. وَلَا إِلَى النَّارِ مَصِيرَنَا. وَلَا تُسَلِّطْ عَلَيْنَا

بِذُنُوبِنَا مَنْ لَا يَخَافُكَ وَلَا يَرْحَمُنَا يَا أَرْحَمَ الرَّاحِمِينَ

يَا رَبَّ الْعَالَمِينَ. (ثَلَاثًا)

أَعُوذُ بِاللهِ السَّمِيعِ الْعَلِيمِ مِنَ الشَّيْطَانِ الرَّجِيمِ. بِسْمِ اللهِ الرَّحْمٰنِ

الرَّحِيمِ وَلَا حَوْلَ وَلَا قُوَّةَ إِلَّا بِاللهِ الْعَلِيِّ الْعَظِيمِ.

Allah is greater than all, and much praise belongs to
Allah and glory be to Allah morning and evening.

Say: 'My Lord has guided me to a straight path, a well-
founded Deen, the religion of Ibrahim, a man of pure
natural belief. He was not one of the mushrikun.'

Say: 'My salat and my rites, my living and my dying, are
for Allah alone, the Lord of all the worlds, Who has no
partner. I am commanded to be like that and I am the
first of the Muslims.'

Allah bears witness that there is no god but Him, as
do the angels and the people of knowledge, upholding
justice. There is no god but Him, the Almighty, the All-
Wise. The Deen with Allah is Islam.

I bear witness to Allah with what Allah bears witness to
Himself and with what His angels and men possessed of
knowledge from His creation bear witness.

There is no god except Allah, alone, with no associate.
To Him belongs the kingdom and praise. He makes to
live and makes to die and He is the living and never dies.
Goodness is in His hand and to Him is the outcome. He
has power over all things.

He is the First and the Last, the Manifest and the
Hidden, the First with no beginning and the Last with no
end, and the Manifest without likeness, and the Hidden
without qualification. He has knowledge of all things.

اَللّٰهُ أَكْبَرُ كَبِيرًا وَالْحَمْدُ لِلّٰهِ كَثِيرًا وَسُبْحَانَ اللّٰهِ بُكْرَةً وَأَصِيلًا.

قُلْ إِنَّنِي هَدَانِي رَبِّي إِلَىٰ صِرَاطٍ مُسْتَقِيمٍ دِينًا قِيَمًا
مِلَّةَ إِبْرَاهِيمَ حَنِيفًا. وَمَا كَانَ مِنَ الْمُشْرِكِينَ.

قُلْ إِنَّ صَلَاتِي وَنُسُكِي وَمَحْيَايَ وَمَمَاتِي لِلّٰهِ رَبِّ الْعَالَمِينَ.
لَا شَرِيكَ لَهُ. وَبِذَٰلِكَ أُمِرْتُ. وَأَنَا أَوَّلُ الْمُسْلِمِينَ.

شَهِدَ اللّٰهُ أَنَّهُ لَا إِلٰهَ إِلَّا هُوَ وَالْمَلَائِكَةُ وَأُولُوا الْعِلْمِ قَائِمًا بِالْقِسْطِ.
لَا إِلٰهَ إِلَّا هُوَ. الْعَزِيزُ الْحَكِيمُ. إِنَّ الدِّينَ عِنْدَ اللّٰهِ الْإِسْلَامُ.

وَأَنَا أَشْهَدُ اللّٰهَ بِمَا شَهِدَ اللّٰهُ بِهِ لِنَفْسِهِ. وَبِمَا شَهِدَتْ لَهُ بِهِ مَلَائِكَتُهُ
وَأُولُوا الْعِلْمِ مِنْ خَلْقِهِ.

لَا إِلٰهَ إِلَّا اللّٰهُ وَحْدَهُ لَا شَرِيكَ لَهُ. لَهُ الْمُلْكُ وَلَهُ الْحَمْدُ. يُحْيِي
وَيُمِيتُ. وَهُوَ حَيٌّ لَا يَمُوتُ أَبَدًا. بِيَدِهِ الْخَيْرُ وَإِلَيْهِ الْمَصِيرُ.
وَهُوَ عَلَىٰ كُلِّ شَيْءٍ قَدِيرٌ.

هُوَ الْأَوَّلُ وَالْآخِرُ وَالظَّاهِرُ وَالْبَاطِنُ. الْأَوَّلُ بِلَا بِدَايَةٍ.
الْآخِرُ بِلَا نِهَايَةٍ. الظَّاهِرُ بِلَا تَشْبِيهٍ. الْبَاطِنُ بِلَا تَكْيِيفٍ.
وَهُوَ بِكُلِّ شَيْءٍ عَلِيمٌ.

In whatever direction you turn, there is the Face of Allah. Every man has his direction to which he turns. And He is with you wherever you are. Allah encompasses all in knowledge and He has numbered everything in numbers.

We created man and We know what his nafs whispers to him. We are nearer to him than his jugular vein.

Shall He not know, He Who created? And He is the All-Subtle, the All-Aware. Allah has created everything and there is nothing like Him, and He is the All-Hearing, the All-Seeing.

Truly, His are the creation and the command. Blessed be Allah, the Lord of all being. Your creation and your uprising are as but a single self. As We originated the first creation so We shall bring it back again – a promise binding on Us, so We shall do.

And it is He Who originates creation then brings it back again, and it is very easy for Him.

Our command is but one word as the twinkling of an eye. There is no creature that crawls but He takes it by the forelock. Surely my Lord is on a straight path.

Not a leaf falls but He knows it. Not a grain in the earth's shadows, not a thing fresh or withered, but it is in a manifest Book.

فَأَيْنَمَا تُوَلُّوا فَثَمَّ وَجْهُ اللهِ. وَلِكُلِّ وِجْهَةٍ هُوَ مُوَلِّيهَا. وَهُوَ مَعَكُمْ أَيْنَمَا كُنْتُمْ. وَأَنَّ اللهَ قَدْ أَحَاطَ بِكُلِّ شَيْءٍ عِلْمًا وَأَحْصَى كُلَّ شَيْءٍ عَدَدًا.

وَلَقَدْ خَلَقْنَا الْإِنْسَانَ وَنَعْلَمُ مَا تُوَسْوِسُ بِهِ نَفْسُهُ وَنَحْنُ أَقْرَبُ إِلَيْهِ مِنْ حَبْلِ الْوَرِيدِ.

أَلَا يَعْلَمُ مَنْ خَلَقَ وَهُوَ اللَّطِيفُ الْخَبِيرُ. اللهُ خَالِقُ كُلِّ شَيْءٍ. لَيْسَ كَمِثْلِهِ شَيْءٌ. وَهُوَ السَّمِيعُ الْبَصِيرُ.

أَلَا لَهُ الْخَلْقُ وَالْأَمْرُ. تَبَارَكَ اللهُ رَبُّ الْعَالَمِينَ. مَا خَلْقُكُمْ وَلَا بَعْثُكُمْ إِلَّا كَنَفْسٍ وَاحِدَةٍ. كَمَا بَدَأْنَا أَوَّلَ خَلْقٍ نُعِيدُهُ. وَعْدًا عَلَيْنَا. إِنَّا كُنَّا فَاعِلِينَ.

وَهُوَ الَّذِي يَبْدَأُ الْخَلْقَ ثُمَّ يُعِيدُهُ. وَهُوَ أَهْوَنُ عَلَيْهِ.

وَمَا أَمْرُنَا إِلَّا وَاحِدَةٌ كَلَمْحٍ بِالْبَصَرِ. مَا مِنْ دَابَّةٍ إِلَّا هُوَ آخِذٌ بِنَاصِيَتِهَا. إِنَّ رَبِّي عَلَى صِرَاطٍ مُسْتَقِيمٍ.

وَمَا تَسْقُطُ مِنْ وَرَقَةٍ إِلَّا يَعْلَمُهَا. وَلَا حَبَّةٍ فِي ظُلُمَاتِ الْأَرْضِ وَلَا رَطْبٍ وَلَا يَابِسٍ إِلَّا فِي كِتَابٍ مُبِينٍ.

And the matter of the Hour is as the twinkling of an eye, or nearer, and in yourselves, so will you not see? Every day He is upon some labour.

Truly your Lord does what He wants. No-one knows how He is, glory be to Him, except Him.

Muhammad is the Messenger of Allah, and those who are with him are fierce to the kafirun, merciful to one another. You see them bowing and prostrating, seeking Allah's good favour and His pleasure.

O Prophet! We have sent you as a witness, and a bringer of good news and a warner, and a caller to Allah by His permission and a light-giving lamp. We have not sent you except to all mankind, good news to carry and a warning. We have not sent you save as a mercy to all beings.

I testify that what our lord and master Muhammad brought, may Allah bless him and his family, and grant them peace, is true.

Allah has been true to His promise and has given victory to His slave. He alone defeats the factions. There is no god save Allah and Allah is greater. Glory be to Allah and praise belongs to Allah. There is no power and no strength except with Allah.

Praise belongs to Allah in every state. A state only exists through the power, strength and support of the Great, the Exalted. Praise be to Allah for His success and His support and His victory and for His forbearance in spite of His knowledge, and for His pardon in spite of His power.

وَمَا أَمْرُ السَّاعَةِ إِلَّا كَلَمْحِ الْبَصَرِ أَوْ هُوَ أَقْرَبُ. وَفِي أَنْفُسِكُمْ أَفَلَا تُبْصِرُونَ. كُلَّ يَوْمٍ هُوَ فِي شَأْنٍ.

إِنَّ رَبَّكَ فَعَّالٌ لِمَا يُرِيدُ. لَا يَعْلَمُ كَيْفَ هُوَ سُبْحَانَهُ إِلَّا هُوَ.

مُحَمَّدٌ رَسُولُ اللهِ. وَالَّذِينَ مَعَهُ أَشِدَّاءُ عَلَى الْكُفَّارِ رُحَمَاءُ بَيْنَهُمْ. تَرَاهُمْ رُكَّعًا سُجَّدًا يَبْتَغُونَ فَضْلًا مِنَ اللهِ وَرِضْوَانًا.

يَا أَيُّهَا النَّبِيُّ إِنَّا أَرْسَلْنَاكَ شَاهِدًا وَمُبَشِّرًا وَنَذِيرًا وَدَاعِيًا إِلَى اللهِ بِإِذْنِهِ وَسِرَاجًا مُنِيرًا. وَمَا أَرْسَلْنَاكَ إِلَّا كَافَّةً لِلنَّاسِ بَشِيرًا وَنَذِيرًا. وَمَا أَرْسَلْنَاكَ إِلَّا رَحْمَةً لِلْعَالَمِينَ.

وَأَشْهَدُ أَنَّ الَّذِي جَاءَ بِهِ سَيِّدُنَا وَمَوْلَانَا مُحَمَّدٌ صَلَّى اللهُ عَلَيْهِ وَسَلَّمَ وَعَلَى ءَالِهِ حَقٌّ.

صَدَقَ اللهُ وَعْدَهُ. وَنَصَرَ عَبْدَهُ. وَهَزَمَ الْأَحْزَابَ وَحْدَهُ. لَا إِلَهَ إِلَّا اللهُ وَاللهُ أَكْبَرُ وَسُبْحَانَ اللهِ وَالْحَمْدُ لِلَّهِ وَلَا حَوْلَ وَلَا قُوَّةَ إِلَّا بِاللهِ.

اَلْحَمْدُ لِلَّهِ عَلَى كُلِّ حَالٍ وَمَا كَانَ مِنْ حَالٍ بِحَوْلٍ وَقُوَّةٍ وَتَأْيِيدِ الْكَبِيرِ الْمُتَعَالِ. الْحَمْدُ لِلَّهِ عَلَى تَوْفِيقِهِ وَتَأْيِيدِهِ وَنَصْرِهِ. وَعَلَى حِلْمِهِ بَعْدَ عِلْمِهِ. وَعَلَى عَفْوِهِ بَعْدَ قُدْرَتِهِ.

O Allah, bless our master Muhammad, your slave and Messenger, the unlettered Prophet, and his family and Companions and grant them peace, by the number of Your creation and Your pleasure and the weight of Your Throne and the ink of Your words.

In the Name of Allah, the Merciful, the Compassionate. Praise be to Allah, the Lord of all the worlds, the All-Merciful, the Most Merciful, the King of the Day of Judgment. You alone we worship. You alone we ask for help. Guide us on the Straight Path, the Path of those You have blessed, not of those with anger on them, nor of the misguided. Amin.

Say: 'My slaves, you who have transgressed against yourselves, do not despair of the mercy of Allah. Truly Allah forgives all wrong actions. He is the Ever-Forgiving, the Most Merciful.' (3)

Your Lord is forgiving to men for all their wrongdoing. (3)

Surely your Lord is wide in His forgiveness. (3)

Your Lord will soon give to you and you will be satisfied. (3)

O Allah, O turner of the hearts and eyes, fix our hearts and eyes on Your Deen with a Muhammadan firmness for ever and ever, by the rank of our Lord and master Muhammad, may Allah bless him and grant him peace and his family and Companions and all the trusting slaves of Allah.

اَللّٰهُمَّ صَلِّ عَلٰى سَيِّدِنَا مُحَمَّدٍ عَبْدِكَ وَرَسُولِكَ النَّبِيِّ الْأُمِّيِّ وَعَلٰى ءَالِهِ
وَصَحْبِهِ وَسَلِّمْ تَسْلِيمًا. عَدَدَ خَلْقِكَ وَرِضٰى نَفْسِكَ
وَزِنَةَ عَرْشِكَ وَمِدَادَ كَلِمَاتِكَ.

بِسْمِ اللهِ الرَّحْمٰنِ الرَّحِيمِ الْحَمْدُ لِلّٰهِ رَبِّ الْعٰلَمِينَ. الرَّحْمٰنِ
الرَّحِيمِ. مَلِكِ يَوْمِ الدِّينِ. إِيَّاكَ نَعْبُدُ وَإِيَّاكَ نَسْتَعِينُ. اهْدِنَا
الصِّرَاطَ الْمُسْتَقِيمَ صِرَاطَ الَّذِينَ أَنْعَمْتَ عَلَيْهِمْ غَيْرِ الْمَغْضُوبِ
عَلَيْهِمْ وَلَا الضَّآلِّينَ. ءَامِين.

قُلْ يَا عِبَادِيَ الَّذِينَ أَسْرَفُوا عَلٰى أَنْفُسِهِمْ لَا تَقْنَطُوا مِنْ رَحْمَةِ اللهِ. إِنَّ
اللهَ يَغْفِرُ الذُّنُوبَ جَمِيعًا. إِنَّهُ هُوَ الْغَفُورُ الرَّحِيمُ. (ثَلاثًا)

وَإِنَّ رَبَّكَ لَذُو مَغْفِرَةٍ لِلنَّاسِ عَلٰى ظُلْمِهِمْ. (ثَلاثًا)

إِنَّ رَبَّكَ وَاسِعُ الْمَغْفِرَةِ. (ثَلاثًا)

وَلَسَوْفَ يُعْطِيكَ رَبُّكَ فَتَرْضٰى. (ثَلاثًا)

اَللّٰهُمَّ يَا مُقَلِّبَ الْقُلُوبِ وَالْأَبْصَارِ ثَبِّتْ قُلُوبَنَا وَأَبْصَارَنَا عَلٰى دِينِكَ
ثَبَاتًا مُحَمَّدِيًّا إِلٰى آبَدِ الْآبَدِ بِجَاهِ سَيِّدِنَا وَمَوْلَانَا مُحَمَّدٍ صَلَّى اللهُ عَلَيْهِ
وَسَلَّمَ وَعَلٰى ءَالِهِ وَأَصْحَابِهِ وَعَلٰى جَمِيعِ عِبَادِ اللهِ الْمُؤْمِنِينَ.

I take refuge with Allah from the accursed shaytan. (3)

In the Name of Allah, the Merciful, the Compassionate. (3)

In the Name of Allah with Whose Name nothing is
harmed in the earth or heaven, and He is the All-
Hearing, the All-Knowing. (3)

Allah is enough for us, He is the best guardian. (3)

There is no power, no strength except with Allah,
the Mighty, the Great. (3)

O Allah, bless our master Muhammad, your slave and
Messenger, the unlettered Prophet, and his family and
Companions and grant them peace, by the number of
Your creation and Your pleasure and the weight of Your
Throne and the ink of Your words.

O Allah, bless our lord and master Muhammad
until nothing remains with which to bless him further.

O Allah bless our lord and master Muhammad among the first
and bless our lord and master Muhammad among the last.

O Allah, bless our lord and master Muhammad among
the heavenly assembly until the Day of Reckoning.
Whatever Allah wills. There is no strength except with
Allah, the High, the Great.

أَعُوذُ بِاللهِ مِنَ الشَّيْطَانِ الرَّجِيمِ. (ثَلَاثًا).

بِسْمِ اللهِ الرَّحْمَٰنِ الرَّحِيمِ. (ثَلَاثًا)

بِسْمِ اللهِ الَّذِي لَا يَضُرُّ مَعَ اسْمِهِ شَيْءٌ فِي الأَرْضِ وَلَا فِي السَّمَاءِ. وَهُوَ السَّمِيعُ الْعَلِيمُ. (ثَلَاثًا)

حَسْبُنَا اللهُ وَنِعْمَ الْوَكِيلُ. (ثَلَاثًا)

وَلَا حَوْلَ وَلَا قُوَّةَ إِلَّا بِاللهِ الْعَلِيِّ الْعَظِيمِ. (ثَلَاثًا)

اَللّٰهُمَّ صَلِّ عَلَىٰ سَيِّدِنَا مُحَمَّدٍ عَبْدِكَ وَرَسُولِكَ النَّبِيِّ الأُمِّيِّ وَعَلَىٰ آلِهِ وَصَحْبِهِ وَسَلِّمْ تَسْلِيمًا. عَدَدَ خَلْقِكَ وَرِضَىٰ نَفْسِكَ وَزِنَةَ عَرْشِكَ وَمِدَادَ كَلِمَاتِكَ.

اَللّٰهُمَّ صَلِّ عَلَىٰ سَيِّدِنَا وَمَوْلَانَا مُحَمَّدٍ حَتَّىٰ لَا يَبْقَىٰ شَيْءٌ مِنَ الصَّلَاةِ عَلَيْهِ.

اَللّٰهُمَّ صَلِّ عَلَىٰ سَيِّدِنَا وَمَوْلَانَا مُحَمَّدٍ فِي الأَوَّلِينَ. وَصَلِّ عَلَىٰ سَيِّدِنَا وَمَوْلَانَا مُحَمَّدٍ فِي الآخِرِينَ.

اَللّٰهُمَّ صَلِّ عَلَىٰ سَيِّدِنَا وَمَوْلَانَا مُحَمَّدٍ فِي الْمَلَإِ الأَعْلَىٰ إِلَىٰ يَوْمِ الدِّينِ. مَا شَاءَ اللهُ لَا قُوَّةَ إِلَّا بِاللهِ الْعَلِيِّ الْعَظِيمِ.

O Allah, bless our lord and master Muhammad and the
family of our lord and master Muhammad, and grant him
means of access to you, merit and high degree, and raise
him to the Praiseworthy Station which You promised
him. Your do not fail the promise.

O Allah, exalt him and clarify his proof and make his
proof to shine and make his goodness evident and accept
his intercession on behalf of his Community and make us
follow his Sunna, O Lord of the worlds and Lord of the
Mighty Throne.

O Allah, gather us in his company under his banner and
give us to drink from his goblet and profit us through his
love. Amin, O Lord of the worlds.

O Allah, O Lord, bring to him the best of greetings
from us, and we ask you to reward him with the best of
that with which you may reward the Prophet from his
Community, O Lord of the worlds.

O Allah, O Lord, I ask You to forgive me and have mercy
upon me and turn to me and protect me from all trials
and afflictions coming out of the earth or descending
from heaven. You are powerful over everything by Your
Mercy. Forgive the trusting-ones, men and women – and the
Muslims – men and women – living and dead.

اَللّٰهُمَّ صَلِّ عَلَى سَيِّدِنَا وَمَوْلَانَا مُحَمَّدٍ وَعَلٰى ءَالِ سَيِّدِنَا وَمَوْلَانَا مُحَمَّدٍ وَأَعْطِهِ الْوَسِيلَةَ وَالْفَضِيلَةَ وَالدَّرَجَةَ الرَّفِيعَةَ وَابْعَثْهُ مَقَامًا مَحْمُودًا الَّذِي وَعَدْتَهُ. إِنَّكَ لَا تُخْلِفُ الْمِيعَادَ.

اَللّٰهُمَّ عَظِّمْ شَأْنَهُ. وَبَيِّنْ بُرْهَانَهُ. وَأَبْلِجْ حُجَّتَهُ. وَبَيِّنْ فَضِيلَتَهُ. وَتَقَبَّلْ شَفَاعَتَهُ فِي أُمَّتِهِ. وَاسْتَعْمِلْنَا بِسُنَّتِهِ. يَا رَبَّ الْعَالَمِينَ وَيَا رَبَّ الْعَرْشِ الْعَظِيمِ.

اَللّٰهُمَّ يَا رَبِّ احْشُرْنَا فِي زُمْرَتِهِ وَتَحْتَ لِوَائِهِ وَأَسْقِنَا بِكَأْسِهِ وَانْفَعْنَا بِمَحَبَّتِهِ. ءَامِين يَا رَبَّ الْعَالَمِينَ.

اَللّٰهُمَّ يَا رَبِّ بَلِّغْهُ عَنَّا أَفْضَلَ السَّلَام وَأَجْزِهِ عَنَّا أَفْضَلَ مَا جَازَيْتَ بِهِ النَّبِيَّ عَنْ أُمَّتِهِ يَا رَبَّ الْعَالَمِينَ.

اَللّٰهُمَّ يَا رَبِّ إِنِّي أَسْأَلُكَ أَنْ تَغْفِرَ لِي وَتَرْحَمَنِي وَتَتُوبَ عَلَيَّ. وَتُعَافِيَنِي مِنْ جَمِيعِ الْبَلَاءِ وَالْبَلْوَآءِ الْخَارِجِ مِنَ الأَرْضِ وَالنَّازِلِ مِنَ السَّمَآءِ. إِنَّكَ عَلَى كُلِّ شَيْءٍ قَدِيرٌ بِرَحْمَتِكَ. وَأَنْ تَغْفِرَ لِلْمُومِنِينَ وَالْمُومِنَاتِ وَالْمُسْلِمِينَ وَالْمُسْلِمَاتِ الأَحْيَآءِ مِنْهُمْ وَالأَمْوَاتِ.

May Allah be pleased with his pure wives,
the mothers of the trusting-ones.

May Allah be pleased with his Companions, the way-
marks, the Imams of guidance, and lamps of the world,
and with the followers, and the followers of the followers.
May He be kind to them until the Day of Reckoning.
Praise belongs to Allah, the Lord of the worlds.

O Allah, bless and grant peace to our lord and master
Muhammad, the first of the lights emanating from the
oceans of the sublimity of the Essence, with every one of
Your perfections in all Your self-manifestations. In the
two worlds – the hidden and the seen –
he realised the meanings of the Names and Attributes.

He is the first to give praise and worship with every
kind of adoration and good action. He is the helper of
all created beings in the world of forms and the world of
spirits. And blessings be upon his family and Companions
with a blessing that will lift the veil from his noble face
for us in visions and in the waking state and will acquaint
us with You and with him in all ranks and presences.

Be gracious to us, O Mawlana, by his rank, in movement
and in stillness, in looks and in thoughts.

Glory be to your Lord, the Lord of might, above all that
they describe, and peace be upon the Messengers,
and praise belongs to Allah, the Lord of the worlds.

وَرَضِيَ اللهُ عَنْ أَزْوَاجِهِ الطَّاهِرَاتِ أُمَّهَاتِ الْمُؤْمِنِينَ.

وَرَضِيَ اللهُ عَنْ أَصْحَابِهِ الأَعْلَامِ أَئِمَّةِ الْهُدَى وَمَصَابِيحِ الدُّنْيَا وَعَنِ التَّابِعِينَ وَتَابِعِ التَّابِعِينَ لَهُمْ بِإِحْسَانٍ إِلَى يَوْمِ الدِّينِ. وَالْحَمْدُ لِلَّهِ رَبِّ الْعَلَمِينَ.

اللَّهُمَّ صَلِّ وَسَلِّمْ بِأَنْوَاعِ كَمَالَاتِكَ فِي جَمِيعِ تَجَلِّيَاتِكَ عَلَى سَيِّدِنَا وَمَوْلَانَا مُحَمَّدٍ أَوَّلِ الأَنْوَارِ الْفَائِضَةِ مِنْ بُحُورِ عَظَمَةِ الذَّاتِ. الْمُتَحَقِّقِ فِي عَالَمَيِ الْبُطُونِ وَالظُّهُورِ بِمَعَانِي الأَسْمَاءِ وَالصِّفَاتِ.

فَهُوَ أَوَّلُ حَامِدٍ وَمُتَعَبِّدٍ بِأَنْوَاعِ الْعِبَادَاتِ وَالْقُرُبَاتِ. وَالْمُمِدُّ فِي عَالَمَيِ الأَرْوَاحِ وَالأَشْبَاحِ بِجَمِيعِ الْمَوْجُودَاتِ. وَعَلَى ءَالِهِ وَأَصْحَابِهِ صَلَاةً تَكْشِفُ لَنَا النِّقَابَ عَنْ وَجْهِهِ الْكَرِيمِ فِي الْمَرَآئِي وَالْيَقَظَاتِ. وَتُعَرِّفُنَا بِكَ وَبِهِ فِي جَمِيعِ الْمَرَاتِبِ وَالْحَضَرَاتِ.

وَالْطُفْ بِنَا يَا مَوْلَانَا بِجَاهِهِ فِي الْحَرَكَاتِ وَالسَّكَنَاتِ وَاللَّحَظَاتِ وَالْخَطَرَاتِ.

سُبْحَانَ رَبِّكَ رَبِّ الْعِزَّةِ عَمَّا يَصِفُونَ. وَسَلَامٌ عَلَى الْمُرْسَلِينَ. وَالْحَمْدُ لِلَّهِ رَبِّ الْعَلَمِينَ.

Allah is enough for you against them. He is the All-
Hearing, the All-Knowing. (3)

Allah is the best protection and the most Merciful of the
Merciful. (3)

I commit my affair to Allah: surely Allah sees His
servants. (3)

There is no god but You! Glory be to You!
Truly I have been one of the wrongdoers. (3)

'Our Lord, give us mercy directly from You and open the
way for us to right guidance in our situation.' (3)

'Our Lord, do not make our hearts swerve aside after
You have guided us. And give us mercy from You. You
are the Ever-Giving.' (3)

O Allah I offer you before every breath, look, glance,
blink made by the people of the heavens and the earth,
and everything which exists in Your knowledge, now or
in the past — before all these I offer You:

Allah, there is no god but Him, the Living, the Self-
Sustaining. He is not subject to drowsiness or sleep.
Everything in the heavens and the earth belongs to Him.
Who can intercede with Him except by His permission?.
He knows what is before them and what is behind them
but they cannot grasp any of His knowledge save what
He wills. His Footstool encompasses the heavens and the
earth and their preservation does not tire Him. He is the
Most High, the Magnificent.

فَسَيَكْفِيكَهُمُ اللهُ وَهُوَ السَّمِيعُ الْعَلِيمُ. (ثَلاثًا)

فَاللهُ خَيْرٌ حِفْظًا وَهُوَ أَرْحَمُ الرَّاحِمِينَ. (ثَلاثًا)

وَأُفَوِّضُ أَمْرِي إِلَى اللهِ. إِنَّ اللهَ بَصِيرٌ بِالْعِبَادِ. (ثَلاثًا)

لَا إِلَهَ إِلَّا أَنْتَ سُبْحَانَكَ إِنِّي كُنْتُ مِنَ الظَّالِمِينَ. (ثَلاثًا)

رَبَّنَا آتِنَا مِنْ لَدُنْكَ رَحْمَةً وَهَيِّئْ لَنَا مِنْ أَمْرِنَا رَشَدًا. (ثَلاثًا)

رَبَّنَا لَا تُزِغْ قُلُوبَنَا بَعْدَ إِذْ هَدَيْتَنَا وَهَبْ لَنَا مِنْ لَدُنْكَ رَحْمَةً. إِنَّكَ أَنْتَ الْوَهَّابُ. (ثَلاثًا)

اَللَّهُمَّ إِنِّي أُقَدِّمُ إِلَيْكَ بَيْنَ يَدَيَّ كُلَّ نَفَسٍ وَلَحْظَةٍ وَلَمْحَةٍ وَطَرْفَةٍ يَطْرُفُ بِهَا أَهْلُ السَّمَوَاتِ وَأَهْلِ الْأَرْضِ.
وَكُلُّ شَيْءٍ هُوَ فِي عِلْمِكَ كَائِنٌ أَوْ قَدْ كَانَ.
أُقَدِّمُ بَيْنَ يَدَيَّ كُلَّ ذَلِكَ كُلِّهِ.

اللهُ لَا إِلَهَ إِلَّا هُوَ الْحَيُّ الْقَيُّومُ. لَا تَأْخُذُهُ سِنَةٌ وَلَا نَوْمٌ.
لَهُ مَا فِي السَّمَوَاتِ وَمَا فِي الْأَرْضِ. مَنْ ذَا الَّذِي يَشْفَعُ عِنْدَهُ إِلَّا بِإِذْنِهِ. يَعْلَمُ مَا بَيْنَ أَيْدِيهِمْ وَمَا خَلْفَهُمْ.
وَلَا يُحِيطُونَ بِشَيْءٍ مِنْ عِلْمِهِ إِلَّا بِمَا شَاءَ. وَسِعَ كُرْسِيُّهُ السَّمَوَاتِ وَالْأَرْضَ. وَلَا يَؤُودُهُ حِفْظُهُمَا وَهُوَ الْعَلِيُّ الْعَظِيمُ.

A Messenger has come to you from among yourselves. Your suffering is distressing to him; he is deeply concerned for you; he is gentle and merciful to the muminun.

But if they turn away, say, 'Allah is enough for me. There is no god but Him. I have put my trust in Him. He is the Lord of the Mighty Throne.' (7)

In the name of Allah, All-Merciful, Most Merciful: Say: 'Kafirun! I do not worship what you worship and you do not worship what I worship. Nor will I worship what you worship nor will you worship what I worship. You have your Deen and I have my Deen.'

In the name of Allah, All-Merciful, Most Merciful: When Allah's help and victory have arrived and you have seen people entering Allah's Deen in droves, then glorify your Lord's praise and ask His forgiveness. He is the Ever-Returning.

In the name of Allah, All-Merciful, Most Merciful: Say: 'He is Allah, Absolute Oneness, Allah, the Everlasting Sustainer of all. He has not given birth and was not born. And no one is comparable to Him.' (3)

In the name of Allah, All-Merciful, Most Merciful: Say: 'I seek refuge with the Lord of Daybreak, from the evil of what He has created and from the evil of the darkness when it gathers and from the evil of women who blow on knots and from the evil of an envier when he envies.' (3)

لَقَدْ جَاءَكُمْ رَسُولٌ مِّنْ أَنْفُسِكُمْ عَزِيزٌ عَلَيْهِ مَا عَنِتُّمْ حَرِيصٌ عَلَيْكُمْ. بِالْمُؤْمِنِينَ رَؤُوفٌ رَحِيمٌ.

فَإِنْ تَوَلَّوْا فَقُلْ حَسْبِيَ اللهُ. لَا إِلَهَ إِلَّا هُوَ. عَلَيْهِ تَوَكَّلْتُ. وَهُوَ رَبُّ الْعَرْشِ الْعَظِيمِ. (سبعًا)

بِسْمِ اللهِ الرَّحْمَـٰنِ الرَّحِيمِ. قُلْ يَا أَيُّهَا الْكَافِرُونَ لَا أَعْبُدُ مَا تَعْبُدُونَ وَلَا أَنْتُمْ عَابِدُونَ مَا أَعْبُدُ. وَلَا أَنَا عَابِدٌ مَا عَبَدْتُمْ وَلَا أَنْتُمْ عَابِدُونَ مَا أَعْبُدُ. لَكُمْ دِينُكُمْ وَلِيَ دِينِ.

بِسْمِ اللهِ الرَّحْمَـٰنِ الرَّحِيمِ. إِذَا جَاءَ نَصْرُ اللهِ وَالْفَتْحُ وَرَأَيْتَ النَّاسَ يَدْخُلُونَ فِي دِينِ اللهِ أَفْوَاجًا فَسَبِّحْ بِحَمْدِ رَبِّكَ وَاسْتَغْفِرْهُ. إِنَّهُ كَانَ تَوَّابًا.

بِسْمِ اللهِ الرَّحْمَـٰنِ الرَّحِيمِ قُلْ هُوَ اللهُ أَحَدٌ. اللهُ الصَّمَدُ. لَمْ يَلِدْ وَلَمْ يُولَدْ. وَلَمْ يَكُنْ لَهُ كُفُوًا أَحَدٌ. (ثلاثًا)

بِسْمِ اللهِ الرَّحْمَـٰنِ الرَّحِيمِ قُلْ أَعُوذُ بِرَبِّ الْفَلَقِ مِنْ شَرِّ مَا خَلَقَ وَمِنْ شَرِّ غَاسِقٍ إِذَا وَقَبَ وَمِنْ شَرِّ النَّفَّاثَاتِ فِي الْعُقَدِ وَمِنْ شَرِّ حَاسِدٍ إِذَا حَسَدَ. (ثلاثًا)

In the name of Allah, All-Merciful, Most Merciful:
Say: 'I seek refuge with the Lord of mankind, the King
of mankind, the God of mankind, from the evil of the
insidious whisperer who whispers in people's breasts and
comes from the jinn and from mankind.' (3)

In the name of Allah, All-Merciful, Most Merciful:
Praise be to Allah, the Lord of all the worlds, the All-
Merciful, the Most Merciful, the King of the Day of
Judgment. You alone we worship. You alone we ask for
help. Guide us on the Straight Path, the Path of those You
have blessed, not of those with anger on them,
nor of the misguided. Amin.

O Allah, bless our master Muhammad, the unlettered
Prophet and his family and Companions and grant them
peace with the most perfect of blessings,
and the purest peace.

O Allah, I seek good from You by Your knowledge and I
ask You for strength by Your power. I ask You for some of
Your great and sublime overflowing. You have power and
I do not. You know and I do not know. And You are the
Knower of the Unseen.

O Allah if You know that my situation – all my
movement and stillness, apparent and hidden, in speech,
deeds, character and state, in spiritual work and daily
life, as regards myself and others, in this night

(or day) and those after it,

بِسْمِ اللهِ الرَّحْمَنِ الرَّحِيمِ قُلْ اَعُوذُ بِرَبِّ النَّاسِ مَلِكِ النَّاسِ
إِلَهِ النَّاسِ مِنْ شَرِّ الْوَسْوَاسِ الْخَنَّاسِ الَّذِي يُوَسْوِسُ فِي صُدُورِ
النَّاسِ مِنَ الْجِنَّةِ وَالنَّاسِ. (ثلاثًا)

بِسْمِ اللهِ الرَّحْمَنِ الرَّحِيمِ الْحَمْدُ لِلَّهِ رَبِّ الْعَالَمِينَ الرَّحْمَنِ الرَّحِيمِ
مَلِكِ يَوْمِ الدِّينِ. إِيَّاكَ نَعْبُدُ وَإِيَّاكَ نَسْتَعِينُ. اهْدِنَا الصِّرَاطَ
الْمُسْتَقِيمَ صِرَاطَ الَّذِينَ أَنْعَمْتَ عَلَيْهِمْ غَيْرِ الْمَغْضُوبِ عَلَيْهِمْ وَلَا
الضَّالِّينَ. ءَامِينَ.

اَللّهُمَّ صَلِّ عَلَى سَيِّدِنَا مُحَمَّدٍ النَّبِيِّ الأُمِّيِّ وَعَلَى ءَالِهِ وَصَحْبِهِ وَسَلِّمْ
أَفْضَلَ الصَّلَاةِ وَأَزْكَى التَّسْلِيمِ. (عشرًا)

اَللّهُمَّ إِنِّي أَسْتَخِيرُكَ بِعِلْمِكَ. وَأَسْتَقْدِرُكَ بِقُدْرَتِكَ. وَأَسْأَلُكَ مِنْ
فَضْلِكَ الْعَظِيمِ الْأَعْظَمِ. فَإِنَّكَ تَقْدِرُ وَلَآ أَقْدِرُ.
وَتَعْلَمُ وَلَآ أَعْلَمُ. وَأَنْتَ عَلَّامُ الْغُيُوبِ.

اَللّهُمَّ إِنْ كُنْتَ تَعْلَمُ أَنَّ هَذَا الْأَمْرَ وَهُوَ جَمِيعُ حَرَكَاتِي وَسَكَنَاتِي
الظَّاهِرَةِ وَالْبَاطِنَةِ. مِنْ قَوْلٍ وَفِعْلٍ وَخُلُقٍ وَحَالٍ. عِبَادَةً وَعَادَةً.
فِي حَقِّي وَفِي حَقِّ غَيْرِي. فِي هَذِهِ اللَّيْلَةِ
(أَوْ: فِي هَذَا الْيَوْمِ) وَفِيمَا بَعْدَهَا (أَوْ بَعْدَهُ)

and for all the rest of my life – is good for me in my Deen and in my worldly existence, in this life and my next life, and my final end, be it sooner or later, then decree it for me, make it easy for me and bless me in it.

But if You know that my situation – all my movement and stillness, apparent and hidden, in speech, deeds, character and state, in spiritual work and daily life, as regards myself and others, in this day or night and those after it, and all the rest of my life – is bad for me in my Deen and in my worldly existence, in this life and my next life, and my final end, be it sooner or later, then divert it from me and divert me from it, and destine the good for me wherever it may be and make me contented with it. You have power over all things.

You who have iman! Have taqwa of Allah and iman in His Messenger. He will give you a double portion of His mercy and grant you a Light by which to walk and forgive you, Allah is Ever-Forgiving, Most Merciful,

so that the People of the Book may know that they have no power at all over any of Allah's favour and that all favour is in the Hand of Allah. He gives it to anyone He wills. Allah's favour is indeed immense.

وَفِي بَقِيَّةِ عُمْرِي خَيْرٌ لِي فِي دِينِي وَدُنْيَايَ

وَمَعَاشِي وَمَعَادِي وَعَاقِبَةِ أَمْرِي وَعَاجِلِهِ وَءَاجِلِهِ.

فَاقْدُرْهُ لِي وَيَسِّرْهُ لِي ثُمَّ بَارِكْ لِي فِيهِ

وَإِنْ كُنْتَ تَعْلَمُ أَنَّ هَذَا الْأَمْرَ وَهُوَ جَمِيعُ حَرَكَاتِي وَسَكَنَاتِي

الظَّاهِرَةِ وَالْبَاطِنَةِ. مِنْ قَوْلٍ وَفِعْلٍ وَخُلُقٍ وَحَالٍ. عِبَادَةً وَعَادَةً.

فِي حَقِّي وَفِي حَقِّ غَيْرِي. فِي هَذِهِ اللَّيْلَةِ (أَوْ: فِي هَذَا الْيَوْمِ)

وَفِيمَا بَعْدَهَا (أَوْ بَعْدَهُ) وَفِي بَقِيَّةِ عُمْرِي شَرٌّ لِي فِي دِينِي وَدُنْيَايَ

وَمَعَاشِي وَمَعَادِي وَعَاقِبَةِ أَمْرِي وَعَاجِلِهِ وَءَاجِلِهِ. فَاصْرِفْهُ عَنِّي

وَاصْرِفْنِي عَنْهُ. وَاقْدُرْ لِي الْخَيْرَ حَيْثُ كَانَ

ثُمَّ رَضِّنِي بِهِ. إِنَّكَ عَلَى كُلِّ شَيْءٍ قَدِيرٌ.

يَآ أَيُّهَا الَّذِينَ ءَامَنُوا اتَّقُوا اللَّهَ وَءَامِنُوا بِرَسُولِهِ يُؤْتِكُمْ كِفْلَيْنِ مِنْ

رَحْمَتِهِ. وَيَجْعَلْ لَكُمْ نُورًا تَمْشُونَ بِهِ وَيَغْفِرْ لَكُمْ.

وَاللَّهُ غَفُورٌ رَحِيمٌ لِئَلَّا يَعْلَمَ أَهْلُ الْكِتَابِ أَلَّا يَقْدِرُونَ عَلَى شَيْءٍ

مِنْ فَضْلِ اللَّهِ وَأَنَّ الْفَضْلَ بِيَدِ اللَّهِ يُؤْتِيهِ مَنْ يَشَآءُ. وَاللَّهُ ذُو

الْفَضْلِ الْعَظِيمِ.

Everything in the heavens and everything in the earth belongs to Allah. Whether you divulge what is in yourselves or keep it hidden, Allah will still call you to account for it. He forgives whoever He wills and He punishes whoever He wills. Allah has power over all things.

The Messenger has iman in what has been sent down to him from his Lord, and so do the muminun. Each one has iman in Allah and His angels and His Books and His Messengers. We do not differentiate between any of His Messengers. They say, 'We hear and we obey.

Forgive us, our Lord! You are our journey's end.' (3)

Allah does not impose on any self any more than it can stand. For it is what it has earned; against it, what it has merited.

Our Lord, do not take us to task if we forget or make a mistake! (3)

Our Lord, do not place on us a load like the one You placed on those before us!

Our Lord, do not place on us a load we have not the strength to bear! (3)

And pardon us; (3)

and forgive us; (3)

and have mercy on us. (3)

لِلَّهِ مَا فِي السَّمَوَاتِ وَمَا فِي الْأَرْضِ. وَإِنْ تُبْدُوا مَا فِي أَنْفُسِكُمْ
أَوْ تُخْفُوهُ يُحَاسِبْكُمْ بِهِ اللهُ فَيَغْفِرُ لِمَنْ يَشَاءُ
وَيُعَذِّبُ مَنْ يَشَاءُ. وَاللهُ عَلَى كُلِّ شَيْءٍ قَدِيرٌ.

ءَامَنَ الرَّسُولُ بِمَا أُنْزِلَ إِلَيْهِ مِنْ رَبِّهِ وَالْمُؤْمِنُونَ. كُلٌّ ءَامَنَ بِاللهِ
وَمَلَائِكَتِهِ وَكُتُبِهِ وَرُسُلِهِ. لَا نُفَرِّقُ بَيْنَ أَحَدٍ مِنْ رُسُلِهِ. وَقَالُوا
سَمِعْنَا وَأَطَعْنَا.

غُفْرَانَكَ رَبَّنَا (ثَلَاثًا) وَإِلَيْكَ الْمَصِيرُ.

لَا يُكَلِّفُ اللهُ نَفْسًا إِلَّا وُسْعَهَا.
لَهَا مَا كَسَبَتْ وَعَلَيْهَا مَا اكْتَسَبَتْ.

رَبَّنَا لَا تُؤَاخِذْنَا إِنْ نَسِينَا أَوْ أَخْطَأْنَا. (ثَلَاثًا)

رَبَّنَا وَلَا تَحْمِلْ عَلَيْنَا إِصْرًا كَمَا حَمَلْتَهُ عَلَى الَّذِينَ مِنْ قَبْلِنَا.

رَبَّنَا وَلَا تُحَمِّلْنَا مَا لَا طَاقَةَ لَنَا بِهِ. (ثَلَاثًا)

وَاعْفُ عَنَّا. (ثَلَاثًا)

وَاغْفِرْ لَنَا. (ثَلَاثًا)

وَارْحَمْنَا. (ثَلَاثًا)

You are our Master, so help us
against the people of the kafirun.

To Allah belong the Most Beautiful Names, so call on
Him by them and abandon those who desecrate His
Names. They will be repaid for what they did.

Say: 'Call on Allah or call on the All-Merciful, whichever
you call upon, the Most Beautiful Names are His.' Do
not be too loud in your salat or too quiet in it, but try
to find a way between the two. And say: 'Praise be to
Allah Who has had no son and Who has no partner in His
Kingdom and Who needs no one to protect Him from
abasement.' And proclaim His Greatness repeatedly!

You who have iman! have taqwa of Allah and let each
self look to what it has sent forward for Tomorrow. Have
taqwa of Allah. Allah is aware of what you do. Do not
be like those who forgot Allah so He made them forget
themselves. Such people are the deviators.

The Companions of the Fire and the Companions of
the Garden are not the same. It is the Companions of
the Garden who are the victors. If We had sent down
this Qur'an onto a mountain, you would have seen it
humbled, crushed to pieces out of fear of Allah. We make
such examples for people
so that hopefully they will reflect.

He is Allah – there is no god but Him. He is the Knower
of the Unseen and the Visible.
He is the All-Merciful, the Most Merciful.

324

أَنْتَ مَوْلَانَا فَانْصُرْنَا عَلَى الْقَوْمِ الْكَافِرِينَ.

وَلِلَّهِ الْأَسْمَاءُ الْحُسْنَى فَادْعُوهُ بِهَا وَذَرُوا الَّذِينَ يُلْحِدُونَ
فِي أَسْمَائِهِ. سَيُجْزَوْنَ مَا كَانُوا يَعْمَلُونَ.

قُلِ ادْعُوا اللَّهَ أَوِ ادْعُوا الرَّحْمَنَ. أَيًّا مَا تَدْعُوا فَلَهُ الْأَسْمَاءُ
الْحُسْنَى. وَلَا تَجْهَرْ بِصَلَاتِكَ وَلَا تُخَافِتْ بِهَا وَابْتَغِ بَيْنَ ذَلِكَ
سَبِيلًا. وَقُلِ الْحَمْدُ لِلَّهِ الَّذِي لَمْ يَتَّخِذْ وَلَدًا وَلَمْ يَكُنْ لَهُ شَرِيكٌ فِي
الْمُلْكِ وَلَمْ يَكُنْ لَهُ وَلِيٌّ مِنَ الذُّلِّ. وَكَبِّرْهُ تَكْبِيرًا.

يَا أَيُّهَا الَّذِينَ ءَامَنُوا اتَّقُوا اللَّهَ وَلْتَنْظُرْ نَفْسٌ مَا قَدَّمَتْ لِغَدٍ.
وَاتَّقُوا اللَّهَ. إِنَّ اللَّهَ خَبِيرٌ بِمَا تَعْمَلُونَ. وَلَا تَكُونُوا كَالَّذِينَ نَسُوا اللَّهَ
فَأَنْسَاهُمْ أَنْفُسَهُمْ. أُولَئِكَ هُمُ الْفَاسِقُونَ.

لَا يَسْتَوِي أَصْحَابُ النَّارِ وَأَصْحَابُ الْجَنَّةِ. أَصْحَابُ الْجَنَّةِ هُمُ
الْفَائِزُونَ. لَوْ أَنْزَلْنَا هَذَا الْقُرْءَانَ عَلَى جَبَلٍ
لَرَأَيْتَهُ خَاشِعًا مُتَصَدِّعًا مِنْ خَشْيَةِ اللَّهِ.
وَتِلْكَ الْأَمْثَالُ نَضْرِبُهَا لِلنَّاسِ لَعَلَّهُمْ يَتَفَكَّرُونَ.
هُوَ اللَّهُ الَّذِي لَا إِلَهَ إِلَّا هُوَ. عَالِمُ الْغَيْبِ وَالشَّهَادَةِ.
هُوَ الرَّحْمَنُ الرَّحِيمُ.

He is Allah – there is no god but Him. He is the King,
the Most Pure, the Perfect Peace, the Trustworthy, the
Safeguarder, the Almighty, the Compeller, the Supremely
Great. Glory be to Allah above all they associate with Him.

He is Allah – the Creator, the Maker, the Giver of Form.
To Him belong the Most Beautiful Names. Everything in
the heavens and earth glorifies Him.
He is the Almighty, the All-Wise.

Glory be to your Lord, the Lord of Might, beyond
anything they describe. And peace be upon the
Messengers. And praise be to Allah,
the Lord of all the worlds!

Glory be to Allah, by His praise,
Glory be to Allah, the Great. (11)

In the name of Allah, All-Merciful, Most Merciful:
Praise be to Allah, the Lord of all the worlds, the All-
Merciful, the Most Merciful, the King of the Day of
Judgment. You alone we worship. You alone we ask for
help. Guide us on the Straight Path, the Path of those You
have blessed, not of those with anger on them,
nor of the misguided. Amin.

O Allah! Guard us with Your eye which never sleeps.
Shelter us in Your hold which is the best possible. Place
us in Your proximity which is unassailed. Do not destroy
us for our wrong actions. You are our trust and our hope.
O Allah! (3)

There is no god but You! Glory be to You!
Truly I have been one of the wrongdoers.

هُوَ اللهُ الَّذِي لَاۤ إِلَهَ إِلَّا هُوَ الْمَلِكُ الْقُدُّوسُ السَّلَامُ الْمُؤْمِنُ الْمُهَيْمِنُ الْعَزِيزُ الْجَبَّارُ الْمُتَكَبِّرُ. سُبْحَانَ اللهِ عَمَّا يُشْرِكُونَ.

هُوَ اللهُ الْخَالِقُ الْبَارِئُ الْمُصَوِّرُ. لَهُ الْاَسْمَاءُ الْحُسْنَى. يُسَبِّحُ لَهُ مَا فِي السَّمَوَاتِ وَالْاَرْضِ. وَهُوَ الْعَزِيزُ الْحَكِيمُ.

سُبْحَانَ رَبِّكَ رَبِّ الْعِزَّةِ عَمَّا يَصِفُونَ. وَسَلَامٌ عَلَى الْمُرْسَلِينَ. وَالْحَمْدُ لِلّهِ رَبِّ الْعَالَمِينَ.

سُبْحَانَ اللهِ وَبِحَمْدِهِ سُبْحَانَ اللهِ الْعَظِيمِ. (إحدى وعشرين مرة)

بِسْمِ اللهِ الرَّحْمَنِ الرَّحِيمِ الْحَمْدُ لِلّهِ رَبِّ الْعَالَمِينَ الرَّحْمَنِ الرَّحِيمِ مَلِكِ يَوْمِ الدِّينِ. إِيَّاكَ نَعْبُدُ وَإِيَّاكَ نَسْتَعِينُ. اِهْدِنَا الصِّرَاطَ الْمُسْتَقِيمَ صِرَاطَ الَّذِينَ أَنْعَمْتَ عَلَيْهِمْ غَيْرِ الْمَغْضُوبِ عَلَيْهِمْ وَلَا الضَّالِّينَ. ءَامِينَ.

اَللّهُمَّ احْرُسْنَا بِعَيْنِكَ الَّتِي لَا تَنَامُ. وَاكْنُفْنَا بِكَنَفِكَ الَّذِي لَا يُرَامُ. وَاجْعَلْنَا فِي جِوَارِكَ الَّذِي لَا يُضَامُ. وَلَا تُهْلِكْنَا بِذُنُوبِنَا فَأَنْتَ ثِقَتُنَا وَرَجَاؤُنَا يَاۤ أَللهُ. (ثلاثًا)

لَاۤ إِلَهَ إِلَّاۤ أَنْتَ سُبْحَانَكَ إِنِّي كُنْتُ مِنَ الظَّالِمِينَ.

O Allah, as You have shown us Your power show us Your
pardon. O Allah. O Allah. O Allah. There is no god
but You! Glory be to You! Truly I have been one of the
wrongdoers. (3)

O Allah, do not expel us from the circle of Lutf
and give us security from what we fear. (3)

O Knower of our secrets, do not rend the veil
covering our wrong actions. (3)

We have come to the morning in Your protection, O
Mawlana, make us come to the evening in Your good
pleasure, O Mawlana. (3)

O Allah, O Turner of the hearts and eyes, fix our hearts
and eyes on Your Deen with a Muhammadan firmness for
ever and ever. (3)

By the rank of our lord and master Muhammad, may
Allah bless him and grant him peace and his family and
Companions and all the believing slaves of Allah.

O Lord, bless him, out of whom secrets and lights have
burst, in whom rose the truth, upon whom devolved
the knowledge of our master Adam, peace be upon
him. Beside him all creatures are incapable, to him
understanding is a trifle. Not one of us has attained his
standard, before or after. The gardens of heaven are
embellished with the beauty of his flowers.

اَللَّهُمَّ كَمَا أَرَيْتَنَا قُدْرَتَكَ فَأَرِنَا عَفْوَكَ. يَا أَللَّهُ يَا أَللَّهُ يَا أَللَّهُ. لَا

إِلَهَ إِلَّا أَنْتَ سُبْحَانَكَ إِنِّي كُنْتُ مِنَ الظَّالِمِينَ. (ثلاثًا)

اَللَّهُمَّ لَا تُخْرِجْنَا مِنْ دَائِرَةِ الْأَلْطَافِ

وَأَمِنَّا مِنْ كُلِّ مَا نَخَافُ. (ثلاثًا)

يَا عَالِمَ السِّرِّ مِنَّا لَا تَهْتِكِ السَّتْرَ عَنَّا. (ثلاثًا)

أَصْبَحْنَا فِي حِمَاكَ يَا مَوْلَانَا

مَسَّنَا فِي رِضَاكَ يَا مَوْلَانَا. (ثلاثًا)

اَللَّهُمَّ يَا مُقَلِّبَ الْقُلُوبِ وَالْأَبْصَارِ ثَبِّتْ قُلُوبَنَا وَأَبْصَارَنَا عَلَى

دِينِكَ ثَبَاتًا مُحَمَّدِيًّا إِلَى أَبَدِ الْآبَدِ. (ثلاثًا)

بِجَاهِ سَيِّدِنَا وَمَوْلَانَا مُحَمَّدٍ صَلَّى اللَّهُ عَلَيْهِ وَسَلَّمَ وَعَلَى ءَالِهِ وَأَصْحَابِهِ

وَعَلَى جَمِيعِ عِبَادِ اللَّهِ الْمُؤمِنِينَ.

اَللَّهُمَّ صَلِّ عَلَى مَنْ مِنْهُ انْشَقَّتِ الْأَسْرَارُ. وَانْفَلَقَتِ الْأَنْوَارُ.

وَفِيهِ ارْتَقَتِ الْحَقَائِقُ. وَتَنَزَّلَتْ عُلُومُ سَيِّدِنَا ءَادَمَ عَلَيْهِ السَّلَامُ

فَأَعْجَزَ الْخَلَائِقَ. وَلَهُ تَضَاءَلَتِ الْفُهُومُ فَلَمْ يُدْرِكْهُ مِنَّا سَابِقٌ وَلَا

لَاحِقٌ. فَرِيَاضُ الْمَلَكُوتِ بِزَهْرِ جَمَالِهِ مُونِقَةٌ.

The cisterns of power spill over with the flood of his lights. There is nothing not dependent on him: for as it was said, 'without the means the end would have escaped us'. Bless him in Your way according to his merits. O Allah, he is your gathered secret that tells of You, Your great veil that stands before You. O Allah, attach me to his descendants, and make me realise his honour. Let me know him with a knowledge by means of which I will be safe from the fountains of ignorance and by which I will sip from the fountains of bounty. Convey me on his way to Your Presence, protected by Your help. Let me face falsehood so that I may conquer it, drive me into the sea of Oneness, snatch me from the mires of belief in Unification (Tawhid) and let me drown in the sea of Unity (Wahda) so much that I may not see, hear, feel or except by It. Make the great veil the life of my spirit and its spirit the secret of my truth and his truth, the integrator of my universe through the realisation of the first truth.

O First! O Last! O Manifest! O Hidden! Hear my cry as you heard the cry of Your slave, our master Zakariah, peace be upon him. Give me victory through You – for You. Support me through You – for You. Join me to You – separate me from other-than-You.

## ALLAH (3)

وَحِيَاضُ الْجَبَرُوتِ بِفَيْضِ أَنْوَارِهِ مُتَدَفِّقَةٌ. وَلَا شَيْءَ إِلَّا وَهُوَ بِهِ
مَنُوطٌ. إِذْ لَوْ لَا الْوَاسِطَةُ لَذَهَبَ كَمَا قِيلَ الْمَوْسُوطُ. صَلَاةً تَلِيقُ
بِكَ مِنْكَ إِلَيْهِ كَمَا هُوَ أَهْلُهُ. اللّهُمَّ إِنَّهُ سِرُّكَ الْجَامِعُ الدَّالُّ عَلَيْكَ.
وَحِجَابُكَ الْأَعْظَمُ الْقَائِمُ لَكَ بَيْنَ يَدَيْكَ. اللّهُمَّ أَلْحِقْنِي بِنَسَبِهِ.
وَحَقِّقْنِي بِحَسَبِهِ. وَعَرِّفْنِي إِيَّاهُ مَعْرِفَةً أَسْلَمُ بِهَا مِنْ مَوَارِدِ الْجَهْلِ.
وَأَكْرَعُ بِهَا مِنْ مَوَارِدِ الْفَضْلِ. وَاحْمِلْنِي عَلَى سَبِيلِهِ إِلَى حَضْرَتِكَ.
حَمْلًا مَحْفُوفًا بِنُصْرَتِكَ. وَاقْذِفْ بِي عَلَى الْبَاطِلِ فَأَدْمَغَهُ. وَزُجَّ بِي
فِي بِحَارِ الْأَحَدِيَّةِ. وَانْشُلْنِي مِنْ أَوْحَالِ التَّوْحِيدِ. وَأَغْرِقْنِي فِي عَيْنِ
بَحْرِ الْوَحْدَةِ. حَتَّى لَا أَرَى وَلَا أَسْمَعَ وَلَا أَجِدَ وَلَا أَحِسَّ إِلَّا
بِهَا. وَاجْعَلِ الْحِجَابَ الْأَعْظَمَ حَيَاةَ رُوحِي. وَرُوحَهُ سِرَّ حَقِيقَتِي.
وَحَقِيقَتَهُ جَامِعَ عَوَالِمِي بِتَحْقِيقِ الْحَقِّ الْأَوَّلِ.

يَا أَوَّلُ يَا آخِرُ يَا ظَاهِرُ يَا بَاطِنُ. اسْمَعْ نِدَائِي بِمَا سَمِعْتَ بِهِ
نِدَاءَ عَبْدِكَ سَيِّدِنَا زَكَرِيَّاءَ عَلَيْهِ السَّلَامُ. وَانْصُرْنِي بِكَ لَكَ.
وَأَيِّدْنِي بِكَ لَكَ. وَاجْمَعْ بَيْنِي وَبَيْنَكَ. وَحُلْ بَيْنِي وَبَيْنَ غَيْرِكَ

اَللّهُ. اَللّهُ. اَللّهُ.

He Who has imposed the Qur'an upon you will surely
bring you home again. Our Lord, give us mercy directly
from You and open the way for us to right guidance in
our situation. (3)

And bless our lord and master Muhammad and his family
and Companions and grant them peace.

Glory be to your Lord, the Lord of Might, beyond
anything they describe. And peace be upon the
Messengers. And praise be to Allah,
the Lord of all the worlds!

Our Lord, give us refreshment of our wives and children
and make us an Imam to the reality-awed. These shall
be recompensed with the highest heaven, because they
endured patiently, and they shall receive there a greeting
and peace. There they shall dwell for ever.
Happy is it as place and station.

Say: 'My Lord would not concern Himself with you but
for your prayers, for you have denied
and there will be judgment.'

Our Lord, grant us contemplation of You accompanied
by conversation, and open our hearing and eyes. If we
grow heedless of You remember us with the best of what
You remember when we remember You. Be merciful to
us when we disobey You with the most perfect of what
You are merciful with when we obey You.
You are powerful over everything.

إِنَّ الَّذِي فَرَضَ عَلَيْكَ الْقُرْءَانَ لَرَآدُّكَ إِلَى مَعَادٍ.

رَبَّنَا ءَاتِنَا مِنْ لَدُنْكَ رَحْمَةً وَهَيِّئْ لَنَا مِنْ أَمْرِنَا رَشَدًا. (ثَلَاثًا)

وَصَلَّى اللهُ عَلَى سَيِّدِنَا وَمَوْلَانَا مُحَمَّدٍ

وَءَالِهِ وَصَحْبِهِ وَسَلَّمَ تَسْلِيمًا.

سُبْحَانَ رَبِّكَ رَبِّ الْعِزَّةِ عَمَّا يَصِفُونَ. وَسَلَامٌ عَلَى الْمُرْسَلِينَ.
وَالْحَمْدُ لِلَّهِ رَبِّ الْعَالَمِينَ.

رَبَّنَا هَبْ لَنَا مِنْ أَزْوَاجِنَا وَذُرِّيَّاتِنَا قُرَّةَ أَعْيُنٍ وَاجْعَلْنَا لِلْمُتَّقِينَ
إِمَامًا. أُولَئِكَ يُجْزَوْنَ الْغُرْفَةَ بِمَا صَبَرُوا وَيُلَقَّوْنَ فِيهَا تَحِيَّةً وَسَلَامًا
خَالِدِينَ فِيهَا. حَسُنَتْ مُسْتَقَرًّا وَمَقَامًا.

قُلْ مَا يَعْبَؤُا بِكُمْ رَبِّي لَوْ لَا دُعَاؤُكُمْ.
فَقَدْ كَذَّبْتُمْ فَسَوْفَ يَكُونُ لِزَامًا.

رَبَّنَا هَبْ لَنَا مُشَاهَدَةً تَصْحَبُهَا مُكَالَمَةً وَافْتَحْ أَسْمَاعَنَا وَأَبْصَارَنَا
وَاذْكُرْنَا إِذَا غَفَلْنَا عَنْكَ بِأَحْسَنِ مَا تَذْكُرُنَا بِهِ إِذَا ذَكَرْنَاكَ.
وَارْحَمْنَا إِذَا عَصَيْنَاكَ بِأَتَمِّ مَا تَرْحَمُنَا بِهِ إِذَا أَطَعْنَاكَ.
إِنَّكَ عَلَى كُلِّ شَيْءٍ قَدِيرٌ.

'Our Lord, accept this from us! You are the All-Hearing, the All-Knowing. Our Lord, make us both Muslims submitted to You, and our descendants a Muslim community submitted to You. Show us our rites of worship and turn towards us. You are the Ever-Returning, the Most Merciful.'

Our Lord, we have wronged ourselves, and if You do not forgive us and have mercy upon us, we shall surely be among the lost. You are our protector, so forgive us and have mercy on us for You are the best of forgivers.

There is no god except You. Glory be to You,
I have been one of the wrongdoers.

O Allah, whatever blessings You have bestowed are from You, by You, for You alone, without partner to You. I cannot render praise to You fittingly. You are as You praise Yourself. (3)

O Allah, we follow the belief of Your Prophet, may Allah bless him and grant him peace, in the perfection of the sublimity of Your Essence and Your Attributes and Your Names and whatever comes from You. We believe as he believed, may Allah bless him and grant him peace in his self. We followed his intention, may Allah bless him and grant him peace, in all kinds of worship and in daily life.

May Allah ta'ala be pleased with our lords and masters, Abu Bakr, 'Umar, 'Uthman, and 'Ali; and Sa'd, Sa'id, Talha, Az-Zubayr, Abdarrahman Ibn 'Awf, Abu 'Ubayda, Hamza, Al-'Abbas, Fatima, 'Aisha, Khadija, Al-Hassan and Al-Hussein: may Allah be pleased with all the Companions of the Messenger of Allah, especially the

رَبَّنَا تَقَبَّلْ مِنَّا إِنَّكَ أَنْتَ السَّمِيعُ الْعَلِيمُ. رَبَّنَا وَاجْعَلْنَا مُسْلِمَيْنِ لَكَ
وَمِنْ ذُرِّيَّتِنَا أُمَّةً مُسْلِمَةً لَكَ. وَأَرِنَا مَنَاسِكًا. وَتُبْ عَلَيْنَا. إِنَّكَ أَنْتَ
التَّوَّابُ الرَّحِيمُ.

رَبَّنَا ظَلَمْنَا أَنْفُسَنَا وَإِنْ لَمْ تَغْفِرْ لَنَا وَتَرْحَمْنَا لَنَكُونَنَّ مِنَ الْخَاسِرِينَ.
أَنْتَ وَلِيُّنَا فَاغْفِرْ لَنَا وَارْحَمْنَا وَأَنْتَ خَيْرُ الْغَافِرِينَ.

لَا إِلَهَ إِلَّا أَنْتَ سُبْحَانَكَ إِنِّي كُنْتُ مِنَ الظَّالِمِينَ.

اَللَّهُمَّ مَا أَنْعَمْتَ بِهِ فَمِنْكَ بِكَ لَكَ وَحْدَكَ لَا شَرِيكَ لَكَ.
لَا أُحْصِي ثَنَاءً عَلَيْكَ. أَنْتَ كَمَا أَثْنَيْتَ عَلَى نَفْسِكَ. (ثَلَاثًا)

اَللَّهُمَّ إِنَّا عَلَى اعْتِقَادِ نَبِيِّكَ ﷺ فِي كَمَالِ عَظَمَةِ ذَاتِكَ وَصِفَاتِكَ
وَأَسْمَائِكَ وَمَا جَاءَ عَنْكَ. وَعَلَى اعْتِقَادِهِ ﷺ فِي نَفْسِهِ وَعَلَى نِيَّتِهِ
ﷺ فِي أَنْوَاعِ الْعِبَادَاتِ وَالْعَادَاتِ.

وَرَضِيَ اللهُ تَعَالَى عَنْ سَادَتِنَا وَمَوَالِينَا أَبِي بَكْرٍ وَعُمَرَ وَعُثْمَانَ
وَعَلِيٍّ. وَسَعْدٍ وَسَعِيدٍ وَطَلْحَةَ وَالزُّبَيْرِ وَعَبْدِ الرَّحْمَنِ بْنِ عَوْفٍ
وَأَبِي عُبَيْدَةَ وَحَمْزَةَ وَالْعَبَّاسِ وَفَاطِمَةَ وَعَائِشَةَ وَخَدِيجَةَ وَالْحَسَنِ
وَالْحُسَيْنِ وَعَنْ أَصْحَابِ رَسُولِ اللهِ أَجْمَعِينَ خُصُوصًا مِنْهُمْ

Muhajirun and the Ansar, and may He be pleased with
their followers who were beloved, and who followed
them with Ihsan until the Day of Reckoning.

O Allah, our Lord, make us among the followers
with Ihsan who are beloved to them until the Day of
Reckoning. (3)

Glory be to your Lord, the Lord of Might, beyond
anything they describe. And peace be upon the
Messengers. And praise be to Allah,
the Lord of all the worlds!

O Allah bless our master Muhammad, Your slave and
Messenger, the unlettered Prophet, and his family and
Companions and grant them peace, as great as the number
of Your creations and Your pleasure and the weight of Your
Throne and the ink of Your words. Amin, Amin, Amin.

O Allah – O Allah. O Allah. O Allah.

O Expander. O Expander. O Expander.

O Irresistible. O Irresistible. O Irresistible.

O Ever-Forgiving. O Ever-Forgiving. O Ever-Forgiving.

O All-Pitying. O All-Pitying. O All-Pitying.

الْمُهَاجِرِينَ وَالْأَنْصَارِ. وَعَنِ التَّابِعِينَ

الْمَحْبُوبِينَ لَهُمْ بِإِحْسَانٍ إِلَىٰ يَوْمِ الدِّينِ.

اَللّٰهُمَّ اجْعَلْنَا يَا مَوْلَانَا مِنَ التَّابِعِينَ

الْمَحْبُوبِينَ لَهُمْ بِإِحْسَانٍ إِلَىٰ يَوْمِ الدِّينِ. (ثَلَاثًا)

سُبْحَانَ رَبِّكَ رَبِّ الْعِزَّةِ عَمَّا يَصِفُونَ. وَسَلَامٌ عَلَى الْمُرْسَلِينَ.

وَالْحَمْدُ لِلّٰهِ رَبِّ الْعَالَمِينَ.

اَللّٰهُمَّ صَلِّ عَلَىٰ سَيِّدِنَا مُحَمَّدٍ عَبْدِكَ وَرَسُولِكَ النَّبِيِّ الْأُمِّيِّ وَعَلَىٰ

ءَالِهِ وَصَحْبِهِ وَسَلِّمْ تَسْلِيمًا. عَدَدَ خَلْقِكَ وَرِضَا نَفْسِكَ وَزِنَةَ

عَرْشِكَ وَمِدَادَ كَلِمَاتِكَ. ءَامِين. ءَامِين. ءَامِين.

اَللّٰهُمَّ يَا أَللّٰهُ يَا أَللّٰهُ يَا أَللّٰهُ يَا أَللّٰهُ.

يَا بَاسِطُ يَا بَاسِطُ يَا بَاسِطُ.

يَا جَبَّارُ يَا جَبَّارُ يَا جَبَّارُ.

يَا غَفَّارُ يَا غَفَّارُ يَا غَفَّارُ.

يَا رَؤُوفُ يَا رَؤُوفُ يَا رَؤُوفُ.

O Ever-Returning. O Ever-Returning.
O Ever-Returning.

O Effacer of wrong actions. (3)

O my help in every trouble, and the answer to my every
prayer, and my refuge in every hardship, and my hope
when my deceptions have come to nothing. O my Helper.
O my Helper. O my Helper. (3)

O Lord, dispel my grief. I have become confused in the
matter, so take me by the hand.
You are all-powerful over everything.

O Light of everything and its Guide. It is You Whose
light rends the darkness. O Light. O Merciful to all who
cry out and are afflicted. You are his help and refuge,
O Merciful.

O Allah, bless and grant peace to our lord and master
Muhammad, the first of the lights emanating from the
oceans of the sublimity of the Essence, with every one of
Your perfections in all Your self-manifestations.. In the
two worlds – the hidden and the seen – he realised the
meanings of the Names and Attributes. He is the first to
give praise and worship with every kind of adoration and
good action. He is the helper of all created beings in the
world of forms and the world of spirits. And blessings be
upon his family and Companions with a blessing that will
lift the veil from his noble face for us in visions and in the
waking state and will acquaint us with You and with him
in all ranks and presences.

يَا تَوَّابُ يَا تَوَّابُ يَا تَوَّابُ يَا تَوَّابُ.

يَا عَفُوُّ يَا عَفُوُّ يَا عَفُوُّ.

يَا غِيَاثِي عِنْدَ كُلِّ كُرْبَةٍ. وَمُجِيبِي عِنْدَ كُلِّ دَعْوَةٍ. وَمَعَاذِي عِنْدَ كُلِّ شِدَّةٍ. وَيَا رَجَآءِي حِينَ تَنْقَطِعُ حِيلَتِي.

يَا غِيَاثِي يَا غِيَاثِي يَا غِيَاثِي. (ثَلَاثًا)

بَارَتْ حِيلَتِي ضَاقَتْ حِيلَتِي يَا رَبِّ فَرِّجْ كُرْبَتِي. قَدْ تَحَيَّرْتُ فِي أَمْرِي خُذْ بِيَدِي. إِنَّكَ عَلَى كُلِّ شَيْءٍ قَدِيرٌ.

يَا نُورَ كُلِّ شَيْءٍ وَهُدَاهُ أَنْتَ الَّذِي فَلَقَ الظُّلُمَاتِ نُورُهُ يَا نُورُ. يَا رَحِيمَ كُلِّ صَرِيخٍ وَمَكْرُوبٍ وَغِيَاثُهُ وَمَعَادَهُ يَا رَحِيمُ. اَللّٰهُمَّ صَلِّ وَسَلِّمْ بِأَنْوَاعِ كَمَالَاتِكَ فِي جَمِيعِ تَجَلِّيَاتِكَ عَلَى سَيِّدِنَا وَمَوْلَانَا مُحَمَّدٍ أَوَّلِ الْأَنْوَارِ الْفَآئِضَةِ مِنْ بُحُورِ عَظَمَةِ الذَّاتِ. الْمُتَحَقِّقِ فِي عَالَمَيِ الْبُطُونِ وَالظُّهُورِ بِمَعَانِي الْأَسْمَآءِ وَالصِّفَاتِ. فَهُوَ أَوَّلُ حَامِدٍ وَمُتَعَبِّدٍ بِأَنْوَاعِ الْعِبَادَاتِ وَالْقُرُبَاتِ. وَالْمُمِدُّ فِي عَالَمَيِ الْأَرْوَاحِ وَالْأَشْبَاحِ بِجَمِيعِ الْمَوْجُودَاتِ. وَعَلَى ءَالِهِ وَأَصْحَابِهِ صَلَاةً تَكْشِفُ لَنَا النِّقَابَ عَنْ وَجْهِهِ الْكَرِيمِ فِي الْمَرَآئِي وَالْيَقَظَاتِ. وَتُعَرِّفُنَا بِكَ وَبِهِ فِي جَمِيعِ الْمَرَاتِبِ وَالْحَضَرَاتِ.

Be gracious to us, O Mawlana, by his rank, in movement

and in stillness, in looks and in thoughts.

Glory be to your Lord, the Lord of might, above all that

they describe. And peace be upon the Messengers. And

praise belongs to Allah, the Lord of the worlds.

O Gentle, O Knower of subtleties, gentleness is Yours!

You are the Gentle, and from You gentleness engulfs us.

Latif, Latif, I beg You

by Your lutf - be lutf to me - and lutf has descended!

Ya Latif, we have sought refuge in Your lutf - we have

gone into the centre of lutf - and lutf has descended.

We have been freed by the lutf of Allah, the Possessor of lutf,

He is Latif, Latif, His lutf is always that.

O Preserver, O Guardian, guardianship is Yours!

You are the Preserver, and from You guardianship

engulfs us.

وَالْطُفْ بِنَا يَا مَوْلَانَا بِجَاهِهِ فِي الْحَرَكَاتِ

وَالسَّكَنَاتِ وَاللَّحَظَاتِ وَانْخَطَرَاتِ.

سُبْحَانَ رَبِّكَ رَبِّ الْعِزَّةِ عَمَّا يَصِفُونَ. وَسَلَامٌ عَلَى الْمُرْسَلِينَ.

وَالْحَمْدُ لِلَّهِ رَبِّ الْعَلَمِينَ.

أَلَا يَا لَطِيفُ يَا لَطِيفُ لَكَ اللُّطْفُ

فَأَنْتَ اللَّطِيفُ مِنْكَ يَشْمَلُنَا اللُّطْفُ

لَطِيفٌ لَطِيفٌ إِنَّنِي مُتَوَسِّلٌ

بِلُطْفِكَ فَالْطُفْ بِي وَقَدْ نَزَلَ اللُّطْفُ

بِلُطْفِكَ عُذْنَا يَا لَطِيفُ وَهَا نَحْنُ

دَخَلْنَا فِي وَسْطِ اللُّطْفِ وَانْسَدَلَ اللُّطْفُ

نَجَوْنَا بِلُطْفِ اللهِ ذِي اللُّطْفِ إِنَّهُ

لَطِيفٌ لَطِيفٌ لُطْفُهُ دَائِمًا لُطْفُ

أَلَا يَا حَفِيظُ يَا حَفِيظُ لَكَ الْحِفْظُ

فَأَنْتَ الْحَفِيظُ مِنْكَ يَشْمَلُنَا الْحِفْظُ

Hafidh, Hafidh, We beg you

by Your hifdh - be hifdh to us - and hifdh has descended.

Ya Hafidh, we have sought refuge in Your hifdh - we have

gone into the centre of hifdh - and hifdh has descended.

We have been freed by the hifdh of Allah,

the Possessor of hifdh.

He is Hafidh, Hafidh, His hifdh is always that.

By the rank of the Imam of the Messengers, Muhammad,

If it were not for him, the source of hifdh,

hifdh would not have descended

Blessings be upon him as long as there is one who chants:

Ya Hafidh, ya Hafidh, the hifdh is Yours!

No God — only Allah

*To the number of three hundred and at the conclusion of each hundred you say:*

Our Master Muhammad is the Messenger of Allah. May Allah bless
him and his family and grant them peace. O Lord, make us firm by its
recital, O Mawlana, give us results from its invocation.
Let us enter into the fortress of its protection

حَفِيظُ حَفِيظُ إِنَّا نَتَوَسَّلُ

بِحِفْظِكَ فَاحْفَظْنَا وَقَدْ نَزَلَ الْحِفْظُ

بِحِفْظِكَ عُذْنَا يَا حَفِيظُ وَهَا نَحْنُ

دَخَلْنَا فِي وَسَطِ الْحِفْظِ وَانْسَدَلَ الْحِفْظُ

نَجَوْنَا بِحِفْظِ اللهِ ذِي الْحِفْظِ إِنَّهُ

حَفِيظٌ حَفِيظٌ حِفْظُهُ دَائِمًا حِفْظُ

بِجَاهِ إِمَامِ الْمُرْسَلِينَ مُحَمَّدٍ

فَلَوْ لَاهُ عَيْنُ الْحِفْظِ مَا نَزَلَ الْحِفْظُ

عَلَيْهِ صَلَاةُ اللهِ مَا قَالَ مُنْشِدٌ

أَلَا يَا حَفِيظُ يَا حَفِيظُ لَكَ الْحِفْظُ

لَا إِلَهَ إِلَّا اللهُ

**(عَدَدَ ثَلَاثِمِائَةِ مَرَّةٍ وَعَلَى رَأْسِ كُلِّ مِائَةِ مَرَّةٍ مَرَّةً نَقُولُ)**

سَيِّدُنَا مُحَمَّدٌ رَسُولُ اللهِ صَلَّى اللهُ عَلَيْهِ وَسَلَّمَ وَعَلَى ءَالِهِ. ثَبِّتْنَا يَا
رَبِّ بِقَوْلِهَا. وَانْفَعْنَا يَا مَوْلَانَا بِذِكْرِهَا. وَأَدْخِلْنَا فِي مَيْدَانِ حِصْنِهَا.

– let us be among its people – and let us say it and know it at the time of

death. Gather us into the company of our lord and master Muhammad,

may Allah bless him and his family and grant them peace.

I ask forgiveness of Allah from what is other than Allah.

I ask forgiveness of Allah. (100)

I ask the forgiveness of Allah, the Great, there is no god

except Him, the Living, the Self-Subsistent, and I turn in

self-renewal to Him.

I ask forgiveness of Allah according to the number of

those who seek His forgiveness, and of what He is asked

forgiveness for, from the people of the heavens and the

earth, an asking forgiveness which surpasses and excels as

does the excelling of Allah over His creation.

O Allah – the Indulgent. (11)

O Allah, there is no god except You. Glory be to You, I

have been one of the wrongdoers.

In the name of Allah, All-Merciful, Most Merciful:

O Allah. (7)

وَاجْعَلْنَا مِنْ أَفْرَادِ أَهْلِهَا. وَعِنْدَ الْمَوْتِ نَاطِقِينَ بِهَا. عَالِمِينَ بِهَا
وَاحْشُرْنَا فِي زُمْرَةِ سَيِّدِنَا مُحَمَّدٍ
صَلَّى اللهُ عَلَيْهِ وَسَلَّمَ وَعَلَىٰ ءَالِهِ.

أَسْتَغْفِرُ اللهَ مِمَّا سِوَى اللهِ.

أَسْتَغْفِرُ اللهَ. (مائة مرّة)

أَسْتَغْفِرُ اللهَ الْعَظِيمَ الَّذِي لَاۤ إِلَهَ إِلَّا هُوَ الْحَيُّ الْقَيُّومُ
وَأَتُوبُ إِلَيْهِ.

أَسْتَغْفِرُ اللهَ عَدَدَ الْمُسْتَغْفِرِينَ وَمَا يَسْتَغْفِرُهُ بِهِ أَهْلُ السَّمَـٰوَاتِ
وَأَهْلُ الْأَرَضِينَ اسْتِغْفَارًا يَفُوقُ وَيَفْضُلُ
كَفَضْلِ اللهِ عَلَىٰ سَآئِرِ خَلْقِهِ.

اللَّهُمَّ يَا حَلِيمُ. (إحدى عشر مرة)

يَاۤ أَللّٰهُ. لَاۤ إِلَهَ إِلَّاۤ أَنْتَ سُبْحَانَكَ إِنِّي كُنْتُ مِنَ الظَّالِمِينَ.

بِسْمِ اللهِ الرَّحْمَـٰنِ الرَّحِيمِ.

يَاۤ أَللّٰهُ. (سبعًا)

O All-Merciful. (7)

O Most Merciful. (7)

O Loving. (7)

O Sublime. (7)

O One Who settles every debt. (7)

O Glorious. (7)

O Allah, forgive the trusting-ones, men and women –
and the Muslims – men and women – living and dead.
And by Your pure love and compassion, forbearance,
kindness, pardon and forgiveness, forgive us and our
fathers and our shaykhs and all the brothers, our
offspring, our country and all its people and all the
people of our age, those who do evil and those who do
good, those who turn to You and those who turn away,
those who give and those who refuse.

Pardon all these with Divine compassion, eternal
sympathy and pre-eternal care which never vanishes
or perishes in the post-eternity of every post-eternity,
through Your mighty Divine Unity which never ends.
Through Your pure excelling, glory be to You and Your
encompassing inclination and the universal mercy and
totality of words – there is no god except You.

يَا رَحْمَنُ. (سبعًا)

يَا رَحِيمُ. (سبعًا)

يَا حَنَّانُ. (سبعًا)

يَا مَنَّانُ. (سبعًا)

يَا دَيَّانُ. (سبعًا)

يَا سُبْحَانُ. (سبعًا)

اَللَّهُمَّ اغْفِرْ لِلْمُؤْمِنِينَ وَالْمُؤْمِنَاتِ

وَالْمُسْلِمِينَ وَالْمُسْلِمَاتِ الْاَحْيَاءِ مِنْهُمْ وَالْاَمْوَاتِ.

وَبِمَحْضِ حَنَانِكَ وَرَأْفَتِكَ وَحِلْمِكَ وَإِحْسَانِكَ وَعَفْوِكَ وَمَغْفِرَتِكَ اغْفِرْ

لَنَا وَلِوَالِدِينَا وَلِمَشَايِخِنَا وَلِجَمِيعِ إِخْوَانِنَا وَذُرِّيَّاتِنَا وَبِلَادِنَا وَجَمِيعِ أَهْلِهَا

وَلِكَافَّةِ أَهْلِ وَقْتِنَا وَلِكُلِّ مَنْ أَحْسَنَ وَأَسَاءَ وَأَقْبَلَ.

وَأَدْبَرَ وَأَعْطَىٰ وَمَنَعَ.

وَلِكُلِّ شَيْءٍ رَأْفَةٌ رَبَّانِيَّةٌ وَعَطْفَةٌ صَمْدَانِيَّةٌ وَعِنَايَةٌ أَزَلِيَّةٌ لَا تَفْنَىٰ وَلَا

تَبِيدُ بِأَبَدِ كُلِّ أَبَدٍ. وَحْدَانِيَّةٌ عَزِيزَةٌ إِلَاهِيَّةٌ غَيْرُ مُتَنَاهِيَةٍ بِمَحْضِ

فَضْلِكَ سُبْحَانَكَ وَعَطْفِكَ الشَّامِلِ وَرَحْمَتِكَ الْعَامَّةِ وَكَلِمَاتِكَ التَّامَّةِ

لَآ إِلَهَ سِوَاكَ

We praise You with Your praise and thank You with
Your thanks: O Praiser! O Thankful! O Rememberer! O
Light! O Living! O Existent! O Hearing!
O Seeing! O Irresistible!

Mend my broken heart and that of every abject
person. Unite with Your Ihsan all those who have been
separated by Your power which is mighty beyond the
comprehension of the intellect.

O Allah! Let love for all the trusting-ones dwell in our
hearts, so that they may be dearer to us than every dear
one, and that everything other than them may be mean,
humble and lowly in our sight. You say to a thing, 'Be!'
and it is. You are a generous, noble Lord, knowing and
bestowing. So we ask You, by You, to hear the entreaty
of him who only sees You.

O most Merciful of the Merciful, (3)
O Lord of the worlds.

O Lord, let me develop with the Latif of Your
sovereignty, with the growth of one who is in need of
You, unable to manage without You, and watch over
me with the eye of Your custody with a watchfulness
that protects me from every calamity which occurs that
might bring torment to my nafs or disturb 'the moment'
for me, or write for me on the tablet of my essence, any
amount of that which amounts to me.

Provide me with the comfort of intimacy with You, and
elevate me to the station of nearness to You, and clothe
me with the robe of acceptance. Let me drink from the
fountains of acceptance and grant me Your mercy which

نَحْمَدُكَ وَنَشْكُرُكَ يَا حَامِدُ يَا شَاكِرُ يَا ذَاكِرُ يَا نُورُ يَا حَيُّ يَا مَوْجُودُ يَا سَمِيعُ يَا بَصِيرُ يَا جَبَّارُ

اجْبُرْ كَسْرَنَا وَكَسْرَ كُلِّ مَكْسُورٍ. وَوَاصِلْ بِإِحْسَانِكَ كُلَّ مَفْصُولٍ بِقُدْرَتِكَ الَّتِي عَزَّتْ عَنِ الْعُقُولِ.

اَللَّهُمَّ سَكِّنْ فِي سُوَيْدَاءِ قُلُوبِنَا مَحَبَّةَ جَمِيعِ الْمُؤْمِنِينَ حَتَّى يَكُونُوا عِنْدَنَا أَعَزَّ مِنْ كُلِّ عَزِيزٍ وَيَكُونَ كُلُّ شَيْءٍ سِوَاهُمْ لَدَيْنَا مَهِينًا ذَلِيلًا حَقِيرًا. فَإِنَّكَ تَقُولُ لِلشَّيْءِ كُنْ فَيَكُونُ. وَرَبُّ جَوَادٌ كَرِيمٌ مُحْسِنٌ وَصُولٌ. فَنَسْأَلُكَ بِكَ سُؤَالَ مَنْ لَا يَرَى سِوَاكَ.

يَا أَرْحَمَ الرَّاحِمِينَ. (ثَلَاثًا) يَا رَبَّ الْعَالَمِينَ

رَبِّ رَبِّنِي بِلَطِيفِ رُبُوبِيَّتِكَ تَرْبِيَةَ مُفْتَقِرٍ إِلَيْكَ لَا يَسْتَغْنِي أَبَدًا عَنْكَ. وَارْقُبْنِي بِعَيْنِ رِعَايَتِكَ مُرَاقَبَةً تَحْفَظُنِي مِنْ كُلِّ طَارِقٍ يَطْرُقُنِي بِأَمْرٍ يَسُوءُنِي فِي نَفْسِي أَوْ يُكَدِّرُ عَلَيَّ وَقْتِي أَوْ يَكْتُبُ فِي لَوْحِ ذَاتِي حَظًّا مِنْ حُظُوظِ حُظُوظِي.

وَارْزُقْنِي رَاحَةَ الْأُنْسِ بِكَ وَرَقِّنِي إِلَى مَقَامِ الْقُرْبِ مِنْكَ وَرَدِّنِي بِرِدَاءِ الرِّضْوَانِ وَأَوْرِدْنِي مَوَارِدَ الْقَبُولِ وَهَبْ لِي رَحْمَةً مِنْكَ

encompasses all things. Straighten my crookedness through Your mercy and perfect my lack. When I wonder – bring me back, and guide me when I am confused. For You are the Lord and teacher of all things.

You had mercy on the essences and raised the degrees.

Your nearness is the refreshment of spirits and sweet basil of delight and the token of success and the comfort of all who enjoy it. You give the baraka, Lord of Lords, Liberator of slaves, and the One Who lifts away torment.

Your mercy and knowledge embrace all things. You forgive wrong actions out of generosity and clemency, and You are the Compassionate, the Merciful.

Praise and thanks belong to Allah. (100)

Praise belongs to Allah, the Lord of the worlds.

O Allah – O Latif. (9)

O Allah – There is no god but You! Glory be to You! Truly I have been one of the wrongdoers.

O Allah – O Latif. (10)

O Allah – There is no god but You! Glory be to You! Truly I have been one of the wrongdoers.

تَلُمُّ بِهَا شَمْلِي وَتُقَوِّمُ بِهَآ إِعْوِجَاجِي وَتُكَمِّلُ نَقْصِي وَتَرُدُّ شَارِدِي

وَتَهْدِي حَائِرِي ۖ فَإِنَّكَ رَبُّ كُلِّ شَيْءٍ وَمُرَبِّيهِ.

رَحِمْتَ الذَّوَاتِ وَرَفَعْتَ الدَّرَجَاتِ

قُرْبُكَ رَوْحُ الْأَرْوَاحِ وَرَيْحَانُ الِارْتِيَاجِ.

وَعُنْوَانُ الْفَلَاحِ وَرَاحَةُ كُلِّ مُرْتَاحٍ تَبَارَكْتَ رَبَّ الْأَرْبَابِ

وَمُعْتِقَ الرِّقَابِ وَكَاشِفَ الْعَذَابِ.

وَسِعْتَ كُلَّ شَيْءٍ رَحْمَةً وَعِلْمًا. وَغَفَرْتَ الذُّنُوبَ كَرَمًا وَحِلْمًا.

وَأَنْتَ الرَّؤُوفُ الرَّحِيمُ.


الْحَمْدُ لِلَّهِ وَالشُّكْرُ لِلَّهِ. (مائة)

الْحَمْدُ لِلَّهِ رَبِّ الْعَٰلَمِينَ.

اَللَّهُمَّ يَا لَطِيفُ. (تسع مرات)

يَآ اَللَّهُ. لَآ إِلَهَ إِلَّآ أَنْتَ سُبْحَانَكَ إِنِّي كُنْتُ مِنَ الظَّالِمِينَ.


اَللَّهُمَّ يَا لَطِيفُ. (عشرًا)


يَآ اَللَّهُ. لَآ إِلَهَ إِلَّآ أَنْتَ سُبْحَانَكَ إِنِّي كُنْتُ مِنَ الظَّالِمِينَ.

O Allah – O Latif. (10)

O Allah – There is no god but You! Glory be to You!
Truly I have been one of the wrongdoers.

O Allah – O Latif. (100)

O Allah – There is no god but You! Glory be to You!
Truly I have been one of the wrongdoers.

O Allah, bless and favour us with good health. Lift Your
wrath from us, for we are powerless before it. Look at us
with the eye of Your approval.

O All-Pitying. (3)

O Allah – There is no god but You! Glory be to You!
Truly I have been one of the wrongdoers. (3)

O Allah. O All-Pitying. (7)

O Allah – There is no god but You! Glory be to You!
Truly I have been one of the wrongdoers.

O Allah. O All-Pitying. (180)

O Allah – There is no god but You! Glory be to You!
Truly I have been one of the wrongdoers.

I have put my trust in the Living Who does not die. And
say: 'Praise be to Allah Who has had no son and Who
has no partner in His Kingdom and Who needs no one to
protect Him from abasement.' And proclaim His Greatness
repeatedly!

اَللّهُمَّ يَا لَطِيفُ. (عشرًا)

يَا اَللّهُ. لَا إِلَهَ إِلَّا أَنْتَ سُبْحَانَكَ إِنِّي كُنْتُ مِنَ الظَّالِمِينَ.

اَللّهُمَّ يَا لَطِيفُ. (مائة مرة)

يَا اَللّهُ. لَا إِلَهَ إِلَّا أَنْتَ سُبْحَانَكَ إِنِّي كُنْتُ مِنَ الظَّالِمِينَ.

اَللّهُمَّ سَلِّمْ وَأَنْعِمْ عَلَيْنَا بِالعَافِيَةِ. وَارْفَعْ عَنَّا غَضَبَكَ. فَإِنَّهُ لَا طَاقَةَ لَنَا عَلَيْهِ. وَانْظُرْ بِعَيْنِ رِضْوَانِكَ إِلَيْنَا.

يَا رَؤُوفُ. (ثلاث مرات)

يَا اَللّهُ. لَا إِلَهَ إِلَّا أَنْتَ سُبْحَانَكَ إِنِّي كُنْتُ مِنَ الظَّالِمِينَ.

(ثلاث مرات)

اَللّهُمَّ يَا رَؤُوفُ. (سبع مرات)

يَا اَللّهُ. لَا إِلَهَ إِلَّا أَنْتَ سُبْحَانَكَ إِنِّي كُنْتُ مِنَ الظَّالِمِينَ.

اَللّهُمَّ يَا رَؤُوفُ. (مائتين وثمانون مرة)

يَا اَللّهُ. لَا إِلَهَ إِلَّا أَنْتَ سُبْحَانَكَ إِنِّي كُنْتُ مِنَ الظَّالِمِينَ.

تَوَكَّلْتُ عَلَى الْحَيِّ الَّذِي لَا يَمُوتُ. وَقُلِ الْحَمْدُ لِلَّهِ الَّذِي لَمْ يَتَّخِذْ وَلَدًا وَلَمْ يَكُنْ لَهُ شَرِيكٌ فِي الْمُلْكِ وَلَمْ يَكُنْ لَهُ وَلِيٌّ مِنَ الذُّلِّ. وَكَبِّرْهُ تَكْبِيرًا.

If Allah helps you, none can overcome you. (3)

Succour! Succour! Messenger of Allah. (25)

May Allah bless him and grant him peace, and his family and Companions, and all the believing slaves of Allah.

Amin, Amin, Amin.

إِنْ يَنْصُرْكُمُ اللهُ فَلَا غَالِبَ لَكُمْ. (ثلاثًا)

الْمَدَدَ الْمَدَدَ يَا رَسُولَ اللهِ. (خمسة وعشرونَ مرة).

صَلَّى اللهُ عَلَيْهِ وَسَلَّمَ وَعَلَى ءَالِهِ وَأَصْحَابِهِ وَعَلَى جَمِيعِ عِبَادِ اللهِ الْمُؤْمِنِينَ ءَامِين ءَامِين ءَامِين.

# Qasida of Ahmad al-Badawi

هذه قصيدة الشيخ سيدي احمد البدوي الفاسي

إِلَاهِي ضَاقَتِ الصُّدُورُ مِنَّا
فَثَبِّتْنَا وَأَيِّدْنَا تَأْيِيدَا

My God, our breasts are constricted,
so strengthen us and help us.

إِلَاهِي حَارَتِ الْأَلْبَابُ مِنَّا
فَمَكِّنَّا وَرَقِّنَا الصُّعُودَا

My God, our minds are confused,
so make us firm and raise us to the heights.

إِلَاهِي عَنْ سِوَاكَ اقْطَعْ رَجَانَا
وَمِنْ بَحْرِ الْمُنَا فَاجْعَلْ وُرُودَا

My God, cut off our hopes from other-than-You,
and let us drink from the sea of raja'.

فَأَنْتَ نَصِيرِي وَالْمُعِينُ حَقًّا

وَفِيكَ رَجَاؤُنَا فَقِنَا الصُّدُودَا

Truly You are my helper and aid.
Our hopes lie with You, so keep us from rejection.

فَإِنَّ الدِّينَ أَمْرُهُ عَظِيمٌ

فَوَفِّقْنَا وَأَكْفِنَا الْوَعِيدَا

The Deen is a vast matter,
so give us success and fulfil the promise.

وَإِنَّ الْوَقْتَ قَدْ أَهَالَ فَأَحْسِنْ

لَنَا الْعُقْبَى وَكُنْ لَنَا رَشِيدَا

The moment has come, so be kind to us
in its results and be our guide.

وَتَوِّجْنَا بِفَرْدِيَّةٍ عَظِيمَهْ

وَأَجْعَلْ مِنْكَ رَبِّ لَنَا الْمَزِيدَا

Crown us with a tremendous uniqueness,
and, O Lord, give us increase from You,

أَفِضْ مَدَدًا لَنَا فِي كُلِّ قُطْرٍ

وَلِلْأَحْبَابِ سَهِّلِ الْوُرُودَا

Pour out help upon us from every quarter
and make the arrival easy for the lovers.

فَيَا فَرْدُ يَا صَمَدُ مُعِزُّ

لِحِصْنِ الْمَجْدِ أَدْخِلَنْ فَرِيدَا

O Self-sufficient, the Goal, the Enhancer!
Bring us alone into the fortress of glory.

وَيَا قَهَّارُ فَاحْمِنَا بِقَهْرٍ

فَأَنْتَ نَصِيرُ مَنْ أَتَىٰ وَحِيدَا

And, O Ever-compelling, protect us with Your force
for You are the helper of whoever comes alone.

فَيَا جَبَّارُ فَاجْبُرْنَا بِخَيْرٍ

وَيَا رَزَّاقُ هَبْ رِزْقًا مَدِيدَا

O Irresistible, help us with the good,
and O Provider, give us adequate provision.

بِعِزِّكَ يَا عَزِيزُ احْرُسْ مَقَامِي

وَوَفِّقْ رَبِّ جَبَّارًا عَنِيدَا

O Almighty, guard my station with Your might,
and O Lord, bring the stubborn tyrant to agreement.

بِحَقِّكَ يَا مُهَيْمِنُ سَلِّمْ أَمْرِي

وَكُنْ يَا رَبِّ لِي رُكْنًا شَدِيدَا

O Protector, protect my affair with Your truth,
and O Lord, be a strong support for me.

كَبِيرُ يَا قَوِيُّ يَا مَتِينُ
وَيَا قَيُّومُ صُنْ سِرَّ الْوَحِيدَا

O Great, Overpoweringly strong, Firm!
O Self-Subsisting, keep my secret, alone.

وَأَبْدِلْ بِدْعَةً بِكُلِّ هَدْيٍ
وَحَقِّقْنَا لِنُدْرِكَ الشُّهُودَا

Replace bida' with every guidance,
and grant us realisation so we may perceive the witnessing.

وَأَمِّنْ خَوْفَنَا وَاقْبَلْ دُعَانَا
فَحَاشَاكَ أَنْ تُخَيِّبَ الْمُرِيدَا

Give us safety from our fear and accept our supplication,
far be it from You that You should disappoint the murid.

بِخَاتِمَةٍ لَنَا فَاخْتِمْ عَظِيمَهْ
وَنَسْلِي كُلَّهُ فَاجْعَلْ سَعِيدَا

Grant us with a mighty seal at the end,
and make all my children fortunate.

بِجَاهِ الْمُصْطَفَى وَالْآلِ مَنْ قَدْ
بِهِ نَالُوا السَّعَادَةَ وَالْمَزِيدَا

By the rank of the Chosen One and his family and all
who have won happiness and increase through him.

360

بِأَصْحَابِهِ وَمَنْ تَبِعُوا وَأَسَّوْا

بِنَـاءَ الدِّينِ حَتَّى غَدَا مَشِيدَا

By his Companions and those who followed him
and helped establish the Deen until it became strong —

لَهُمْ أُهْدِي الصَّلَاةَ بِكُلِّ لَفْظِ

يُرَى فِي الْحِسِّ وَالْمَعْنَى فَرِيدَا

I bestow a prayer on them with every word
seen to be one in spiritual and material meaning.

وَيَتْبَعُهَا سَلَامٌ مُسْتَمِرٌّ

عَلَى مَرِّ الزَّمَانِ يُرَى جَدِيدَا

The prayer is followed by peace extending throughout time,
yet seen to be renewed over the passage of time.

صَلَاةً تَمْلَأُ الْأَكْوَانُ نُورًا

وَتُسْعِدُ وَقْتَنَا فَيَكُونُ عِيدَا

It is a prayer which fills beings with light,
and makes our age happy so that it becomes a festival,

وَيَظْهَرُ خَيْرُهَا فَنَفُوزُ فَوْزًا

عَظِيمًا وَافِرَ الْمَعْنَى مَدِيدَا

whose goodness is clearly manifest,
so we win a great victory full of vastness and meaning.

تَشَفَّعْ يَا رَسُولَ اللهِ فِينَا
فَمَا نَرْجُو الشَّفَاعَةَ مِنْ سِوَاكَا

O Messenger of Allah, intercede for us,
we do not hope for intercession from anyone except you.

أَغِثْ يَا خَيْرَ خَلْقِ اللهِ قَوْمًا
ضِعَافًا ظِلُّهُمْ أَبَدًا لِوَاكَا

O Best of Allah's creation, grant help
to a weak people whose protection is always your banner.

وَأَسْرِعْ فِي إِغَاثَتِنَا فَإِنَّا
نَرَى الْمَوْلَىٰ يُسَارِعُ فِي رِضَاكَا

Hasten to aid us, for we see
that the Lord is swift to approve of you.

عَلَيْكَ صَلَاةُ رَبِّنَا كُلَّ حِينٍ
وَآلِكَ كُلِّهِمْ وَمَنْ وَالَاكَا ۞

May the blessings of your Lord be upon you at every instant
and on all your family and those who are your friends.

لَا إِلَهَ إِلَّا اللهُ مُحَمَّدٌ رَسُولُ اللهِ. (ثَلاَثًا).

There is no god except Allah, Muhammad is the Messenger of Allah (3)

صَلَّى اللهُ عَلَيْهِ وَ سَلَّمَ وَعَلَى ءَالِهِ وَأَصْحَابِهِ وَعَلَى جَمِيعِ عِبَادِ اللهِ الْمُؤْمِنِينَ. ءَامِين. ءَامِين. ءَامِين.

— may Allah bless him and his family and grant them peace, and his Companions and all the believing slaves of Allah. Amin. Amin. Amin.

وَسَلَامٌ عَلَى الاَنْبِيَاءِ وَالْمُرْسَلِينَ. (ثلاثًا)

And peace be upon the Prophets and the Messengers (3)

وَعَلَى جَمِيعِ عِبَادِ اللهِ الصَّالِحِينَ.

and on all the slaves of Allah who are Saliheen.

وَءَاخِرُ دَعْوَانَا أَنِ الْحَمْدُ لِلَّهِ رَبِّ الْعَلَمِينَ. وَلَا حَوْلَ وَلَا قُوَّةَ إِلَّا بِاللهِ الْعَلِيِّ الْعَظِيمِ. وَمَا تَوْفِيقِي إِلَّا بِاللهِ. عَلَيْهِ تَوَكَّلْتُ وَإِلَيْهِ أُنِيبُ. الْحَمْدُ لِلَّهِ عَلَى نِعْمَةِ الاِسْلَامِ وَكَفَى بِهَا نِعْمَةً.

The last of our prayer is: Praise be to Allah, the Lord of the worlds. There is no power and no strength but through Allah, the Mighty, the Great. My help is only with Allah. In Him I have put my trust — and to Him I turn in renewal. Praise belongs to Allah for the blessing of Islam, and it is blessing enough.

# Surah Yasin

In the name of Allah, All-Merciful, Most Merciful

Ya Sin. By the Wise Qur'an. Truly you are one of the Messengers on
a Straight Path. The revelation of the Almighty, the Most Merciful so
that you may warn a people whose fathers were not warned
and who are therefore unaware.
The Word has been justly carried out against most of them so they
have no iman. We have put iron collars round their necks reaching
up to the chin, so that their heads are forced back. We have placed a
barrier in front of them and a barrier behind them,
blindfolding them so that they cannot see.
It makes no difference to them whether you warn them
or do not warn them: they will not have iman.
You can only warn those who act on the Reminder and fear the All-
Merciful in the Unseen. Give them the good news of forgiveness and a
generous reward. We bring the dead to life and We record what they
send ahead and what they leave behind.
We have listed everything in a clear register.

بِسْمِ اللهِ الرَّحْمَنِ الرَّحِيمِ

يسٓ ۝ وَالْقُرْءَانِ الْحَكِيمِ ۝ إِنَّكَ لَمِنَ الْمُرْسَلِينَ ۝ عَلَىٰ صِرَٰطٍ
مُّسْتَقِيمٍ ۝ تَنزِيلَ الْعَزِيزِ الرَّحِيمِ ۝ لِتُنذِرَ قَوْمًا مَّآ أُنذِرَ
ءَابَآؤُهُمْ فَهُمْ غَٰفِلُونَ ۝ لَقَدْ حَقَّ الْقَوْلُ عَلَىٰٓ أَكْثَرِهِمْ فَهُمْ لَا
يُؤْمِنُونَ ۝ إِنَّا جَعَلْنَا فِىٓ أَعْنَٰقِهِمْ أَغْلَٰلًا فَهِىَ إِلَى الْأَذْقَانِ فَهُم
مُّقْمَحُونَ ۝ وَجَعَلْنَا مِنۢ بَيْنِ أَيْدِيهِمْ سَدًّا وَمِنْ خَلْفِهِمْ سَدًّا
فَأَغْشَيْنَٰهُمْ فَهُمْ لَا يُبْصِرُونَ ۝ وَسَوَآءٌ عَلَيْهِمْ ءَأَنذَرْتَهُمْ أَمْ لَمْ
تُنذِرْهُمْ لَا يُؤْمِنُونَ ۝ إِنَّمَا تُنذِرُ مَنِ اتَّبَعَ الذِّكْرَ وَخَشِىَ الرَّحْمَٰنَ
بِالْغَيْبِ فَبَشِّرْهُ بِمَغْفِرَةٍ وَأَجْرٍ كَرِيمٍ ۝ إِنَّا نَحْنُ نُحْىِ الْمَوْتَىٰ وَنَكْتُبُ
مَا قَدَّمُوا۟ وَءَاثَٰرَهُمْ وَكُلَّ شَىْءٍ أَحْصَيْنَٰهُ فِىٓ إِمَامٍ مُّبِينٍ ۝

365

Make an example for them of the inhabitants of the city
when the Messengers came to it.
We sent them two and they denied them both,
so We reinforced them with a third.
They said, 'Truly We have been sent to you as Messengers.'
They said, 'You are nothing but human beings like ourselves.
The All-Merciful has not sent down anything.
You are simply lying.'
They said, 'Our Lord knows we have been sent as Messengers to you.
We are only responsible for clear transmission.'
They said, 'We see an evil omen in you.
If you do not stop we will stone you
and you will suffer a painful punishment at our hands.'
They said, 'Your evil omen is in yourselves. Is it not just that you have
been reminded? No, you are an unbridled people!'


A man came running from the far side of the city, saying,
'My people! follow the Messengers! Follow those who do not ask you
for any wage and who have received guidance.
Why indeed should I not worship Him Who brought me into being,
Him to Whom you will be returned?
Am I to take as gods instead of Him those whose intercession, if the
All-Merciful desires harm for me, will not help me at all
and cannot save me? In that case I would clearly be misguided. I have
iman in your Lord so listen to me!' He was told, 'Enter the Garden!'
He said, 'If my people only knew how my Lord has forgiven me
and placed me among the honoured ones!'

وَاضْرِبْ لَهُم مَّثَلًا أَصْحَٰبَ الْقَرْيَةِ إِذْ جَاءَهَا الْمُرْسَلُونَ ۝

إِذْ أَرْسَلْنَا إِلَيْهِمُ اثْنَيْنِ فَكَذَّبُوهُمَا فَعَزَّزْنَا بِثَالِثٍ فَقَالُوا إِنَّا إِلَيْكُم مُّرْسَلُونَ ۝ قَالُوا مَا أَنتُمْ إِلَّا بَشَرٌ مِّثْلُنَا وَمَا أَنزَلَ الرَّحْمَٰنُ مِن شَيْءٍ إِنْ أَنتُمْ إِلَّا تَكْذِبُونَ ۝ قَالُوا رَبُّنَا يَعْلَمُ إِنَّا إِلَيْكُمْ لَمُرْسَلُونَ ۝ وَمَا عَلَيْنَا إِلَّا الْبَلَٰغُ الْمُبِينُ ۝ قَالُوا إِنَّا تَطَيَّرْنَا بِكُمْ لَئِن لَّمْ تَنتَهُوا لَنَرْجُمَنَّكُمْ وَلَيَمَسَّنَّكُم مِّنَّا عَذَابٌ أَلِيمٌ ۝ قَالُوا طَائِرُكُم مَّعَكُمْ أَئِن ذُكِّرْتُم بَلْ أَنتُمْ قَوْمٌ مُّسْرِفُونَ ۝ وَجَاءَ مِنْ أَقْصَا الْمَدِينَةِ رَجُلٌ يَسْعَىٰ قَالَ يَٰقَوْمِ اتَّبِعُوا الْمُرْسَلِينَ ۝ اتَّبِعُوا مَن لَّا يَسْأَلُكُمْ أَجْرًا وَهُم مُّهْتَدُونَ ۝ وَمَا لِيَ لَا أَعْبُدُ الَّذِي فَطَرَنِي وَإِلَيْهِ تُرْجَعُونَ ۝ أَأَتَّخِذُ مِن دُونِهِ آلِهَةً إِن يُرِدْنِ الرَّحْمَٰنُ بِضُرٍّ لَّا تُغْنِ عَنِّي شَفَٰعَتُهُمْ شَيْئًا وَلَا يُنقِذُونِ ۝ إِنِّي إِذًا لَّفِي ضَلَٰلٍ مُّبِينٍ ۝ إِنِّي آمَنتُ بِرَبِّكُمْ فَاسْمَعُونِ ۝ قِيلَ ادْخُلِ الْجَنَّةَ قَالَ يَٰلَيْتَ قَوْمِي يَعْلَمُونَ ۝ بِمَا غَفَرَ لِي رَبِّي وَجَعَلَنِي مِنَ الْمُكْرَمِينَ ۝

We did not send down to his people any host from heaven after him
nor would We send one down.
It was but one Great Blast and they were extinct.
Alas for My slaves! No Messenger comes to them
without their mocking him.
Do they not see how many generations before them We have destroyed
and that they will not return to them?
Each and every one will be summoned to Our presence.

A Sign for them is the dead land which We bring to life and from which
We bring forth grain of which they eat.
We place in it gardens of dates and grapes,
and cause springs to gush out in it, so they may eat its fruits –
they did not do it themselves.
So will they not be thankful? Glory be to Him Who created all the
pairs: from what the earth produces and from themselves
and from things unknown to them.

A Sign for them is the night: We peel the day away from it
and there they are in darkness.
And the sun runs to its resting place.
That is the decree of the Almighty, the All-Knowing.
And We have decreed set phases for the moon,
until it ends up looking like an old palm spathe.

It is not for the sun to overtake the moon
nor for the night to outstrip the day;
each one is swimming in a sphere.

وَمَا أَنزَلْنَا عَلَىٰ قَوْمِهِ مِنۢ بَعْدِهِ مِن جُندٍ مِّنَ ٱلسَّمَآءِ وَمَا كُنَّا مُنزِلِينَ ۝ إِن كَانَتْ إِلَّا صَيْحَةً وَٰحِدَةً فَإِذَا هُمْ خَٰمِدُونَ ۝

يَٰحَسْرَةً عَلَى ٱلْعِبَادِ مَا يَأْتِيهِم مِّن رَّسُولٍ إِلَّا كَانُوا بِهِ يَسْتَهْزِءُونَ ۝ أَلَمْ يَرَوْا كَمْ أَهْلَكْنَا قَبْلَهُم مِّنَ ٱلْقُرُونِ أَنَّهُمْ إِلَيْهِمْ لَا يَرْجِعُونَ ۝ وَإِن كُلٌّ لَّمَّا جَمِيعٌ لَّدَيْنَا مُحْضَرُونَ ۝

وَءَايَةٌ لَّهُمُ ٱلْأَرْضُ ٱلْمَيْتَةُ أَحْيَيْنَٰهَا وَأَخْرَجْنَا مِنْهَا حَبًّا فَمِنْهُ يَأْكُلُونَ ۝ وَجَعَلْنَا فِيهَا جَنَّٰتٍ مِّن نَّخِيلٍ وَأَعْنَٰبٍ وَفَجَّرْنَا فِيهَا مِنَ ٱلْعُيُونِ ۝ لِيَأْكُلُوا مِن ثَمَرِهِ وَمَا عَمِلَتْهُ أَيْدِيهِمْ أَفَلَا يَشْكُرُونَ ۝ سُبْحَٰنَ ٱلَّذِي خَلَقَ ٱلْأَزْوَٰجَ كُلَّهَا مِمَّا تُنۢبِتُ ٱلْأَرْضُ وَمِنْ أَنفُسِهِمْ وَمِمَّا لَا يَعْلَمُونَ ۝ وَءَايَةٌ لَّهُمُ ٱلَّيْلُ نَسْلَخُ مِنْهُ ٱلنَّهَارَ فَإِذَا هُم مُّظْلِمُونَ ۝ وَٱلشَّمْسُ تَجْرِي لِمُسْتَقَرٍّ لَّهَا ذَٰلِكَ تَقْدِيرُ ٱلْعَزِيزِ ٱلْعَلِيمِ ۝ وَٱلْقَمَرَ قَدَّرْنَٰهُ مَنَازِلَ حَتَّىٰ عَادَ كَٱلْعُرْجُونِ ٱلْقَدِيمِ ۝ لَا ٱلشَّمْسُ يَنۢبَغِي لَهَآ أَن تُدْرِكَ ٱلْقَمَرَ وَلَا ٱلَّيْلُ سَابِقُ ٱلنَّهَارِ وَكُلٌّ فِي فَلَكٍ يَسْبَحُونَ ۝

A Sign for them is that We carried their families in the laden ship.
And We have created for them the like of it in which they sail.
If We wished, We could drown them with no one to hear their cry, and
then they would not be saved – except as an act of mercy from Us,
to give them enjoyment for a time.

They are told, 'Have taqwa of what is before you and behind you
so that hopefully you will have mercy shown to you.'
Not one of your Lord's Signs comes to them
without their turning away from it.
And when they are told, 'Spend from the provision Allah has given
you,' those who are kafir say to those who have iman, 'Why should we
feed someone whom, if He wished, Allah would feed Himself?
You are clearly in error.'
And they say, 'When will this promise come about if you are telling the
truth?' What are they waiting for but one Great Blast to seize them while
they are quibbling? They will not be able to make a will
or return to their families.
The Trumpet will be blown and at once
they will be sliding from their graves towards their Lord.

They will say, 'Alas for us! Who has raised us from our resting-place?
This is what the All-Merciful promised us.
The Messengers were telling the truth.'
It will be but one Great Blast,
and they will all be summoned to Our presence.
Today no self will be wronged in any way.
You will only be repaid for what you did.

وَءَايَةٌ لَّهُمْ أَنَّا حَمَلْنَا ذُرِّيَّتَهُمْ فِي ٱلْفُلْكِ ٱلْمَشْحُونِ ۝

وَخَلَقْنَا لَهُم مِّن مِّثْلِهِۦ مَا يَرْكَبُونَ ۝ وَإِن نَّشَأْ نُغْرِقْهُمْ فَلَا

صَرِيخَ لَهُمْ وَلَا هُمْ يُنقَذُونَ ۝ إِلَّا رَحْمَةً مِّنَّا وَمَتَٰعًا إِلَىٰ حِينٍ ۝

وَإِذَا قِيلَ لَهُمُ ٱتَّقُوا۟ مَا بَيْنَ أَيْدِيكُمْ وَمَا خَلْفَكُمْ لَعَلَّكُمْ تُرْحَمُونَ ۝

وَمَا تَأْتِيهِم مِّنْ ءَايَةٍ مِّنْ ءَايَٰتِ رَبِّهِمْ إِلَّا كَانُوا۟ عَنْهَا مُعْرِضِينَ ۝

وَإِذَا قِيلَ لَهُمْ أَنفِقُوا۟ مِمَّا رَزَقَكُمُ ٱللَّهُ قَالَ ٱلَّذِينَ كَفَرُوا۟ لِلَّذِينَ

ءَامَنُوٓا۟ أَنُطْعِمُ مَن لَّوْ يَشَآءُ ٱللَّهُ أَطْعَمَهُۥٓ إِنْ أَنتُمْ إِلَّا فِي ضَلَٰلٍ

مُّبِينٍ ۝ وَيَقُولُونَ مَتَىٰ هَٰذَا ٱلْوَعْدُ إِن كُنتُمْ صَٰدِقِينَ ۝

مَا يَنظُرُونَ إِلَّا صَيْحَةً وَٰحِدَةً تَأْخُذُهُمْ وَهُمْ يَخِصِّمُونَ ۝ فَلَا

يَسْتَطِيعُونَ تَوْصِيَةً وَلَآ إِلَىٰٓ أَهْلِهِمْ يَرْجِعُونَ ۝ وَنُفِخَ فِي

ٱلصُّورِ فَإِذَا هُم مِّنَ ٱلْأَجْدَاثِ إِلَىٰ رَبِّهِمْ يَنسِلُونَ ۝

قَالُوا۟ يَٰوَيْلَنَا مَنۢ بَعَثَنَا مِن مَّرْقَدِنَا هَٰذَا مَا وَعَدَ ٱلرَّحْمَٰنُ

وَصَدَقَ ٱلْمُرْسَلُونَ ۝ إِن كَانَتْ إِلَّا صَيْحَةً وَٰحِدَةً

فَإِذَا هُمْ جَمِيعٌ لَّدَيْنَا مُحْضَرُونَ ۝ فَٱلْيَوْمَ لَا تُظْلَمُ

نَفْسٌ شَيْـًٔا وَلَا تُجْزَوْنَ إِلَّا مَا كُنتُمْ تَعْمَلُونَ ۝

371

The Companions of the Garden are busy enjoying themselves today,
they and their wives reclining on couches in the shade.
They will have fruits there and whatever they request.


'Peace!'
A word from a Merciful Lord.
'Keep yourselves apart today, you evildoers!


Did I not make a contract with you, tribe of Adam, not to worship
Shaytan, who truly is an outright enemy to you, but to worship Me?
That is a straight path.
He has led huge numbers of you into error.
Why did you not use your intellect?
This is the Hell that you were promised.


Roast in it today because you were kafirun.'
Today We seal up their mouths and their hands speak to us,
and their feet bear witness to what they have earned.


If We wished, We could put out their eyes. Then, though they might
race for the path, how would they see?
If We wished, We could transform them where they stand so they
would neither be able to go out nor return.
When We grant long life to people, We return them to their primal
state. So will you not use your intellect?


We did not teach him poetry nor would it be right for him.
It is simply a reminder and a clear Qur'an

إِنَّ أَصْحَبَ الْجَنَّةِ الْيَوْمَ فِى شُغُلٍ فَكِهُونَ ۝ هُمْ

وَأَزْوَجُهُمْ فِى ظِلَلٍ عَلَى الْأَرَآئِكِ مُتَّكِئُونَ ۝

لَهُمْ فِيهَا فَكِهَةٌ وَلَهُم مَّا يَدَّعُونَ ۝ سَلَمٌ قَوْلًا مِّن

رَّبٍّ رَّحِيمٍ ۝ وَامْتَزُوا الْيَوْمَ أَيُّهَا الْمُجْرِمُونَ ۝

أَلَمْ أَعْهَدْ إِلَيْكُمْ يَبَنِى ءَادَمَ أَن لَّا تَعْبُدُوا الشَّيْطَنَ

إِنَّهُ لَكُمْ عَدُوٌّ مُّبِينٌ ۝ وَأَنِ اعْبُدُونِى هَذَا صِرَطٌ

مُّسْتَقِيمٌ ۝ وَلَقَدْ أَضَلَّ مِنكُمْ جِبِلًّا كَثِيرًا أَفَلَمْ

تَكُونُوا تَعْقِلُونَ ۝ هَذِهِ جَهَنَّمُ الَّتِى كُنتُمْ تُوعَدُونَ ۝

اصْلَوْهَا الْيَوْمَ بِمَا كُنتُمْ تَكْفُرُونَ ۝ الْيَوْمَ نَخْتِمُ عَلَى

أَفْوَهِهِمْ وَتُكَلِّمُنَا أَيْدِيهِمْ وَتَشْهَدُ أَرْجُلُهُم بِمَا كَانُوا

يَكْسِبُونَ ۝ وَلَوْ نَشَآءُ لَطَمَسْنَا عَلَى أَعْيُنِهِمْ فَاسْتَبَقُوا

الصِّرَطَ فَأَنَّى يُبْصِرُونَ ۝ وَلَوْ نَشَآءُ لَمَسَخْنَهُمْ عَلَى مَكَانَتِهِمْ

فَمَا اسْتَطَعُوا مُضِيًّا وَلَا يَرْجِعُونَ ۝ وَمَن نُّعَمِّرْهُ

نُنَكِّسْهُ فِى الْخَلْقِ أَفَلَا تَعْقِلُونَ ۝ وَمَا عَلَّمْنَهُ الشِّعْرَ

وَمَا يَنبَغِى لَهُ إِنْ هُوَ إِلَّا ذِكْرٌ وَقُرْءَانٌ مُّبِينٌ ۝

so that you may warn those who are truly alive and so that the Word
may be carried out against the kafirun.

Have they not seen how We created for them, by Our own handiwork,
livestock which are under their control?

We have made them tame for them and some they ride
and some they eat. And they have other uses for them, and milk to
drink. So will they not be thankful?

They have taken gods besides Allah so that perhaps they may be helped.

They cannot help them even though they are an army
mobilised in their support.

So do not let their words distress you.

We know what they keep secret and what they divulge.


Does not man see that We created him from a drop yet
there he is, an open antagonist!

He makes likenesses of Us and forgets his own creation,
saying, 'Who will give life to bones when they are decayed?'

Say 'He Who made them in the first place will bring them back to life.

He has total knowledge of each created thing;

He Who produces fire for you from green trees
so that you use them to light your fires.'

Does He Who created the heavens and earth
not have the power to create the same again?

Yes indeed! He is the Creator, the All-Knowing.

His command when He desires a thing is just to say to it, 'Be!' and it is.


Glory be to Him Who has the Dominion of all things in His Hand.

To Him you will be returned.

لِّتُنذِرَ مَن كَانَ حَيًّا وَيَحِقَّ ٱلْقَوْلُ عَلَى ٱلْكَٰفِرِينَ ۝

أَوَلَمْ يَرَوْا۟ أَنَّا خَلَقْنَا لَهُم مِّمَّا عَمِلَتْ أَيْدِينَآ أَنْعَٰمًا فَهُمْ لَهَا مَٰلِكُونَ ۝ وَذَلَّلْنَٰهَا لَهُمْ فَمِنْهَا رَكُوبُهُمْ وَمِنْهَا يَأْكُلُونَ ۝

وَلَهُمْ فِيهَا مَنَٰفِعُ وَمَشَارِبُ أَفَلَا يَشْكُرُونَ ۝ وَٱتَّخَذُوا۟ مِن دُونِ ٱللَّهِ ءَالِهَةً لَّعَلَّهُمْ يُنصَرُونَ ۝ لَا يَسْتَطِيعُونَ نَصْرَهُمْ وَهُمْ لَهُمْ جُندٌ مُّحْضَرُونَ ۝ فَلَا يَحْزُنكَ قَوْلُهُمْ ۝ إِنَّا نَعْلَمُ مَا يُسِرُّونَ وَمَا يُعْلِنُونَ ۝ أَوَلَمْ يَرَ ٱلْإِنسَٰنُ أَنَّا خَلَقْنَٰهُ مِن نُّطْفَةٍ فَإِذَا هُوَ خَصِيمٌ مُّبِينٌ ۝ وَضَرَبَ لَنَا مَثَلًا وَنَسِيَ خَلْقَهُۥ قَالَ مَن يُحْىِ ٱلْعِظَٰمَ وَهِىَ رَمِيمٌ ۝ قُلْ يُحْيِيهَا ٱلَّذِىٓ أَنشَأَهَآ أَوَّلَ مَرَّةٍ وَهُوَ بِكُلِّ خَلْقٍ عَلِيمٌ ۝ ٱلَّذِى جَعَلَ لَكُم مِّنَ ٱلشَّجَرِ ٱلْأَخْضَرِ نَارًا فَإِذَآ أَنتُم مِّنْهُ تُوقِدُونَ ۝ أَوَلَيْسَ ٱلَّذِى خَلَقَ ٱلسَّمَٰوَٰتِ وَٱلْأَرْضَ بِقَٰدِرٍ عَلَىٰٓ أَن يَخْلُقَ مِثْلَهُم بَلَىٰ وَهُوَ ٱلْخَلَّٰقُ ٱلْعَلِيمُ ۝ إِنَّمَآ أَمْرُهُۥٓ إِذَآ أَرَادَ شَيْـًٔا أَن يَقُولَ لَهُۥ كُن فَيَكُونُ ۝ فَسُبْحَٰنَ ٱلَّذِى بِيَدِهِۦ مَلَكُوتُ كُلِّ شَىْءٍ وَإِلَيْهِ تُرْجَعُونَ ۝

Allah, there is no god but Him, the Living, the Self-
Sustaining. He is not subject to drowsiness or sleep.
Everything in the heavens and the earth belongs to Him.
Who can intercede with Him except by His permission?
He knows what is before them and what is behind them
but they cannot grasp any of His knowledge save what
He wills. His Footstool encompasses the heavens and the
earth and their preservation does not tire Him. He is the
Most High, the Magnificent.

O Allah, we take refuge in Your satisfaction from Your
wrath and in Your gifts from Your punishment and in
You from You. I am unable to praise You adequately as
You have praised Yourself.
There is no god but You! Glory be to You!
Truly I have been one of the wrongdoers.

Glory be to You, O Allah, and by Your praise I witness
that there is no god except You. I ask forgiveness of You
and I turn to You in self-renewal. I have done wrong and
I have wronged myself, so forgive me, for none forgives
wrong actions except You. There is no god but You!
Glory be to You!
Truly I have been one of the wrongdoers.

O Allah, bless our master Muhammad, Your slave,
Prophet and Messenger, the unlettered Prophet and his
family and Companions and grant them peace by the
measure of the sublimity of Your Essence at every time
and in every age. Amin. Amin. Amin.

اللهُ لَا إِلَهَ إِلَّا هُوَ الْحَيُّ الْقَيُّومُ. لَا تَأْخُذُهُ سِنَةٌ وَلَا نَوْمٌ. لَهُ مَا فِي السَّمَوَاتِ وَمَا فِي الْأَرْضِ. مَنْ ذَا الَّذِي يَشْفَعُ عِنْدَهُ إِلَّا بِإِذْنِهِ. يَعْلَمُ مَا بَيْنَ أَيْدِيهِمْ وَمَا خَلْفَهُمْ. وَلَا يُحِيطُونَ بِشَيْءٍ مِنْ عِلْمِهِ إِلَّا بِمَا شَاءَ. وَسِعَ كُرْسِيُّهُ السَّمَوَاتِ وَالْأَرْضَ. وَلَا يَؤُودُهُ حِفْظُهُمَا. وَهُوَ الْعَلِيُّ الْعَظِيمُ.

اَللّٰهُمَّ إِنَّا نَعُوذُ بِرِضَاكَ مِنْ سَخَطِكَ. وَبِمُعَافَاتِكَ مِنْ عُقُوبَتِكَ. وَبِكَ مِنْكَ. لَا أُحْصِي ثَنَاءً عَلَيْكَ. أَنْتَ كَمَا أَثْنَيْتَ عَلَى نَفْسِكَ. لَا إِلَهَ إِلَّا أَنْتَ سُبْحَانَكَ إِنِّي كُنْتُ مِنَ الظَّالِمِينَ.

سُبْحَانَكَ اللّٰهُمَّ وَبِحَمْدِكَ أَشْهَدُ أَنْ لَا إِلَهَ إِلَّا أَنْتَ أَسْتَغْفِرُكَ وَأَتُوبُ إِلَيْكَ. عَمِلْتُ سُوءًا وَظَلَمْتُ نَفْسِي فَاغْفِرْ لِي فَإِنَّهُ لَا يَغْفِرُ الذُّنُوبَ إِلَّا أَنْتَ. لَا إِلَهَ إِلَّا أَنْتَ.
سُبْحَانَكَ إِنِّي كُنْتُ مِنَ الظَّالِمِينَ.

اَللّٰهُمَّ صَلِّ عَلَى سَيِّدِنَا مُحَمَّدٍ عَبْدِكَ وَنَبِيِّكَ وَرَسُولِكَ النَّبِيِّ الْأُمِّيِّ وَعَلَى آلِهِ وَصَحْبِهِ وَسَلِّمْ تَسْلِيمًا. بِقَدْرِ عَظَمَةِ ذَاتِكَ فِي كُلِّ وَقْتٍ وَحِينٍ. ءَامِينْ ءَامِينْ ءَامِينْ.

In the name of Allah, All-Merciful, Most Merciful:
Praise be to Allah, the Lord of all the worlds, the All-
Merciful, the Most Merciful, the King of the Day of
Judgment. You alone we worship. You alone we ask for
help. Guide us on the Straight Path, the Path of those You
have blessed, not of those with anger on them,
nor of the misguided. Amin.

Glory be to your Lord, the Lord of might, above all that
they describe. And peace be upon the Messengers. And
praise belongs to Allah, the Lord of the worlds.

O Lord, lead me in with a just ingoing and lead me out
with a just outgoing: grant me authority from You to help
me. There is no god but You! Glory be to You!
Truly I have been one of the wrongdoers.

Glory be to You, O Allah, and by Your Praise I bear
witness that there is no god except You. I ask forgiveness
of You and I turn to you in self-renewal. I have done
wrong and I have wronged myself, so forgive me, for
none forgives wrong actions except You. There is no god
but You! Glory be to You! Truly I have been one of the
wrongdoers.

O Allah, bless our master Muhammad, Your slave,
Prophet and Messenger, the unlettered Prophet and his
family and Companions and grant them peace by the
measure of the sublimity of Your Essence at every time
and in every age. Amin. Amin. Amin.

بِسْمِ اللهِ الرَّحْمَنِ الرَّحِيمِ الْحَمْدُ لِلّهِ رَبِّ الْعَلَمِينَ الرَّحْمَنِ الرَّحِيمِ
مَلِكِ يَوْمِ الدِّينِ. إِيَّاكَ نَعْبُدُ وَإِيَّاكَ نَسْتَعِينُ. اهْدِنَا الصِّرَاطَ
الْمُسْتَقِيمَ صِرَاطَ الَّذِينَ أَنْعَمْتَ عَلَيْهِمْ
غَيْرِ الْمَغْضُوبِ عَلَيْهِمْ وَلَا الضَّالِّينَ. ءَامِين.

سُبْحَانَ رَبِّكَ رَبِّ الْعِزَّةِ عَمَّا يَصِفُونَ. وَسَلَامٌ عَلَى الْمُرْسَلِينَ.
وَالْحَمْدُ لِلّهِ رَبِّ الْعَلَمِينَ.

رَبِّ أَدْخِلْنِي مُدْخَلَ صِدْقٍ وَأَخْرِجْنِي مُخْرَجَ صِدْقٍ وَاجْعَلْ لِي
مِنْ لَدُنْكَ سُلْطَانًا نَصِيرًا. لَآ إِلَهَ إِلَّا أَنْتَ
سُبْحَانَكَ إِنِّي كُنْتُ مِنَ الظَّالِمِينَ.

سُبْحَانَكَ اللَّهُمَّ وَبِحَمْدِكَ أَشْهَدُ أَنْ لَآ إِلَهَ إِلَّا أَنْتَ أَسْتَغْفِرُكَ
وَأَتُوبُ إِلَيْكَ. عَمِلْتُ سُوءًا وَظَلَمْتُ نَفْسِي فَاغْفِرْ لِي فَإِنَّهُ لَا يَغْفِرُ
الذُّنُوبَ إِلَّا أَنْتَ. لَآ إِلَهَ إِلَّا أَنْتَ
سُبْحَانَكَ إِنِّي كُنْتُ مِنَ الظَّالِمِينَ.

اَللَّهُمَّ صَلِّ عَلَى سَيِّدِنَا مُحَمَّدٍ عَبْدِكَ وَنَبِيِّكَ وَرَسُولِكَ النَّبِيِّ الْأُمِّيِّ
وَعَلَى ءَالِهِ وَصَحْبِهِ وَسَلِّمْ تَسْلِيمًا. بِقَدْرِ عَظَمَةِ ذَاتِكَ فِي كُلِّ وَقْتٍ
وَحِينٍ. ءَامِين ءَامِين ءَامِين.

In the name of Allah, All-Merciful, Most Merciful:
Praise be to Allah, the Lord of all the worlds, the All-
Merciful, the Most Merciful, the King of the Day of
Judgment. You alone we worship. You alone we ask for
help. Guide us on the Straight Path, the Path of those You
have blessed, not of those with anger on them, nor of the
misguided.

Glory be to your Lord, the Lord of might, above all that
they describe. And peace be upon the Messengers.
And praise belongs to Allah, the Lord of the worlds.

O Allah, bless us in our provision, our Deen and our
children, and our country. We take refuge with You from
the evil of our nafs and from the evil of all that is evil.
There is no god but You! Glory be to You!
Truly I have been one of the wrongdoers.

O Allah, You are my Lord, there is no god except You.
You created me and I am your slave, and I follow Your
command and promise as much as I am able. I take refuge
with You from the wrong I have done. I acknowledge to
you Your blessing upon me, and I acknowledge my wrong
actions, so forgive me, for none forgives wrong actions
except You.

O Allah, bless our master Muhammad, Your slave,
Prophet and Messenger, the unlettered Prophet and his
family and Companions and grant them peace by the
measure of the sublimity of Your Essence at every time
and in every age. Amin. Amin. Amin.

بِسْمِ اللهِ الرَّحْمٰنِ الرَّحِيمِ الْحَمْدُ لِلّٰهِ رَبِّ الْعَٰلَمِينَ الرَّحْمٰنِ الرَّحِيمِ
مَٰلِكِ يَوْمِ الدِّينِ. إِيَّاكَ نَعْبُدُ وَإِيَّاكَ نَسْتَعِينُ. اِهْدِنَا الصِّرَاطَ
الْمُسْتَقِيمَ صِرَاطَ الَّذِينَ أَنْعَمْتَ عَلَيْهِمْ غَيْرِ الْمَغْضُوبِ عَلَيْهِمْ وَلَا
الضَّآلِّينَ. ءَامِين.

سُبْحَانَ رَبِّكَ رَبِّ الْعِزَّةِ عَمَّا يَصِفُونَ. وَسَلَامٌ عَلَى الْمُرْسَلِينَ.
وَالْحَمْدُ لِلّٰهِ رَبِّ الْعَٰلَمِينَ.

اَللّٰهُمَّ بَارِكْ لَنَا فِي رِزْقِنَا وَدِينِنَا وَذُرِّيَّاتِنَا وَبِلَادِنَا وَنَعُوذُ بِكَ مِنْ
شَرِّ أَنْفُسِنَا وَمِنْ شَرِّ كُلِّ ذِي شَرٍّ. لَآ إِلٰهَ إِلَّا أَنْتَ سُبْحَانَكَ إِنِّي
كُنْتُ مِنَ الظَّالِمِينَ.

اَللّٰهُمَّ أَنْتَ رَبِّي لَآ إِلٰهَ إِلَّا أَنْتَ خَلَقْتَنِي وَأَنَا عَبْدُكَ وَأَنَا عَلَى
عَهْدِكَ وَوَعْدِكَ مَا اسْتَطَعْتُ. أَعُوذُ بِكَ مِنْ شَرِّ مَا صَنَعْتُ. أَبُوءُ
لَكَ بِنِعْمَتِكَ عَلَيَّ وَأَبُوءُ بِذَنْبِي. فَاغْفِرْ لِي
فَإِنَّهُ لَا يَغْفِرُ الذُّنُوبَ إِلَّا أَنْتَ.

اَللّٰهُمَّ صَلِّ عَلَى سَيِّدِنَا مُحَمَّدٍ عَبْدِكَ وَنَبِيِّكَ وَرَسُولِكَ النَّبِيِّ الْأُمِّيِّ
وَعَلَى ءَالِهِ وَصَحْبِهِ وَسَلِّمْ تَسْلِيمًا. بِقَدْرِ عَظَمَةِ ذَاتِكَ فِي كُلِّ وَقْتٍ
وَحِينٍ. ءَامِين ءَامِين ءَامِين

381

In the name of Allah, All-Merciful, Most Merciful:
Praise be to Allah, the Lord of all the worlds, the All-
Merciful, the Most Merciful, the King of the Day of
Judgment. You alone we worship. You alone we ask for
help. Guide us on the Straight Path, the Path of those You
have blessed, not of those with anger on them, nor of the
misguided. Amin. Amin. Amin.

Glory be to your Lord, the Lord of might, above all that
they describe. And peace be upon the Messengers. And
praise belongs to Allah, the Lord of the worlds.

Allah. (7)

Allah is greater. (3)

Allah is greater and much praise is due to Allah. Glory be
to Allah in the morning and evening.

I have turned my face to Him Who originated the
heavens and the earth, a man of the ancient way. I am not
of the mushrikin.

Say: 'My salat and my rites, my living and my dying, are
for Allah alone, the Lord of all the worlds, Who has no
partner. I am commanded to be like that and I am the
first of the Muslims.'

Glory be to your Lord, the Lord of might, above all that
they describe. And peace be upon the Messengers. And
praise belongs to Allah, the Lord of the worlds.

بِسْمِ اللهِ الرَّحْمَـٰنِ الرَّحِيمِ الْحَمْدُ لِلَّهِ رَبِّ الْعَـٰلَمِينَ الرَّحْمَـٰنِ الرَّحِيمِ
مَـٰلِكِ يَوْمِ الدِّينِ. إِيَّاكَ نَعْبُدُ وَإِيَّاكَ نَسْتَعِينُ.

اِهْدِنَا الصِّرَاطَ الْمُسْتَقِيمَ صِرَاطَ الَّذِينَ أَنْعَمْتَ عَلَيْهِمْ
غَيْرِ الْمَغْضُوبِ عَلَيْهِمْ وَلَا الضَّآلِّينَ. ءَامِين. ءَامِين. ءَامِين.

سُبْحَانَ رَبِّكَ رَبِّ الْعِزَّةِ عَمَّا يَصِفُونَ. وَسَلَامٌ عَلَى الْمُرْسَلِينَ.
وَالْحَمْدُ لِلَّهِ رَبِّ الْعَـٰلَمِينَ.

اللهُ. (سَبْعًا)

اللهُ أَكْبَرُ. (ثَلَاثًا)

اللهُ أَكْبَرُ كَبِيرًا وَالْحَمْدُ لِلَّهِ حَمْدًا كَثِيرًا
وَسُبْحَانَ اللهِ بُكْرَةً وَأَصِيلًا.

إِنِّي وَجَّهْتُ وَجْهِيَ لِلَّذِي فَطَرَ السَّمَـٰوَٰتِ وَالْأَرْضَ حَنِيفًا وَمَآ
أَنَا مِنَ الْمُشْرِكِينَ.

قُلِ اِنَّ صَلَاتِي وَنُسُكِي وَمَحْيَايَ وَمَمَاتِي لِلَّهِ رَبِّ الْعَـٰلَمِينَ
لَا شَرِيكَ لَهُ. وَبِذَٰلِكَ أُمِرْتُ. وَأَنَا أَوَّلُ الْمُسْلِمِينَ.

سُبْحَانَ رَبِّكَ رَبِّ الْعِزَّةِ عَمَّا يَصِفُونَ. وَسَلَامٌ عَلَى الْمُرْسَلِينَ.
وَالْحَمْدُ لِلَّهِ رَبِّ الْعَـٰلَمِينَ.

383

# The 99 Beautiful Names

هذه القصيدة الرائية في التوسّل بأسماء الله (تعالى) الحسنى
للسيد أحمد بن عبد العزيز الفيلاني

بَدَأَتْ بِبِسْمِ اللهِ في أَوَّلِ السَّطْرِ
فَأَسْمَاؤُهُ حِصْنٌ مَنِيعٌ مِنَ الضَّرِّ

I have begun with the name of Allah in the first line,
for His most Beautiful Names are a fortress invincible against harm.

وَصَلَّيْتُ في الثَّانِي عَلَى خَيْرِ خَلْقِهِ
مُحَمَّدٍ الْمَبْعُوثِ بِالفَتحِ وَالنَّصرِ

In the second, I pray for blessings on the Best of Creation,
Muhammad, who was sent with an opening and triumph.

إِذَا اسْتَفْتَحَ القُرَّاءُ في مُحْكَمِ الذِّكْرِ
فَبِاسْمِكَ يَا ذَا العَرْشِ يَسْتَفْتِحُ المُقْرِى

When they begin in the circle of dhikr it is with Your name,
O Lord of the Throne, that the reciter must begin.

384

إِذَا نَابَنِي خَطْبٌ وَضَاقَ بِهِ صَدْرِي
تَلَافَاهُ لُطْفُ اللهِ مِنْ حَيْثُ لَا أَدْرِي

When I am in trouble and my breast constricts,
the lutf of Allah enters it, coming from where I do not know.

وَلَا سِيَّمَا إِذْ جِئْتُه مُتَوَسِّلًا
بِأَسْمَآئِهِ الْحُسْنَى الْمُعَظَّمَةِ الْقَدْرِ

Especially when I come to Him, entreating Him
by His most beautiful and mighty Names.

فَيَا اللَّهُ يَا رَحْمَنُ إِنِّي لَذُو فَقْرٍ
وَأَنْتَ رَحِيمٌ مَالِكُ الْخَلْقِ وَالْأَمْرِ

So Allah, O All-Merciful, truly I am in dire poverty,
You are Compassionate, the Lord of Creation and the command.

بِقُدْسِكَ قُدُّوسٌ سَلَامٌ ومؤمِنٌ
مُهَيْمِنٌ قَدِّسْنِي لَدَى السِّرِّ وَالْجَهْرِ

By Your purity, O Pure, O Peace, O Safety-giver,
O Protector, purify me both inside and outside.

عَزِيزٌ وَجَبَّارٌ وَيَا مُتَكَبِّرُ
وَيَا خَالِقَ الْخَلْقِ اكْفِنِي أَزْمَةَ الدَّهْرِ

O Hard of Access, Irresistible, Rightly Proud,
Creator of creation, shelter me on the Day of Reckoning.

وَيَا بَارِئُ مَالِي سِوَاكَ مُصَوِّرٌ
وَغَفَّارُ يَا قَهَّارُ جَبْرًا لِذِى كَسْرِ

O first Creator and Giver of Form, I have none but You.
O Forgiving, O Compeller, mend the one who has been broken.

وَهَبْ لِي يَا وَهَّابُ رَزَّاقُ مَطْلَبِي
وَفَتَّاحُ أَشْرِقْ يَا عَلِيمُ دُجَىٰ فِكْرِي

O Giver, give me what I seek, O Provider.
O Opener, All-Knowing, illumine the darkness of my thoughts.

وَيَا قَابِضُ يَا بَاسِطُ خَافِضُ الْعِدَا
وَيَا رَافِعُ ارْفَعْ بِالتِّبَاعِ الْهُدَىٰ ذِكْرِي

O He-Who-contracts, He-Who-expands, O Abaser, O Exalter,
exalt my dhikr by making me follow guidance.

مُعِزٌّ مُذِلٌّ يَا سَمِيعُ بَصِيرُ جُدْ
عَلَىٰ مَا تَرَىٰ مِنْ فَادِحِ الْعَيْبِ بِالسِّتْرِ

O Enacter, O One Who humbles, O Hearing O Seeing,
Draw Your veil and cover the ugliness of my faults.

وَيَا حَكَمُ عَدْلُ لَطِيفُ خَبِيرُ مَا
لَنَا وِزْرُ إِلَّاكَ فِي الضِّيقِ وَالْعُسْرِ

O the Just, O the Judge, the Latif, Aware of all things,
We are overcome unless we have You in distress and hardship.

حَلِيمُ عَظِيمُ يَا غَفُورُ شَكُورُ لَنْ

يُخِيبَ امْرُءًا يَرْجُوكَ بِالْحِلْمِ وَالْغَفْرِ

O Indulgent, Immense, Utterly Forgiving, Grateful,
You do not disappoint the one who hopes for gentle pardon from You.

عَلِيُّ كَبِيرُ يَا حَفِيظُ مُقِيتُ هَبْ

لَنَا حِفْظَكَ الْاَحْمَى لَدَى الْحَادِثِ الْوَعْرِ

O High, Great, All-Preserver, Nourisher, grant us
Your sheltering protection in every difficult event.

حَسِيبُ جَلِيلُ يَا رَقِيبُ كَرِيمُ مَنْ

سِوَاكَ نُرَجِّيهِ لِخَلَّةِ ذِي فَقْرِ

O All-Reckoning, Majestic, Ever-Watchful, Generous,
who other than You can we hope will be a friend for one in poverty?

مُجِيبُ أَجِبْ يَا وَاسِعُ يَا حَكِيمُ يَا

وَدُودُ دُعَا دَاعٍ لِفَضْلِكَ مُضْطَرِ

O Answerer, Utterly Vast beyond measure, Ever-Wise, Loving,
answer the prayers of the one who, hard-pressed, prays for Your bounty.

مَجِيدُ مُجِدْ يَا بَاعِثُ يَا شَهِيدُ بِا

لَّذِي نَرْتَجِي يَا حَقُّ مِنْ جُودِكَ الْغَمْرِ

O Glorious, Raiser of the Dead, Directly-perceiving Haqiqa,
by Whom we hope, be generous with Your all-engulfing generosity.

وَكِيلُ قَوِيٌّ يَا مَتِينُ وَلِيُّ كُنْ

وَلِيًّا لِعَبْدٍ مِنْ خَطَايَاهُ فِي أَسْرِ

O Reliable Guardian, Overpoweringly Strong, Firm, Protector,
protect Your slave from falling into the captivity of wrong action.

حَمِيدُ وَمُحْصِي مُبْدِئُ وَمُعِيدُ لَنْ

يَزَلْ مِنْكَ جُودٌ يَنْتَحِنَّ بِلَا حَصْرِ

O Praiseworthy, Knower of each separate thing, O Bringer-into-Being
and Bringer-Back, Your incalculable giving never ceases.

وَمُحْيِي مُمِيتٌ حَيٌّ قَيُّومُ وَاجِدُ

وَيَا مَاجِدُ لَا تُوْلِنِي الْخِزْيَ فِي النَّشْرِ

O Life-Giver, Life-Taker, Living, Self-Sustaining, Un-needing, All-Glorious,
do not assign me to punishment on the Day of Gathering.

وَيَا أَحَدُ نَرْجُوكَ يَا صَمَدُ إِذَا

تَضِيقُ بِنَا يَا قَادِرُ فُسْحَةُ الْعُمْرِ

O One, Self-Sufficient, All-Powerful Lord,
we have hope in You when the fullness of life becomes narrow.

وَمُقْتَدِرُ ارْفَعْ يَا مُقَدِّمُ رُتْبَتِي

مُؤَخِّرُ أَخِّرْ كُلَّ مَنْ يَبْتَغِي ضُرِّي

O Determiner, the Bringer-Near, the One Who puts it far, raise my rank
and put all who wish me harm far away from me.

وَيَـا أَوَّلُ يَـا آخِرُ ظَـاهِرُ وَبَـا
طِنُ وَالٍ اِجْذِبْنِي إِلَىٰ حَضْرَةِ الطُّهْرِ

O First, Last, Outwardly Manifest, Inwardly Hidden,
Protecting Master, draw me into the presence of purity.

وَيَـا مُتَعَـالٍ بَرُّ تَوَّابُ جُدْ وَتُبْ
وَمُنْتَقِمُ حُلْ بَيْنَنَـا وَذَوِي الشَّرِّ

O Sublime, Benign, Relenting – be generous to us and turn to us,
and, O Avenger, defend me against those who are evil.

عَفُوُّ رَءُوفُ مَـالِكُ الْمُلْكِ أَنْتَ ذُو
الْجَلَالِ وَالاِكْرَامِ اعْفُ عَنْ كُلِّ مَا وِزْرِ

O Effacer of wrong actions, All-Pitying, Possessor of the kingdom,
You are the Lord of Majesty and Gifts – forgive every wrong action.

وَمُقْسِطُ جَـامِعُ غَنِيُّ فَأَغْنِنَـا
غِنَى الْقَلْبِ يَـا مُغْنِي لِنَغْنَ عَنِ الْوَفْرِ

O Equitable, O Gatherer, O Rich, Enricher,
enrich our hearts so that they may be rich to overflowing.

وَيَـا مَـانِعُ يَـا ضَـارُّ يا نَـافِعُ اِهْدِنَا
بِنُورِكَ يَـا نُورُ وَهَـادٍ إِلَى الْيُسْرِ

O Preventer, Harmer, and Benefitter, Light and Guide –
guide us by Your light to tranquillity.

بَدِيعُ وَبَـاقٍ وَارِثُ يَا رَشِيدُ يَا
صَبُورُ أَتِحْ لِي الرُّشْدَ لِلشُّكْرِ وَالصَّبْرِ

O Originator, O Enduring, Inheritor, Infallible-Guide,
All-Patient, give me right guidance in gratitude and fortitude.

بِأَسْمَـائِكَ الْحُسْنَىٰ دَعَوْنَـاكَ نَبْتَغِي
رِضَـاكَ وَلُطْفًا فِي الْحَيَـاةِ وَفِي الْقَبْرِ

We beg You by Your most beautiful Names,
seeking Your approval and lutf in this life and the grave.

وَفِي النَّشْرِ ثُمَّ الْحَشْرِ وَالْمَوْقِفِ الَّذِي
تُحَـاسَبُ فِيهِ الْخَلْقَ يَا عَـالِمَ السِّرِّ

And on the Day of Rising and Gathering at the stopping place
where creation will be taken to account, O Knower of secrets!

وَفِي حَالِ اَخْذِ الصُّحْفِ وَالْوَزْنِ بَعْدَهَا
كَذَالِكَ فِي حَـالِ الْمُرُورِ عَلَى الْجَسْرِ

When the books of actions are taken and weighed
and at the arrival and when we pass over the bridge.

وَعَـافِيَةَ دِينًـا وَدُنْيًـا وَرَحْمَةً
بِفَضْلِكَ فِي الدَّارَيْنِ يَا وَاسِعَ الْبِرِّ

O Vast in Goodness, give us health in our Deen,
and this world, and mercy in the two abodes by Your generosity.

وَخَتْمًا بِحُسْنَىٰ مَعْ جِوَارِ نَبِينَا

مُحَمَّدٍ الْمَحْمُودِ فِي الْمَوْقِفِ الْحَشْرِ

We ask for a seal of goodness, and to be near the Prophet Muhammad,
the Praiseworthy, in the Station of Gathering.

عَلَيْهِ صَلَاةُ اللهِ ثُمَّ سَلَامُهْ

بِلَا مُنْتَهَىٰ وَالْآلِ مَعْ صَحْبِهِ الْغُرِّ

May the blessings of Allah be upon him, and His peace without end,
and on his family and glorious Companions.

وَلِلنَّاظِمِ اغْفِرْ يَا إِلَهِي وَأَهْلِهِ

وَأَحْبَابِهِ وَاسْتُرْهُمْ دَائِمَ السِّتْرِ

O my God, pardon the poet and his family and loved ones,
and always veil and conceal their wrong actions,

وَقَارِئِهَا وَالْمُسْلِمِينَ جَمِيعِهِمْ

وَلِلَّهِ رَبِّ دَائِمُ الْحَمْدِ وَالشُّكْرِ ۞

And pardon the reader and all the Muslims.
Praise and thanks endlessly belongs to Allah, my Lord.

# This Qasida in Fa by its Author
## as-Sayyid Ahmad al-Hilali

هذه القصيدة الفائيّة لناظمها السيد أحمد الهيلالي

لَكَ الْحَمْدُ كُلَّ الْحَمْدِ يَا رَاحِمَ الضُّعْفِ

وَيَا دَائِمَ الاِحْسَانِ وَالرِّفْقِ وَاللُّطْفِ

All praise is due to You, O You Who are merciful to the weak,
and constant in kindness, gentleness and Lutf.

لَكَ الْحَمْدُ ثُمَّ الشُّكْرُ دُونَ نِهَايَةٍ

عَلَى نِعَمٍ جَلَّتْ عَنِ الْعَدِّ وَالْوَصْفِ

Endless praise and thanks belong to You
for Your blessings which are beyond number and description.

صَرَفْتَ مِنَ الاَسْوَاءِ مَا لَا يُطِيقُهُ

مُطِيقٌ فَأَنْتَ اللهُ ذُو الْكَرَمِ الصِّرْفِ

You are pure of evil as no-one else can be,
for You are Allah, the Lord of Pure Generosity.

وَجُدْكَ وَأَسْدَيْتَ الْجَمِيلَ تَفَضُّلاً

وَزِدْتَ مِنَ الْإِنْعَـامِ ضِعْفًا عَلَى ضِعْفِ

You are generous and You have extended Your favours with kindness
and You have increased Your blessings many times over.

لَكَ الْحَمْدُ يَـا قَهَّـارُ وَالْأَمْرُ كُلُّهُ

إِذَا قُلْتَ كُنْ كَـانَ الْمُرَادُ بِلَا خُلْفِ

Praise belongs to You, O Conquerer, and the command belongs to You,
when You say, 'Be!' what You have willed happens without opposition.

إِلَيْكَ مَدَدْنَا الْكَفَّ كَيْ مَا تُمِدُّنَـا

بِمَـا نَرْتَجِي يَـا مَالِكَ الْبَسْطِ وَالْكَفّ

We stretch out our hands to You, that You may provide us
with what we hope for, O Lord of restraint and extension.

فَعَـافٍ وَدَافِعْ وَارْحَمْ يَـا رَبِّ وَاكْفِنَا

بِحِفْظِكَ مَـا نَخْشَى فَغَيْرُكَ لَا يَكْفِي

Pardon us, defend us and have mercy on us, O Lord, suffice us
with Your protection from what we fear, for other than You is not enough.

وَأَبْقِ عَلَيْنَـا السِّتْرَ فِي كُلِّ حَـالَةٍ

بِفَضْلِكَ فِي الدُّنْيَا وَالْأُخْرَى بِلَا كَشْفِ

Spare us by veiling our wrong actions in every state by Your overflowing
in this world and the next with a veil that is not drawn aside.

وَأَعْظِمْ وَأَعْزِزْ يَـا عَزِيزُ جَنَـابَنَـا

وَحُطْنَا مِنَ انْخِذْلَانِ وَالضَّيمِ وَالْخَسْفِ

O Powerful, exalt us and strengthen us
and protect us from disappointment, in fair times and in shame.

وَزِدْنَـا مِنَ النَّعْمَـاءِ فَوْقَ مَرَامِنَـا

بِمَنِّكَ يَـا مَوْلَايْ تَعَالَىٰ عَنِ الْكَيْفِ

Increase us in blessings beyond our desire with Your graciousness,
O my Master, exalted above qualification.

وَصَلِّ وَسَلِّمْ ثُمَّ بَـارِكْ عَلَى الشَّفِيعْ

بِهِ نَرْتَجِي مِنْكَ الامَـانَ مِنَ الْخَوْفِ

Bless and grant peace to the Intercessor and bless him again.
Through him we hope You will grant us security from fear.

وَصَلِّ وَسَلِّمْ ثُمَّ بَـارِكْ عَلَى الْحَبِيبْ

بِهِ نَطْلُبُ مِنْكَ الامَـانَ مِنَ الرَّجْفِ

Bless and grant peace to the Beloved and bless him again!
Through him we look to You for security from trembling.

مُحَمَّدٍ الْمُخْتَـارِ وَالْغُرِّ أَهْلِهِ

وَأَصْحَـابِهِ الأُسْدِ الْغِضَابِ يَوْمَ الرَّجْفِ

Muhammad, the Chosen. O grant the same to his mighty family
and his Companions – the raging lions – on the Day of Trembling.

وَوَاصِلْ عَلَيْهِمْ ذَاكَ مَا لَاذَ خَائِفٌ

بِهِمْ فَتَحَلَّى بِالْأَمَانِ مِنَ الْخَوْفِ

Bestow safety on them as long as there is one who fears (Allah)
seeking refuge with them, so that he may be robed in security from fear

وَمَا قَالَ مَرْحُومٌ عَلَى حَالِ ضُعْفِهِ

لَكَ الْحَمْدُ كُلَّ الْحَمْدِ يَا رَاحِمَ الضُّعْفِ ۝

And as long as there is one in a state of weakness
to whom You have shown mercy,
saying: 'All praise is due to You Who are merciful to the weak.'

# A Tawassul composition
## by the Gnostic of Allah Shaykh Zarruq

توسل من نظم العارف بالله الشيخ زروق

فَيَا نَفْحَةَ الْآلْطَافِ مِنْ لُطْفِ رَبِّنَا
وَيَا سُرْعَةَ الْيُسْرِ الْمُشَتِّتِ لِلْعُسْرِ

O Gust of Goodness from the Lutf of our Lord,
O Swift Help Who scatters our difficulties.

وَيَا رَحْمَةَ الْمَوْلَى السَّمَاوِيَّةَ الَّتِي
تَهِبُّ هُبُوبَ الرِّيحِ مِنْ حَيْثُ لَا أَدْرِي

O Celestial Mercy of the Lord which comes,
blowing like the wind, from where I know not.

إِغَاثَةَ مَلْهُوفٍ أَضَرَّتْ بِحَالِهِ
نَوَائِبُ لَا تَخْفَاكَ يَا عَالِمَ السِّرِّ

You are the help of the one who is troubled, oppressed by his state
and his misfortunes which hold no fear for You, O Knower of Secrets.

وَلَمَّا دَهَانِي الْحَالُ وَاشْتَدَّ خَطْبُهُ

شَكَوْتُ إِلَىٰ رُحْمَاكَ يَا رَبِّ مِنْ ضُرِّي

When a state overtakes me and misfortune is violent,
I complain to Your mercy, O Lord of my affliction.

فَعَجِّلْ وَسَارِعْ يَا سَرِيعُ بِحَالِ مَا

تَضَايَقَ بِي يَا وَاسِعَ الْفَضْلِ وَالْبِرِّ

O Swift, make haste, and quickly help me in the state
which distresses me, O Vast Overflowing Kindness.

فَمَنْ ذَا الَّذِي أَرْجُو سِوَاكَ لِحَاجَتِي

وَفَقْرِي فَدَارِكْ حَالِي يَا مَالِكَ الْأَمْرِ

In my need and poverty who can I have hope in, except You?
So, O master of the command, overtake my state.

فَأَنْتَ الْقَرِيبُ الْمُسْتَجِيبُ لِمَنْ دَعَا

غَنِيٌّ كَرِيمٌ دَائِمُ الْعَفْوِ وَالسِّتْرِ

You are the Near, the One Who answers whoever prays to You;
You are the Rich, the Generous, with perpetual pardon of wrong actions.

وَصَلِّ عَلَىٰ خَيْرِ الْأَنَامِ مُحَمَّدٍ

مَا دَامَتْ لَكَ الْأَحْكَامُ فِي تَصْرِيفِ الْأَمْرِ ۞

And bless the best of mankind, Muhammad,
as long as Your judgments in the disposition of the command remain.

# Here ends the Noble Hafidha

With praise of Allah and His excellent help — and there is no power and no strength but by Allah, the High, the Vast.
In the Hafidha:

The *'Asma l-Husna* was written by Sayyidi 'Abdalaziz Hilali of Marrakesh

The first two qasidas were added by Sayyidi Tayyib.

The *Laka' l-hamd* was written by Sayyidi Muluqsur of Marrakesh.

*Fa ya nafhata' l-altafi* — and also the *Tashaffa ya Rasula' llah* — written by: Sayyidi Ahmad Mowla Milyana of Algeria.

*Ala ya Latifu* was written by Shaykh Moulay al-'Arabi ad-Darqawi

*Ilahi daqati's-sudura minna* — written by Shaykh Ahmad al-Badawi

*Allahumma salli 'ala man minhu'nshaqqati' l-asrar* — written by Shaykh 'Abdassalam al-Mashish

*Allahumma salli wa sallim bi anwa'i kamalatika* — is from Shaykh Muhammad Ibn al-Habib

# A Story by Abu Hafs Umar

حكاية تشوِّقُ الراغبين في الطريق

وتُثبِّت أقدام السائرين عليها

بِسْمِ اللهِ الرَّحْمَنِ الرَّحِيمِ

الْحَمْدُ للهِ الْحَمْدُ للهِ الْحَمْدُ للهِ الَّذِي بِسَابِقِ عِنَايَتِهِ تَسَابَقَتْ هِمَمُ الْعَابِدِينَ الْمُخْلِصِينَ. فَتَعَطَّشَتْ قُلُوبُهُمْ لِمَعْرِفَتِهِ. وَبِعَظِيمِ تَوْفِيقِهِ عَظُمَتِ النِّعْمَةُ عَلَى الْمُرِيدِينَ الصَّادِقِينَ. فَتَاقَتْ أَرْوَاحُهُمْ لِلتَّطَلُّعِ عَلَى أَهْلِ حِزْبِهِ وَوِلَايَتِهِ. وَبِتَمَامِ لُطْفِهِ تَمَّتِ الْمِنْحَةُ عَلَى الْمَحْبُوبِينَ الْمُحْسِنِينَ. فَاتَّصَلَتْ أَشْبَاحُهُمْ بِخَاصَّةِ أَهْلِ وَقْتِهِمْ حَسْبَمَا وَقَعَ التَّعَارُفُ الرُّوحِي فِي عَالَمِ مَلَكُوتِهِ

Praise be to Allah. Praise be to Allah. Praise be to Allah Whose concern existed before the himmas of the sincere worshippers vied against one another so that their hearts thirsted for gnosis of Him. By His vast bestowal of success, the true murids received an immense blessing and so their arwah yearned to see the people of His Party and His awliya'. By His undiminished lutf He bestowed the complete gift on the lovers who do good, received the perfect gift and their physical forms joined the elite people of their time, commensurate with their spiritual mutual recognition in the world of His Malakut.

أَحْمَدُهُ سُبْحَانَهُ وَتَعَالَى حَمْدَ عَبْدٍ أَنْعَمَ اللهُ عَلَيْهِ بِنِعْمَتَيِ الْإِسْلَامِ وَالتَّصْدِيقِ. وَأَشْكُرُهُ جَلَّ وَعَلَا شُكْرَ مَنْ أَكْرَمَهُ مَوْلَاهُ بِمُوَالَاةِ أَهْلِ التَّشْرِيعِ وَالتَّحْقِيقِ. وَأَشْهَدُ أَنْ لَا إِلَهَ إِلَّا اللهُ الْوَاحِدُ الْأَحَدُ الصَّمَدُ الْمَعْبُودُ.

I praise Him — glory be to Him and may He be exalted! — with the praise of a slave on whom Allah has bestowed the twin blessings of Islam and affirmation. I thank Him, the Majestic and High, with the thankfulness of someone who has been granted by his Master the friendship of the people of the Shari'a and the Haqiqa. I testify that there is no god but Allah, the One, the Unique, the Everlasting Support, the Worshipped.

وَأَشْهَدُ أَنَّ سَيِّدَنَا وَمَوْلَانَا مُحَمَّدًا عَبْدُهُ وَرَسُولُهُ الْمُفَضَّلُ عَلَى سَائِرِ الْوُجُودِ ٠ وَعَلَى آلِهِ وَأَصْحَابِهِ أَهْلِ الْكَرَمِ وَالْجُودِ. وَعَلَى كَافَّةِ عِبَادِ اللهِ الصَّالِحِينَ الْبَاذِلِينَ فِي نُصْحِ عَبِيدِ رَبِّهِمْ أَنْفُسَهُمْ وَكُلٌّ بِهَا يَجُودُ.

I testify that our master Muhammad is His slave and Messenger, preferred over all existence. May Allah bless him and grant him peace, and bless his family and Companions, the people of nobility and generosity, and all the righteous slaves of Allah who expend themselves in giving good counsel to the slaves of their Lord, and all who are generous with it.

وَبَعْدُ فَيَقُولُ الْعُبَيْدُ الْمُفْتَقِرُ، أَبُو حَفْصٍ عُمَرُ، بَلَّغَهُ اللهُ الْآمَالَ، وَلَطَفَ بِهِ فِي جَمِيعِ الْأَحْوَالِ: لَمَّا كَانَ الدِّيوَانُ الْعَدِيمُ النَّظِيرِ: دِيوَانُ الْعَارِفِ بِاللهِ الشَّيْخِ الْأَكْبَرِ، وَالْأُسْتَاذِ الْأَشْهَرِ، عَلَّامَةِ الزَّمَانِ، وَنُورُ حَدِيقَةِ الْعِرْفَانِ، الْعَلَّامَةُ اللَّوْذَعِي، وَالْقُطْبِ الْغَوْثِ الْكَبِيرِ الْأَلْمَعِيّ، الْعَلَّامَةَ الرَّبَّانِيّ، وَالْفَرْدِ الْمُحَمَّدِي النُّورَانِي. أَبُو الْفُيُوضَاتِ وَالْإِمْدَادَاتِ وَمَعْدِنِ الْأَسْرَارِ وَالْبَرَكَاتِ، مَوْلَانَا أَبُو عَبْدِ اللهِ سَيِّدُنَا الشَّيْخُ مُحَمَّدُ بْنُ سَيِّدِنَا الْحَبِيبِ الْأَمْغَارِي الْإِدْرِيسِيّ الْحَسَنِيّ نَسَبًا الْمَالِكِي مَذْهَبًا الشَّاذَلِي الدَّرْقَاوِي طَرِيقَةً وَانْتِسَابًا الْمُحَمَّدِي فَيْضًا وَمَشْرَبًا الْفَاسِي ثُمَّ الْمَكَّاسِيّ مَنْشَأً وَدَارًا،

The needy slave, Abu Hafs 'Umar, whose hopes were realised by Allah Who showed kindness to him in his every state, says concerning the unique and unparalleled Diwan, the Diwan of the gnostic of Allah, the greatest shaykh and most famous master, the guidepost of his time and light of the garden of gnosis, the brilliant Guidepost and Qutb and Greatest Ghawth, the radiant sovereign guide and luminous Muhammadan individual, who possesses overflowing effulgence and assistance, a veritable lode of secrets and blessings, our master Abu 'Abdullah, our shaykh, Shaykh Muhammad ibn al-Habib al-Amghari al-Idrisi al-Hasani al-Maliki ash-Shadhili ad-Darqawi of Fes and then Meknes.

لَمْ تَسْمَحْ قَرِيحَةٌ بِمِثَالِهِ وَلَمْ يُنْسَجْ عَلَى مِنْوَالِهِ. وَأَنَّهُ مَا تَأَمَّلَهُ سَالِكٌ ذَائِقٌ إِلَّا
وَمَا عِنْدَهُ نَمَا وَرَبَا وَمَا تَصَفَّحَهُ مُرِيدٌ صَادِقٌ إِلَّا وَتَهَذَّبَ وَتَرَبَّى وَمَا طَرَقَ سَمْعَ
خَالِي الذِّهْنِ شَائِقٍ إِلَّا وَدَخَلَ فِي الطَّرِيقِ وَلَبَّى ثُمَّ بَعْدَ طَبْعِهِ أَوَّلًا نَبَعَتْ مَعَارِفُ
مِنْ فُيُوضَاتِ أَسْرَارِ مُؤَلِّفِهِ، رَضِيَ اللهُ عَنْهُ لِذَلِكَ عَزَمَ خَوَاصُّ الْفُقَرَاءِ وَأَعْيَانُ
الْأَحْبَابِ عَلَى طَبْعِهِ ثَانِيًا

No spring has burst forth like it and it is totally unique. No wayfarer with spiritual tasting reflects on it but that what he already has grows and increases, and no sincere murid studies it but that he is taught and instructed. No one with an open mind happens to hears it but that he enters the Tariq and turns to Allah. After it was published the first time, gnoses flowed forth from the overflowing of the secrets of its author, may Allah be pleased with him. That is why the elite fuqara' and lovers resolved to publish it a second time.

فَنَاسَبَ أَنْ يُدْخَلَ ذَلِكَ الْمَزِيدَ مَعَ بَعْضِ قَصَائِدَ أَنْشَأَهَا بَعْضُ التَّلَامِذَةِ فِي شَيْءٍ
مِنْ شَمَائِلِ صَاحِبِ الدِّيوَانِ الْمَذْكُورِ، وَلِتِلْكَ الْمُنَاسَبَةِ أَذْكُرُ نُبْذَةً قَلِيلَةً مِنْ حِكَايَةٍ
عَجِيبَةٍ فِي السَّبَبِ الْجَامِعِ لِي بِهَذَا السَّيِّدِ الْجَلِيلِ:

Therefore it seemed fitting that this murid should include some qasidas which some of his students wrote, on some of the virtues of the author of this Diwan. It also provides an opportunity to mention a small part of an extraordinary story about the manner in which I met this illustrious master.

(أَقُولُ أَنَّهَا لَمَّا هَبَّتْ رِيَاحُ الْعَطَايَا وَالْمِنَنِ وَقَرُبَتْ سُوَيْعَاتُ الِاتِّصَالِ بِخَاصَّةِ
أَهْلِ هَذَا تَشَوَّشَ بَالِي وَتَغَيَّرَتْ أَحْوَالِي فَتَعَلَّقْتُ بِأَذْيَالِ الصَّلَاةِ عَلَى سَيِّدِ الْأَنَامِ
وَتَوَسَّلْتُ بِجَاهِهِ لِلرَّبِّ الَّذِي لَا يَنَامُ طَالِبًا مِنْهُ سُبْحَانَهُ أَنْ يَجْمَعَنِي بِشَيْخٍ مُرَبِّي،
فَأَلْهَمَنِي اللهُ لِقِرَاءَةِ عَدَدٍ مَعْلُومٍ مِنَ الصَّلَاةِ الْكَامِلَةِ. فَلَمَّا أَتْمَمْتُ الْعَدَدَ ظَهَرَتْ
عَلَامَاتُ الْقَبُولِ، ثُمَّ تَشَوَّقْتُ لِلسَّفَرِ فَخَرَجْتُ مُتَوَجِّهًا نَحْوَ الْمَغْرِبِ

When the winds of gifts and presents blew, and the time of joining the elite of the people of this time was close at hand, my mind became confused and my circumstances changed. After the prayer, I turned myself to the Master of Mankind and sought intercession by his rank with the Lord Who does not sleep, asking Him to take me to a shaykh of instruction. Allah inspired me to recite the well-known number of the perfect prayer. When I completed the number, the signs of its acceptance appeared. Then I yearned to travel and set out in the direction of Morocco.

فَلَمَّا وَصَلْتُ مَدِينَةَ تِيَارِتْ لَقِيَنِي رَجُلٌ عَلَيْهِ سِيمَةُ الصَّالِحِينَ وَقَالَ مِنْ أَيْنَ الرَّجُلُ، قُلْتُ مِنْ وَرْقَلَهْ، وَقَالَ وَهَلْ فِيهَا شُيُوخُ تَرْبِيَةٍ قُلْتُ لَا عِلْمَ لِي بِذَلِكَ، قَالَ أَمَّا أَنَا فَقَدْ اجْتَمَعْتُ بِرَجُلٍ عَالِمٍ مِنْ عُلَمَاءِ الْمَغْرِبِ الاقْصَى فِي الْبُلَيْدَةِ اسْمُهُ سَيِّدِي مُحَمَّدُ بْنُ الْحَبِيبِ فَإِنْ كَانَ فِي هَذَا الْعَصْرِ شَيْخُ تَرْبِيَةٍ فَهُوَ ذَاكَ وَسُكْنَاهُ فِي مَدِينَةِ فَاس

When I reached the city of Tiaret, I met a man who had the appearance of one of the righteous. He asked, "Where are you from?" I replied, "From Ouargla." He inquired, "Are there shaykhs of teaching there?" I answered, "I have no knowledge of that." He said, "As for myself, I have met one of the men of knowledge in a town in Morocco. His name is Sayyidi Muhammad ibn al-Habib. If there is a shaykh of teaching in this time, it is him. He lives in the city of Fes."

فَقَصَدْتُهَا وَتَيَمَّمْتُ جَامِعَهَا الاعْظَمَ جَامِعَ الْقَرَوِيِّينْ، فَلَمَّا دَخَلْتُهُ وَجَدْتُ رَجُلاً فِي نَاحِيَةٍ وَبِيَدِهِ دِيوَانُ سَيِّدِي عُمَرَ بْنِ الْفَارِضِ فَاسْتَأْذَنْتُهُ فِي الْاسْتِمَاعِ فَأَذَنَ لِي وَرَفَعَ صَوْتَهُ بِالْقِرَاءَةِ فَلَمَّا سَكَتَ قُلْتُ سَيِّدِي أَمَوْجُودُونَ الآنَ أَرْبَابُ هَذَا الْفَنِّ؟ قَالَ أَجَلْ كَيْفَ لَا وَالنَّبِيُّ يَقُولُ : ( لَا تَزَالُ طَائِفَةٌ مِنْ أُمَّتِي ) . الحديث.

I went there and made for its greatest mosque, the Qarawiyyin Mosque. When I entered it, I found a man in a corner who had the Diwan of Sayyidi 'Umar ibn al-Farid in his hand. I asked for permission to listen and he gave me permission. He raised his voice and read. When he was silent I asked, "Sayyidi, are there now any masters of this science?" "Certainly," he replied, "How could there not be when the Prophet, may Allah bless him and grant him peace, said, 'There will continue to be a group of my Community…' (the hadith)."

فَقُلْتُ لَهُ وَهَذِهِ مَدِينَةٌ عَظِيمَةٌ لَمَّا فِيهَا مِنْ أَكَابِرِ الْعُلَمَاءِ وَأَعْيَانِ الشَّرَفَاءِ وَخَوَاصِّ الصُّلَحَاءِ قَدِيمًا وَحَدِيثًا. فَهَلْ مِنْ شَيْخٍ فِيهَا قَالَ نَعَمْ هُوَ هَذَا سَيِّدِي مُحَمَّدُ بْنُ الْحَبِيبِ مَشْهُورُ الزَّاوِيَةِ وَالسُّكْنَى فِي قَصْبَةِ النُّوَّارِ فَأَخَذْتُ الْعُنْوَانَ وَذَهَبْتُ

مُسْرِعًا وَبِمُجَرَّدِ مَا دَخَلْتُ تِلْكَ الزَّاوِيَةِ زَالَ عَنِّي كُلُّ مَا كُنْتُ أَجِدُهُ قَبْلُ مِنَ التَّشْوِيشِ وَالتَّغْيِيرِ وَطَابَ وَقْتِي وَوَجَدْتُ تَلامِيذَةً مُهَذَّبِينَ، وَأَخْبَرُونِي بِأَنَّ سَيِّدَنَا الشَّيْخَ مَشْغُولٌ بِشُؤُونِ الارْتِحَالِ إِلَى زَاوِيَتِهِ الْعُظْمَى بِمَكْنَاسَ،

I asked him, "This great city has had notable scholars and noble individuals and elite righteous people, both old and modern. Is there a shaykh in it?" "Yes," he replied. "There is Sayyidi Muhammad ibn al-Habib. His zawiyya and home is well known in the Qasba an-Nuwar." So I took the address and went there immediately. The moment I entered that zawiyya, all the confusion and change that I had experienced before vanished, and I felt good. I found well-mannered disciples who told me that Sayyiduna Shaykh was busy preparing to travel to his main zawiyya in Meknes.

وَبَقِيتُ مَعَ الْفُقَرَاءِ حَتَّى طَلَعَ عَلَيْنَا الأُسْتَاذُ وَقْتَ صَلاةِ الْعَصْرِ مِنَ الْيَوْمِ الثَّالِثِ فَتَنَوَّرَتْ قُلُوبُنَا بِرُؤْيَتِهِ وَأَذْكَارِهِ وَطَابَتْ أَوْقَاتُنَا بِأَسْرَارِهِ وَأَنْوَارِهِ وَتَرَوَّحَتْ أَرْوَاحُنَا بِإِشَارَاتِهِ وَتَذْكَارِهِ، وَوَجَدْتُ مِنْ قَلْبِي مَا اللهُ أَعْلَمُ بِهِ ثُمَّ سَأَلَنِي عَنْ سَبَبِ سِيَاحَتِي، قُلْتُ طَمَعًا فِي مُلاقَاةِ أَمْثَالِكُمْ وَتَعَرُّضًا لِلانْخِرَاطِ فِي أَحْزَابِكُمْ

I remained with the fuqara' until the master came out to us at the time of the 'Asr prayer on the third day. Our hearts were filled with light at the sight of him and his dhikr. Our moments were made delightful by his secrets and lights, and our spirits revived by his indications and reminders. I felt in my heart what Allah knows best. Then he asked me what the reason for my journey was and I said, "The desire to meet those like you and to be included in your party."

فَعِنْدَ ذَلِكَ قَرَّبِنِي إِلَيْهِ وَأَجْلَسَنِي بَيْنَ يَدَيْهِ وَهُوَ يَقُولُ أَهْلاً وَسَهْلاً وَمَرْحَبًا وَبَايَعْتُهُ وَلَقَّنَنِي وِرْدَهُ الشَّرِيفَ وَأَذِنَ لِي فِي ذِكْرِهِ وَاجْتَمَعَتْ بِحَمْدِ اللهِ هِمَّتِي عَلَيْهِ

Then he drew me to him and had me sit before him, saying, "Welcome! Welcome!" So I gave him ba'ya and he taught me his noble wird and gave me idhn to recite it. Praise be to Allah, my himma was concentrated on it.

ثُمَّ ارْتَحَلْنَا إِلَى مَكْنَاسَ وَجَعَلَتْ تَرِدُ عَلَيْنَا خَوَاصُّ الْفُقَرَاءِ وَأَعْيَانُ الْمُحِبِّينَ مِنْ كُلِّ فَجٍّ عَمِيقٍ لِحَفْلَةِ سَابِعِ الْمِيلادِ الْمُحَمَّدِيِّ ثُمَّ بَعْدَ تَفَرُّقِ الْوَافِدِينَ مِنْ ذَلِكَ

الْمَوْسِمِ بَقِيتُ مَعَ سَادَتِي الْفُقَرَاءِ الْمُتَجَرِّدِينَ فِي الزَّاوِيَةِ نَحْوًا مِنْ ثَلَاثَةِ أَشْهُرٍ

Then we travelled to Meknes and the elite of the fuqara' and lovers began to come to us from every deep ravine to attend the gathering held on the Mawlud of the Prophet Muhammad. When those who came to that moussem departed, I remained with my masters, the fuqara' who were divested, in the zawiyya for about three months.

ثُمَّ أَمَرَنِي بِالرُّجُوعِ إِلَى الْوَطَنِ لِنَشْرِ الطَّرِيقِ وَالدَّلَالَةِ وَالْإِرْشَادِ، بَعْدَمَا أَوْصَانِي بِمَا وَصَانِي، وَذَاكَرَنِي بِمَا ذَاكَرَنِي، وَأَخْبَرَنِي بِشَيْءٍ مِمَّا أَكْرَمَهُ بِهِ مَوْلَاهُ وَذَلِكَ عَلَى يَدِ الْوَاسِطَةِ الْعُظْمَى سَيِّدِ الْأَنَامِ عَلَيْهِ أَفْضَلُ الصَّلَاةِ وَأَزْكَى السَّلَامِ.

Then he told me to return to my homeland to spread the Tariq and to guide and direct people after he gave me some advice, reminded me and told me about some of that with which his Master had honoured him. That was all at the hand of the greatest means, the Master of Mankind, may the best blessing and purest peace be upon him.

ثُمَّ سَافَرْتُ بَاكِيَ الْعَيْنِ حَزِينَ الْقَلْبِ مِنْ أَلَمِ الْفِرَاقِ، وَوَدَّعَنِي الْأُسْتَاذُ وَشَيَّعَنِي بِنَفْسِهِ إِلَى خَارِجِ الزَّاوِيَةِ، وَدَعَا بِمَا شَاءَ اللهُ أَنْ يَدْعُو وَرَجَعْتُ إِلَى وَطَنِي وَتَكَوَّنَتْ طَائِفَةٌ مِنَ الْفُقَرَاءِ مُتَنَوِّرَةٌ وَذَلِكَ كُلُّهُ بِبَرَكَةِ الْاِتِّصَالِ بِصَاحِبِ الْوَقْتِ وَسِرِّ إِذْنِهِ.

Then I departed in tears, with a heart filled with sorrow at the pain of parting. The master bade me farewell and he himself accompanied me to the exit of the zawiyya and made whatever supplication Allah wished for him to make. I returned to my homeland and an illuminated group of fuqara' formed. All of that was due to the baraka of meeting the master of the moment and of the secret of his idhn.

وَالْحَمْدُ لِلَّهِ عَلَى ذَلِكَ. مَتَّعَنَا اللهُ بُرْهَةً مِنَ الزَّمَانِ بِحَيَاتِهِ، آمِين آمِين آمِين وَهَذَا مَا دَعَتِ الْحَاجَةُ إِلَى ذِكْرِهِ.

وبه أبو حفص المذكور

Praise belongs to Allah for that. May Allah let us enjoy his life for an instant of time. Amin. Amin Amin.

Abu Hafs.

# The Isnad of the Tariq

Sayyiduna
## Muhammad
blessings and peace of Allah be upon him

Sayyiduna 'Ali ibn Abi Talib

Sayyidi al-Hasan ibn 'Ali
Sayyidi Abu Muhammad Jabir
Sayyidi Sa'id al-Ghazwani
Sayyidi Fathu's-Su'ud
Sayyidi Sa'd
Sayyidi Sa'id
Sayyidi Ahmad al-Marwani
Sayyidi Ibrahim al-Basri
Sayyidi Zaynu'd-Din al-Qazwini
Sayyidi Muhammad Shamsu'd-Din
Sayyidi Muhammad Taju'd-Din
Sayyidi Nuru'd-Din Abu'l-Hasan 'Ali
Sayyidi Fakhru'd-Din
Sayyidi Taqiyyu'd-Din

> In the name of Allah,
> All-Merciful,
> Most Merciful
> Say: 'He is Allah,
> Absolute Oneness,
> Allah, the Everlasting
> Sustainer of all.
> He has not given birth
> and was not born.
> And no one is
> comparable to Him.'

Sayyidi al-Hasan al-Basri
Sayyidi Habib al-'Ajami
Sayyidi Da'ud at-Ta'i
Sayyidi Ma'ruf al-Karkhi
Sayyidi Sari as-Saqati
al-Imam al-Junayd
Sayyidi ash-Shibli
Sayyidi at-Tartusi
Sayyidi Abu-l-Hasan al-Hukkari
Sayyidi Abu Sa'id al-Mubarak
**Mawlana 'Abd al-Qadir al-Jilani**
Sayyidi Abu Madyan al-Ghawth
Sayyidi Muhammad Salih
Sayyidi Muhammad ibn Harazim
Sayyidi 'Abd ar-Rahman al-'Attar
Sayyidi 'Abdu's-Salam ibn Mashish
**Sayyidi Abu'l-Hasan ash-Shadhili**
Sayyidi Abu'l-'Abbas al-Mursi
Sayyidi Ahmad ibn 'Ata'illah
Sayyidi Da'ud al-Bakhili
Sayyidi Muhammad Wafa
Sayyidi 'Ali Wafa
Sayyidi Yahya al-Qadiri
Sayyidi Ahmad al-Hadrami
Sayyidi Ahmad Zarruq
Sayyidi Ibrahim al-Fahham
Sayyidi 'Ali ad-Dawwar
Sayyidi 'Abd ar-Rahman al-Majdhub
Sayyidi Yusuf al-Fasi
Sayyidi Muhammad ibn 'Abdillah
Sayyidi Qasim al-Khassasi
Sayyidi Ahmad ibn 'Abdillah
Sayyidi al-'Arabi ibn 'Abdillah
Sayyidi 'Ali al-Jamal
**Mawlana al-'Arabi ibn Ahmad ad-Darqawi**

Sayyidi Abu Ya'za al-Muhaji
Sayyidi Muhammad 'Abd al-Qadir al-Basha
Sayyidi Muhammad ibn Qudur
Sayyidi ibn al-Habib al-Buzidi
Mawlana Ahmad ibn Mustafa al-'Alawi
Sayyidi Muhammad al-Fayturi Hamuda

> A man came running
> from the far side of
> the city, saying, 'My
> people! follow the
> Messengers!'

Sayyidi Ahmad al-Badawi
Sayyidi Muhammad al-'Arabi
Sayyidi al-'Arabi al-Hawwari
Sayyidi Muhammad ibn 'Ali
**Sayyidi Muhammad ibn al-Habib**

**Sayyidi 'Abdalqadir as-Sufi**
**Moulay Murtada al-Boumas-houli**

إسناد الطريق

سيدنا

محمد ﷺ

سيدنا علي بن أبي طالب

سيدي الحسن بن علي

سيدي أبو محمد جابر

سيدي سعيد الغزواني

سيدي فتح السعود

سيدي سعد

سيدي سعيد

سيدي أحمد المرواني

سيدي إبراهيم البصري

سيدي زين الدين القزويني

سيدي محمد شمس الدين

سيدي محمد تاج الدين

سيدي نور الدين أبو الحسن علي

سيدي فخر الدين

سيدي تقي الدين

سيدي عبد الرحمن العطار

سيدي عبد السلام بن مشيش

سيدي الحسن البصري

سيدي حبيب العجمي

سيدي داوود الطائي

سيدي معروف الكرخي

سيدي ساري السقطي

الإمام جنيد

سيدي الشبلي

سيدي الطرطوسي

سيدي أبو الحسن الهكاري

سيدي أبو سعيد المبارك

مولانا عبد القادر الجيلاني

سيدي أبو مدين الغوث

سيدي محمد صالح

سيدي محمد بن حرازم

بِسْمِ اللهِ الرَّحْمَنِ الرَّحِيمِ قُلْ هُوَ اللهُ أَحَدٌ. اللهُ الصَّمَدُ. لَمْ يَلِدْ وَلَمْ يُولَدْ. وَلَمْ يَكُنْ لَهُ كُفُوًا أَحَدٌ.

سيدي أبو الحسن الشاذلي

سيدي أبو العباس المرسي

سيدي أحمد بن عطاء الله

سيدي داود الباخلي

سيدي محمد وفا

سيدي علي وفا

سيدي يحيى القادري

سيدي أحمد الحضرمي

سيدي أحمد زروق

سيدي إبراهيم الفحام

سيدي علي الدوار

سيدي عبد الرحمن المجذوب

سيدي يوسف الفاسي

سيدي عبد الرحمان الفاسي

سيدي محمد بن عبد الله

سيدي قاسم الخصاصي

سيدي أحمد بن عبد الله

سيدي العربي بن عبد الله

سيدي علي الجمل

مولانا العربي بن أحمد الدرقاوي

سيدي أحمد البدوي

سيدي محمد العربي

سيدي العربي الهواري

سيدي محمد بن علي

سيدي محمد بن الحبيب

وَجَاءَ مِنْ أَقْصَا الْمَدِينَةِ رَجُلٌ يَسْعَى قَالَ يَقَوْمِ اتَّبِعُوا الْمُرْسَلِينَ

سيدي أبو يعزى المحاجي

سيدي محمد عبد القادر الباشا

سيدي محمد بن قدور

سيدي ابن الحبيب البوزيدي

سيدي أحمد بن مصطفى العلوي

سيدي محمد الفيتوري حمودة

سيدي عبد القادر الصوفي

مولاي مرتضى البومسهولي

# The Isnad of the Tariq
## سند الطريق

تلقيتها عن العارف بالله العلّامة الربّاني سيّدنا الشيخ محمد بن سيدي الحبيب، عن سيدي محمد بن علي، عن سيدي العربي الهواري، عن سيدي محمد العربيّ، عن سيدي أحمد البدويّ، عن سيدي مولاي العربيّ الدرقاويّ، عن سيدي علي الجمل، عن سيدي العربيّ بن عبد الله، عن سيدي أحمد بن عبد الله، عن سيدي قاسم الخصاصيّ، عن سيدي محمد بن عبد الله، عن سيدي عبد الرحمان الفاسي، عن سيدي يوسف الفاسي، عن سيدي عبد الرحمان المجذوب، عن سيدي علي الدوار، عن سيدي إبراهيم الفحام، عن سيدي أحمد زروق، عن سيدي أحمد الحضرميّ، عن سيدي يحي القادريّ، عن سيدي علي وفا، عن سيدي محمد وفا، عن سيدي داود الباخليّ، عن سيدي أحمد بن عطاء الله، عن سيدي أبي العبّاس المرسيّ، عن سيدي أبي الحسن الشاذليّ، عن سيدي عبد السلام ابن مشيش ۰ وأخذ القطب الشاذليّ أيضًا عن سيدي محمد بن حرازم، عن سيدي محمد صالح، عن سيدي أبي مدين الغوث، عن مولانا عبد القادر الجيلاني، عن سيدي أبي سعيد المبارك، عن سيدي أبي الحسن الهكاري، عن سيدي الطرطوسيّ، عن سيدي الشبليّ، عن الإمام الجنيد، عن سيدي السري السقطيّ، عن سيدي معروف الكرخيّ، عن سيدي داود الطائي، عن سيدي حبيب العجميّ، عن سيدي الحسن البصريّ، عن سيّدنا علي بن أبي طالب رضي الله عنه و كرّم الله وجهَه، عن سيد الأوّلين والآخرين، عن سيدنا جبريل الأمين، عن مَن جلت عظمته وتقدّست أسماؤهُ وصِفاته ربِّ العالَمِين ۰

I took it from the gnostic of Allah and scholar, Sayyiduna Shaykh Muhammad ibn al-Habib, from Sayyidi Muhammad ibn 'Ali from Sayyidi al-'Arabi al-Huwari from Sayyidi Muhammad al-'Arabi from Sayyidi Ahmad al-Badawi from Sayyidi Moulay'l-'Arabi ad-

Darqawi from Sayyidi 'Ali al-Jamal from Sayyidi al-'Arabi ibn 'Abdullah from Sayyidi Ahmad ibn 'Abdullah from Sayyidi Qasim al-Khassasi from Sayyidi Muhammad ibn 'Abdullah from Sayyidi Sayyidi 'Abdu'r-Rahman al-Fasi from Sayyidi Yusuf al-Fasi from Sayyidi 'Abdu'r-Rahman al-Majdhub from Sayyidi 'Ali ad-Duwwar from Sayyidi Ibrahim al-Fahham from Sayyidi Ahmad Zarruq from Sayyidi Ahmad al-Hadrami from Sayyidi Yahya al-Qadiri, from Sayyidi 'Ali Wafa from Sayyidi Muhammad Wafa from Sayyidi Dawud al-Bakhili from Sayyidi Ahmad ibn 'Ata'illah from Sayyidi Abu'l-'Abbas al-Mursi from Sayyidi Abu'l-Hasan ash-Shadhili who took from Sayyidi 'Abdu's-Salam ibn Mashish, and the Shadhili Qutb also took from Sayyidi Muhammad ibn Harazim from Sayyidi Muhammad Salih from Sayyidi Abu Madyan al-Ghawth from Mawlana 'Abdu'l-Qadir al-Jilani from Sayyidi Abu Sa'id al-Mubarak, from Sayyidi Abu'l-Hasan al-Hukkari from Sayyidi at-Tartusi from Sayyidi ash-Shibli from Imam al-Junayd from Sayyidi as-Sari as-Saqati from Sayyidi Ma'ruf al-Karkhi from Sayyidi Da'ud at-Ta'i from Sayyidi Habib al-'Ajami from Sayyidi al-Hasan al-Basri from Sayyiduna 'Ali ibn Abi Talib, may Allah be pleased with him and honour his face, from the Master of the first and the last, from our master Jibril, the Trusty, from the One Whose majesty is vast, and Names and Attributes are pure, the Lord of the Worlds.

ثُمَّ نَظَمْتُ ذَلِكَ تَسْهِيلًا لِلْحِفْظِ لِمَنْ رَامَهُ. قُلْتُ :

Then I turned that into verse to make it easy to memorise
if someone wishes to do so.

فَإِنْ شِئْتَ أَنْ تُعْزَىٰ إِلَىٰ خَيْرِ فِرْقَةٍ
فَصَاحِبْ إِمَامَ الْعَارِفِينَ الْأَجِلَّةِ

If you wish to be ascribed to the best party,
then accompany the Imam of the lofty gnostics,

سَلِيلَ النَّبِيِّ وَارِثَ السِّرِّ مَنْ بَدَا
يَتِيمًا لِذَا الْأَوَانِ مِنْ دُونِ شُبْهَةَ

The descendant of the Prophet, heir of the secret
of the one who appeared as an orphan at that time without doubt,

سَلِيلَ الْمُحَبِّ الْحَبِيبِ الشَّرِيفِ مَنْ
يُسمَّى مُحمَّدًا بَدِيعَ الْعِبَارَة

The descendant of the beloved sharif al-Habib.
His name is Muhammad, and he has extraordinary expression.

فَعنْهُ أَخَذْتُ الْعَهْدَ بِاللهِ وَاثِقًا
عَنْ ابْنِ عَلِيٍّ ذِي الْحِبَا وَالْبِشَارَة

I took the contract with Allah from him with trust
from Ibn 'Ali who had gifts and good news,

وَعَنِ الْعَالِمِ الرَّاسِخِ فِي الْحَقِيقَة
سَيِّدِي الْعَرَبِي الْهُوَارِي ذِي الْمَحَبَّة

And from the scholar who is firmly rooted in the Reality,
Sayyidi al-'Arabi al-Huwari, master of love,

عَنْ أُسْتَاذِهِ مُحمَّدِ الْعَرَبِي السَّرِي
عَنِ الْبَدَوِيِّ ذِي الْعُلُومِ الْغَزِيرَة

From his teacher, the noble Muhammad al-'Arabi,
from al-Badawi, master of innate knowledges,

عَنِ الدَّرْقَاوِي الزَّكِي الشَّهِيرِ الْمُعَظَّمِ
عَنِ الْجَبَلِ الطَّوْدِ الْكَثِيرِ الإِنَابَة

From ad-Darqawi, pure, famous and exalted,
from the lofty mountain with much repentance,

عَنِ ابْنِ عُبَيْدِ اللهِ مَنْ فَاقَ عَصْرِ

عَنِ ابْنِ عُبَيْدِ اللهِ أَحْمَدَ فِرْقَة

From Ibn 'Abdullah, pre-eminent in his time
a group from Ahmad ibn 'Abdullah,

عَنِ الْقَاسِمِ الْخَصَّاصِي مَنْ صَارَ لَا

عَنِ ابْنِ عُبَيْدِ اللهِ بَحْرِ الْكَرَامَة

From al-Qasim al-Khassasi who was a refuge,
from Ibn 'Abdullah, the sea of nobility,

عَنِ الْفَاسِي مَنْ رَقَّ ذُرَى الْمَجْدِ وَالتُّ

عَنِ الْفَاسِي حَاوِي الْفَنِّ بَحْرِ الشَّرِيـ

from al-Fasi who ascended to the peaks of glory and taqwa,
from al-Fasi, Master of the Art, the Sea of the Shari'a,

عَنِ الْبَطَلِ الْمَجْذُوبِ تَاجِ طَرِيقِنَا

عَنِ الصَّنْهَاجِي الدُّوَّارِ كَنْزِ الطَّرِيـ

From the hero al-Majdhub, the Crown of our Tariq,
from as-Sanhaji, ad-Duwwar, the treasure of the Tariqa,

عَنْ إِبْرَاهِيمَ الْفَحَّامِ زِينَةِ وَقْتِهِ

عَنِ الْجَهْبَذِ الزَّرُّوقِ وِتْرِ الْأَئِمَّة

From Ibrahim al-Fahham, the adornment of his time,
from the brilliant Zarruq, the unique Imam,

عَنِ الْحَضْرَمِي بْنِ عُقْبَةَ السَّيِّدِ الذَّكِي
عَنِ الْقَادِرِيّ يَحْيَ لَطِيفِ الاِشَارَةِ

From al-Hadrami ibn 'Uqba, the intelligent sayyid,
from Yahya al-Qadiri, with subtle indications,

عَنِ السَّيِّدِ الصَّفِي الْمُسَمَّىٰ عَلِي وَفَا
عَنْ أُسْتَاذِه مُحَمَّدٍ ذِي الْمُروءَةِ

From the pure Sayyid called 'Ali Wafa
from his teacher Muhammad, master of chivalry,

عَنِ الْبَاخِلِي الصِّدِّيقِ يُدْعَىٰ بِدَاوُدٍ
عَنِ ابْنِ عَطَاءِ اللهِ مُسْدِي النَّصِيحَةِ

From al-Bakhili the truthful, called Da'ud,
from Ibn 'Ata'illah, who gave us good advice,

عَنِ السَّيِّدِ الْمَرْسِيِّ مَنْ جَا بِحُلَّةٍ
عَنِ الشَّاذِلِيّ الْقُطْبِ غَوْثِ الْجَمَاعَةِ

From the Sayyid al-Mursi who brought a robe of honour,
from the Qutb ash-Shadhili, the Ghawth of the Community.

لَقَدْ شَرِبَ السِّرَّ الْمَصُونَ الْمُحَجَّبَا
تَلَقَّاهُ عَنْ قَوْمٍ كِرَامٍ أَعِزَّةٍ

He drank the veiled protected secret,
which he received from noble mighty people,

كَنَجْلِ مَشِيشٍ الْحَرِي نَخْرِ غَرْبِنَا
وَنَجْلِ حَرَازِمِ شَهِيرِ الْمَحَجَّة

Like the worthy son of Mashish, the glory of our West,
and the son of Harazim, whose path is famous,

عَنْ أُسْتَاذِهِ مُحَمَّدٍ صَالِحِ الْخَنَا
عَنِ اللَّذْ قَدِ اشْتَهَرْ بِغَوْثٍ وَكُنْيَةٍ

From his teacher, Muhammad Salih of the tavern,
from the one who is known as a Ghawth and by his kunya,

عَنِ الْقُطْبِ غَوْثِ الْكُلِّ عَبْدِ لِقَادِرٍ
عَنِ اللَّذْ يُدْعَىٰ مُبَارَكًا ذَا سَعَادَةٍ

From the Qutb, the Ghawth of all, 'Abdu'l-Qadir,
from the one called Mubarak, who possessed true happiness,

عَنِ الْأُسْتَاذِ الْهُكَّارِ يُدْعَىٰ أَبَا الْحَسَنْ
عَنِ الطَّرْطُوسِيِّ ذِي الْحَيَا وَالْمَهَابَةِ

From the master al-Hukkari called Abu'l-Hasan,
from at-Tartusi who had modesty and awe,

عَنِ الشِّبْلِيِّ الْمَشْهُورِ شِبْلِ زَمَانِه
عَنِ الْمُرْتَضَى الْجُنَيْدِ مُبْدِي الْحَقِيقَةِ

From ash-Shibli famous as the lion of his time,
from the pleasing al-Junayd, who brought the Reality to light,

عَنِ السَّقْطِي مَنْ غَدَا عَظِيمًا مُعَظَّمًا

عَنِ الْكَرْخِي مَنْ سَقَا أُنَاسًا بِسُرْعَةٍ

From as-Saqati who became great and venerated,
from al-Karkhi who swiftly quenched people's thirst,

عَنِ الطَّائِي مَنْ بَدَا إِمَامًا وَقُدْوَةً

عَنِ الْعَجَمِيِّ ذِي الْفُنُونِ الْغَرِيبَةِ

From at-Ta'i who was an imam and model,
from al-'Ajami, master of rare sciences,

عَنِ الْحَسَنِ الْبَصْرِيِّ ذُخْرِ سَبِيلِنَا

عَنِ اللَّذْ لَه يَدٌ عَلَى كُلِّ نِسْبَةِ

From al-Hasan al-Basri, the treasure-house of our Path,
from the one who has a place in every ascription,

وَزِيرُ النَّبِيِّ صِهْرُه وَابْنُ عَمِّه

عَنِ الْمُصْطَفَى الْمُخْتَارِ سِرِّ الْخَلِيقَةِ

The wazir of the Prophet, his in-law and nephew,
from the Chosen Selected one, the secret of creation,

عَنِ الْقَوِيِّ الْأَمِينِ نَامُوسِ رُسْلِنَا

عَنِ الصَّمَدِ الْمُعْطِي الطَّرِيقَ السَّوِيَّةِ

From the strong Trusty One, the Namus of our Messengers,
from the Eternal Support, the Giver of the Straight Path.

أَبُو حَفْصٍ الْمِسْكِينُ يَدْعُوكَ دَائِمًا

لِـمَا قَدَّمَتْ يَدَاهُ مِنْ فَرْطِ غَفْلَةِ

Abu Hafs, the impoverished, prays to You always
on account of the excessive heedlessness he has sent ahead.

تَوَسَّلْتُ بِالْهَادِي الشَّفِيعِ الْمُشَفَّعِ

إِلَيْكَ إِلَاهِي أَنْ تُقِيلَ خَطِيئَتِي

I turn for help to the interceding guide who is granted intercession
with You, my God, to cancel my errors.

عَلَيْهِ صَلَاةُ اللهِ مَا حَنَّ شَائِقٌ

إِلَى الْحَضْرَةِ الْعَلْيَا مُقَامِ الْأَحِبَّةِ

On him be the blessing of Allah as long as someone yearns
for the sublime Presence, the station of the lovers,

وَءَالِهِ وَالصَّحْبِ الْكِرَامِ وَكُلِّ مَنْ

تَصَدَّرَ لِلْإِرْشَادِ مِنْ خَيْرِ أُمَّةِ ۝

And on his family and noble Companions and everyone
among the best of the Community who is sent to guide.

انتهى بحمد الله وحسن عونه غرة ربيع الأول عال ١٣٦٨ من هجرة خير الأنام

عليه أفضل الصلاة وأزكى السلام .

Completed with praise of Allah and His help
Rabi' al-Awwal 1368 AH

# The Salat of Ibn Mashish

الصلاة المشيشية

اَللَّهُمَّ صَلِّ عَلَى مَنْ مِنْهُ انْشَقَّتِ الأَسْرَارُ. وَانْفَلَقَتِ الأَنْوَارُ.
وَفِيهِ ارْتَقَتِ الْحَقَآئِقُ. وَتَنَزَّلَتْ عُلُومُ سَيِّدِنَا ءَادَمَ عَلَيْهِ السَّلَامُ
فَأَعْجَزَ الْخَلَآئِقَ. وَلَهُ تَضَآءَلَتِ الْفُهُومُ
فَلَمْ يُدْرِكْهُ مِنَّا سَابِقٌ وَلَا لَاحِقٌ

O Lord, bless him, out of whom secrets and lights have burst, in whom
rose the truth, upon whom devolved the knowledge of our master
Adam, peace be upon him. Beside him all creatures are incapable, to
him understanding is a trifle. Not one of us has attained his standard,
before or after.

فَرِيَاضُ الْمَلَكُوتِ بِزَهْرِ جَمَالِهِ مُونِقَةٌ.
وَحِيَاضُ الْجَبَرُوتِ بِفَيْضِ أَنْوَارِهِ مُتَدَفِّقَةٌ.

The gardens of heaven are embellished with the beauty of his flowers.
The cisterns of power spill over with the flood of his lights.

وَلَا شَيْءَ إِلَّا وَهُوَ بِهِ مَنُوطٌ. إِذْ لَوْ لَا الْوَاسِطَةُ لَذَهَبَ كَمَا قِيلَ
الْمَوْسُوطُ. صَلَاةً تَلِيقُ بِكَ مِنْكَ إِلَيْهِ كَمَا هُوَ أَهْلُهُ.

There is nothing not dependent on him: for as it was said, 'without the
means the end would have escaped us'.
Bless him in Your way according to his merits.

415

اَللّٰهُمَّ إِنَّهُ سِرُّكَ الْجَامِعُ الدَّالُّ عَلَيْكَ.
وَحِجَابُكَ الْاَعْظَمُ الْقَائِمُ لَكَ بَيْنَ يَدَيْكَ.

O Allah, he is your gathered secret that tells of You,
Your great veil that stands before You.

اَللّٰهُمَّ أَلْحِقْنِي بِنَسَبِهِ. وَحَقِّقْنِي بِحَسَبِهِ. وَعَرِّفْنِي إِيَّاهُ مَعْرِفَةً أَسْلَمُ
بِهَا مِنْ مَوَارِدِ الْجَهْلِ. وَأَكْرَعُ بِهَا مِنْ مَوَارِدِ الْفَضْلِ.

O Allah, attach me to his descendants, and make me realise his honour. Let
me know him with a knowledge by means of which I will be safe from the
fountains of ignorance and bring me to the fountains of goodness.

وَاحْمِلْنِي عَلَى سَبِيلِهِ إِلَى حَضْرَتِكَ. حَمْلاً مَحْفُوفاً بِنُصْرَتِكَ. وَاقْذِفْ
بِي عَلَى الْبَاطِلِ فَأَدْمَغَهُ. وَزُجَّ بِي فِي بِحَارِ الْاَحَدِيَّةِ. وَانْشُلْنِي مِنْ
أَوْحَالِ التَّوْحِيدِ. وَأَغْرِقْنِي فِي عَيْنِ بَحْرِ الْوَحْدَةِ. حَتَّى لَاَ أَرَى
وَلَاَ أَسْمَعَ وَلَاَ أَجِدَ وَلَاَ أُحِسَّ إِلَّا بِهَا.

Convey me on his way to Your Presence, protected by Your help. Let me
face falsehood so that I may conquer it, drive me into the sea of Oneness,
snatch me from the mires of belief in Unification (Tawhid) and let me
drown in the sea of Unity (Wahda) so much that I may not see, hear,
feel or sense except by It.

وَاجْعَلِ الْحِجَابَ الْاَعْظَمَ حَيَاةَ رُوحِي. وَرُوحَهُ سِرَّ حَقِيقَتِي.
وَحَقِيقَتَهُ جَامِعَ عَوَالِمِي بِتَحْقِيقِ الْحَقِّ الْاَوَّلِ.

Make the great veil the life of my spirit and its spirit the secret of my truth
and his truth, the integrator of my universe through the realisation of the
first truth.

يَاۤ اَوَّلُ يَاۤ ءَاخِرُ يَا ظَاهِرُ يَا بَاطِنُ.

O First! O Last! O Manifest! O Hidden!

اِسْمَعْ نِدَاۤئِي بِمَا سَمِعْتَ بِهِ نِدَاۤءَ عَبْدِكَ سَيِّدِنَا زَكَرِيَّاۤءَ عَلَيْهِ السَّلَامُ.
وَانْصُرْنِي بِكَ لَكَ. وَاَيِّدْنِي بِكَ لَكَ. وَاجْمَعْ بَيْنِي وَبَيْنَكَ.
وَحُلْ بَيْنِي وَبَيْنَ غَيْرِكَ.

Hear my cry as you heard the cry of Your slave, our master Zakariah,
peace be upon him. Give me victory through You – for You. Support
me through You – for You. Join me to You – separate me from other-
than-You.

اَللّٰهُ اللّٰهُ اللّٰهُ

ALLAH (3)

417

إِنَّ الَّذِي فَرَضَ عَلَيْكَ الْقُرْءَانَ لَرَآدُّكَ إِلَىٰ مَعَادٍ.

He Who has imposed the Qur'an upon you
will surely bring you home again.

رَبَّنَآ ءَاتِنَا مِنْ لَدُنْكَ رَحْمَةً وَهَيِّئْ لَنَا مِنْ أَمْرِنَا رَشَدًا. (ثلاثًا)

Our Lord, give us mercy directly from You and open the way for us to
right guidance in our situation. (3)

# From the Diwan
## of Shaykh Muhammad al-Fayturi Hamuda

# Hamuda

مِن ديوان الشيخ محمد الفيتوري حمودة

# 1

يَا طَالِبَ الْمَعْرِفَة   وَمَقَامَاتِ الصَّفَا

اِصْحَبْ خِلًّا قَدْ وَفَىٰ   بِعُبُودِيَّةِ اللّٰه

O seeker of gnosis and the stations of serenity!
Keep the company of a close friend
who has fully met the obligation of slavehood to Allah.

لَا تَكْتَفِ بِالْأَقْوَالْ   اِنْهَضْ بَادِرْ بِالْأَعْمَالْ

تَبْلُغْ مَقَامَ الْكَمَالْ   لَا إِلٰهَ إِلَّا اللّٰه

Do not be content with words. Arise and embark on deeds without delay!
You will reach the Station of perfection – there is no god except Allah.

وَإِنْ تُرِيدُ الْمَعْنَىٰ   فِي اسْمِ ذَاتِهِ فَافْنَىٰ

كَرِّرًا مُعْلِنًا   تُحْظَىٰ بِلِقَاءِ اللّٰه

If you desire the meaning, then seek annihilation in the name of His essence.
Often and openly – you will obtain encounter with Allah.

بِهِ تَبْلُغُ الْمَقْصُودْ     تُسْقَى بِكَأْسِ الشُّهُودْ

فَتَرَى كُلَّ الْوُجُودْ     ظَاهِرًا بِنُورِ اللهْ

You will obtain the goal by it —

you will be given the cup of witnessing to drink.

Then you will see all of existence outwardly manifest by the light of Allah.

اذْكُرْهُ مَعْنًى وَحِسّْ     مِنَ النُّورِ تَقْتَبِسْ

تَدْخُلْ فِي مَقَامِ الْأُنْسْ     دَائِمًا فَرْحَكَ بِاللهْ

Remember Him in meaning and the senses — you will acquire light.

You will enter the Station of intimacy — your joy constantly with Allah.

قُلِ اللهُ جَهْرَةً     وَسِرًّا وَخَلْوَةً

فَيَأْتِيكَ نَفْحَةٌ     تُفْنِيكَ فِي ذَاتِ اللهْ

Say 'Allah!' openly, secretly, and in retreat,

A breath of fragrance will come to you

which will annihilate you in the essence of Allah.

رَاقِبْ جَمَالَ الْحَبِيبْ     هُوَ الْقَرِيبُ الْمُجِيبْ

يَأْتِيكَ فَتْحٌ غَرِيبْ     تُحْيَى بِشُهُودِ اللهْ

Watch the beauty of the Beloved with fear —

He is the Near, the Answerer —

A startling opening will come to you —

you will be brought to life by the witnessing of Allah.

تَوَضَّأْ بِمَاءِ الْغَيْبْ  وَيَمِّمْ نَحْوَ الْحَبِيبْ

فَثَمَّ سِرٌّ عَجِيبْ  تَشْهَدِ اللّٰهَ بِاللّٰهْ

Do wudu with the water of the unseen
and direct yourself toward the Beloved.
There is a wondrous secret! You will see Allah by Allah!

وَإِنْ تُرِيدِ التَّمْكِينْ  وَأَذْوَاقَ الْعَارِفِينْ

أُسْتَاذِي عَيْنُ التَّعْيِينْ  الْعَلَوِي سِرُّ اللّٰهْ

If you desire the firm establishment and the tasting of the gnostics,
My master is the very one designated, al-'Alawi, the secret of Allah.

فَهَيَّمِنِي بِالْوِدَادْ  مِنْهُ أَتَتْنِي الْامْدَادْ

فَنِلْتُ أَعْلَا الْمُرَادْ  صِرْتُ غَنِيًّا بِاللّٰهْ

He bewildered me in love. Help has come to me from him,
So I obtained the highest desire — I became rich in Allah.

يَا مَنْ تُرِيدِ الدَّوَا  وَالْغَيْبْ عَنِ السِّوَىٰ

اِشْرَبْ مِنْ خَمْرِي تُرْوَىٰ  فَتَنْظُرْ جَمَالَ اللّٰهْ

O you who desire the cure and withdrawal from other!
Drink from my wine and you will be quenched.
Then you will see the beauty of Allah.

تَبْرُزْ لَكَ شُمُوسُ الذَّاتْ بِالاَسْمَاءِ وَالصِّفَاتْ

فِي جَمِيعِ الْكَائِنَاتْ كَانَ اللهُ وَبَاقِ اللهُ

The suns of the essence will bring you the names and the attributes
in all beings. Allah was and Allah remains.

حَدِّدْ بَصَرَ الاِيمَانْ تَرَى اللهَ لَا الاَكْوَانْ

هَذَا مَقَامُ الاِحْسَانْ اِخْتِصَاصًا مِنَ اللهْ

Make the eye of Iman keen –
you will see Allah, not phenomenal beings.
This is the Station of Ihsan, a special favour from Allah.

لَا بِجِدٍّ وَاجْتِهَـادْ عَطَاءٌ مِنَ الْجَوَادْ

اَلرَّؤُوفُ بِالْعِبَـادْ شُكْرًا وَحَمْدًا لِلَّهْ

Not by diligence or striving – a gift from the Generous,
the Compassionate to the slaves. Thanks and praise be to Allah!

مُحَمَّدُ الْفِيتُورِي مُعْتَرِفٌ بِالْقُصُورِ

بِهِ تَمَّ سُرُورِي فَانٍ وَبَـاقِ بِـاللهْ

Muhammad al-Fayturi admits his incapacity,
In Him my happiness was complete – annihilated and going-on in Allah.

صَلِّ مَوْلَانَا الْعَظِيمْ   عَلَى الرَّؤُوفِ الرَّحِيمْ

هُوَ الصِّرَاطُ الْقَوِيمْ   هَادِيًا بِإِذْنِ اللهُ ۞

Our Master, the Great, bless the gentle, the merciful.
He is the straight path, guiding by the permission of Allah.

# 2

أَضْرَمَتْ نَارُ الْهَوَىٰ      لَدَعَتْ قَلْبِي انْكَوَىٰ

لَنْ تَذَرْ فِيهِ السِّوَىٰ      عَـادَ فَرْعِي لِأَصْلِي

The fire of passion was kindled and it called my heart: Be burned!
It will not leave other in it, so it became a branch of my root.

خِلِّي ظَـاهِرْ فِي مَجْلَاهْ      أَضَاءَ الْكَوْنَ سَنَاهْ

ظَهَرَتْ شَمْسٌ بَهَـاهْ      مَا أَبْدَعُ التَّجَلِّي

My close Friend is outwardly manifest in His place of tajalli.
The cosmos illuminated His radiance.
The sun of His splendour appeared – how marvellous the tajalli is!

فَهُوَ سِرُّ الْوُجُودْ      هُوَ الشَّـاهِدْ وَالْمَشْهُودْ

إِلَـيْهِ الْأَمْرُ يَعُـودْ      هُوَ مُرْشِدُ الْكُلِّ

He is the secret of existence. He is the Witness and the Witnessed.
The command returns to Him. He is the guide of all.

أَوْقَاتِي بِهِ هَنَا   لَمَّا فَهِمْتُ الْمَعْنَى

حَبِيبِي مِنِّي دَنَا   وَمَطْلُوبِي حَصَلْ لِي

My moments were full of delight with Him
when I understood the meaning –
My Beloved drew near me and my goal was obtained for me.

أَطْلَقَنِي مِنَ الْقُيُودْ   سَقَانِي كَأْسَ الشُّهُودْ

سِوَاهُ عِنْدِي مَفْقُودْ   مِنْهُ نُطْقِي وَفِعْلِي

He freed me of fetters and let me drink from the glass of witnessing.
Other-than-Him is lost with me. My speech and action is from Him.

شَرِبْتُ خَمْرَ الْاَذْوَاقْ   مِنْ رَاحَتْ سَاقِي الْعُشَّاقِ

بَرَزَتْ شَمْسُ الْاِطْلَاقْ   بَدَى حُسْنُ التَّحَلِّي

I drank the wine of tasting
from the hands of the cupbearer of the passionate ones.
The sun of liberation emerged and the beauty of adornment appeared.

نَظَرْتُ خَلْفَ السِّتَارْ   مَا لَا تُدْرِكُ الْاَبْصَارْ

غِبْتُ فِي بَحْرِ الْاَنْوَارْ   صَارَ بَعْضِي كُلِّي

I looked behind the veil at what the eyes do not perceive,
I withdrew into the sea of lights – part of me became all of me.

دَارَتْ كُؤُوسُ الطَّرِيقْ     أُذنْ مِنِّي يَا رَفِيقْ

نُسْقِيكَ خَمْرَ عَتِيقْ     تُحْظَىٰ بِرُوحِ الْكُلِّ

The goblets of the Path were passed around:

'Come near Me, My friend!

We will let you drink an ancient wine – you will obtain the joy of all!'

أُسْتَاذِي نُقْطَةُ الْبَاءْ     مِنْهُ كَانَ الِابْتِدَاءْ

ظُهُورًا وَانْتِهَا     فَافْهَمُو يَا عُذَالِي

My master is the dot of the ba'. The beginning was from him,

Outwardly as well as at the end. Understand then, O critic!

هَلُمُّوا أَهْلَ الْعِرْفَانْ     إِلَىٰ مِنْهَلِ الْإِحْسَانْ

اَلْعَلَوِي غَوْثُ الزَّمَانْ     بِهِ تَمَّ وِصَالِي

People of gnosis! Come now to the spring of Ihsan!

Al-'Alawi, the ghawth of the age. My arrival was completed by him.

فَهُوَ فَخْرُ الْاسْرَارْ     وَهُوَ الْكَأْسُ وَالْخَمَّارْ

وَهُوَ السَّاقِي لِلْاحْبَارْ     مِنْ خَمْرَةِ الْكَمَالْ

He is the glory of the secrets. He is the glass and the wine.

He is the Cupbearer of the wine of perfection to the learned.

فَيتُورِي بِهِ وَلَهَانْ      شَارِبْ مِنْ خَمْرِهْ نَشْوَانْ

إِنِّي لَفَرْدُ الزَّمَانْ      عَبْدًا بِلَا انْفِصَالِ

Al-Fayturi is out of his head with love from him —
he drinks intoxicated from his wine.
I am an individual of the age, a slave without interruption.

فَصَلُّوا يَا فُقَرَا      عَلَى أَعْظَمِ الْوَرَى

خَيْرُ مَنْ بِهِ أَسْرِي      مَغْنَاطِيسُ الْكَمَالِ ۝

Fuqara! Then ask for blessings on the greatest of mankind,
The best, by whom the magnet of perfection flows!

# 3

تَجَلَّى حِبِّي    اِفْرَحْ يَا قَلْبِي

اِحْرِمْ وَلِّي    لِجَرِّي تَبَسَّم

My Beloved appeared to me in tajalli! Rejoice, my heart!
Divest yourself while my core, my glory smiles.

غَرَامِي زَادَ    سَاقِيهِ نَادَى

أَخْذَ الْفُؤَادَ    بِالْخَفْضِ وَالضَّمّ

My passion increased – His cupbearer called –
He took the heart with joining and subduing.

دَارَتْ كُؤُوسِي أَحْيَتْ نُفُوسِي

لَاحَتْ شُمُوسِي مِنْ حُلْوِ الْمَبْسَمْ

My cups went around – my selves gave life –
my suns shone because of the sweetness of the smile.

هُوَ حَيَاتِي مَحْوَىٰ ثَبَاتِي
أَفْنَ فِي الذَّاتِ لِلسَّيْرِ تَفْهَمْ

He is my life, the focus of my firmness –
annihilate yourself in the essence for the journey,
then you will understand!

مَوْتِي وُجُودِي غَيْبِي شُهُودِي
فَالْجُودُ جُودِي وَالْحَيْرَهْ تَمْتَمْ

My death is my existence, my withdrawal is my witnessing –
so generosity is my generosity and confusion stutters.

هَذَا تَلْوِينِي فِي كُلِّ حِينٍ
أَبْصِرْ بِعَيْنِي لِكَنْزِكَ تَغْنَمْ

This is my sign in every time.
Look with my eye at your treasure, you will obtain booty.

أُنْظُرْ فِي ذَاتِكْ تَحْيَا حَيَاتِكْ
رُوحُكْ نَادَاتِكْ لِفَكَّ الطَّلْسَمْ

Look at your essence – you will be brought to life by your life.
Your spirit called to you to unwind the talisman.

سِرُّ الْهِدَايَهْ    كَهْفُ الْوِلَايَهْ

سَيِّدِي مَوْلَايَ لِلْكُلِّ أَنْعَمْ

The secret of guidance is the cavern of wilaya,
my master, my lord giving favours to all.

الْعُرْوَةُ الْوَثِيقَهْ    عَيْنُ الطَّرِيقَهْ

كَنْزُ الْحَقِيقَهْ    الْفَرْدُ الْخَاتِمْ

The firm grip, the source of the Path,
the treasury of the Haqiqa, the unique individual, the seal.

هُوَ سُلْطَانِي فِي كُلِّ آنِ

شَمْسُ الْعِرْفَانِ الْعَلَوِي الاَعْظَمْ

He is my sultan at every moment,
the sun of gnosis, al-'Alawi, the greatest.

صَرِّحْ يَا حَادِي فِي كُلِّ نَادِ

عُبَيْدُ أُسْيَادِي الْفَيْتُورِي فَاعْلَمْ

Announce, caravan leader! to every circle
the little slave of my lords, al-Fayturi, and learn!

صَلِّ يَا رَبِّ عَلَى الْمُرَبِّي

أَحْيَا لِي قَلْبِي بِفَكِّ الطَّلْسَم ۝

O Lord! Bless the one who tends

he brought my heart to life by unwinding the talisman.

# 4

نَادَانِي حِبِّي مِنْ حَضْرَهِ قُرْبِي

قُمْتُ مُلَبِّي لِنِدَاءِ اللّٰهْ

My Beloved called me from the presence of my nearness –
I stood up to answer the call of Allah.

أَتَيْتُ لِلْبَابْ مِنْ غَيْرِ ارْتِيَابْ

وَجَدْتُ الأَحْبَابْ فِي حَضْرَةِ اللّٰهْ

I came to the door without hesitation
I found the lovers in the presence of Allah.

شَرِبْتُ بِالأَقْدَاحْ مِنْ دَنَدَاتِ الرَّاحْ

فَاهْتَزَّتِ الأَشْبَاحْ طَرَبًا بِاللّٰهْ

I drank cups from the wine-jars of joy,
so the forms quivered out of rapture with Allah.

شَرَابٌ قَدِيمٌ قَدْرُهُ عَظِيمٌ

صِرَاطٌ قَوِيمٌ لِمُرِيدِ اللّٰه

A timeless drink whose value is immense,
a straight path for the one who desires Allah.

طَلَعَ الصَّبَاحْ بِنُورِ الْفَلَاحْ

صِرْنَا بِالاَرْوَاحْ مِنْ مَلَكُوتِ اللّٰه

The morning came with the light of success –
we went with the spirits from the Malakut of Allah.

لَاقِينَا الْحَكِيمْ اَلْغَوْثَ الْعَظِيمْ

اَلْعَلَوِي الْمُقِيمْ فِي جَبَرُوتِ اللّٰه

We met the wise, the great ghawth,
al-'Alawi, residing in the Jabarut of Allah.

لِكَوْنِي طَوَىٰ فَغَابَ السِّوَىٰ

فَقُلْتُ هُوَ هُوَ هُوَ اللّٰه

He crossed to my being and Other withdrew.
Then I said: He! He! He! Allah!

نَـاصِحُ الأُمَّةْ مُجَلِّي الغُمَّهْ

صَـاحِبُ الْهِمَّةْ فِي طَرِيقِ اللهْ

The counsellor of the community, he who manifests sorrow,
the possessor of himma in the Path of Allah.

وَارِثُ الرَّسُولْ بِالْفِعْلِ وَالْقَوْلْ

حَضْرَةُ الْقَبُولْ لِأَحْكَـامِ اللهْ

The heir of the Messenger in action and word,
the presence of acceptance of the judgments of Allah.

سَيْفُ الإِسْلَامِ مُحْيِي الأنَـامِ

حَـازَ الْمَقَامِ اِصْطَفَـاهُ اللهْ

The sword of Islam, the reviver of people,
he won the station which Allah chose.

آدَمُ الزَّمَـانْ خَلَّفَهُ الرَّحْمَـنْ

لَا تَكُنْ شَيْطَـانْ تُشْقَى بِلِقَـاهْ

The Adam of the age whom the Merciful made a Khalifa.
Do not be a shaytan, you will have trouble when you meet him.

أَتُوا إِلَيْهِ وَهِيمُوا بِهِ

خَرُّوا إِلَيْهِ سُجَّدًا لِلَّه

They came to him and thirsted with passionate love for him.
They swooned before him, prostrating to Allah.

أَسْكَرَنِي شَذَاهْ حَيَّرَنِي مَعْنَاهْ

أَدْهَشَنِي بَهَاهْ سَجَدْتُ لِلَّه

His fragrance intoxicated me and his meaning put me in confusion –
his radiance dazzled me, I prostrated to Allah.

يَا مُرِيدْ أَقْدِم إِنْ شِئْتَ تَغْنَم

اُذْكُرْ وَسَلِّم تَحْظَى بِلِقَاهْ

O murid! Advance if you desire booty!
Do dhikr and greet, you will obtain his encounter.

غِبْ عَنِ الصِّفَاتْ وَأَفْنَ فِي الذَّاتْ

تُحْيِيكَ الْحَيَاهْ تَبْقَى بِبَقَاهْ

Withdraw from the attributes and annihilate yourself in the essence
– it will bring you completely to life and you will go on
with His going-on.

437

صَلِّ يَا سَلَامْ    عَلَىٰ قُطْبِ الانَامْ

بِهِ قَلْبِي هَامْ    فُزْتُ بِلِقَاهْ ۞

O peace! Bless the pole of men!

My heart thirsts after him with passionate love, so I won his encounter.

# 5

اُتْرُكْ يَا مُرِيدْ   نَفْسَكَ مَا تُرِيدْ

إِنْ رُمْتَ الْمَزِيدْ   مِنْ أَسْرَارِ اللهْ

O murid! Abandon your self and what it wants
if you desire increase from the secrets of Allah!

اُدْخُلِ الطَّرِيقْ   وَالْزَمِ الرَّفِيقْ

يُسْقِيكَ الْعَتِيقْ   مِنْ خَمْرَةِ اللهْ

Enter the path and cling to the friend —
he will give you an ancient vintage of the wine of Allah to drink.

يُعْطِيكَ الْحَبِيبْ   سِرَّهُ الْعَجِيبْ

هِمْ بِهِ وَغِبْ   فِي أَنْوَارِ اللهْ

The Beloved will give you His wondrous secret —
thirst with love for him and withdraw into the lights of Allah.

ذَابَتِ الاَشْبَاحْ  لَمَّا حِبِّي بَاحْ

بِإِسْمِ الْفَتَّاحْ  لِمُرِيدِ اللهْ

The forms melted away when my Beloved divulged
the name of opening for the one who desires Allah.

دَارَتِ الاَقْدَاحْ  بَيْنَنَا يَا صَاحْ

فَاحَ السِّرُّ فَاحْ  مِنْ مِشْكَاةِ اللهْ

The cups went around among us, O friend,
the secret diffused a fragrant scent from the niche of Allah.

أَدْنَ لَدُنِ الرَّاحْ  شُرْبه مُبَاحْ

بِهِ حَقًّا تَرْتَاحْ  تَرَىٰ وَجْهَ اللهْ

Draw near to the wine whose drink is permitted.
By it you will truly be pleased, you will see the face of Allah.

اِرْجِعْ يَا جَاحِدْ  فَلَا تُعَانِدْ

لِلْفَرْدِ الْمُرْشِدْ  هُوَ نُورُ اللهْ

O denier! Refrain and do not be stubborn
towards the unique individual, the guide who is the light of Allah.

يُرَبِّي بِالنَّظْرَه يُدَخِّلْ لِلْحَضْرَه

صَاحِبُ الاسْرَا فِي جَبَرُوتِ اللهْ

He teaches with the glance and he admits
the possessor of the night-journey in the Jabarut of Allah to the Presence.

فَهِمْتُ بِهِ مِنْهُ إِلَيْهِ

مَنْ ذَا يُدْرِيهِ جَامِعَ سِرِّ اللهْ

I understood by him, from him, to him
whoever knows him to contain the secret of Allah.

مِنْهَجُ الطَّرِيقْ سُلْطَانُ التَّحْقِيقْ

فَنِعْمَ الرَّفِيقْ لِمُرِيدِ اللهْ

The open road of the Path, the Sultan of realisation!
How excellent is the friend for the one who desires Allah!

اَلْعَلَوِي سَيِّدِي إِبْنُ الْبُوزِيدِي

أَطْلَقَ لِي قَيْدِي أَصْبَحْتُ لِلّهْ

Al-'Alawi is my master, the son of al-Buzidi.
He set me free from my fetters and I was sent forth to the company of Allah.

عَرَّفَنِي نَفْسِي   أَدْخَلَنِي أُنْسِي

فِي حَضْرَهِ قُدْسِي   غِبْتُ عَنْ سِوَاهْ

He made me recognise my self, he made me enter my intimacy –
I withdrew from other-than-Him in the presence of purity.

فَيْتُورِي سَقِيمْ   أَتَىٰ بِالتَّسْلِيمْ

لِلْغَوْثِ الْعَظِيمْ   مِنْهَلِ عِلْمِ اللهْ

Fayturi is wasting-away and brings the greeting
to the great Ghawth, the spring of the knowledge of Allah.

صَلِّ الْمَوْلَىٰ   عَلَىٰ نُورِ الْهُدَىٰ

أَحْيَا لِي قَلْبِي   شَاهَدْتُ الْمَوْلَىٰ ۞

May the Master bless the light of guidance!
He brought my heart to life and I saw the Master.

# Refuge Prayer

BY SHAYKH MUHAMMAD WAFA
(FROM SEASONS OF THE REALITIES)

المعاوذة للشيخ محمد وفى

من كتاب فصول الحقائق

بسم الله الرحمن الرحيم

In the Name of Allah, the All-Merciful, Most Merciful

أَعُوذُ بِاللهِ مِنْ شَيَاطِينِ الخْلَقِ وَالْكَوْنِ

I seek refuge with Allah from the shaytans of creation and existence,

وَأَبَالِسَةِ الْعِلْمِ وَالْجَهْلِ وَأَغْيَارِ الْمَعْرِفَةِ وَالنَّكِرَةِ

and from the devils of knowledge and ignorance, and from otherness
resulting from recognition and denial.

اَللَّهُمَّ إِنِّي أَعُوذُ بِكَ وَبِسَبْقِ قِدَمِكَ مِنْ سِرِّ حُدُودِكَ
وَبِظُلْمَةِ ذَاتِكَ مِنْ نُورِ صِفَاتِكَ

O Allah, I seek refuge with You and Your prior timelessness from the
secret of the limits You set, and with the darkness of Your Essence from
the light of Your Attributes,

وَبِقُوَّةِ سُلُوبِكَ مِنْ ضَعْفِ إِيجَادِكَ

and with the strength of Your negation from the weakness of what You bring into existence,

وَبِظُلْمَةِ عَدَمِكَ مِنْ نُورِ تَأْضِوَاتِكَ

and with the darkness of Your void from the light of what You make shine.

وَأَعِذْنِي اللّهُمَّ بِكَ مِنْكَ فِي كُلِّ ذَالِكَ

O Allah, give me refuge with You from You in all of that,

كَذَالِكَ مِنْ وَجْهِ الْعِلْمِ وَلَا كَيْفَ

as well as from superficial knowledge and "without how",

كَذَالِكَ مِنْ حَيْثُ الْعَقْلِ وَلَا

as well as from the "where" of the intellect and "no",

كَذَالِكَ مِنْ جِهَةِ قَصْدِ النَّفْسِ وَلَا

as well as from the control of the intent of the self and "no",

كَذَالِكَ مِنْ حَيْثُ تَصَوُّرِ الْوَهْمِ

as well as from the "where" of the conceptualisation of the imagination.

أَعُوذُ بِكَ مِنْ كُلِّ ذَالِكَ

I seek refuge with You from all of that

كَذَٰلِكَ مِنْ حَيْثُ إِنَّهُ كَذَٰلِكَ

inasmuch as it is like that,

لَا مِنْ حَيْثُ إِنَّكَ وَلِيَّ ذَٰلِكَ.

not inasmuch as You are the Master of that.

اَللَّهُمَّ اغْنِنِي بِدَيْمُومَتِكَ عَنْ بَقَاءِ آلَاتِكَ وَبِإِحَاطَةِ وُجُودِكَ عَنْ
تَصَوُّرِ الْوَاحِدِ الْأَحَدِ

O Allah, by Your perpetuity free me of the need of the continuance of Your blessings and by Your all-encompassing existence from conceptualising the One, Unique,

وَبِقَيُّومِيَّةِ قِيَامِكَ عَنْ إِسْتِقَامَةِ تَقْوِيمِ الْمَدَدِ

and by the everlastingness of Your support from seeking to arrange help,

وَغَيْبَتِي فِي ظُلْمَةِ ذَٰلِكَ الَّتِي تَعْجِزُ فِيهَا الْأَبْصَارُ وَالْبَصَائِرُ
وَيَسْتَحِيلُ فِيهَا مَعَارِفُ الْعُقُولِ الْإِلَهِيَّةِ ذَاتِ الْأَسْرَارِ وَالسَّرَائِرِ

and make me withdraw into the darkness of that in which both eyes and inner eyes are powerless and in which the divine gnoses of intellects which possess secrets and inner secrets are transformed.

وَأَسْتَغْفِرُكَ بِلِسَانِ الْحَقِّ لَا بِلِسَانِ الْوِقَايَةِ وَالنَّظَرِ بِعَيْنِ التَّلَاشِي

I ask You for forgiveness with the tongue of the Truth, not with the tongue of precaution, while looking with the eye of disappearance,

لَا بِعَيْنِ الرِّعَايَةِ

not the eye of attention,

وَالْجَذْبِ بِسِرِّ الْعَدَمِ لَا بِقُوَّةِ الْهِدَايَةِ

and attraction by the secret of non-existence, not the strength of guidance,

وَالتَّلَاشِي بِنَفِي الرَّسْمِ لَا بِرُسُومِ الْوِلَايَةِ

and disappearance by the negation of forms, not the formalities of wilaya.

سُبْحَانَكَ مِنْ وَجْهِ مَا أَنْتَ لَا مِنْ وَجْهِ مَا أَنَا

Glory be to You by the standpoint of Yourself, not by my standpoint.

سُبْحَانَكَ مِنْ وَجْهِ الْوَجْهِ الْمُنَزَّهِ عَنْ وَسْمِ الِاسْمَاءِ وَالْكُنَى

Glory be to You by the Face which is disconnected from the designation
of the Names and allusions!

سُبْحَانَكَ فِي الْحَيْثِ الَّذِي لَا يَلْتَحِقُ بِهِ الْبَقَاءُ وَلَا الْفَنَاءُ

Glory be to You in the "where"
which is not connected to going-on or annihilation!

أُحَاشِيكَ عَنِ الْعِلْمِ وَالْقَوْلِ وَأُنَزِّهُكَ عَنِ الْقُوَّةِ وَالْحَوْلِ وَأُشَاعِلُ
لَا فِي الْمِنَّةِ وَالطَّوْلِ

I proclaim You far from knowledge and words and I disconnect You
from strength and power. I am not distracted by favour or generosity.

446

وَأَمُدُّ لَكَ يَدَ التَّأْبِيدِ لَا يَدَ الْوَسِيلَةِ

I stretch out to you the hand of support, not the hand of means.

وَأَسْأَلُكَ بِسَبْحِ التَّفْضِيلِ لَا فَضْلَ الْفَضِيلَةِ

I ask You by the glorification of granting favour, not the excellence of virtue,

وَأَعُوذُ بِكَ مِنْ تَخْلِيلِ التَّحْوِيلِ وَمُحَاوَلَاتِ الْحِيلَةِ

and I seek refuge with You from allowing transference and from the
ruses of stratagems.

اَللَّهُمَّ أَرِنِي وَجْهَكَ لَا مِنْ حَيْثُ كُلِّ شَيْءٍ هَالِكٌ

O Allah, show me Your Face, not inasmuch as all things pass away.

وَأَسْأَلُكَ بِي لَا سَبِيلَ الْمَهَالِكِ لِهَالِكٌ

I ask You for me not the path of perils by which one perishes.

اَللَّهُمَّ إِنِّي أَسْأَلُكَ بِذَاتِ عَدَمِكَ وَبِذَاتِ ذَاتِكَ وَبِالذَّاتِ
الْمُجَرَّدَةِ وَبِالذَّاتِ الْمُتَّصِفَةِ بِذَاتِ وِينٍ وَالتَّلْوِينِ وَبِالذَّاتِ
الْفَاعِلَةِ وَبِالذَّاتِ الْمُنْفَعِلَةِ

O Allah, I ask You by the essence of Your non-existence and the essence
of Your essence, and by the Essence of Your Essence and by the divested
Essence and by the Essence described by the essence of where and
change, and by the active Essence and by the reactive Essence!

ثُمَّ اجْعَلْنِي عَيْنًا لِذَاتِ الذَّوَاتِ وَمَشْرِقًا لِأَنْوَارِهَا الْمُشْرِقَاتِ

Then make me a source for the Essence of Essences and a place where
its radiant lights rise,

وَمُسْتَوْدَعًا أَسْرَارِهَا الْمُكْتَتِمَةِ فِي عُيُوبِهَا الْمُهِمَّاتِ

and a repository for its secrets concealed in its dark unseen worlds.

اَللَّهُمَّ إِنِّي أُنَزِّهُكَ لَا لِتَنْزِيهِ الْحُسْنِ لَكَ عَنْ الْجِسْمِ وَالنَّفْسِ

O Allah, I disconnect You, but not to disconnect Your beauty,
from the body and soul,

عَنْ شَهَوَاتِ الطَّبْعِ وَالْعَقْلِ وَعَلَاقِ النَّفْسِ وَالْقَلْبِ وَأُنَزِّهُكَ عَنْ
كُلِّ ذَالِكَ وَيَدِهِ وَخِلَافِهِ وَغَيْرِهِ تَنْزِيهًا مَعْجُوزًا
عَنْ تَصَوُّرِهِ وَتَوَهُّمِهِ ۞

from the appetites of nature and the intellect and the attachment of the
self and heart. I disconnect You from all of that, and from its hand and
its opposite and other than it, with a disconnection which cannot be
conceptualised or imagined.

# Qasidas of Shaykh Moulay Murtada al-Boumas-houli

# Treasured Letters

A Qasida about Shaykh Abdalqadir as-Sufi

قصيدة في حق الشيخ عبد القادر الصوفي

يَحْيَا بِهِ كُلُّ قَلْبٍ قَدْ أَحَاطَ بِهِ
رَانٌ يَـزُولُ بِنَظْرَةٍ وَبِـالنَّظَرِ

Through him every rusted heart is brought to life
and the rust is removed by a single glance.

يَشْفِي الْعَلِيلَ بِحُلْوِ مَاءٍ يُطْعِمُهُ
ذَوِي الْمَحَبَّةِ وَالاِخْلَاصِ وَالنُّورِ

He cures the sick with the sweetness of the water he gives
to the people of love, true sincerity and light.

فَعَيْنُهُ مَعِينٌ لَا يَنْضُبُ أَبَدًا
وَبَـاؤُهُ وَبَـاءٌ عَلَى ذَوِي الشَّرَرِ

His 'Ain is an ever-flowing spring,
His Baa a plague upon the wicked.

451

وَدَالُهُ دَائِمًا يَدُلُّ عَلَى اللهِ

وَأَلِفُ أَلِفَ الْاِحْسَانَ بِالْفَقِيرِ

His Daal always leads to Allah,
His Alif has made the Faqir intimate with Ihsan.

وَلَامُهُ لَامَ كُلَّ نَفْسٍ أَمَّارَةٍ

بِالْقَافِ أَوْقَفَهَا عَنْ كُلِّ سُوءٍ شَرِّ

His Laam condemns every nafs commanding to wrong,
his Qaaf stops them from all wickedness and harm.

وَأَلِفُ أَلَّفَ لِلنَّاسِ مَوْسُوعَةً

بِدَالِهِ أَدْنَاهُ لِلدِّينِ وَالنُّورِ

His Alif has composed a vast oeuvre for the people,
His Daal has drawn them near to the Deen and the Light.

فَالرَّاءُ رَبَّى شَبَابَ الْجِيلِ تَرْبِيَةً

أَخْلَاقُهُمْ قَدْ بَدَتْ فِي جُودِهِمْ وَالْخَيْرِ

His Raa has raised a generation's youth,
Their good character manifesting in their generosity and fineness.

وَهَذِهِ حُرُوفُ الْكُنُوزِ قَدْ ظَهَرَتْ

مِنْ إِسْمِهِ خَيْرُ أَسْمَاءٍ بِلَا فَخَرِ

These are the treasured letters manifest in his name,
The best of names, and that is no boast.

أَدِمْ إِلَهِي عَفْواً وَصِحَّةً دَائِماً

عَلَى شَيْخٍ خَـادِمٍ لِكُلِّ أَهْلِ الذِّكْرِ

Oh Allah, grant always wellbeing and good health
To a Shaykh, a servant of all the people of dhikr.

ثُمَّ الصَّلَاةُ عَلَى مَنْ قَالَ حِينَ دَنَا

مِنْ رَبِّهِ أُمَّتِي وَأُمَّتِي فِي الْحَشْرِ

Peace be upon the one who, when brought near to his Lord
on the Day of Gathering, says, "My Ummah, my Ummah."

وَآلِـــهِ وَالصَّـحْبِ كُلِّـــهِـــمْ

وَمَنْ خَطَى خَطْوَهُمْ بِالنَّهْجِ وَالاثَرِ ۞

And upon his family and all the noble companions,
And all who follow and tread in their footsteps.

# The True Shaykh

قصيدة رائية في حق الشيخ عبد القادر الصوفي الدرقاوي
عنوانها الشيخ الصادق

كَيْفَ أَبْدَأُ إِنْ لَمْ أَبْدَأْ بِـسْمِ اللهِ
الرَّحْمٰنِ الرَّحِيمِ وَهُوَ الْكَبِيرُ

How should I begin other than with the name of Allah,
The All-Merciful, the Most Merciful? He is the Great.

أَسْأَلُ اللهَ أَن يُصَلِّيَ عَلَىٰ مَنْ
بِهِ نِلْنَا الْمُنَى النَّذِيرُ الْبَشِيرُ

I ask Allah for blessings upon the one
by whom we achieved our desire –
The Warner and Bringer of Good News.

وَارْضَ يَا رَبَّـنَا عَنِ الآلِ وَالصَّحْبِ
مَعَ التَّـابِعِينَ أَنْتَ النَّصِـيرُ

And be pleased, our Lord, with his family and companions,
And the followers – you are the Helper who gives Victory.

قَدْ بَدَا لِلاَنَامِ خَيْرٌ كَثِيرٌ
بِظُهُورِ الْمُرَبِّي شَيْخٌ كَبِيرٌ

A source of immense good has appeared to humanity.
In the emergence of the Great Shaykh of Instruction.

وَهْوَ الدَّالُّ عَلَى الالَهِ الْعَلِيِّ
قَدْ أَنَارَ الطَّرِيقَ وَهْوَ الْمُنِيرُ

He is the one who indicates the way to God, the High.
He has shed light on the Way – he is the illuminator.

أَكْرَمَ اللهُ بِالْهِدَايَةِ قَوْمًا
بَلْ بِهِ شَرَحَ الصُّدُورَ الْقَدِيرُ

Allah has honoured a people by guidance.
Moreover, through the Shaykh, the All-Powerful has opened hearts.

فَلَأَنْ يَهْدِيَ الالَهُ رِجَالًا
بِرَجَالٍ فَذَاكَ هُوَ الاكْسِيرُ

The fact that Allah guides men
through other men – that is the rare elixir.

اَلصُّوفِيُّ الدَّرْقَاوِيُّ الَّذِي قَدْ عَرَفَ
مَعْنَى الاَسْرَارِ وَهْوَ الْخَبِيرُ

As-Sufi, ad-Darqawi, the one who knows
The meanings of the secrets, he is the expert.

سَقَاهُ ابْنُ الْحَبِيبِ شُرْبَةَ سِرٍّ

فَسَقَاهَا الافْرَادَ وَهْوَ الامِيرُ

Ibn al-Habib gave him a drink from a drink of secrets;
He then gave to the others – he is the commander.

فَالْمُرِيدُ الَّذِي لَهُ أَدَبٌ مَعْ

حَضْرَةٍ وَذِكْرٍ فَهَذَا فَقِيرُ

The Murid who has Adab in the Hadra and the Dhikr
– He is the genuine Faqir.

فَتَرَاهُ لَمَّا أَتَى الشَّيْخَ قَدْ طَوَىٰ

رُكْبَيْهِ أَلَيْسَ هَذَا مُثِيرُ

When the Shaykh comes you see him
Drawing in his outstretched feet. Is that not striking?

فَفَضْلُهُ بِاللهِ ثُمَّ بِكُمْ يَا

مَنْ جَعَلْتَ تَعْسِيرهم تَيْسِيرُ

His favour is by Allah, then by you
Who has made his difficulties easy.

أَلَّفْتَ لِلاِسْلاَمِ شَيْئًا عَظِيمًا

وَبَيَّنْتَ الصَّحِيحَ مِنْهُ الْيَسِيرُ

You have written great works for Islam,
And you have clarified and made simple what is correct in it.

فَجَعَلْتَ التَّوْحِيدَ أَوَّلَ شَيْءٍ
عَرَّفْتَهُ الْمُرِيدَ نِعْمَ التَّفْكِيرِ

You began by teaching Tawhid to the Murid.
What a great inspiration!

وَثُنِّيتَ بِحُبِّ اللهِ وَحُبِّ
رَسُولِنَا الطَّهُورِ نِعْمَ الْبَشِيرُ

You made the second subject Love of Allah and Love of our Messenger,
The pure one and the best bringer of news.

وَنَشَرْتَ الْمَحبَّةَ بَيْنَ قَوْمٍ
أَلِفُوا الْحُبَّ إِنَّهُمْ أَبْرَارُ

You have spread this love among a people
Who have become accustomed to it. They are the people of Birr.

وَجَعَلْتَ الْاَعْمَالَ خَيْرَ خِتَامٍ
خَتَمَ الدِّينَ لِلْعِبَادِ الْبَصِيرُ

And you made 'Amal the best possible seal
May the All-Seeing seal the Deen for the slaves.

وَعَمَّرْتَ الزَّوَايَا فِي كُلِّ وَجْهٍ
فِي أُورُوبَّا إِفْرِيقْيَا نِعْمَ التَّعْمِيرُ

And you have filled zawiyyas everywhere
In Europe, in Africa — what an excellent achievement!

وَفِي آسِيَا وَأَمْرِيكَا وَأَسْتَرَالِيَا
أَنْتَ وَاللهِ شَيْخُنَا وَالْمُشِيرُ

And in Asia, America and Australia,
You are, by Allah, our Shaykh and the one to ask for counsel.

وَهَذَا فَيْضُكُمْ وَفِي كُلِّ يَوْمٍ
يَنْطِقُ بِالتَّوْحِيدِ أَهْلُ التَّكْفِيرِ

This is your overflowing gift. And every day
The kuffar pronounce the word of Tawhid.

شَرَحَ اللهُ لِلْعِبَادِ قُلُوبًا
نِسَاءً وَرِجَالاً كُلُّ فَقِيرٌ

Allah has opened the hearts of many slaves,
Women and men, all fuqara.

أَيَا شَيْخَ الطَّرِيقِ قَدْ نِلْتُمُ الْحَظَّ
فِي قَلْبِي وِدَّاً فَأَنَا الْفَخُورُ

O Shaykh of the Path! You have made good fortune
Reach my heart with affection, and I am proud.

قَدْ شَكَرْتُ الالَهَ إِذْ أَيَسَرَ لِي
نَظْرَةً فِي وُجُوهِكُمُ الْمُنِيرُ

I have thanked Allah, as He has permitted me
To see your illuminating face.

أَسْأَلُ اللهَ أَنْ تَمُنُّوا عَلَيْنَا

بِرُجُوعٍ فَأَنْتُمُ الْاَمْطَارُ

I ask Allah to bless us with a return,
For you are the rains that fall.

وَبِكُمْ تَحْيَا أَرْضُنَا وَالْاَرَاضِي

وَبِكُمْ نَسْتَضِيءُ فَأَنْتُم أَنْوَارُ

By you our land came alive, and other lands too.
We seek light in you, for you are lights.

رَحِمَ اللهُ شَيْخَنَا ابْنَ الْحَبِيبِ

وَجَزَاكُمْ عَنَّا الْجَزَاءَ الْوَفِيرُ

May Allah have mercy upon our Shaykh, Ibn al-Habib,
And may He reward you for us with an abundant reward.

وَتَغَمَّدْ بِرَحْمَةٍ وَرِضْوَانٍ

شَيْخَنَا الْفَتُورِي فَأَنْتَ الْجَدِيرُ

And cover with mercy and pleasure Our Shaykh,
Al-Fayturi – as You are well able.

وَصَلَاةٌ عَلَى النَّبِيِّ الْمُمَجَّدْ

وَعَلَى الْآلِ وَالصِّحَابِ الْاَخْيَارُ

Blessings be upon the Prophet, the honoured one,
And upon his family and excellent companions

وَالْحَمْدُ لِلْاِلَهِ وَهْوَ الْعَلِيُّ

نِعْمَ الْمَوْلَىٰ وَنِعْمَ اللهُ النَّصِيرُ

Praise be to the God, He is the High,
The best Protector, the best Helper.

اِنْتَهَىٰ قَصْدِي بَعْدَ سَرْدِي لِأَبْيَا

 تٍ عَدُّهَا عُمْرِي وَأَنَا الْفَقِيرُ ۝

I have achieved my aim by completing these verses,
The number of which is my age – and I am the faqir.

# The Strength of the Shaykh

قَصِيدَةٌ فِي حَقِّ الشَّيْخ عَبْدِ الْقَادِرِ الصُّوفِي
تَحْتَ عَنْوَانِ قُوَّةِ الشَّيْخ

يَا مَنْ يُرِدْ أَنْ يَعْرِفَ الْحَقَّ أَيْنَ هُوْ
فَانْظُرْ جَبِينَ الشَّيْخِ فِيهِ الَّذِي تَرَى

O you who desire to know where the truth is,
look upon the Shaykh's forehead,  that is what you will see.

نُورٌ يَلُوحُ عَلَى الانَامِ بِسِرِّهِ
فِي ظَاهِرٍ يَسْقِي الْفَقِيرَ وَمَا حَوَى

A light which shines over all mankind by his secret
giving the Faqeer to drink in the inward and outward.

إِنْ غِبْتَ أَعْوَامًا وَعُدْتَ إِلَيْهِمُ
مَا غَيَّرَ الدَّهْرُ الطَّوِيلُ وَمَا انْطَوَى

If you are absent for years and then return to them
you will find time has not changed him nor bent his back.

فَتَرَاهُ فِي ذَا الْمَوْسِمِ مَا زَادَهُ

إِلَّا الشَّجَـاعَةَ وَالْمُروؤَةَ وَالْقُوَىٰ

You see him in this Mawsim – it only increased him
in courage, manliness and strength.

حَلَفَ الزَّمَـانُ لَيَـاتِيَنَّ بِمِثْلِهِ

حَنَثَ الزَّمَانُ بِلَا شَكٍّ فِي مَا ادَّعَىٰ

Had time swore it would bring another like him
time would doubtless not have been true to its word.

بِـاللهِ يَـا مَنْ زُرتهِ وَشَهدْتهِ

أَرَأَيْتَ شَيْخًا مِثْلَهُ يَـا ذَا الْفَتَىٰ

By Allah, O you who have visited and seen him,
O youth, have you seen a Shaykh anywhere like him?

أَيَا فُقَرَا يَا مَنْ حَضَرتُمْ مَوْسِماً

فَهُوَ الْمَعِينُ لَمَنْ أَرَادَ الارْتِوَىٰ

O Fuqara, O you who have attended a Mawsim
he is the spring that satisfies the thirst of every drinker.

شَرِبنَا مِنْ نَظْرتِهِ تعُمُّ جُموعَنَا

فَلَا عَطشٌ بَعْدَ اللِّقَاءِ وَلَا ظَمَىٰ

We drank from his glance which encompassed everyone,
so that no thirst remained after the encounter.

رَحِمَ الالٰهُ شَيْخَنَا الاَمْغَارِيَّ

وَالْفَيْتُورِي يَا رَبِّي فِي جَنَّةِ الْمَأْوَىٰ

May Allah have mercy on our Amghari Shaykh
and al-Fayturi, O Lord, in the Garden of Refuge.

وَأَدِمْ إِلٰهِي حِفْظَكَ يَا ذَا الْعُلَىٰ

عَلَىٰ شَيْخِنَا وَمَنْ لَهُ قَدِ اقْتَفَىٰ ۞

And protect forever, O Exalted God,
our Shaykh and all those who follow him.

# Commentary on the Qasida
# 'Counsel on Death'

تخميس قصيدة «نصيحة»

لمولاى المرتضى البومسْهُولِ الله وليُّه

يَا مَنْ بِدُنْيَاهُ عَنْ دِينِهِ مُنْشَغِلُ

وَغَرَّهُ شَهْـوَةً ثَرْوَةٌ ومَـالُ

هَلْ تَدْرِي أَنَّكَ لَا بُدَّ رَاحِلُ

تَزَوَّدْ أَخِي لِلْمَوْتِ إِنَّهُ نَـازِلُ

وَلَا تُطِلِ الآمَالَ يَقْسُو لَكَ الْقَلْبُ

O you who are busy with your world and neglect your deen,
whose appetite for wealth has deceived him,
do you not realise that you will have to depart?
*Prepare yourself for death, O my brother, for it will descend.*
*Do not draw out your hopes, in case your heart becomes hard.*

وَأَكْثِرْ مِنْ ذِكْرٍ وَفِكْرٍ مِنْ غَيْرِ عَدٍّ

وَبَـادِرْ بِكُلِّ خَيْرٍ مِنْ غَيْرِ حَدٍّ

وَإِيَّـاكَ أَنْ تَنْسَى هَادِمًا لِلْمَلَاذِ

وَوَاظِبْ عَلَى الْفِكْرِ الْمُعِينِ عَلَى الْجِدِّ

وَسَارِعْ إِلَى الأَعْمَالِ فَالْعُمْرُ يَذْهَبُ

Engage a great deal in dhikr and reflection without counting
and hasten to do every good action without limit.
Beware of forgetting the demolisher of pleasures.
*Persevere in reflection which will make you aware*
*and move you to do good works, for life will soon depart.*

وَأَعْطِ ذَوِي الْحُقُوقِ حَقَّهُمْ دَائِمًا

وَلَا تَنْسَـاهُ حَدِيثًا كَانَ أَوْ قَدِيمًا

فَبِذَا تَكُونُ بِحَوْلِ اللهِ غَانِمًا

وَفِكِّرْ فِي أَحْوَالِ الْقِيَامَةِ دَائِمًا

كَبَعْثٍ وَنَشْرٍ وَالْمَوَازِينُ تُنْصَبُ

Always fulfil the rights of those who have rights
and do not forget it whether it is recent or old
for by means of that, by the power of Allah, you will be successful.
*Constantly reflect on the states of the Last Hour, the Rising,*
*the Gathering and the Balance of actions which is set up.*

وَإِيَّاكَ مِنْ فِكْرٍ بِلَا اعْتِبَارٍ يَحُولْ

فَفِيهِ خِلَافٌ لِمِنْهَجِ كُلِّ الرُّسُلْ

فَحِمْلُ الْعَاصِي لِوِزْرٍ يَوْمَ الدِّينِ يَثْقُلْ

وَكَالصِّرَاطِ الَّذِي لَهُ عَقَبَاتُهُ

تَطُولُ عَلَى الْعَاصِي وَمَشْيُهُ يَصْعُبُ

Beware of thinking without consideration
because in that you are at variance with the way of all the Messengers.
The disobedient's burden on the Day of Reckoning is heavy.
*Then there is the Bridge which has its steep and difficult ascents;*
*it will be lengthy for the disobedient and walking on it will be hard,*

وَلَكِنَّ مَنْ قَدْ تَابَ لِلَّه خَالِصًا

وَيَنْهَلُ عِبْرَةً فِي الْقُرْءَانِ قَصَصًا

وَيَرَىٰ فِيهِ نَصِيبَ الْمُطِيعِ حِصَصًا

وَمَنْ كَانَ طَائِعًا وَلِلَّه مُخْلِصًا

يَمُرُّ كَبَرْقٍ أَوْ كَرِيحٍ فَيَذْهَبُ

However, whoever has turned sincerely to Allah in tawba
and drinks an admonition from the stories of the Qur'an
and sees in it the portion of the obedient
*while whoever was obedient and sincere towards Allah*
*will pass over it like lightning or a wind and will go on.*

أَ يَـا مَنْ أَرَدْتَ أَنْ تَنْهَجَ نِعْمَ السَّيْرِ

وَخِفْتَ مِنْ هَوْلِ قَبْرٍ وَمَطْلَعَ النَّشْرِ

أَوْ ظَمَإٍ تَخْشَاهُ يَوْمَئِذٍ مِنْ حَرِّ

وَإِنْ شِئْتَ أَنْ تُسْقَى مِنَ الحَوْضِ فِي الْحَشْرِ

فَلَازِمْ حُبَّ النَّبِي وَمَنْ لَهُ يُنْسَبُ

O you who want to travel the easiest of journeys
and are afraid of the terror of the grave and the coming of the gathering
or the thirst which you fear on that day from the great heat.
*If you wish to be given a drink from the Basin on the Day of Gathering,*
*you must love the Prophet and his descendants.*

فَاشْرَبْ فِيهِ شُرْبَةً هَنِيَّةً لِتُرْوَى

وَاعْلَمْ أَنَّ فَضْلَ اللهِ مِنْ صَاحِبِ الشَّكْوَى

فَسَلِّمْ عَلَيْهِ بِالسِّرِّ ثُمَّ بِالنَّجْوَى

وَصَلِّ عَلَى الْهَادِي الْمُشَفَّعِ فِي الْوَرَى

يَقُولُ أَنَا لَهَا إِذَا الْخَلْقُ يَرْهَبُ

Then drink a pleasant drink in order to be slaked.
Know that the bounty of Allah comes from the Owner of the Complaint.
Ask for peace for him in secret and then in intimate converse.
*And bless the Guide whose intercession for mankind is accepted,*
*for he is the one who intercedes when people are terrified.*

فَـا بَعْدَ شُفْعَةِ الْمُخْتَارِ مِنْ حَزَنٍ

تَحْتَ لِوَا الْمُصطَفَى تَنْسَى كُلَّ مِحَنِ

فَأَحبَّ ءَالَهُ فَأَنْتَ فِي أَمَانٍ

عَلَيْهِ صَلَاةُ اللهِ فِي كُلِّ مَوْطِنٍ

وَءَالٍ وَأَصْحَابٍ وَمَنْ يَتَحَبَّبُ

There is no grief after the intercession of the Chosen One
under the banner of the Mustafa, you will forget every trial
so love his family and you will be safe.
*May the blessings of Allah be upon him in every land,
and on his family and Companions and those who show love for him.*

فَيَا رَبِّ بِالنَّبِيِّ صَاحِبِ دَعْوَةٍ

تَغَمَّدِ الشَّيْخَ ابْنَ الْحَبِيبِ بِرَحْمَةٍ

وَمَنْ نَالَ سِرَّهُ مِنْ شَيْخٍ بِحُجَّةٍ

وَأَسْأَلُ رَبِّ اللَّهَ نَيْلَ سَعَادَةٍ

لِي وَلِلْأَحْبَابِ وَمَنْ يَتَقَرَّبُ ۞

O my Lord, by the Prophet, the owner of da'wah
enfold Shaykh Muhammad ibn al-Habib in mercy
and enfold whatever Shaykh obtains his secret with a proof.
*I ask my Lord, Allah, for the gift of true happiness
for me and the beloved ones and those who draw near.*

# Commentary on the Qasida 'Ahimu Wahdi'

تخميس قصيدة «أهيم وحدي»
لمولاي المرتضى البومسهولي الله وليّه

فَإِنْ ضَاقَ الصَّدْرُ مَعَ قَلْبِي
وَاشْتَدَّ هَمِّي وَغَمِّي بِي
أَوْ أَزْمَةٌ أَوْ دَاءٌ إِشْتَدَّ بِي
أَهِيمُ وَحْدِي بِذِكْرِ رَبِّي
فَذِكْرُ رَبِّي هُوَ الشِّفَاءُ

When my heart and breast become oppressed
and my worries and sorrows are severe
and a crisis or affliction overcomes me,
*I am ecstatic, alone, in the dhikr of my Lord,*
*for the dhikr of my Lord — it is the cure.*

إِنْ كَانَ لِلْقَوْمِ حُبٌّ بَادِي

فِي مَالِهِمْ وَدُنْيَا الْوُجُودِ

أَوْ لَيْسَ لِي حِيلَةُ الصُّعُودِ

أَحْبَبْتُ رَبًّا هُوَ اعْتِمَادِي

لِكُلِّ شَيْءٍ هُوَ يَشَاءُ

If the People have a manifest love
for their wealth and this world,
and I don't find a way of getting on,
*I have loved a Lord — on Whom I rely;*
*in each single thing — it is He Who wills it.*

يَا مَنْ أَضَاعَ عُمْرًا فِي حُبٍّ

أَلْقَيْتَهُ كُلَّهُ فِي جُبٍّ

أَتْعَبْتَ نَفْسًا بِكُلِّ صَعْبٍ

وَكُلُّ حُبٍّ لِغَيْرِ رَبِّي

فِيهِ الْعَذَابُ فِيهِ الشَّقَاءُ

Oh you who have wasted your life in vain love,
you have thrown it all into the bottom of a well.
You have tired yourself with every trouble.
*In every love for other than my Lord*
*there is torment and grief.*

إِنْ شِئْتَ عَجِّلْ بِطِبِّ الدَّاءِ

بِوَصْلِكَ الرُّوحَ بِالسَّمَـــاءِ

بِـغَيْبَةٍ وَصفَا صَفَـاءِ

يَا فَوْزَ فَانٍ عَنِ الْفَنَاءِ

لَهُ الْحَيَاةُ لَهُ الْبَقَاءُ

If you wish it, hasten to the cure of the disease
by directing your Ruh to Heaven,
withdrawing into Him and cleansing yourself totally.
*Oh the victory of the one annihilated to annihilation,*
*he will have life and going on.*

فَطَهِّرِ الْقَلْبَ مِنَ الْحَسَدِ

مِنْ كُلِّ عِلْمٍ فَهِمٍ تَجَرَّدْ

وَقُلْ فِي كُلِّ جَمْعٍ مُمجَّدْ

يَا رَبِّ صَلِّ عَلَى مُحَمَّدْ

مِنْ ذَاتِهِ النُّورُ وَالضِّيَاءُ

Purify the heart of envy,
strip away all knowledge and understanding,
and in every exalted meeting say:
*O my Lord, bless Muhammad.*
*From his essence there is light and radiance.*

وَإِنْ تُرِدْ حِصْنًا مِنْ حَرَامِ

فَاتَّبِعِ الشَّيْخَ فِي الْكَلَامِ

وَنَبِيَّ اللهِ فِي السَّلَامِ

وَءَالِهِ وَالصَّحْبِ الْكِرَامِ

لَهُمْ عُهُودٌ لَهُمْ وَفَاءُ ﴿۩﴾

And if you wish protection from the Haram,
follow the Shaykh in what he says,
and the Prophet of Allah regarding the prayer on him –
*And bless his family and noble Companions.*
*They have covenants; they fulfil them.*

عَنْهُ (وَصَلِّ صَلَاةَ الظُّهْرِ فِي أَوَّلِ العَصْرِ) أَيْ صَلِّ الظُّهْرَ، أَيْ ظُهُورَ مَا فِي
إِدَارَتِكَ لِرَبِّكَ وَهِيَ دَوَامُ الشُّهُودِ لِحَضْرَةِ المَلِكِ المَعْبُودِ، كَمَا تَقَدَّمَ فِي أَوَّلِ العَصْرِ
أَيْ مُعَاصَرَتِكَ لِشَيْخِكَ وَسَلْكِكَ الإِرَادَةَ لَهُ، وَلَيْسَ مُرَادُهُ رَضِيَ اللهُ عَنْهُ، صَلَاةَ
الظُّهْرِ وَالعَصْرِ المُشْتَمِلَةِ عَلَى الرُّكُوعِ وَالسُّجُودِ، لِأَنَّ الظُّهْرَ المَعْلُومَ يُطْلَبُ فِيهَا
أَنْ تُصَلَّى فِي أَوَّلِ وَقْتِهَا لَا فِي أَوَّلِ العَصْرِ، فَمِنْ ثَمَّ حَمَلْنَاهَا عَلَى مَا ذَكَرْنَا فَافْهَمْ
تُرْشَدْ وَاللهُ يَتَوَلَّى هُدَانَا وَهُدَى العَلَمِينَ، ءَامِينَ. وَقَوْلُهُ: (فَتِلْكَ صَلَاةُ العَارِفِينَ
بِرَبِّهِمْ) وَهِيَ دَوَامُ الشُّهُودِ لِحَضْرَةِ المَلِكِ المَعْبُودِ فَلَا تَنْقَطِعُ صَلَاتُهُمْ لِكَوْنِهِمْ
مِنَ الَّذِينَ هُمْ عَلَى صَلَاتِهِمْ دَائِمُونَ، أَيْ عَلَى شُهُودِهِمْ لِرَبِّهِمْ مُوَاظِبُونَ، وَقَوْلُهُ
(فَإِنْ كُنْتَ مِنْهُمْ فَانْضِحِ البَرَّ بِالْبَحْرِ)، فَإِنْ كُنْتَ مِنَ العَارِفِينَ وَهُمُ الَّذِينَ لَا
يُحْجَبُونَ بِالْخَلْقِ عَنِ الْحَقِّ وَلَا بِالْحَقِّ عَنِ الْخَلْقِ، فَانْضِحْ أَيْ رُشَّ بَرَّ شَرِيعَتِكَ
بِبَحْرِ حَقِيقَتِكَ وَكُنْ مِنَ الجَامِعِينَ بَيْنَهُمَا، كَمَا قَالَ إِمَامُنَا مَالِكٌ، رَضِيَ اللهُ عَنْهُ :
(مَنْ تَشَرَّعَ وَلَمْ يَتَحَقَّقْ فَقَدْ تَفَسَّقَ وَمَنْ تَحَقَّقَ وَلَمْ يَتَشَرَّعْ فَقَدْ تَزَنْدَقَ، وَمَنْ جَمَعَ
بَيْنَهُمَا فَقَدْ تَحَقَّقَ) أَيْ تَحَقَّقَ بِالْعُبُودِيَّتَيْنِ: عُبُودِيَّةِ التَّكْلِيفِ وَعُبُودِيَّةِ التَّعْرِيفِ.

أَمَرَ رَضِيَ اللَّهُ عَنْهُ الْمُرِيدَ بِالتَّطْهِيرِ بِمَاءِ الْغَيْبِ وَيُؤْخَذُ مِنْهُ أَنَّ الطَّهَارَةَ عَلَى قِسْمَيْنِ: طَهَارَةٌ حِسِّيَّةٌ وَتَكُونُ بِالْمَاءِ الْحِسِّيِّ، وَمُتَعَلِّقُهَا الْبَدَنُ كُلُّهُ إِنْ كَانَ الْحَدَثُ أَكْبَرَ أَوِ الْأَعْضَاءُ الْمَخْصُوصَةُ إِنْ كَانَ الْحَدَثُ أَصْغَرَ وَلَيْسَتْ هَذِهِ مُرَادَةً لِلنَّاظِمِ، رَضِيَ اللَّهُ عَنْهُ، وَالْقِسْمُ الثَّانِي الطَّهَارَةُ الْمَعْنَوِيَّةُ، وَهِيَ طَهَارَةُ الْقُلُوبِ مِنَ الْأَمْرَاضِ الْحَاجِبَةِ لَهَا عَنْ حَضْرَةِ عَلَّامِ الْغُيُوبِ، وَهَذِهِ الطَّهَارَةُ لَا تَكُونُ إِلَّا بِالْمَاءِ الْمَعْنَوِيِّ وَهُوَ مَاءُ الْعُلُومِ وَالْمَعَارِفِ وَالْأَسْرَارِ الْجَارِي مِنْ حَضْرَةِ الْغَيْبِ إِلَى قَلْبِ الشَّيْخِ الْعَارِفِ بِاللَّهِ الْمُطَهَّرِ مِنَ الْغَيْبِ الَّذِي يُفِيضُهُ الشَّيْخُ عَلَى الْمُرِيدِ، فَيَتَطَهَّرُ قَلْبُهُ مِنَ الْأَغْيَارِ وَيَمْلَأُ بِالْمَعَارِفِ وَالْأَسْرَارِ، وَهَذَا إِنْ كَانَ الْمُرِيدُ صَاحِبَ سِرٍّ أَيْ بَصِيرَةٍ يَتَوَصَّلُ بِهَا إِلَى مَنْ يَأْخُذُ بِيَدِهِ وَهُوَ الشَّيْخُ الَّذِي يَسْتَمِدُّ مِنْ حَضْرَةِ الْغَيْبِ كَمَا قَدَّمْنَا، وَإِنْ لَمْ يَكُنِ الْمُرِيدُ صَاحِبَ سِرٍّ وَبَصِيرَةٍ فَلْيَتَيَمَّمْ بِصَعِيدِ الْأَعْمَالِ الظَّاهِرَةِ وَالْعُلُومِ الرَّسْمِيَّةِ حَتَّى يَفْتَحَ اللَّهُ عَلَيْهِ بِالسِّرِّ وَالْبَصِيرَةِ. وَأَشَارَ رَضِيَ اللَّهُ عَنْهُ بِقَوْلِهِ: (وَقَدِّمْ إِمَامًا كُنْتَ أَنْتَ أَمَامَهُ) إِلَى أَنَّ الْمُرِيدَ يَجِبُ عَلَيْهِ أَنْ يُقَدِّمَ إِمَامًا شَيْخًا عَارِفًا بِاللَّهِ يَقْتَدِي بِهِ فِي الصَّلَاةِ الْمَعْنَوِيَّةِ الَّتِي هِيَ الشُّهُودُ لِحَضْرَةِ الْمَلِكِ الْمَعْبُودِ كَمَا أَنَّ الْمَأْمُومَ يَجِبُ عَلَيْهِ أَنْ يَقْتَدِيَ بِإِمَامٍ فِي الصَّلَاةِ ذَاتِ الرُّكُوعِ وَالسُّجُودِ، وَقَوْلِهِ (كُنْتَ أَنْتَ أَمَامَهُ) أَشَارَ بِهِ رَضِيَ اللَّهُ عَنْهُ إِلَى أَنَّ الْمُرِيدَ لَا يَقْتَدِي بِشَيْخٍ مِنَ الشُّيُوخِ إِلَّا إِذَا حَصَلَ التَّعَارُفُ بَيْنَهُمَا فِي عَالَمِ الْأَرْوَاحِ، قَالَ عَلَيْهِ السَّلَامُ: (الْأَرْوَاحُ جُنُودٌ مُجَنَّدَةٌ مَا تَعَارَفَ مِنْهَا ائْتَلَفَ وَمَا تَنَاكَرَ مِنْهَا اخْتَلَفَ)، فَيَكُونُ الْمَعْنَى عَلَى هَذَا وَقَدِّمْ إِمَامًا فِي عَالَمِ الْأَشْبَاحِ كُنْتَ أَمَامَهُ فِي عَالَمِ الْأَرْوَاحِ، وَلِأَجْلِ الْمُقَابَلَةِ وَالتَّعَارُفِ الَّذِي حَصَلَ فِي عَالَمِ الْأَرْوَاحِ حَصَلَ الِائْتِلَافُ فِي عَالَمِ الْأَشْبَاحِ، وَقَوْلُهُ رَضِيَ اللَّهُ

فَإِنْ كَانَ مِنْهُ اللَّفْظُ جَاءَ بِحُلَّةٍ

وَأَعْنِي بِهَا الْأَسْرَارَ تَسْرِي بِسُرْعَةٍ

لِقَلْبِ مُرِيدِ الْحَقِّ مِنْ غَيْرِ شِرْكَةٍ

وَزُهْدُهُ فِي الْأُكْوَانِ عُمْدَةُ سَيْرِهِ

وَشُغْلٌ بِإِفْرَادِ الْحَبِيبِ بِرُؤْيَةٍ

وَتَصْرِيحُهُ بِالْإِذْنِ مِنْ خَيْرِ أُمَّةٍ

عَلَيْهِ اعْتِمَادُ الصَّادِقِينَ الْأَجِلَّةِ

فَإِنْ حَصَلَ الْمَقْصُودُ مِمَّا ذَكَرْتُهُ

قَبَادِرْ وَأَعْطِ النَّفْسَ مِنْ غَيْرِ مُهْلَةٍ

وَلَا تَعْتَبِرْ شَيْئًا سِوَى مَا رَسَمْتُهُ

فَفِيهِ الَّذِي يُغْنِي وَكُلُّ الْمَسَرَّةِ


وَقَالَ الْجُنَيْدُ رَضِيَ اللهُ عَنْهُ:


تَطَهَّرْ بِمَاءِ الْغَيْبِ إِنْ كُنْتَ ذَا سِرٍّ

وَإِلَّا تَيَمَّمْ بِالصَّعِيدِ أَوِ الصَّخْرِ

وَقَدِّمْ إِمَامًا كُنْتَ أَنْتَ أَمَامَهُ

وَصَلِّ صَلَاةَ الظُّهْرِ فِي أَوَّلِ الْعَصْرِ

فَتِلْكَ صَلَاةُ الْعَارِفِينَ بِرَبِّهِمْ

فَإِنْ كُنْتَ مِنْهُمْ فَانْضَحِ الْبَرَّ بِالْبَحْرِ

يَتَمَسَّكُ بِمَنْ حَسُنَتْ نِيَّتُهُ فِيهِ مِنْ مَشَائِخِ الْعَصْرِ. وَقَالَ سِيِّدِي عَبْدُ الْوَاحِدِ بْنُ عَاشِرٍ:

بِيَصْحَبُ شَيْخًا عَارِفَ الْمَسَالِكْ

يَقِيهِ فِي طَرِيقِهِ الْمَهَالِكْ

يُذَكِّرُهُ اللّهَ إِذَا رَآهُ

وَيُوصِلُ الْعَبْدَ إِلَى مَوْلَاهُ

اُنْظُرْ مَا قَالَهُ الشُّرَّاحُ فِي هَذِهِ الْأَبْيَاتِ يَزُولُ عَنْكَ الْإِشْكَالَ، وَقَالَ ابْنُ عَطَاءِ اللّهِ رَضِيَ اللّهُ عَنْهُ فِي حِكَمِهِ مَنْ لَا تَصْحَبْ مَنْ لَا يُنْهِضُكَ حَالُهُ وَلَا يَدُلُّكَ عَلَى اللّهِ مَقَالُهُ فَإِنْهَاضُ الْحَالِ وَدَلَالَةُ الْمَقَالِ مِنْ نَتِيجَةِ الصُّحْبَةِ فَمَنْ لَمْ يَجِدْ هَذِهِ الْحَالَةَ مِنْ صَاحِبِهِ فَلْيَتْرُكْهُ لِلّهِ وَلْيَبْحَثْ عَلَى مَنْ هَذِهِ صِفَتُهُ فَإِنَّهُ يَظْفِرُ بِهِ عَلَى حَسَبِ صِدْقِهِ وَقُوَّةِ عَزْمِهِ وَاللّهُ الْمُسْتَعَانُ. وَقُلْتُ فِي قَصِيدَةٍ لِي تَائِيَّةٍ ذَكَرْتُ فِيهَا أَوْصَافَ الشَّيْخِ الْمُرَبِّي وَنَصَّ الْمَقْصُودِ مِنْهَا:

وَهَيْلَلَةٌ تَنْفِي جَمِيعَ الْوَسَاوِسِ

بِتَلْقِينِ شَيْخٍ عَارِفٍ بِالْحَقِيقَةِ

وَآيَاتُهُ نُورٌ يَلُوحُ بِظَاهِرٍ

وَسِرٌّ بَدَا مِنْ بَاطِنٍ مَعَ هِمَّةٍ

وَتَرْقِيَةٌ بِاللَّحْظِ قَبْلَ تَلَفُّظِ

التَّهْدِيدُ عَلَى البُرُوزِ فَبَرَزْتُ لِخَلْقِ بِاللهِ وَلِلَّهِ، وَقُلْتُ كَمَا قَالَ ابْنُ عَطَاءِ اللهِ فِي حِكَمِهِ إِلَهِي أَمَرْتَ بِالرُّجُوعِ إِلَى الأَثَرِ فَارْجِعْنِي إِلَيْهَا بِكِسْوَةِ الأَنْوَارِ وَهِدَايَةِ الاسْتِبْصَارِ حَتَّى أَرْجِعَ إِلَيْكَ مِنْهَا كَمَا دَخَلْتُ عَلَيْكَ مِنْهَا مَصُونَ السِّرِّ عَنِ النَّظَرِ إِلَيْهَا وَمَرْفُوعَ الهِمَّةِ عَنِ الاعْتِمَادِ عَلَيْهَا إِنَّكَ عَلَى كُلِّ شَيْءٍ قَدِيرٌ، وَاعْلَمُوا سَادَتِي، أَنَّ اتِّخَاذَ الشَّيْخِ الحَيِّ وَاجِبٌ عَلَى كُلِّ مُرِيدٍ طَالِبٍ لِحَضْرَةِ اللهِ وَدَلِيلُ الوُجُوبِ قَوْلُهُ تَعَالَى : ﴿يَا أَيُّهَا الَّذِينَ ءَامَنُوا اتَّقُوا اللهَ وَكُونُوا مَعَ الصَّادِقِينَ﴾. وَالمَعِيَّةُ تَقْتَضِي المُصَاحَبَةَ بِالأَشْبَاحِ لَا بِالأَرْوَاحِ وَقَالَ تَعَالَى :﴿وَاتَّبِعْ سَبِيلَ مَنْ أَنَابَ إِلَيَّ﴾. فَأَمَرَ تَعَالَى فِي هَذِهِ الآيَةِ الوَلَدَ بِمُتَابَعَةِ وَالِدِ الأَرْوَاحِ دُونَ مُتَابَعَةِ وَالِدِ الأَشْبَاحِ لِأَنَّ وَالِدَ الرُّوحِ يُرَبِّي المَعْنَى وَوَالِدَ الجِسْمِ يُرَبِّي لَكَ الحِسَّ وَشَتَّانَ مَا بَيْنَ مَنْ هَمُّهُ الحِسُّ وَمِنْ هِمَّتُهُ المَعْنَى، وَقَالَ ﷺ (المَرْءُ عَلَى دِينِ خَلِيلِهِ فَلْيَنْظُرْ أَحَدُكُمْ مَنْ يُخَالِلْ). وَوَقَعَ الاتِّفَاقُ مِنْ هَذِهِ الأُمَّةِ المُحَمَّدِيَّةِ سَلَفًا عَنْ خَلَفٍ عَلَى أَنَّ أَوَّلَ مَا يَجِبُ عَلَى المُرِيدِ بَعْدَ انْتِبَاهِهِ مِنَ الغَفْلَةِ أَنْ يَعْمَدَ إِلَى شَيْخٍ نَاصِحٍ مُرْشِدٍ عَالِمٍ بِعُيُوبِ النَّفْسِ وَدَوَاعِيهَا وَأَدْوِيَةِ أَمْرَاضِهَا فَارِغٍ مِنْ تَهْذِيبِ نَفْسِهِ وَأَغْرَاضِهَا يُبَصِّرُهُ بِعُيُوبِ نَفْسِهِ وَيُخْرِجُهُ مِنْ دَائِرَةِ حِسِّهِ لِأَنَّ مَنْ لَمْ يَكُنْ لَهُ شَيْخٌ يَقُودُهُ إِلَى طَرِيقِ الهُدَى قَادَهُ الشَّيْطَانُ لَا مَحَالَةَ إِلَى طَرِيقِ الرَّدَى، وَالمُرِيدُ مُشْتَقٌّ مِنَ الإِرَادَةِ وَمُتَعَلَّقُهَا الإِخْلَاصُ وَحَقِيقَةُ المُرِيدِ أَنَّهُ المُتَجَرِّدُ عَنْ إِرَادَتِهِ لِمَا أَرَادَ اللهُ مِنْهُ وَهُوَ عِبَادَةُ اللهِ، لِقَوْمِهِ تَعَالَى : ﴿وَمَا خَلَقْتُ الجِنَّ وَالإِنْسَ إِلَّا لِيَعْبُدُونَ....﴾ وَلَمَّا كَانَ المُرِيدُ ضَعِيفًا عَنْ تَهْذِيبِ نَفْسِهِ إِذِ الوِلَايَةُ فِي البَاطِنِ لِلنَّفْسِ وَالشَّيْطَانِ فَإِذَا كَانَ فِي حُكْمِ الشَّيْخِ تَحْتَ كَنَفِ وِلَايَتِهِ أَعَانَهُ عَلَى طَاعَةِ اللهِ وَعِبَادَتِهِ بِهِمَّتِهِ العَامِلَةِ بِإِذْنِ اللهِ وَكَلَامِهِ المُؤَثِّرِ بِفَضْلِ اللهِ فَوَجَبَ عَلَيْهِ أَنْ

وَمَوْلَانَا أَحْمَدُ الْبَدَوِيُّ رَضِيَ اللهُ عَنْهُ:

وَفَيْضُكُمْ فِي ازْدِيَادِ
وَجُودكُمْ فِي تَوَالِي

وَقَدْ أَشَرْتُ فِي قَصِيدَةٍ لِي إِلَى بَعْضِ مَا خَصَّنِي اللهُ بِهِ تَحَدُّثًا بِنِعَمِ اللهِ وَنَصُّهَا:

قَدْ كَسَانَا ذِكْرُ الْحَبِيبِ جَمَالًا
وَبَهَاءً وَرِفْعَةً وَسُرُورًا
وَخَلَعْنَا الْعِذَارَ عِنْدَ التَّدَانِي
وَجَهَرْنَا بِمَنْ نُحِبُّ افْتِخَارَا

وَهِيَ قَصِيدَةٌ مَشْهُورَةٌ مَذْكُورَةٌ فِي هَذَا الدِّيوَانِ الْمُبَارَكِ فِيهَا عِشْرُونَ بَيْتًا فِي صَفْحَةٍ طَالِعهَا تَجِدُ مَا أَشَرْتُ لَكَ، وَمُنْذُ تُوُفِّيَ الشَّيْخُ سَيِّدِي مُحَمَّدُ بْنُ عَلِيٍّ رَضِيَ اللهُ عَنْهُ، وَالْإِذْنُ يَتَجَدَّدُ عَلَيَّ وَأَنَا أَسْتَحْقِرُ نَفْسِي وَأَرَاهَا لَيْسَتْ أَهْلًا لِذَلِكَ الْمَقَامِ حَتَّى أَتَانِي الْمَشَايِخُ الْأَرْبَعَةُ، وَهُمْ سَيِّدِي مُحَمَّدُ بْنُ عَلِيٍّ رَضِيَ اللهُ عَنْهُ، وَسَيِّدِي الْعَرَبِيُّ بْنُ الْهُوَارِيِّ رَضِيَ اللهُ عَنْهُ، وَسَيِّدِي مُحَمَّدُ الْعَرَبِيُّ رَضِيَ اللهُ عَنْهُ، وَسَيِّدِي أَحْمَدُ الْبَدَوِيُّ رَضِيَ اللهُ عَنْهُمْ وَأَمَرُونِي بِالْبُرُوزِ إِلَى الْخَلْقِ وَدَلَالَتِهِمْ عَلَى الْمَلِكِ الْحَقِّ، وَقَالُوا إِنَّ الْمَاءَ الَّذِي شَرِبْتَهُ مِنَّا هُوَ أَعْذَبُ الْمِيَاهِ وَأَحْلَاهَا فَمُدَّ يَدَكَ شَرْقًا وَغَرْبًا وَلَا تَخَفْ مِنْ أَحَدٍ، ثُمَّ بَعْدَ هَذَا وَقَعَ الْإِذْنُ مِنَ الْمُصْطَفَى ﷺ وَوَقَعَ

اللهُ. وَقَدْ حَقَّقَ اللهُ رَجَاءَهُ فِينَا، فَوَاللهِ ثُمَّ وَاللهِ مَا مَرَرْنَا عَلَى مَدِينَةٍ وَلَا قَرْيَةٍ وَلَا بَادِيَةٍ إِلَّا وَشَهِدَ أَهْلُهَا بِوُصُولِ الْمَدَدِ إِلَيْهِمْ وَسَرَيَانِ الْحَيَاةِ فِي قُلُوبِهِمْ، وَذَلِكَ سِرُّ الْإِذْنِ، وَمَا جَلَسَ مَعَنَا، وَالْحَمْدُ لِلهِ، فَقِيرٌ إِلَّا وَازْدَادَ عِلْمًا لَمْ يَكُنْ عِنْدَهُ، وَحَصَلَ مِنْهُ خُضُوعٌ وَانْكِسَارٌ وَلَا جَلَسَ مَعَنَا مُرِيدُ الطَّرِيقَةِ إِلَّا وَقَوِيَتْ قَرِيحَتُهُ وَعَلَتْ هِمَّتُهُ لِطَلَبِ مَعْرِفَةِ اللهِ وَلَا شَيْخٌ مِنْ مَشَايِخِ الْعَصْرِ إِلَّا وَازْدَادَ ذَوْقًا إِلَى ذَوْقِهِ وَاسْتَفَادَ مِنَّا شَيْئًا لَمْ يَكُنْ عِنْدَهُ، وَذَلِكَ كُلُّهُ مِنْ سِرِّ الْإِذْنِ وَبَرَكَتِهِ، قَالَ ابْنُ عَطَاءِ اللهِ فِي حِكَمِهِ (مَنْ أُذِنَ لَهُ فِي التَّعْبِيرِ فُهِمَتْ فِي مَسَامِعِ الْخَلْقِ عِبَارَتُهُ وَجُلِّيَتْ إِلَيْهِمْ إِشَارَتُهُ) وَالْمَأْذُونُ هُوَ الَّذِي يَتَكَلَّمُ بِاللهِ وَلِلهِ، وَلِذَلِكَ أَثَّرَ كَلَامُهُ فِي الْقُلُوبِ وَانْقَادَ إِلَيْهِ كُلُّ مَخْصُوصٍ وَمَحْبُوبٍ، وَقَدْ قَالَ شَيْخُ شَيْخِنَا سَيِّدِي مُحَمَّدٌ الْعَرَبِيُّ، رَضِيَ اللهُ عَنْهُ وَاللهِ لَا يَأْتِينِي إِلَّا الْمَقْبُولُ وَأَنَا أَقُولُ تَحَدُّثًا بِنِعَمِ اللهِ وَاللهِ لَا يَأْتِينِي إِلَّا الْمَحْبُوبُ، وَقَدْ قَالَ لِي ﷺ فِي بِشَارَةٍ: اعْلَمْ يَا وَلَدِي أَنَّ اللهَ يُكْرِمُكَ بِمِيَاهٍ عَذْبَةٍ حُلْوَةٍ قُلْتُ يَا رَسُولَ اللهِ هَذِهِ الْمِيَاهُ هِيَ مِيَاهُ الْإِسْلَامِ وَالْإِيمَانِ وَالْإِحْسَانِ قَالَ لِي ﷺ هِيَ قُلْتُ يَا رَسُولَ اللهِ هَذِهِ الْمِيَاهُ أَشْرَبُهَا وَحْدِي أَوْ أَنَا وَكُلُّ مَنِ اقْتَدَى بِي فَقَالَ تَشْرَبُهَا أَنْتَ وَكُلُّ مَنِ اقْتَدَى بِكَ مِنْ أُمَّتِي. وَقَدْ حَقَّقَ اللهُ لَنَا مَا وَعَدَنَا بِهِ ﷺ، فَوَاللهِ لَقَدْ شَرِبْنَا هَذِهِ الْمِيَاهَ وَكُلُّ مَنْ صَحِبَنَا بِالصِّدْقِ يَشْرَبُهَا فِي أَقْرَبِ زَمَنٍ فَاحْمَدُوا اللهَ سَادَتِي وَاشْكُرُوهُ عَلَى مَا أَكْرَمَكُمْ بِهِ مَوْلَاكُمْ فِي وَقْتِكُمْ. قَالَ تَعَالَى ﴿مَا نَنسَخْ مِنْ ءَايَةٍ أَوْ نُنسِهَا نَأْتِ بِخَيْرٍ مِّنْهَا أَوْ مِثْلِهَا﴾. وَقَدَّمَ اللهُ تَعَالَى الْخَيْرِيَّةَ عَلَى الْمِثْلِيَّةِ إِشَارَةً إِلَى أَنَّ الْوَلِيَّ الْكَامِلَ لَا بُدَّ أَنْ يَظْهَرَ وَارِثُهُ وَلَوْ بَعْدَ حِينٍ وَيَكُونُ أَكْمَلَ مِنْهُ فِي الْعِلْمِ وَالْمَعْرِفَةِ بِاللهِ تَعَالَى كَرَامَةً لِذَلِكَ الْوَلِيِّ الْكَامِلِ، وَلِأَنَّ مَدَدَ اللهِ تَعَالَى وَفَيْضَهُ فِي الزِّيَادَةِ، قَالَ الشَّيْخُ سَيِّدُنَا

المَأْذُونُ مِنَ اللهِ وَرَسُولِهِ وَمِنْ سَائِرِ أَوْلِيَاءِ اللهِ وَهُوَ الفَرْدُ المُحَمَّدِيُّ الَّذِي لَا يَكُونُ فِي كُلِّ وَقْتٍ مِنْهُ إِلَّا وَاحِدٌ وَإِنْ كَثُرَ المَشَائِخُ فِي عَصْرِهِ فَالحُكْمُ لِذَلِكَ الفَرْدِ عَلَيْهِمْ شَعَرُوا أَوْ لَمْ يَشْعُرُوا. وَقَدْ كَثُرَ المُدَّعُونَ لِمَقَامِ الفَرْدَانِيَّةِ بِالبُهْتَانِ وَالزُّورِ طَلَبًا لِلرِّيَاسَةِ وَاسْتِجْلَابًا لِلدُّنْيَا الفَانِيَةِ وَمَا شَعَرَ هَذَا المُدَّعِي أَنَّ مَنِ ادَّعَى مَا لَيْسَ فِيهِ كَذَّبَتْهُ شَوَاهِدُ الامْتِحَانِ لِأَنَّ عِنْدَهَا يَعِزُّ المَرْءُ أَوْ يُهَانُ. وَقَدْ كَانَ المَشَائِخُ الصَّادِقُونَ يَكْتَفُونَ بِعِلْمِ اللهِ وَلَا يَتَعَلَّقُونَ بِأَحَدٍ سِوَى اللهِ، وَإِنْ بَرَزَ مِنْهُمْ شَيْءٌ فَعَلَى وَجْهِ التَّحَدُّثِ بِنِعَمِ اللهِ. قَالَ تَعَالَى ﴿ وَأَمَّا بِنِعْمَةِ رَبِّكَ فَحَدِّثْ﴾.

فَهَا هُوَ العَبْدُ الفَقِيرُ إِلَى مَوْلَاهُ الغَنِيِّ بِهِ عَمَّا سِوَاهُ مُحَمَّدُ بْنُ الحَبِيبِ الأَمْغَارِي الحَسَنِي نَسَبًا الفَاسِي مَنْشَئًا وَدَارًا يَقُولُ عَلَى وَجْهِ التَّحَدُّثِ بِنِعَمِ اللهِ، قَدْ وَقَعَ لَنَا الإِذْنُ مِنَ اللهِ وَمِنْ رَسُولِ اللهِ وَمِنْ سَائِرِ أَوْلِيَاءِ اللهِ. وَأَفْرَدَنِي بِعُلُومٍ وَأَسْرَارٍ لَمْ تَكُنْ إِلَّا عِنْدَ الفَرْدِ المُحَمَّدِيِّ وَلَوْ أَرَدْنَا بَسْطَ مَا أَنْعَمَ اللهُ بِهِ عَلَيْنَا لَاحْتَجْنَا إِلَى مُجَلَّدَاتٍ، وَلَكِنْ نَذْكُرُ إِلَى الفُقَرَاءِ مَا خَصَّنِي بِهِ شَيْخِي وَأُسْتَاذِي سَيِّدِي مُحَمَّدُ بْنُ عَلِيٍّ وَذَلِكَ أَنَّهُ لَمَّا تَصَدَّرَ، رَضِيَ اللهُ عَنْهُ، كَتَبْتُ لَهُ رِسَالَةً فِي تَجْدِيدِ العَهْدِ مَعَهُ بَعْدَ أَنْ كُنْتُ أَخَذْتُ الطَّرِيقَ عَلَى الشَّيْخِ العَارِفِ بِاللهِ سَيِّدِي العَرَبِي بْنِ الهُوَّارِي فَكَتَبَ إِلَيَّ رَضِيَ اللهُ عَنْهُ وَأَمَرَنِي بِالقُدُومِ إِلَى حَضْرَتِهِ فَامْتَثَلْتُ أَمْرَهُ وَقَدِمْتُ إِلَى مُرَاكُشَةَ، فَلَمَّا دَخَلْتُ عَلَيْهِ رَضِيَ اللهُ عَنْهُ، دَخَلَ عَلَيْهِ مِنَ الفَرَحِ وَالسُّرُورِ مَا لَا يَدْخُلُ تَحْتَ حَصْرٍ، وَقَالَ لِي جَاءَتْنِي الطَّائِفَةُ كُلُّهَا لَمَّا جِئْتَنِي أَنْتَ. وَقَالَ لِي مَرَّةً أُخْرَى فِي بِشَارَةٍ يَطُولُ ذِكْرُهَا: أَنْتَ عِنْدَنَا فِي طَائِفَتِنَا بِمَنْزِلَةِ ابْنِ عَطَاءِ اللهِ مِنَ الطَّائِفَةِ الشَّاذِلِيَّةِ،فَكَمَا أَنَّ اللهَ أَحْيَا الطَّرِيقَةَ الشَّاذِلِيَّةَ بِابْنِ عَطَاءِ اللهِ كَذَلِكَ يُحْيِ اللهُ هَذِهِ الطَّرِيقَةَ المُبَارَكَةَ بِكَ إِنْ شَاءَ

# مقدمة الشيخ محمد بن الحبيب

## بسم الله الرحمن الرحيم

قَالَ رَضِيَ اللهُ عَنْهُ وَأَرْضَاهُ، الْحَمْدُ لِلَّهِ الَّذِي أَقَامَ فِي كُلِّ وَقْتٍ لِإِحْيَاءِ طَرِيقَتِهِ أَفْرَادًا وَبَسَطَ عَلَيْهِمْ مِنَ الْأَنْوَارِ الْمُحَمَّدِيَّةِ مَا يَسْتَمِدُّ بِهِ كُلُّ مَنِ اقْتَدَى بِهِمْ مِنَ الْمُحِبِّينَ أَزْوَاجًا وَأَفْرَادًا. نَحْمَدُهُ سُبْحَانَهُ وَتَعَالَى عَلَى مَا خَصَّنَا بِهِ مِنَ الْأَسْرَارِ وَمَا أَفَاضَهُ عَلَيْنَا مِنَ الْعُلُومِ وَالْمَعَارِفِ وَالْأَنْوَارِ وَنَشْكُرُهُ جَلَّ جَلَالُهُ شُكْرًا يَسْتَغْرِقُ سَائِرَ النِّعَمِ الْوَاصِلَةِ إِلَيْنَا وَإِلَى جَمِيعِ عِبَادِ اللهِ الْعَبِيدِ وَالْأَحْرَارِ. وَنَشْهَدُ أَنْ لَا إِلَهَ إِلَّا اللهُ وَحْدَهُ لَا شَرِيكَ لَهُ شَهَادَةَ أَهْلِ الْفَنَاءِ فِي التَّوْحِيدِ مِنَ الْمُقَرَّبِينَ. وَنَشْهَدُ أَنَّ سَيِّدَنَا مُحَمَّدًا عَبْدُهُ وَرَسُولُهُ الَّذِي أَرْسَلَهُ اللهُ رَحْمَةً لِلْعَالَمِينَ صَلَّى اللهُ عَلَيْهِ وَعَلَى آلِهِ وَأَصْحَابِهِ الَّذِينَ بَذَلُوا أَنْفُسَهُمْ وَأَمْوَالَهُمْ فِي إِحْيَاءِ طَرِيقَتِهِ وَإِقَامَةِ سُنَّتِهِ وَمَا الْتَفَتُوا إِلَى إِذَايَةِ الْمُنَافِقِينَ وَالْمَحْجُوبِينَ.

وَبَعْدُ، فَاعْلَمُوا عِلْمًا يَقِينًا يَا مَعْشَرَ الْإِخْوَانِ مِنَ الطَّائِفَةِ الدَّرْقَاوِيَّةِ الشَّاذِلِيَّةِ وَغَيْرِهِمْ مِنْ كُلِّ مَنْ أَرَادَ الْاقْتِدَاءَ مِنْ عَبِيدِ رَبِّنَا فِي سَائِرِ بِلَادِ اللهِ وَعِبَادِ اللهِ أَنَّ اللهَ تَبَارَكَ وَتَعَالَى قَيَّضَ لِهَذِهِ الطَّرِيقَةِ الْمُبَارَكَةِ فِي كُلِّ وَقْتٍ مَنْ يَقُومُ اعْوِجَاجَهَا وَيُظْهِرُ أَسْرَارَهَا وَأَنْوَارَهَا وَهُوَ الشَّيْخُ الْجَامِعُ بَيْنَ الْحَقِيقَةِ وَالشَّرِيعَةِ

ولذا فقد أذن الشيخ عبد القادر رضي الله عنه بتحقيق وطبع الديوان مرة أخرى في نسخته الجديدة وسأل أن أكتب مقدمة له،وبدورنا نبارك هذا الإذن راجين من الله أن يجعله خالصا لوجهه ونافعا لعباده وكل من قرأه أوسمعه أو نظر فيه ولم يكن ذا اختبارا.

وصلى الله على واسطتنا إليه وقدوتنا سيدنا محمد وعلى آله وصحبه وسلم تسليما.

خادم أهل الله محمد المرتضى البومسهولي الله وليه.

# مقدمة الشيخ محمد المرتضى البومسهولي

بسم الله الرحمن الرحيم وصلى الله وسلم وبارك على سيدنا
ونبينا ومولانا محمد وعلى آله وصحبه وسلم تسليما.
ولا حول ولا قوة الا بالله العلي العظيم

مِنَ الْمُؤْمِنِينَ رِجَالٌ صَدَقُوا مَا عَاهَدُوا اللَّهَ عَلَيْهِ ص
فَمِنْهُم مَّن قَضَى نَحْبَهُ وَمِنْهُم مَّن يَنتَظِرُ ص
وَمَا بَدَّلُوا تَبْدِيلًا ص

إن رسالة الشيخ سيدي محمد ابن الحبيب رضي الله عنه وأرضاه التي تتضمن
أوراده الشريفة ووظيفته الحفيظة وقصائده الهادفة لها تأثير في نفوس كل قارئ
وسامع في أقطار العالم وخصوصا بعد ترجمتها الى لغات عديدة مكنت الغربيين
وغيرهم من فهم المضمون ،وإن هذا كل بفضل الله وفضل سر الإذن منه
رضي الله عنه، إذ لما أذن للشيخ عبد القادر الصوفي رضي الله عنه في تلقينه
للأوراد وطبع ديوانه ،ظهرت بركاته بإقبال الناس عليه ،حيث أصبح لكل
مريد (ديوان) في حقيبته وخزانته،وما يدل على تزايد المريدين حاجتنا للمزيد
من النسخ منه.

بِسْمِ اللهِ الرَّحْمٰنِ الرَّحِيمِ

وَصَلَّى اللهُ عَلَى سَيِّدِنَا مُحَمَّدٍ وَءَالِهِ

دِيوَانُ الْعَارِفِ بِاللهِ وَالدَّالِّ عَلَى اللهِ أَبِي الْقُيُوضَاتِ وَالْإِمْدَادَاتِ، وَمَعْدِنُ الْأَسْرَارِ وَالْبَرَكَاتِ الْعَلَّامَةُ الرَّبَّانِيُّ وَالْفَرْدُ الْمُحَمَّدِيُّ النُّورَانِيُّ مَوْلَانَا أَبُو عَبْدِ اللهِ الشَّيْخُ سَيِّدُنَا مُحَمَّدُ بْنُ الْحَبِيبِ الْأَمْغَارِيُّ الْإِدْرِيسِيُّ الْحَسَنِيُّ نَسَبًا الْمَالِكِيُّ مَذْهَبًا الشَّاذِلِيُّ طَرِيقَةً وَانْتِسَابًا الْمُحَمَّدِيُّ فَيْضًا وَمَشْرَبًا الْفَاسِيُّ ثُمَّ الْمَكَّاسِيُّ مَنْشَئًا وَدَارًا

مَتَّعَ اللهُ الْمُسْلِمِينَ بِحَيَاتِهِ ءَامِين

# بُغْيَةُ الْمُرِيدِينَ السَّائِرِينَ وَتُحْفَةُ السَّالِكِينَ الْعَارِفِينَ

ديوان

الشيخ العارف بالله

سيدي محمد بن الحبيب

الأمغاري الإدريسي الحسني

ديوان
الشيخ سيدي محمد بن الحبيب

9 781908 892478